How European Citizens Understand the Economy

AFE43300

This book argues that the European public sphere functions to help citizens understand complex economic issues and discuss them meaningfully across borders. Through original research conducted on citizens' perceptions of European economic issues, it explores a mechanism that allows people to make sense of such complex issues – national anchoring – and shows that the way issues are politicized today in a national public sphere will shape citizens' understandings of novel issues tomorrow.

The book demonstrates that debates in the European public sphere spread knowledge to the population just as national debates do, thus allowing transnational deliberation to function in the EU and potentially advance an European identity. The book thus draws optimistic conclusions with regard to EU legitimacy, with the European public sphere functioning rather well and problems of complexity and compatibility seeming less pronounced than often expected in public opinion research and European studies.

This book will be of key interest to scholars and students of public opinion, European studies, political attitudes, austerity politics and more broadly to political science, sociology and social psychology.

Dorian Alt is a postdoctoral researcher at the Institute of Comparative Constitutionalism at Charles University, Prague. His research interests lie at the intersection of Political Sociology and European Studies. Dorian holds a Ph.D. in Politics from Freie Universität Berlin, an M.Sc. in Philosophy from LSE and a BA in European Studies from Maastricht University

Routledge / UACES Contemporary European Studies

The primary objective of the new Contemporary European Studies series is to provide a research outlet for scholars of European Studies from all disciplines. The series publishes important scholarly works and aims to forge for itself an international reputation.

The Politics of Legitimation in the European Union
Legitimacy Recovered?
Edited by Christopher Lord, Peter Bursens, Dirk De Bièvre, Jarle Trondal and Ramses A. Wessel

European Banking Nationalism
State Power and Troubled Banks
Shawn Donnelly and Gaia Pometto

How European Citizens Understand the Economy
Knowledge, Politicization and Anchoring in the European Public Sphere
Dorian Alt

How European Citizens Understand the Economy

Knowledge, Politicization and Anchoring in the European Public Sphere

Dorian Alt

Routledge
Taylor & Francis Group
LONDON AND NEW YORK

UACES

First published 2023
by Routledge
4 Park Square, Milton Park, Abingdon, Oxon OX14 4RN

and by Routledge
605 Third Avenue, New York, NY 10158

Routledge is an imprint of the Taylor & Francis Group, an informa business

British Library Cataloguing-in-Publication Data
A catalogue record for this book is available from the British Library

Library of Congress Cataloging-in-Publication Data
Names: Alt, Dorian, author.
Title: How European citizens understand the economy : knowledge, politicization and anchoring in the European public sphere / Dorian Alt.
Description: Abingdon, Oxon ; New York, NY : Routledge, 2023. |
Series: Routledge/UACES contemporary European studies |
Includes bibliographical references and index.
Identifiers: LCCN 2022058343 (print) | LCCN 2022058344 (ebook) |
ISBN 9781032371559 (hardback) | ISBN 9781032371658 (paperback) |
ISBN 9781003335610 (ebook)
Subjects: LCSH: Economics–Europe. | Public opinion–Europe. |
Europe–Economic conditions–21st century. |
Europe–Economic conditions–Public opinion.
Classification: LCC HC240 .A78283 2023 (print) |
LCC HC240 (ebook) | DDC 330.94–dc23/eng/20230118
LC record available at https://lccn.loc.gov/2022058343
LC ebook record available at https://lccn.loc.gov/2022058344

ISBN: 9781032371559 (hbk)
ISBN: 9781032371658 (pbk)
ISBN: 9781003335610 (ebk)

DOI: 10.4324/9781003335610

Typeset in Times New Roman
by Newgen Publishing UK

Contents

Figures

Tables

Acknowledgments

I am immensely grateful to many people for supporting me during the four and half years it took to write this book. No word could have been written without their emotional, practical and intellectual support.

The success of this project owes to my supervisor (or doctoral father as we say in German), Thomas Risse, to a large extent. Thanks for making this journey possible, for encouraging me or hitting the breaks when necessary. It's simply unthinkable that I could have written this thesis without your intellectual guidance. The same is true for my doctoral mother, Florence Haegel, who adopted me at the Centre d'Études Européennes in Paris, making my field research in France possible in the first place. Thank you for being an anchor of qualitative thinking in this quantitative academic world.

I am also very grateful to a number of academics who commented on my research at different stages of the project. Thanks to Jürgen Gerhards, Colin Hay, Emiliano Grossmann and the participants of the dejeuner textuel, Agnieszka Chmielewska, Piotr Filipkowski and Thomasz Zarycki. I am particularly grateful to Barbara Pfetsch, who hosted me twice in her Colloquium, and to Jonathan White, who has been a continuous inspiration for and supporter of the project.

But it's not only to academics this project owes its success to. My family supported me the entire time. Thanks to my parents for providing enormous amounts of care and love, and, rather practically, for hosting me during my moody fieldwork visits to Berlin. Thanks to my sister-in-law and my brother who actually managed to visit me at any place I ever lived at during my studies. Thanks to my nephew for teaching me how to make phone calls with a banana.

My friends have been just like a family to me during this time. Thanks for bearing my occasional desperation or outbursts of enthusiasm (the latter potentially being more annoying). Thanks for consoling me, discussing with me, celebrating with me. I particularly want to thank my roommates in the various cities of my fieldwork to whom I am so incredibly grateful for keeping me in the balance of life. Thanks to David, Ilja and Tiffany in Berlin, to Caro, Sami and Nantke in Paris, to Ewa and Stephan in Warsaw, and to Gemina in the very long end.

Some of these roommates have also taken upon themselves the arduous task of teaching me their language. My capacity to communicate in French and Polish is owed to many generous and patient speakers and listeners. Some deserve special mention, simply because I spent so much time learning from them when I was still not a very fluent conversation partner in the respective language. Thanks to Ewa, Julia and Edyta to whom I owe my Polish. Thanks Renata and Sami for the French. And to the theatre crew of la tempête, which is also responsible for some of the most beautiful diversions during my Ph.D.

There are some forms of support that fit in none of the categories mentioned so far. Thanks to the participants of my focus group discussions for donating an hour of their time to a stranger with a weird accent and even weirder questions. Thanks to Konrad for providing escapes when I needed them, be it to Brighton or Brussels. Thanks to Gerhild Arjes for pulling me out of the hole I fell into. Thanks to Mme Illiadis for being such a continuous source of laughter. Thanks to Justin for always being there. Thanks to Lua for your sensibility and love.

Abbreviations

CETA	Comprehensive Economic and Trade Agreement
ENF	Europe of Nations and Freedom
EPP	European People's Party
EPS	European Public Sphere
EU	European Union
MEP	Member of European Parliament
S&D	Socialists & Democrats

Introduction

How the European Public Overcomes Problems of Understanding

PSUM2: "In Poland for example something good we have in that direction is *500+* because that creates jobs. I would say it increases domestic demand because one knows that this money goes into consumption."

– Polish soccer players discussing 'expenditure'

FSTM6: "Look for example at the workers here, you call them *travailleurs détachés*. What is a *travailleur détaché*? The people coming from Romania to work in France. But they do the same work for two times less than a French salary."

– French soccer players discussing 'workers' rights'

GSUM4: "I think interest rates are low enough. […]"
GSUM2: "As things stand Mr. Draghi is living the opposite. You permanently hear the interest screw should go up again at some point."

– German soccer players discussing 'interest'

The idea to write this book was born during the economic crisis. I was 16 when the 2008 financial crisis hit Europe and I entered university at the peak of the eurozone crisis in 2012. During this time, a question formed in my mind: How were people supposed to understand, discuss and form an opinion on the economic events of the day? How were we to meaningfully debate austerity, quantitative easing, labor regulation, trade balances and so on? And how do people in other EU countries think about these issues?

As I found out later during my degree in European studies, I was not alone in asking these questions. The European public sphere is frequently diagnosed with problems of understanding, both by scholars and in the broader public. European politics tend to be viewed as distant, obscure and complex, while citizens are described as uninformed or preoccupied with national affairs. The question is thus not only if European citizens understand complex economic issues, but also if they understand each other, given that they are caught up in their own national perspectives. Throughout this book, I call these two interrelated problems of understanding the **complexity** problem and the **compatibility** problem, respectively.

DOI: 10.4324/9781003335610-1

It was these two problems that sent me off during my PhD in 2018 and 2019 to conduct 18 focus group discussions with citizens in France, Germany and Poland. These discussions left the strong impressions that the European public sphere functions much better than often assumed. The quotes at the beginning of the chapter exemplify why. First, they reveal that citizens were surprisingly well able to make sense of complex economic issues. In the quotes, amateur soccer players debate issues as complex as Keynesian economic policy (quote 1), factor-price equalization resulting from international migration flows (quote 2) and the ECB's interest rate policy (quote 3). In their own words, these citizens pointedly describe highly complex economic processes and theories. Second, while the discussions gravitated on different issues in each country, they were hardly incompatible. In different national contexts, certain arguments become more frequent and persuasive. But the arguments are never exclusive to one nation and completely alien to another. While the concept of a posted worker means little to Germans, they understand the basic implications of work migration. And French citizens sometimes rely on Keynesian reasoning too, even without being able to connect it to a recent government program such as *500+*. Both with respect to complexity and compatibility, the European public sphere seems to do better than expected by many.

The impression that European publics can overcome problems of understanding has become the central argument of this book. More precisely, I argue that **European citizens are able (1) to understand complex economic issues and (2) to discuss them across borders in the European public sphere.** In my view, this is very good news for EU legitimacy. A functioning public sphere is essential to a democratic system and the compatibility and complexity problems have been some of the most potent arguments challenging the functioning of the European public sphere. In an age in which highly complex political issues are increasingly decided at the European level, it is reassuring to see that such decisions can be flanked by meaningful public deliberation. The fact that European citizens understand complex economic issues and each other makes EU democracy look more healthy.

This optimistic evaluation of the state of the European public sphere requires explanation. Let us take a step back. The interviews from which quotes are provided at the beginning of the chapter were conducted with groups of amateur soccer players after training, beer in hand. The fact that these discussions were both informed and transnationally compatible cannot be taken for granted. Few people (me included) would have expected such a quality of debate in the locker rooms of Europe. So how is it possible that citizens without economic training understand complex economic issues so well and, often, so transnationally similar?

The explanation I want to present in this book is **national anchoring**. The concept of national anchoring unites two theories. The term anchoring is drawn from social representation theory and it is based on the idea that citizens draw on familiar bodies of knowledge to render the unfamiliar intelligible. To this, I add a conception of nationhood as a cultural reservoir, with debates in the public sphere creating specific national meaning structures and linguistic expressions. National anchoring thus denotes the process in which citizens draw on pre-existing knowledge acquired during past national debates to render new information intelligible. Periods of intense politicization in the public sphere popularize specific meaning structures and thus shape citizens' perceptions of future issues.

This conception of national anchoring helps to explain how citizens were able to overcome the complexity problem in the issue area of economics. Mobilizing knowledge of salient past debates was the most prominent strategy of complexity reduction found in the empirical material. The quotes at the beginning of the chapter provide evidence of this. In all three quotes, complex issues are anchored in knowledge drawn from salient national debates. In the Polish case, the debate over the PiS government's heavily contested child-support policy of *500+* spread Keynesian arguments to the population. In the French case, the polarization surrounding the 2005 referendum on the European constitution popularized economic vocabulary to describe adverse effects of integration, including the notion of *travailleur détaché*. In Germany, entrenched ordoliberal academics waged a public campaign on the European Central Bank's (ECB) interest rate policy, leading to Berlin soccer players informedly debating the need to tighten "the interest screw". In all these cases, knowledge of past national debate was used to make sense of complex economic questions.

Yet, national anchoring does not only help explain how complexity is overcome but also provides a partial explanation of why debates are transnationally compatible. The same mechanism that is at work in national publics is also at work in the European public sphere. Economic debates in the European public sphere (e.g., surrounding the euro crisis or certain trade deals) popularize certain conceptions of the European economy or of a European economic identity. In other words, politicization in the European public sphere seems to create the elements of a transnationally shared European political culture. The fact that debates are transnationally compatible is partly due to the availability of such transnationally shared assumptions, for example, regarding the existence of a European social model. If national anchoring is part of the answer to the complexity question, 'European anchoring' is partly responsible for solving the compatibility puzzle.

While national anchoring is a novel concept, complexity and compatibility are old problems. The rest of the introduction provides a brief overview of the state of the art in both areas of research and sets out this book's contribution to these ongoing debates in greater detail. The introduction concludes with a brief overview of the book's methodology and structure.

I.1 Complexity and Citizen Competence

A central function of a public sphere in a democratic system is to convey information to the citizenry (e.g., Gerhards, 1998, p. 273). In modern societies, this task arguably becomes more difficult to fulfill as increasingly complex scientific issues come on the political agenda (Beck, 1999, pp. 109–110; Giddens, 1994, pp. 1–5; Susen, 2015, p. 229). Climate change, pandemics or economic crises are issues that keep legions of highly specialized scientists busy, while still regularly dominating public debates. Yet, if issues get so complex that even highly trained experts struggle to grasp their implications, we need to wonder how ordinary citizens are supposed to form an opinion on them. In modern, functionally differentiated societies, citizens will possess expert knowledge only in very limited domains, while being laypeople[1] in 99% of all other public debates. This is what I will henceforth call the **complexity problem**: How can a lay citizenry understand and discuss complex issues?

In the European context, the complexity problem is particularly salient in the issue area of economics. The EU's economic powers are highly specific and often technically complex. The regulation of the single market, the negotiation of trade deals or the setting of interest rates require a significant degree of expert knowledge. At the same time, transnational debates are most intense in precisely those areas in which the EU boosts considerable economic competences. Koopmans (2014) demonstrates that Europe-wide debate on issues such as monetary policy reaches a level of transnational intensity roughly similar to the degree of inter-regional communication in federal states. This Europeanization of national public spheres for common economic issues was further intensified by the euro crisis (Hutter & Grande, 2014, p. 1006; Risse, 2014a). This intensity of debate on economic matters in the European public sphere is puzzling given the complexity of the issues at stake (Hepp et al., 2016, pp. 195–197; Lingenberg, 2010, p. 210). How are adequately informative economic debates possible with the largest part of the European citizenry lacking training in economics?

The European public sphere's complexity problem in the issue area of economics is the first research question this book addresses.

> **RQ1 (complexity):** How do European citizens manage to understand complex economic arguments circulating in the European public sphere?

There are three prominent approaches in public opinion research that provide answers to this question. The most pessimistic of them is rooted in the literature on the public understanding of science. This literature initially relied on a **deficit model**, diagnosing a lack of scientific knowledge among laypeople and proposing strategies to educate the public (Cortassa, 2016, pp. 448–450). A similar position can be discerned in political science. Since the 1960s (Converse, 2006 [1964]), studies of public levels of information regularly found citizens to be ill-informed about politics, volatile in their opinions and incapable of spelling out even some of the most basic ideological principles. Until today, many researchers still subscribe to the view that contemporary democracies face a serious legitimacy problem because their citizens are simply not qualified enough to decide the issues of the day (Flynn et al., 2017; Gunn, 2014). In the issue area of economics, proponents of the deficit model maintain that citizens are subject to biases in their reasoning and thus do not understand the implications of economic policies on individual and societal welfare (e.g., Bartels, 2005; Caplan, 2011). Social representations of economics thus are assumed to differ from economic theory; they are diverse but uninformed.

An opposing position is – often implicitly – taken by some scholars working within a **rational choice** framework. In rational choice inspired studies, public opinion is often explained as a function of individual cost–benefit calculations. Citizens experience the effects of economic processes on their personal economic situation and make political decisions accordingly (e.g., Brinegar & Jolly, 2005; Ehrlich, 2010; Fraile & Ferrer, 2005; O'Rourke et al., 2001; Rehm, 2011, 2016). In proposing this line of reasoning, rational choice approaches often make very optimistic assumptions about citizen competence. Assessing the effects of trade deals, economic crises or government spending on personal finances requires citizens to possess high levels of economic knowledge. Citizens are supposed to see the economy exactly as economic experts would. Social representations of economics thus are assumed to closely mirror economic theory. Social representations of the economy are uniform (i.e., equivalent to economic theory) and thus informed.

A third approach is rooted in the **interpretive** turn that has swept through the social sciences since the 1980s. In the literature on the public understanding of science, this "ethnographic" or "contextual" approach paid closer attention to the creative strategies citizens employ to adapt knowledge at their disposal in order to make informed judgments (Cortassa, 2016, pp. 448–450). In political science, this approach is mostly exemplified by studies focusing on heuristics and the idiosyncrasies of citizens' reasoning (e.g., Gamson, 1992; Jayet, 2020; Sniderman et al., 1993; White, 2011; Zaller, 1992). While some of these studies have touched on economic issues, a comprehensive study of "folk economics" is still missing (Swedberg, 2018; see also Mau, 2005). One of the aims of this book is to fill this gap.

Being rooted in the interpretive tradition, this book ultimately provides a critique of the deficit model and of rational choice approaches. My exact argument with regard to the complexity problem is that lay perceptions of the economy are **diverse but informed**. Citizens' perceptions of the economy don't simply correspond to economic theory (as the rational choice model would have it), but this does not mean that they are random, meaningless or uninformed (as the deficit model suggests; see Table I.1). The fact that most citizens do not hold the same views as experts must not be considered a deficit, but rather a difference in opinion reflecting the diversity of legitimate positions present in politics and academia. The harsh criticisms voiced by proponents of the deficit model as much as the overly optimistic assumptions of rational choice scholars result from a lack of engagement with the intricacies of lay reasoning.

So what does lay reasoning look like if it is not characterized by ignorance or rational calculation? How can we understand how citizens make

Table I.1 Three approaches to public opinion of economics

	Deficit Model	Rational Choice Model	Anchoring Model
Lay representations of economics	Diverse Uninformed	Uniform Informed	Diverse Informed

sense of complex issues? Throughout this book, the central concept I employ to explain lay reasoning is **anchoring**, as it is defined in **social representation theory**. A social representation is a construction of reality (a representation) valid for a specific social group. The central idea of social representation theory is that individuals need to mobilize pre-existing stocks of knowledge if they are confronted with a new idea. In the words of its inventor, social representation theory describes the process of making "the unfamiliar familiar" (Moscovici, 1984, p. 30, 2004 [1961]). The process of connecting alien concepts to more familiar stocks of knowledge is called anchoring; I will refer to the pre-existing stocks of knowledge that are mobilized to anchor a concept as **anchoring domains**. The content of a social representation depends on the anchoring domain that was mobilized for its creation. For me, then, investigating how citizens understand complex economic issues means uncovering the anchoring domains they employ and showing which social representations of the economy they entail. Anchoring is the key to understanding lay reasoning.

In my empirical material, I was able to differentiate five anchoring domains that citizens employed to understand complex economic processes. Each of them is discussed in a different chapter of this book.

- **National political culture** (i.e., collective meaning structures resulting from politicization in the national public sphere and often sedimented into language; Chapter 2)
- **The worth of nations** (i.e., knowledge of the characteristics of the national economy either assessed through neoliberal or social-ecological discourses and spread through politicization; Chapter 3)
- **A discourse of the common people** (i.e., an experience-based discourse depicting the common people as victims of big business and immoral management elites; Chapter 4)
- **Economic theory** (i.e., knowledge of economic theory acquired in high school or university depicting the market as efficient and mutually beneficial; Chapter 5)
- An emergent **European political culture** (i.e., transnationally shared meaning structures comprising memories of recent EU politics and a vision of a European social model; Chapter 7)

Of these five anchoring domains, I subsume three under the label **national anchoring** because knowledge of all three is produced and transmitted in a similar manner. Knowledge of national political culture, the worth of nations and European political culture is spread through politicization in the public sphere. Salient debates popularize specific conceptions and linguistic expressions that will be mobilized in future debates. Given this similarity between multiple anchoring domains, national anchoring is the most common form of anchoring that I find, accounting for approximately 40% of social representations identified.

While these findings are of limited generalizability, they testify to the capacity of many citizens to make sense of complex issues. This study certainly has a rather explorative character with regard to the complexity problem, rather than providing a fully representative test. Nonetheless, the results warrant optimism for the debate on citizen competence. If we adopt a broad understanding of citizen competence focused on the capacity to creatively process new information (Cramer & Toff, 2017; Goren, 2012; Lupia, 2016), the European public seems up to the task. Anchoring processes more generally and national anchoring in particular make the complexity problem look surmountable. In this line of reasoning, **European citizens are able to understand complex economic issues**.

I.2 Compatibility and the Functioning of the European Public Sphere

While national anchoring should boost our confidence in citizens' capacity to understand complex issues, it potentially creates a new problem for the European public sphere. If national knowledge is used as an anchoring domain, this might significantly impede citizens' capacity to understand the arguments of their counterparts in different nations. This incompatibility of arguments might undermine the functioning of the European public sphere.

In the recurring debate concerning the EU's democratic deficit, a number of criteria have been developed to assess whether the European public sphere can bestow legitimacy on the EU (Eder & Kantner, 2000; Kantner, 2014; Risse, 2010, 2014a, 2014b; Statham, 2010). One of these criteria demands that frames of reference are compatible. Compatibility in this case implies mutual understanding, rather than the existence of a single perspective. The existence of different perspectives in itself is not problematic, as long as participants in the debates understand the different lines of argument they are confronted with. Acknowledging, however, that European debates are transnational in nature (i.e., they take place in separate national publics) and that national knowledge is a probable anchoring domain (thus generating social representations that differ between countries), it seems questionable whether Europeans in different countries will interpret economic arguments in a compatible manner. This is what I call the **compatibility problem**: given the need for interpretation of complex economic issues, will citizens' representations be transnationally compatible?

As pointed out before, the compatibility problem is closely linked to the complexity problem. The greater the complexity, the greater the need for anchoring in more familiar knowledge and hence the greater the danger that incompatible anchoring domains are mobilized. Given the prominence of complex economic issues, complexity and compatibility form a **twin problem** in the European public sphere. Research question two thus arises logically from research question one:

> **RQ2 (compatibility):** Do inter-national[2] differences in social representations inhibit the functioning of the European public sphere?

Answering this compatibility question is an important step in assessing the EU's democratic legitimacy. A functioning public sphere constitutes an element of most theories of democracy (e.g., Habermas, 1992b, p. 452). The compatibility criterion is one of three criteria for the functioning of a transnational public sphere and thus its investigation ultimately contributes to an assessment of the EU's legitimacy. Yet, whereas the other two criteria for the functioning of the European public sphere have been comprehensively addressed (e.g., Koopmans, 2014; Risse, 2010, 2014a, 2014b; Statham, 2010), transnational compatibility has so far been studied mostly with regard to media frames (Eder & Kantner, 2000; Kantner, 2014). This book contributes to the study of the European public sphere by providing an assessment on the citizen level, which so far has been largely ignored (with Lingenberg, 2010, being the notable exception). Arguably, it is citizens' understanding rather than media reporting that ultimately matters for an assessment of the public sphere's functioning. What is more, this book is also the first to develop a precise operationalization of compatibility. These compatibility criteria are needed, for example, to distinguish misunderstandings from disagreements and to establish a national standard of comparison. The assessment of compatibility as proposed here thus makes important contributions to the literature on the European public sphere. Should inter-national incompatibilities between citizens prove to be insignificant, concerns about the malfunctioning of the European public sphere should cease to persist.

The systematic assessment of the compatibility criteria shows that **the European public sphere functions as well as national publics**. In Chapter 6, I compare interpretive problems in the European public sphere to those in national publics, thus establishing a national standard of comparison. My empirical material shows that national anchoring does indeed produce misunderstandings in the European public sphere. Yet, these misunderstandings seem to be no more pronounced than the hermeneutic differences we find among citizens of the same nation. What is more, while the research was designed to maximize inter-national differences (see following section on research design), intra-national differences should be expected to be much stronger and diverse beyond the sample. If the European public sphere prevailed even under these very unfavorable conditions, it is likely to function in terms of compatibility in most other scenarios too.

The finding that compatibility problems in the European public sphere seem to be minor is not only good news for EU legitimacy. It is also somewhat puzzling. How is it possible that citizens understand each other so well across borders? A national political culture – understood as a reservoir of meaning providing all members of the political community with the means to participate in public debate (Calhoun, 1997, p. 4; Hearn, 2006, p. 12; Lamont & Thévenot, 2000; Özkirimli, 2005, pp. 29–30) – has often been perceived as a precondition for the functioning of a public sphere. The relevance of national anchoring seems to confirm this point, as memories of recent politics serve as shared reference points facilitating debates in national publics. The finding that the European public sphere functions in terms of compatibility, then, inevitably contributes to the discussion about the European demos. In Chapter 7, I argue that many social representations are indeed transnationally shared by European citizens and that these elements of a shared political culture might be the nucleus of a self-conscious political community. Analogous to national anchoring, a form of 'European anchoring' is discernable. Like on the national level, **a European political culture seems to emerge as the result of politicization** of shared problems in the European public sphere. This finding seems to be further good news for EU legitimacy. Just like the European public sphere, the European demos has prominently featured debates concerning the EU's alleged democratic deficit. The investigation of compatibility thus warrants optimism for these two crucial domains of EU legitimacy. The following section will spell out by what means I attempted to ensure that these results are not only normatively encouraging, but also empirically valid.

I.3 Research Design: Simulating Transnational Debates under Unfavorable Conditions

To assess complexity and compatibility in the European public sphere, the research design for this book needs to balance three demands. First, due to the nature of the research object, I opt for a qualitative and interpretive approach. Social representations essentially are intersubjectively shared meaning structures and such structures are most reliably uncovered by in-depth qualitative approaches. Second, the research design needs to mirror the transnational functioning of the European public sphere. The aim is not simply to take stock of social representations, but to reveal how they are used in the specific context of European debates. Finally, and most challengingly, despite the need for qualitative depth and for the generation of context-specific observations, the research design needs to guarantee a certain degree of external validity to allow for conclusions about the European public sphere at large. In other words, the design must allow an inference to a very big phenomenon from a very limited number of in-depth observations. Roughly speaking, the research design combines these demands by using focus group methodology, by employing triggers from real EU-level sources in realistic national contexts, and by constructing very unfavorable conditions for transnational communication.

The empirical material on which this book is based was collected in 18 focus group discussions conducted in France, Germany and Poland between March 2018 and March 2019. Focus groups are an excellent way of studying social representations (e.g., Gamson, 1992; Krzyzanowski, 2008, p. 169). They reveal how intersubjective meaning is collectively constructed, negotiated and mobilized in specific contexts. Rather than treating individuals as coherent agents holding stable opinions, it can be observed which patterns of arguments are socially accepted as legitimate. In other words, focus groups allow the study of arguments as reservoirs of meaning individuals selectively draw on (Lamont & Molnár, 2002; Lamont & Thévenot, 2000; Swidler, 1986). For the study of social representations, this is advantageous as it allows an identification of the various anchoring domains participants have access to. The focus group methodology I employ, then, is qualitative and interpretive in nature. Apart from meeting the specific demands of my research questions, this approach also contributes to the growing body of literature that imports **the methods of interpretive political sociology** into European studies (Duchesne et al., 2013; Lingenberg, 2010; White, 2011).

The content and structure of the focus group discussions were chosen in order to reflect the characteristics of the European public sphere. The European public sphere, first, operates in a transnational fashion, and second, as most public spheres today, in a rather top-down manner (Gerhards, 1998; Habermas, 1992). In other words, European debates tend to be triggered by events or arguments appearing on the European level and are consequently passed on by national media into the respective national spheres. My focus groups were organized in a similar manner: participants were confronted with arguments drawn from real European level debates. These trigger arguments were translated into the respective national languages, but they remained essentially the same in each discussion. The arguments were chosen in order to reflect the complex nature of most issues on which the European public sphere unfolds. They come from two domains of economic policy in which EU institutions have shown persistent activity in the past decade: trade and unemployment. Structure and content of the focus groups, then, mirror the transnational structure of the European public sphere and the complexity of issues discussed therein.

Country selection and the selection of participants, finally, were driven by a desire to create highly unfavorable conditions for the European public sphere. Practically, this implies maximizing the potential for inter-national differences. Such differences increase the potential for national perspectives to be incompatible and thus of a malfunctioning of the European public sphere. As for country selection, France, Germany and Poland meet this imperative as they are ideal types of different varieties of capitalism (Farkas, 2011; Nölke & Vliegenthart, 2009; Schmidt, 2003). Accordingly, citizens of these countries are likely to have **different economic experiences** and are probably exposed to **different national cultures**. In other words, France, Germany and Poland are very likely to provide diverging national anchoring domains. The second step in the quest for the maximization of inter-national differences, then, consists in identifying citizens that are likely to draw on these national anchoring domains. To achieve this end, teachers, estate agents and amateur soccer players were chosen as focus group participants. Regarding national culture, in particular teachers are well-suited to observe the mobilization of this anchoring domain as they play a key role in its transfer to the citizenry. The school is the school of the nation, as the theory of nationalism has it. Apart from this prominent access to national culture, the sample was chosen to cover a wide range of employment groups which are likely to have different experiences in the respective national varieties of capitalism. Among teachers, soccer player and estate agents, we find public and private sector employees, entrepreneurs and blue- and white-collar workers. The sample thus covers a wide range of potentially different economic experiences while also including those groups most likely to draw on national culture. Taken together, then, country and participant selection maximize the potential for inter-national differences. The focus groups were conducted in countries whose national repertoires of knowledge might fundamentally differ and they assembled participants very likely to use these repertoires as anchoring domains.

The advantage of reproducing these very unfavorable conditions is that it allows to reach conclusions about the severity of inter-national incompatibilities. In other words, the worst-case assumption can serve as a yardstick to assess the external validity of the findings of this study. This approach has been labelled the **Sinatra condition** as it allows for an inference to all more favorable conditions (Leuffen, 2007, pp. 152–153): if the European public sphere can make it here, it can make it anywhere. If national differences turn out to be insignificant even where I tried to stimulate them, it might be safe to assume that transnational debates will function in other, less problematic circumstances too.

Where the compatibility problem is concerned, the design thus allows for inferences beyond the sample. The external validity of my findings regarding the complexity problem is somewhat weaker. As participants were partly selected for their privileged access to specific anchoring domains, these anchoring strategies might be less common in other parts of the population. For some of my participants, it might have been easier to overcome complexity than for the average citizen. While for the compatibility problem, then, this study amounts to a full-flung test with decent external validity, for the complexity problem the aim of this investigation is more **exploratory**. The study can prove the existence and utility of multiple anchoring strategies, while not being indicative about their spread in the overall population.

I.4 Structure of the Book

The book is divided into three main parts, with the first developing the concept of national anchoring and the latter two spelling out its implications for the complexity and compatibility problems. Prior to Part I, Chapter 1 spells out the **theory and method** in greater detail. With regard to complexity, this implies a more elaborate introduction of social representation theory and a theoretical introduction of the various anchoring domains that will be discussed throughout the book (national culture, worth of nations, economic experiences and economic theory). Regarding compatibility, the chapter is mainly concerned with developing the three criteria to operationalize compatibility in the European public sphere. Furthermore, the chapter also elaborates how participant selection, focus group design and country selection combine into a worst-case scenario for the European public sphere. The chapter proceeds with a discussion of how the empirical material was analyzed, in particular focusing on the coding strategy and questions of internal validity. Finally, the chapter explains the structure of **Appendix 1**, a neutral overview of social representations of the economy designed for scholars more interested in lay perceptions of economics generally and not so much in the specific questions of this book.

Part I of the book introduces the concept of **national anchoring**. Empirically, this means that both Chapters 2 and 3 tackle differences in understanding between French, German and Polish participants. Both chapters also provide evidence for the central mechanism underlying national anchoring: the spread of knowledge via politicization, its sedimentation into national languages and its later mobilization by citizens in order to anchor complex economic arguments. The chapters focus, however, on different aspects of national knowledge, with Chapter 2 assessing various elements of national culture (recent politicization, academic cultures and grand history) and Chapter 3 discussing the worth of nations (representations of the characteristics of the national economy placed in transnational discourses of evaluation).

Part II of the book discusses the implications of national anchoring for the complexity problem in the European public sphere. It does so by addressing (and criticizing) two prominent approaches to public opinion research on economic issues. Chapter 4 addresses rational-choice-based approaches which tacitly assume that citizens hold perfect information on the distributional effects of economic consequences. It is shown that economic experiences do not guarantee inferences to objective economic conditions, but rather fuel a morally loaded discourse of the common people. Given the diversity of lay representations and their diversion from economic theory, Chapter 5 then turns to the deficit model, the assumption that lay representations of economics are uniformed and biased. The chapter diagnoses significant differences between participants with and without economic training, with the former entertaining much more positive representations of the market mechanism. Despite this diversion from economic theory, I argue that lay representations simply voice heterodox economic positions and can thus be viewed as informed. The negative judgments of the proponents of the deficit model for economics are often based on inadequate data, which obscures the quality of lay perceptions. Both Chapters 4 and 5 then combine into the argument that **citizens' representations of economics are diverse, but informed**. In both chapters, established theories of public opinion are found wanting because they fail to engage with this diversity of lay representations. The central take-away of Part II, therefore, is that public opinion research needs to take lay representations seriously and study them empirically in their own right. If this is done, the European public seems capable of overcoming the complexity problem.

Part III spells out how national anchoring affects compatibility in the European public sphere. Chapter 6 tests the three compatibility criteria developed in Chapter 1, comparing the inter-national differences found in Chapters 2 and 3 to the intra-national differences discussed in Chapter 5. It also conducts an analysis of alternative representations in order to distinguish misunderstandings from disagreements. Finding that compatibility issues in the European public sphere seem to be less pronounced than in national publics, Chapter 7 then proceeds to explore a potential explanation for this. It asks if the European public sphere functions so smoothly due to the existence of shared European anchoring domains. The chapter tests a range of theories that conceptualize the European demos in economic terms, including neoliberal conceptions and a vision based on a European social model. Yet, like on the national level, the most promising conception of a European community seems to be in terms of a European political culture, emerging from the politicization of shared problems that arise from market integration. Far from undermining the European public sphere, then, the concept of national anchoring might actually illuminate why it functions. **The European public sphere functions despite and because of national anchoring**.

In the conclusion, I review these results while drawing out promising avenues of further application and research. For public opinion research, I recommend a more pronounced focus on the idiosyncrasies of citizens' thought coupled with analyses of official discourse to develop a theory of political resonance. For European studies, I maintain that the results strengthen those voices of the debate that see the EU increasingly resembling national polities. Given the functioning of the European public sphere with regard to questions of understanding, the EU increasingly resembles a proper transnational democracy.

Notes

1 I am aware that the terms "experts" and "laypeople" come with strong normative baggage, implying some positions to be superior or better than others. It should be clear, however, that I employ these terms due to their currency in the literature on the public understanding of science and not to express a judgment or a hierarchization.

2 I use the term "inter-national" to refer to differences between citizens of different nations, i.e., citizens with access to different bodies of national knowledge. I use the hyphen to differentiate it from the term "international" which refers to relationships between states rather than to differences between the people living in the nation state. It should also be distinguished from "transnational" as this is mainly employed to designate similarities and relationships across national societies, rather than differences between them ("transnational differences" seem to be a bit of an oxymoron). Finally, I often employ the term "intra-national" in opposition to "inter-national". "Intra-national", then, refers to differences appearing between citizens within the same nation or national public sphere.

Bibliography

Bartels, L. M. (2005). Homer Gets a Tax Cut: Inequality and Public Policy in the American Mind. *Perspectives on Politics*, *3*(1), 15–31. https://doi.org/10.1017/S1537592705050036

Beck, U. (1999). *World Risk Society*. Wiley.

Brinegar, A. P. & Jolly, S. K. (2005). Location, Location, Location: National Contextual Factors and Public Support for European Integration. *European Union Politics*, *6*(2), 155–180. https://doi.org/10.1177/1465116505051981

Calhoun, C. J. (1997). *Nationalism*. University of Minnesota Press.

Caplan, B. (2011). The Myth of the Rational Voter. In *The Myth of the Rational Voter*. Princeton University Press. www.degruyter.com/document/doi/10.1515/9781400828821/html

Converse, P. E. (2006) [1964]. The Nature of Belief Systems in Mass Publics. *Critical Review*, *18*(1–3), 1–74. https://doi.org/10.1080/08913810608443650

Cortassa, C. (2016). In Science Communication, Why Does the Idea of a Public Deficit Always Return? The Eternal Recurrence of the Public Deficit. *Public Understanding of Science*, *25*(4), 447–459. https://doi.org/10.1177/0963662516629745

Cramer, K. J. & Toff, B. (2017). The Fact of Experience: Rethinking Political Knowledge and Civic Competence. *Perspectives on Politics*, *15*(3), 754–770. https://doi.org/10.1017/S1537592717000949

Duchesne, S., Ingelgom, V. V., Frazer, E., Haegel, F., & Van Ingelgom, V. (2013). *Citizens' Reactions to European Integration Compared: Overlooking Europe* (2013 edition). Palgrave Macmillan.

Eder, K., & Kantner, C. (2000). Transnationale Resonanzstrukturen in Europa. In M. Bach (Ed.), *Die Europäisierung nationaler Gesellchaften. Sonderheft 40 der Kölner Zeitschrift für Soziologie und Sozialpsychologie* (pp. 306–331). https://doi.org/10.1007/978-3-322-80390-0_13

Ehrlich, S. D. (2010). Who Supports Compensation? Individual Preferences for Trade-Related Unemployment Insurance. *Business and Politics*, *12*(1), 1–22. https://doi.org/10.2202/1469-3569.1289

Farkas, B. (2011). The Central and Eastern European Model of Capitalism. *Post-Communist Economies*, *23*(1), 15–34. https://doi.org/10.1080/14631377.2011.546972

Flynn, D. J., Nyhan, B. & Reifler, J. (2017). The Nature and Origins of Misperceptions: Understanding False and Unsupported Beliefs About Politics. *Political Psychology*, *38*(S1), 127–150. https://doi.org/10.1111/pops.12394

Fraile, M. & Ferrer, M. (2005). Explaining the Determinants of Public Support for Cuts in Unemployment Benefits Spending across OECD Countries. *International Sociology*, *20*(4), 459–481. https://doi.org/10.1177/0268580905058327

Gamson, G. & William, A. (1992). *Talking Politics*. Cambridge University Press.

Gerhards, J. (1998). Öffentlichkeit. In O. Jarren, U. Sarcinelli, & U. Saxer (Eds.), *Politische Kommunikation in der demokratischen Gesellschaft: Ein Handbuch mit Lexikonteil* (pp. 268–274). VS Verlag für Sozialwissenschaften. https://doi.org/10.1007/978-3-322-80348-1_14

Giddens, A. (1994). *Beyond Left and Right: The Future of Radical Politics*. Stanford University Press.

Goren, P. (2012). *On Voter Competence*. Oxford University Press.

Gunn, P. (2014). Democracy and Epistocracy. *Critical Review*, *26*(1–2), 59–79. https://doi.org/10.1080/08913811.2014.907041

Habermas, J. (1992). Further Reflections on the Public Sphere. In C. J. Calhoun (Ed.), *Habermas and the Public Sphere* (pp. 421–461). MIT Press.

Hearn, J. (2006). *Rethinking Nationalism: A Critical Introduction*. Palgrave Macmillan.

Hepp, A., Elsler, M., Lingenberg, S., Mollen, A., Möller, J., Offerhaus, A., Sword, K. & Pospielovsky, D. V. (2016). *The Communicative Construction of Europe: Cultures of Political Discourse, Public Sphere, and the Euro Crisis*. Palgrave Macmillan UK. https://doi.org/10.1057/9781137453136

Hutter, S. & Grande, E. (2014). Politicizing Europe in the National Electoral Arena: A Comparative Analysis of Five West European Countries, 1970–2010. *JCMS: Journal of Common Market Studies*, *52*(5), 1002–1018. https://doi.org/10.1111/jcms.12133

Jayet, C. (2020). The Meaning of the European Union and Public Support for European Integration. *JCMS: Journal of Common Market Studies*, *58*(5), 1144–1164. https://doi.org/10.1111/jcms.13022

Kantner, C. (2014). The European Public Sphere and the Debate about Humanitarian Military Interventions. *European Security*, *23*(4), 409–429. https://doi.org/10.1080/09662839.2014.890595

Koopmans, R. (2014). How Advanced is the Europeanization of Public Spheres? Comparing German and European Structures of Political Communication. In T. Risse (Ed.), *European Public Spheres: Politics Is Back* (pp. 63–96). Cambridge University Press. https://doi.org/10.1017/CBO9781139963343.005

Krzyzanowski, M. (2008). Analyzing Focus Group Discussions. In R. Wodak & M. Krzyzanowski (Eds.), *Qualitative Discourse Analysis in the Social Sciences* (pp. 273–306). Palgrave Macmillan.

Lamont, M., & Molnár, V. (2002). The Study of Boundaries in the Social Sciences. *Annual Review of Sociology*, *28*(1), 167–195. https://doi.org/10.1146/annurev.soc.28.110601.141107

Lamont, M., & Thévenot, L. (2000). Introduction: Toward a Renewed Comparative Cultural Sociology. In L. Thévenot & M. Lamont (Eds.), *Rethinking Comparative Cultural Sociology: Repertoires of Evaluation in France and the United States* (pp. 1–22). Cambridge University Press. https://doi.org/10.1017/CBO9780511628108.001

Leuffen, D. (2007). Case Selection and Selection Bias in Small-*n* Research. In T. Gschwend & F. Schimmelfennig (Eds.), *Research Design in Political Science: How to Practice What They Preach* (pp. 145–160). Palgrave Macmillan UK. https://doi.org/10.1057/9780230598881_8

Lingenberg, S. (2010). Fallstudien zur europäischen Verfassungsdebatte. In S. Lingenberg (Ed.), *Europäische Publikumsöffentlichkeiten: Ein pragmatischer Ansatz* (pp. 183–226). VS Verlag für Sozialwissenschaften. https://doi.org/10.1007/978-3-531-92120-4_5

Lupia, A. (2016). *Uninformed: Why People Know So Little about Politics and What We Can Do about It*. Oxford University Press.
Mau, S. (2005). Europe from the Bottom: Assessing Personal Gains and Losses and Its Effects on EU Support. *Journal of Public Policy*, *25*(3), 289–311. https://doi.org/10.1017/S0143814X05000346
Moscovici, S. (1984). The Phenomenon of Social Representations. In R. M. Farr & S. Moscovici (Eds.), *Social representations* (pp. 1–67). TPB.
Moscovici, S. (2004). *La psychanalyse, son image et son public*. Presses Universitaires de France. https://doi.org/10.3917/puf.mosco.2004.01
Nölke, A., & Vliegenthart, A. (2009). Enlarging the Varieties of Capitalism: The Emergence of Dependent Market Economies in East Central Europe. *World Politics*, *61*(4), 670–702. https://doi.org/10.1017/S0043887109990098
O'Rourke, K. H., Sinnott, R., Richardson, J. D. & Rodrik, D. (2001). The Determinants of Individual Trade Policy Preferences: International Survey Evidence [with Comments and Discussion]. *Brookings Trade Forum*, 157–206. JSTOR.
Özkirimli, U. (2005). *Contemporary Debates on Nationalism: A Critical Engagement*. Macmillan Education UK.
Rehm, P. (2011). Social Policy by Popular Demand. *World Politics*, *63*(2), 271–299. https://doi.org/10.1017/S0043887111000037
Rehm, P. (2016). *Risk Inequality and Welfare States: Social Policy Preferences, Development, and Dynamics*. Cambridge University Press.
Risse, T. (2010). *A Community of Europeans?: Transnational Identities and Public Spheres*. Cornell University Press.
Risse, T. (2014a). No Demos? Identities and Public Spheres in the Euro Crisis. *JCMS: Journal of Common Market Studies*, *52*(6), 1207–1215. https://doi.org/10.1111/jcms.12189
Risse, T. (2014b, November). *Introduction*. European Public Spheres: Politics Is Back. https://doi.org/10.1017/CBO9781139963343.002
Schmidt, V. (2003). French Capitalism Transformed, Yet Still a Third Variety of Capitalism. *Economy and Society*, *32*(4), 526–554. https://doi.org/10.1080/0308514032000141693
Sniderman, P. M., Brody, R. A., & Tetlock, P. E. (1993). *Reasoning and Choice: Explorations in Political Psychology*. Cambridge University Press.
Statham, P. (2010). Europe's Search for a Public. In R. Koopmans & P. Statham (Eds.), *The Making of a European Public Sphere: Media Discourse and Political Contention* (pp. 1–11). Cambridge University Press.
Susen, S. (2015). *The 'Postmodern Turn' in the Social Sciences*. Springer.
Swedberg, R. (2018). Folk Economics and Its Role in Trump's Presidential Campaign: An Exploratory Study. *Theory and Society*, *47*(1), 1–36. https://doi.org/10.1007/s11186-018-9308-8
Swidler, A. (1986). Culture in Action: Symbols and Strategies. *American Sociological Review*, *51*(2), 273–286. JSTOR. https://doi.org/10.2307/2095521
White, J. (2011). *Political Allegiance After European Integration*. Palgrave Macmillan. www.palgrave.com/gp/book/9780230279780
Zaller, J. R. (1992). *The Nature and Origins of Mass Opinion*. Cambridge University Press.

1 Investigating Complexity and Compatibility in the European Public Sphere

1.1 Introduction

The European public sphere has received an increasing amount of scholarly attention in the past two decades. In this vast literature, there are two findings which seem to produce a twin problem. First, the European public sphere is **transnational in nature**. It emerges where the same European issues are discussed at the same time in separate national publics, rather than in a unified supranational communicative space (Risse, 2014a, 2014b; Statham, 2010). The second feature is issue **complexity**. The European public sphere is most developed in areas where the EU commands considerable competences and these, alas, often tend to be quite complex (Koopmans, 2014). Taken together, issue complexity and the transnational mode of functioning create a twin problem that this book is dedicated to. How can compatibility be maintained under conditions of issue complexity?

This chapter outlines how the complexity and the compatibility problems can be investigated. For each of these problems, the chapter will present central **concepts**, an **operationalization** of these concepts and **hypotheses** providing potential answers to the problems. Section 1.2 does this for the complexity problem while Section 1.3 is dedicated to compatibility. Section 1.4 then describes the **research design**, that is, the way the data necessary to answer the research questions was collected. This section centers on focus group design, participant selection and country selection. The final section of the chapter presents the **method** of analysis for the data thus gathered.

1.2 The Complexity Problem

Investigating the complexity problem is essentially a quest of the sociology of knowledge. The object of analysis is people's perceptions of complex phenomena. I have already pointed out in the introduction that I rely on social representation theory to describe the way complex or novel issues are appropriated by a largely lay public. I also already introduced the concepts of anchoring and of anchoring domains to describe this process in greater detail. Citizens employ pre-existing stocks of knowledge (anchoring domains) to

DOI: 10.4324/9781003335610-2

render new concepts intelligible (anchoring; Moscovici, 1984; Wagner et al., 1999, p. 98; Höijer, 2011, pp. 7–13). The result of an anchoring process, then, is called a representation. Social representations are intersubjectively shared meaning structures, that is, patterns of knowledge that exist across minds (Wagner et al., 1999, pp. 95–96). As such, they are the object of sociology of knowledge and thus a perfect point of departure to investigate the complexity problem.

Yet, answering the complexity question is trickier than just establishing these concepts. This is so because social representations are not uniform in modern societies. For each complex issue, there are a variety of anchoring domains that could potentially make it more understandable for citizens. Accordingly, there will also be a variety of representations of complex issues depending on the anchoring domains mobilized. It is important to note that the concept of social representations was developed in response to the Durkheimian idea of collective representations (Gillespie, 2008, p. 375). While thus remaining close to a Durkheimian ontology in its focus on intersubjective rather than purely individual meaning structures, social representation theory diagnoses a coexistence of knowledge authorities in modern societies (Voelklein & Howarth, 2005, p. 433). Unlike traditional societies, modern society is a "diverse symbolic space" (Jovchelovitch, 2006, p. 118) and individuals in it have access to competing forms of knowledge.

The answer to the complexity problem thus lies in exploring the different ways complex issues can be understood by a lay public. Issue complexity gives rise to a diversity of lay representations. The following sections outline the tools necessary to grasp this diversity. The conceptual section (1.2.1) deals with the fact that representations are always social, that is, that they always exist for a social group. In doing so, it discusses the relationship between social structure and individual agency, which is crucial in this context. The following section (1.2.2), then, attempts to operationalize the link between groups of individuals and knowledge structures. It is only once we understood how individuals have access to specific anchoring domains that we can formulate hypotheses for the complexity problem (Section 1.2.3).

1.2.1 Concepts: Linking Anchoring Domains and Social Groups

In social representation theory, a social representation (a construction of reality) is always valid for a specific **social group** (Elcheroth et al., 2011, pp. 739–741; Wagner et al., 1999, pp. 96–97). The size of this community can vary; it can be a civilization, a nation or even a family (Jovchelovitch, 2006, pp. 71–72). The idea that knowledge is bounded to a community is also widely shared beyond social representation theory: it features, for instance, notions of culture (e.g., Lamont & Thévenot, 2000, p.5) or even the Habermasian concept of a lifeworld (Jovchelovitch, 2006, pp. 91–97). What is common to these approaches, then, is that there is a link between social groups and the knowledge they hold. In this study thus, I will identify social groups via their access to bodies of knowledge, that is, via their **access to anchoring domains**.

At first sight, this proposition might seem to have heavy structuralist undertones. Can we reduce an individual to what she was taught in school or to what he read in the news? Doesn't this reduce individual agency in forming opinions to an unacceptable minimum? The answer to this concern is similar in many areas of the social sciences today: acknowledging the impact of knowledge structures need not eliminate the space for agency. Rather, knowledge can be treated as a *reservoir* individuals selectively draw on (Lamont & Molnár, 2002; Lamont & Thévenot, 2000; Swidler, 1986). The fact that modern society is characterized by a variety of knowledge authorities also implies that individuals have a variety of knowledges at their disposal (Jovchelovitch, 2006, pp. 118–120; Provencher, 2011, pp. 380–385; Strauss, 2005, p. 223). Knowledge, in this understanding, is not determining, it is *available* (White, 2011, pp. 62–63). In selectively drawing on these reservoirs of knowledge, individuals are able re-interpret and re-shape the social structure they are surrounded by (Quinn, 2005, p. 22). Within social representation theory, this approach has been known under the label of "thinking society" (Farr, 1993; Moscovici, 1984; see also Duveen, 2007, p. 545; Marková et al., 1998, p. 455; Voelklein & Howarth, 2005, pp. 439–443). Rather than taking a side, this approach resolves the structure–agency dilemma by granting the individual an interpretive autonomy.

Accordingly, in my study, anchoring domains are understood as reservoirs of knowledge citizens selectively draw on. Statements in the empirical material are not necessarily viewed as fixed opinions but rather as reactions provoked by a specific combination of contextual factors (Duchesne et al., 2013; White, 2011, pp. 34–39). This view has the advantage of not excluding the possibility that individuals might choose to react differently in a different setting. Nevertheless, this kind of approach still reveals what forms of knowledge were available. Defining social groups based on access to anchoring domains thus does not presuppose a determination of individual arguments by knowledge structures while still allowing to identify social representations that are particular to specific groups. Thus, the diversity of social representation in modern societies becomes explainable as it results from different social groups' access to different anchoring domains. The following section explains how this link between social groups and anchoring domains can be empirically traced.

1.2.2 Operationalization: Transmission Mechanisms and Language Use

In order to identify which social groups have access to which anchoring domains, I mainly rely on two empirical indicators: transmission mechanisms and language use. Although both require rather different methods to be empirically shown, they equally serve the purpose of revealing the anchoring domains individuals draw on to render complex issues intelligible.

Let us begin with transmission mechanisms. Under the term transmission mechanism, I subsume the events or institutions that bring knowledge to an individual. Put differently, transmission mechanisms refer to the way communities perpetuate and produce knowledge. In this study, I consider three such transmission mechanisms: education, media and personal experience. All three are generally acknowledged as extremely central mechanisms of knowledge transmission in any society (e.g., Prior, 2007).

Transmission mechanisms help to operationalize the link between social groups and anchoring domains as they are empirically traceable. They exemplify how different communities of knowledge are produced at different spatial levels. Let us consider the example of **education**: while some elements of educational curricula (e.g., math) have an almost global status, for most other subjects the content is decided by local authorities (e.g., history). Beyond differences of location, knowledge communities can be distinguished along professional lines, with academic disciplines or university faculties being examples of educational institutions maintaining such communities. Similarly, public spheres and the **media** available in them provide different forms of knowledge for spatial and professional communities. Media outlets differ widely in their reach, and expert publics provide knowledge to very specific audiences. Assessing the educational institutions and the media individuals are exposed to thus can lead a long way in identifying which anchoring domains they have access to. We can trace an individual's access to such domains by inquiring about her educational past, her media consumption and even about the location where she passed most of her life.

The same is true of **personal experience**, the third transmission mechanism to be discussed here. Personal experience has been repeatedly shown to be an important aspect of anchoring domains, in particular for political issues (Gamson, 1992, pp. 153–155; Stoker et al., 2016, p. 15). Thus, experience can be crucial in reducing complexity. Linking unknown ideas to episodes of one's own life seems to be a natural and quite individual way of making sense of the world.[1] What is more, we can empirically trace some experiences an individual has made by acquiring biographical information. Some jobs, for example, come with a greater probability of experiencing strikes; old age comes with a higher probability of having experienced retirement. Experiences thus form important anchoring domains and, in many cases, the structural reason why the experience was made can be empirically traced.

Apart from transmission mechanisms such as education, media and experience, another important indicator of access to anchoring domains is **language use**. The process of anchoring has an important linguistic dimension. Naming or labelling an unknown phenomenon is a very common first step when individuals are confronted with new ideas. The unknown object is thus placed within a pre-existing category, which will determine its future understanding (Moscovici, 1984, pp. 30–36; Wagner et al., 1999, pp. 97–98).[2] Language thus is an important part of anchoring domains individuals can mobilize. Furthermore, the use of specific vocabularies, jargons, concepts, expressions and metaphors can be indicative of the anchoring domain mobilized. Empirically, we will be able to recognize scientific jargon or specific metaphors that are current within a certain political camp. The language being used for a social representation thus can allow us to empirically trace the anchoring domain mobilized for its construction.

In identifying social groups, then, attention must be paid to the experiences and vocabularies members of these groups share as well as to their media exposure and education. In the rest of the book, I use these indicators to trace social groups' access to anchoring domains. Taken together, they should allow us to grasp the diversity of anchoring domains present in modern societies and thus will help to illuminate the various ways complex phenomena are understood by a lay citizenry.

1.2.3 Hypotheses Regarding the Complexity Problem

In order to provide potential solutions to the complexity problem, the hypotheses incorporate the concepts developed in the previous sections. To do so each of the hypothesis will identify, first, an anchoring domain; second, a social group having access to this domain through a specific transmission mechanism; and finally, the content of social representations of the economy formed when the anchoring domain is mobilized. Regarding the last point, particular attention is paid to representations of causal processes and to the normative reference points employed. Each hypothesis thus predicts how a specific social group will understand and judge complex economic phenomena. An overview of the four hypotheses and of their predictions regarding these dimensions can be found in Table 1.1.

1.2.3.1 The Market Experience Hypothesis

Public opinion research is a natural place to start looking for potential hypothesis as it has the same research object as the present study: in both cases, the focus is on citizens' perceptions. Yet, some rational-choice-inspired branches of public opinion research seem to be quite unconcerned by the complexity problem. Rather than worrying about lay representations, these branches of literature seem to rely on the optimistic assumption that lay citizens will understand complex economic issues in just the same way as they are described by expert theory. Borrowing from statistics, I would suggest to think of this conception as a kind of null hypothesis for the complexity problem. Just as a null hypothesis stipulates that there is no correlation between two phenomena, the **market experience hypothesis** predicts that there is no complexity problem after all. Which representations of economics should we expect to find then? And how is this knowledge transmitted to the citizenry?

The central assumption in these branches of public opinion research seems to be a vision of a homo economicus capable of making correct inferences to larger economic processes from his experiences in the market. The idea of the

Table 1.1 Hypotheses with regard to complexity problem. Which group has access to which forms of knowledge and how does this shape representations of economic processes and normative judgment thereof?

	Anchoring domain mobilized to accommodate complexity	**Transmission mechanism to social group**	**Social representations**	
			Representations of economic processes	**Normative reference points**
Market experience (null hypothesis: no complexity problem)	• Anchoring in experience of market processes	• Experience (exposure to relevant market process)	• Accurate inference from experience to economic theory (uniform representations)	• Individual benefit (differences in judgment based on position in the economy)
Economic theory	• Anchoring knowledge of economic theory	• Education (economic training in school or university)	• Differences between experts and laypeople	• Market as mutually beneficial (experts)
Worth of nations	• Anchoring in knowledge of characteristics of national economy	• Public sphere/ education (higher education level, higher exposure)	• Inter-nationally different representations	• Benefit for nation (differences in judgment based on strengths/ weaknesses of national economy)
National culture	• Anchoring in national language, history and academic culture	• Education/ public sphere (higher education level, higher exposure)	• Inter-nationally different representations	• Normative judgments implicit in language or in collective memories

homo economicus can be characterized by two features. It contains, first, an assumption about self-interest being the most important normative consideration and, second, a capacity for rational cost–benefit calculation (Pettit, 1995). Individuals are thus understood as rational agents primarily concerned with their own advantage. Based on this assumption, explanations of individuals' assessment of public policies can be generated. By calculating how (mainly material) costs and benefits are distributed in society individuals' preferences can be inferred. In other words, it is an individual's **position in the economy** that determines her opinion.

What kind of social representations of economic processes should we expect to find if this assumption was correct? Public opinion studies using such an approach cover a wide range of economic issues. Yet, for sake of brevity, I only review studies dealing with the economic issues under scrutiny in this book: trade and unemployment. Regarding trade, a common approach to determine citizens' opinions on trade policy relies on the Heckscher–Ohlin model (Brinegar & Jolly, 2005, pp. 156–158; O'Rourke et al., 2001). This economic model predicts costs and benefits of factor mobility, assuming that scarce factors of production will lose out. In a country with high employment levels (i.e., where labor is scarce), for example, wages might drop as a result of international factor mobility. More workers might move to the country, thus increasing labor supply and decreasing the profitability of the formerly scarce factor. For public opinion, then, it is assumed that attitudes toward trade can be derived from a country's factor endowments in combination with the individuals' position in the economy. Workers in low-wage countries should favor liberalization, capital owners should oppose it (and vice versa in high wage countries). According to this approach, individuals calculate their personal costs and benefits from trade to determine their opinion on it. The approach has frequently been applied in European studies too. Conceptualizing the EU as a common market (i.e., a space of factor mobility), individuals are supposed to derive their attitudes toward the EU from a utilitarian calculation of the costs and benefits of market integration (Gabel, 1998; for a summary see Hobolt & de Vries, 2016, p. 420).

Similar arguments circulate in the literature on public opinion on unemployment, or, more precisely, on unemployment benefits. Unemployment benefits in this branch of theory are viewed as an insurance paid for by tax money. Support or opposition to welfare policies, then, depends on individuals' risk assessment: the more vulnerable a citizen is to unemployment, the greater her support for generous benefits (Blekesaune, 2007, pp. 393–394; Ehrlich, 2010; Fraile & Ferrer, 2005, pp. 461–462; Rehm, 2016). The mechanism is concisely summarized by Rehm (2011, p. 272):

> There is strong evidence that demand for unemployment benefits increases with the risk of unemployment (due to an increase in the expected utility from them) and that it decreases with income (since the costs of unemployment insurance are related to income). On average,

citizens seem to comprehend the redistributive and insuring function of unemployment benefits rather well.

For unemployment just as much as far trade, individuals are supposed to form their opinions based on a self-interested cost–benefit calculation.

Yet how do citizens acquire the information necessary for such cost–benefit calculation? How is knowledge of the economic effect of a policy transmitted to the citizenry? The approaches discussed above suggest that citizens are capable of **understanding complex economic processes in a uniform manner**. More precisely, rational citizens should be able to make inferences to larger economic processes from their personal experience. In the unemployment example, the notion of risk refers to such a highly complex economic issue. Citizens are supposed to assess job risk in the economy from the assessment of their own workplace, so it seems. Moreover, this inference is supposed to be 'correct' in the sense that citizens reach the same conclusions as economic experts analyzing the state of the economy. In the trade example, similarly, citizens are supposed to do a calculation equivalent to the Heckscher–Ohlin model based on their personal economic situation. From the development of personal income or product prices, an inference is to be made to the workings of a trade deal. The utilitarian approach, then, might be said to operate under an assumption of quasi-perfect information (Darriet & Bourgeois-Gironde, 2015, p. 246; Mau, 2005). It trusts individuals to reach the same conclusions as economic theories based on an **inference from market experience**.

The market experience hypothesis, thus, seems to deny the existence of a complexity problem. The usage of market experience as an anchoring domain is taken to guarantee an 'adequate' understanding economic arguments (i.e., an understanding akin to economic theory). Accordingly, there would be no more reason to investigate the specificities of lay representations generated in the attempt to render complex issues more intelligible. This view is challenged by some branches of economic sociology that view knowledge of economic theory as a product of education rather than as the result of an inference. Based on this literature, a hypothesis opposing the market experience hypothesis is developed in the following section.

1.2.3.2 The Economic Theory Hypothesis

Rather than by inference from market experience, citizens might understand complex economic issues simply because they know **economic theory**. While it seems unrealistic to assume that all citizens possess such knowledge, it might well be true for some. The economic theory hypothesis thus predicts that there will be differences between expert and lay understandings, that is, differences between those with access to economic theory and those not familiar with this anchoring domain.

What kind of representations of economics should we expect to find among those familiar with economic theory? What are the central elements of economic theory as an anchoring domain? Economic theory is a scientific paradigm that evolved over the past 200 years. It constitutes a distinguishable body of thought providing a specific vocabulary and a number of paradigmatic assumptions that might serve as a primary anchoring domain for those having had access to economic training. It is obviously beyond the scope of this literature review to point out all the patterns of argument particular to economic theory. I mainly wish to point to one substantive argument which has long been at the core of economic theory: the belief in **mutual benefit generated by the workings of the free market**. This belief in the positive effects of competition characterized the paradigmatic shift from mercantilism to early liberal thought and it has remained center stage since ever since (despite changing conception of how exactly competition comes about; Foucault, 2006a [1979], pp. 168–175).

Due to the centrality of the mutual benefit argument, its traces can be found in a number of economic theories. For reasons of brevity again, I will only briefly highlight some applications to the issue areas of trade and unemployment. For trade, the classical school of economics already developed the model of comparative advantage. In opposition to earlier models of absolute advantage, this theory states that trade is beneficial even if all the products of one trading partner are superior to those of the other. Relying on a conception of opportunity cost, the argument postulates that specialization of countries creates advantages for both sides even if one side's products are inferior (Brue & Grant, 2007 chapter 5–7). Trade thus is shown to produce benefits to all parties involved. A similar argument about liberty, specialization and mutual benefits underpins the neoclassical conception of the labor market. Here, the free interplay between supply and demand of labor is taken to bring unemployment down to a natural minimum level (Baxandall, 2004; Brue & Grant, 2007, chapters 15 and 18). Like in trade, barriers to this free exchange are depicted as deadweight losses to society overall; a free market, on the other hand, engenders mutual benefits.

How is this knowledge of economic theory transmitted to the population, then? How can we identify the social group that is likely to employ the representations described above? Two transmission mechanisms seem to be promising candidates: First, economic theory might be transmitted via the public sphere, for example, via expert journals and media. More frequent (or at least: much more frequently observed in empirical studies) is a second transmission mechanism: **education**. Empirical studies have repeatedly shown individuals with access to economic training to behave and argue differently than those who have never studied economics. Although some have argued that behavioral differences might result from a self-selection bias (i.e., people with a specific mindset chose to study economics; Carter & Irons, 1991), other studies have shown the performativity of economic theories (i.e., economic theory shapes actors' behavior rather than just describing it; Mackenzie, 2008). On a discursive level, most studies find significant differences between those who do and who do not have access to economic theories (Działo &

Gawrońska-Nowak, 2017, pp. 121–133; Leiser et al., 2010). The economically trained have been shown to use deductive reasoning, employing tenants of economic theory as an initial anchor (van Bavel & Gaskell, 2004). Access to economic theory thus might engender specific social representations of economic processes not shared by those who never studied economics.

Having established education as the most prominent transmission mechanism also explains the narrow focus on mutual benefit arguments in the paragraphs above. The neoclassical theories cited above have, of course, been significantly amended; modern economics provides a more complex view of these phenomena and a multitude of diverging theories explaining them. Yet, the aim here was not to give an overview of present economic debates. Rather, I tried to identify central tenets which are transmitted via economic education in schools or universities. It is no coincidence that the citations above were drawn from economic textbooks: the models presented above are objects of study in most university or high school classes in economics. Mutual benefit arguments, then, make up an essential element of the economic knowledge transmitted to students of these disciplines. Citizens having been confronted with them in education might be more likely to mobilize them as anchoring domain for European policy issues.

A last factor that might help us in the identification of individuals with access to economic training is language use. Apart from certain paradigmatic arguments, economic theory also provides a specific jargon, a body of discipline-specific vocabulary allowing the designation of economic phenomena in accordance with theory. The vocabulary of economic theory is a highly metaphorical one, frequently adapting terms from modern physics (e.g., equilibrium, elasticity, inflation; Mitchell, 1998, pp. 86–87). Another set of frequent economic **metaphors** depicts the economy as a machine in need of careful engineering (van Bavel & Gaskell, 2004, p. 432). The presence of such discipline-specific expressions might help us to detect when economic theory is used as an anchoring domain.

To sum up then, economic knowledge can be conceptualized as an anchoring domain, and depending on the transmission mechanism, different conclusions for the complexity problem are reached. If understood as an inference from market experience, economic knowledge might generate uniform representations of economic phenomena. If understood as the body of knowledge generated by an academic discipline and transmitted via educational institutions, economic theory might produce differences between those with access to economic theory and those who never studied it. The market experience and the economic theory hypotheses thus set the baseline for the investigation of the complexity problem. While the former suggests that no complexity problem exists, the latter affirms that lay representations of economics differ from economic theory. Should the latter be the case, we would have to wonder in what way lay representations are different from economic theory. That is, an investigation of non-economic anchoring domains would be necessary. Which other anchoring domains could be available to citizens to render complex economic questions intelligible? The following sections conceptualize national knowledge as such a potential solution to the complexity problem.

1.2.3.3 The Worth of Nations Hypothesis

In the introduction, I have argued that nationalism can engender bodies of knowledge to which people living in the nation-state often have privileged access. In the words of social representation theory, nationalism can create anchoring domains, and it guarantees access to these anchoring domains via various transmission mechanisms. National knowledge, then, can probably solve the complexity problem by providing nationally specific representations of complex issues.

The first hypothesis that can be derived from this understanding of nationalism is based on the literature on neoliberal nationalism (and, in turn, methodological nationalism). A central observation of this literature is that citizens are aware of the specific characteristics of their national economies. Citizens might know specific strengths and weaknesses of their national economy and they might mobilize this knowledge to comprehend and judge complex economic processes. Comparisons of status of the national economy to other countries, then, produce an economic hierarchy of states, giving citizens the reason to take pride or pity in the state of their nation. The strength of the national economy thus determines **the worth of nations** (Greenfeld, 1995). Transmitted mainly through media, such knowledge of the state of the national economy could be a suitable anchoring domain allowing citizens to render complex economic issues intelligible.

In order to understand how knowledge of the worth of nations is produced and how it is transmitted to citizens, it is instructive to review the literature on methodological nationalism. Two inter-related processes can be distinguished here. On the one hand, methodological nationalism implies that nations are treated as an ontological category in many social sciences.[3] In many disciplines, nation-states are accepted as the appropriate object of analysis (Chernilo, 2006). The concept of society, for example, is most frequently operationalized as the social system within a nation state.[4] Ulrich Beck has referred to this equation of nation-state and society as a paradigm of sociology (Beck, 2007, p. 286). This approach is reinforced, on the other hand, by the availability of data on the national level. With the establishment of the modern state, new forms of government emerge that require knowledge about the state of affairs within the nation (Foucault, 2006b, pp. 400–402 & 449–513, 2006a, pp. 13–40; Nassehi, 2019, pp. 54–59; Offe, 2005, p. 141). A prime example of this new mode of knowledge generation is the birth of the statistic; to this day, most statistical data available specifically refers to national populations. By providing the necessary means for analysis, the nation-state thus reinforced tendencies in the social sciences which viewed the nation as the adequate focus of research. Modern social sciences thus constitute the **nation as a knowable object**.

Little surprisingly, methodological nationalism also pertains to economics. A tendency to treat the nation as a natural unit of analysis is already discernable in its foundational work, Adam Smith's *Wealth of Nations.* Arguably, however, the impact of methodological nationalism on economic thought becomes more visible in the 20th century. The notion of the economy, for example, only emerges in the beginning of the century. While the expression 'economies' was priorly used as a reference to the savings of a household, in Keynesian economics 'the economy' came to denote the totality of economic relationships (Mitchell, 1998; Nakano, 2004). Keynesian economics tellingly distinguishes between an inside and an outside of the economy – thus clearly incorporating a foreign–domestic distinction. Like the term society, the notion of the economy thus presupposes the nation-state as the natural unit of analysis. Moreover, with the emergence of the concept of the economy comes a need of knowing and measuring it. The first half of the 20th century, then, witnesses the exponential growth of economic statistics. Indicators such as unemployment rate or economic growth are naturally calculated on a national basis (Mitchell, 1998). In economics as much as in other domains of science, then, we see the impact of nationalism as a paradigm and its reinforcement through the establishment of statistical data on a national level. Economic science constitutes the **national economy** as a knowable object.

Based on this vision of the national economy as a unit of analysis with discernable features, a specific vision of the international order emerges in the second half of 20th century. This vision of international relations as an economic competition of states has most forcefully been highlighted by the literature on neoliberalism standing in a Foucauldian tradition (Foucault, 2006a, pp. 300–324 [1979]; Fougner, 2008). Broadly speaking, Foucault defines neoliberalism as the application of market principles to areas thus far not governed by economic rationalities. In combination with methodological nationalism, this allows for the application of economic concepts originally developed for firms to entire nations and their population. By analogy with firms competing in the market, nation-states can be described as economic subjects whose fate it is to succeed or fail in a global competition (Rosamond, 2002, p. 164). Nation-states are expected to raise their economic competitiveness by creating a favorable environment for the market; they compete for investment and qualified specialists, just as companies compete for labor and profit (Fougner, 2008; for specific country cases see Kangas, 2013; O'Toole, 2003; Peet, 2002). While neoliberalism is frequently seen as a counter-current to Keynesianism, in both schools of thought an ontology of nations persists. Neoliberalism relies on a vision of the nation-state as an economic subject competing with other states in the international arena.

Just as the concept of the economy produced new forms of measurement within nation-states, the conceptualization of the economic world order as a race for competitiveness generates its own form of knowledge production. A major role in this process is played by international mechanisms of evaluation. Multiple, mostly neoliberally oriented institutions rank states according to their competitiveness, the freedom of their economy or their capacity for innovation (Fougner, 2008). Bond and currency markets permanently judge the economic attractiveness of states (White, 2019, pp. 69–73). Thus, they establish a hierarchy of states, showing the worth rather than the wealth of nations (Greenfeld, 1995, p. 555). The national economy thus is not only knowable through statistical measurement on the nation-state level. Placed within an international competition, it also becomes the object of **benchmarking and ranking**.

How does this knowledge of the state of the nation and of the international competition of states reach the citizenry? And, more importantly, how can we empirically identify the moments in which this anchoring domain is mobilized? For the worth of nations hypothesis, the most relevant transmission mechanism seems to be the **media** (although education might also play a marginal role). To begin with, many characteristics of the national economy are updated on a regular basis and frequently are reported on in the news. Examples of such economic statistics that are highly visible are unemployment levels, trade deficits or economic growth. Consequently, studies of levels of political knowledge highlight that this knowledge still mainly covers the national political and economic system (e.g., Armingeon & Ceka, 2014). Apart from national statistics, then, international rankings appear frequently in the national media, too. This might be so as such rankings lend themselves easily to a simplified phrasing in terms of 'winning or losing', 'catching up or falling behind'. They produce 'export world champions' or identify the current 'sick man of Europe'. Thus it doesn't come as a surprise that such international rankings of the national economy frequently make the headlines (e.g., SPIEGEL, 2020). In order to trace access to knowledge of the state of the nation, then, it seems most promising to rely on media exposure. Being exposed for a longer period of time to the discussions in a national public sphere inevitably produces access to this form of knowledge. What is more, we might be able to identify the moments in which this anchoring domain is used by paying close attention to language use. The **metaphors** of ranking, race, competition and sports discussed above can serve as indicators for the mobilization of the state of the nation, too.

It should be noted that the mechanisms producing knowledge about the national economy operate in other areas as well. Like the economy, language, history or art are divided into national categories. And again, these national languages, histories or arts have been subject to systematic study in the past, thus generating substantial bodies of knowledge. Taken together, all these forms of national knowledge constitute what I call – for lack of a better term – national culture. National culture is an anchoring domain made available to citizens mainly through the institutions of public education. It is this potentially most far-reaching understanding of nationalism that the final hypothesis is dedicated to.

1.2.3.4 The National Culture Hypothesis

The final branch of the literature on nationalism I wish to review here understands nationalism as a symbolic structure which establishes de-contested patterns of meaning within the national society (e.g., Bonikowski, 2017, p. 149; Greenfeld, 1995, p. 3; Lamont & Thévenot, 2000). Nations thus understood are "zones of conflict" in which meaning is constantly re-negotiated (Delanty et al., 2008). This implies that the de-contestation of meaning structures is rarely achieved in entirety (Eder & Kantner, 2000, pp. 308–309; Jovchelovitch, 2012, p. 442; Wodak, 2009). Rather, there is a permanent struggle over the interpretation of the inherited symbols and narratives (Chernilo, 2006). At the same time, a certain degree of stability is achieved in the meaning structure – otherwise it would be pointless to characterize nationalism as a structure in this sense (Freeden, 1998, p. 749; Norval, 2000; Smith, 1998). I refer to the temporary result of this struggle for interpretation of inherited meaning structures as **national culture** (for a similar usage of the term culture see Geertz, 2000; Pfetsch, 2014, pp. 1–2; Swidler, 1986). Although the term might suggest a greater degree of cohesion than I assume to be present within nations, I still use it because of the breadth of phenomena it can serve to describe.

Two points are of particular importance in the following discussion. First, national culture comprises multiple bodies of knowledge which can serve as anchoring domains. Among these elements of national culture, I particularly stress language, history and the cultures of national academic fields. These elements of national culture, second, are upheld and transmitted by a specific set of institutions (mainly the public sphere and public schools) and thus structure social hierarchies within nations. These conceptualizations imply that national culture can be understood as an anchoring domain, which is particularly available to social groups with rather elevated social status. The following paragraphs show how this knowledge–power nexus structures national languages, histories and the cultures of national academic fields.

National culture comprises multiple bodies of knowledge that are predominantly available within the national society. A seemingly obvious element of national culture is the command of the national language. But while the existence of national languages seems natural to us, these languages have been actively constructed in the past. In the middle ages, language is rather a spectrum of understandability, which decreases with distance from an individual's native village. The canonization of vocabulary, spelling and grammar thus can be understood as a disciplinary mechanism emerging in the modern (nation-)state (Billig, 1995, pp. 28–32). Appropriate ways of speaking and writing are spread, on the one hand, via the public sphere, as reading publics require a relatively standardized medium of communication, and on the other hand, via the institutions of public education. Bearing this origin of national languages in mind, it becomes clear how the command of language bestows symbolic capital on individuals. While national languages of course are subject to continuous evolution and change, language is still sufficiently codified to function as a status indicator. Within national spaces, language use is stratified (Collins, 2009; Gal, 1989, pp. 354–358). Language thus is a perfect example of how shared meaning patterns are established within nations, and how these meaning structures then engender social hierarchies.

In a similar manner, national history is an actively constructed body of knowledge bestowing status on those who can mobilize it. The re-writing of history in national terms has been at the core of the nation building process. The invention of tradition, the designation of *lieu de mémoires*, the active formation of collective memories – all these strategies have contributed to a self-understanding of nations as historical communities of fate (e.g., Hobsbawm & Ranger, 1992; Kaneva, 2006, p. 2). School teaching in history to this day maintains an essentially national focus, and studies on public perceptions of history reveal the dominance of national perspectives (Gerhards et al., 2017, pp. 37–38; Killingsworth et al., 2010, pp. 1167–1170). The capacity to use this body of historical knowledge in public debates can be a source of power. Schmidt (2014, pp. 191–194), for example, has shown how memories of economic crisis are selectively mobilized in Germany to link specific economic policies to the rise of Nazism and thus to undermine the legitimacy of counterarguments. Again, it is those with rather high levels of education and social status that are most likely to mobilize history as an argumentative resource (Haegel, 2013). National history, like language, constitutes a shared meaning structure privileging those who can command it.

A final aspect of national culture I would like to highlight is the existence of field-specific expert cultures that might differ between national contexts. National expert communities are high-status groups which have repeatedly been shown to perpetuate rather specific bodies of thought (Bourdieu, 1998; Fourcade-Gourinchas, 2001; Mérand, 2006, pp. 132–137). A major role in this is played by the institutions of higher education which might serve to perpetuate locally specific academic traditions. Yet, through dominance in the respective national academic fields, nationally specific bodies of knowledge might be spread to the national public sphere as well. Such nationally specific expert cultures also exist in economics. The dominance of ordoliberal thought in the German field of economics has long been noted (e.g., Foucault, 2006a [1979]), but it has also been shown to penetrate the framing of economic issues in the public sphere (Díez Medrano & Gray, 2010). Such different meaning structures for economics have been shown to exist in many nations, partly due to the different evolution of the respective academic fields (e.g., Moody & Thévenot, 2000 for France and the US; Zarycki, 2014, 2015 for Poland). The meaning structures by which economic ideas are publicly assessed, then, might differ significantly between nations, and they might do so in particular among educated strata.

As the previous discussion of language, history and academic culture might have shown, national culture is a source of discursive power (Hearn, 2006, p. 12; Özkirimli, 2005, p. 33). The literature on nationalism has highlighted this knowledge–power nexus within national societies and it has identified the institutions that perpetuate it. National educational systems are the most prominent institutions of transmission (Waks, 2006, pp. 405 & 409). While for some 19th century thinkers the army was considered the school of the nation, it is now agreed that this function is mainly fulfilled by the school (for a foundational study on the subject see Weber, 1976). School education transmits many elements of national culture, and at the same time assesses pupils by their capacity to appropriate them. A perfect example of this mechanism is the French concours system, a nation-wide contest containing a considerable amount of general (read national) knowledge questions. Being knowledgeable about (mainly national) history, art or politics and commanding the appropriate vocabulary to express one's thoughts are essential resources to succeed in such contests. Among other things, the concourse is used to distribute places at France's most prestigious universities and in public administration (Beattie, 1996). This aspect of the education system therefore exemplifies very well how status and command of national culture are interlinked in national societies.

Beyond the education system, national culture is transmitted in the public sphere (Hepp & Wessler, 2009, pp. 180–181; Pfetsch, 2014, pp. 1–2). Again, the literature on nationalism has been vocal in highlighting this link. In particular Benedict Anderson's (1991) conception of nations as imagined communities is based on an analysis of early modern reading publics. In the public sphere, similar topics are simultaneously discussed by a community of readers. Thus, a common reservoir of cultural references emerges. Just like the education system, then, the public sphere does not only transmit knowledge, it also sets common standards of evaluation. In other words, using appropriate references to national culture increases the credibility of the speaker and thus the persuasiveness of arguments. National culture again appears as a mechanism yielding discursive power.

National culture, then, can function as an anchoring domain for complex economic issues. Specific historical or linguistic references as well as knowledge drawn from academic cultures could facilitate the understanding of issues in the European public sphere. The elements of national culture, moreover, are transmitted to the citizenry through the public sphere and through the national education system. Being able to draw on national culture can function as a marker of status. Using national culture as an anchor for complexity reduction, therefore, might be more frequent among the formally educated strata. According to the national culture hypothesis, then, lay citizens grasp complex issues by anchoring them in specifically national symbolic reservoirs. Lay representations of economics differ between citizens of different nations and they do so increasingly among citizens with high levels of formal education.

It has been the purpose of the sections above to develop predictions regarding the complexity problem. In total, I have described four hypotheses, each of which will be empirically tested in one chapter of this book (Chapters 2–5). The last two of these hypotheses predicted social representations of economics to be anchored in national knowledge, implying that citizens' understandings of the economy might be internationally different. This potential diagnosis brings us to another problem public spheres face.

1.3 The Compatibility Problem

I have previously described complexity and compatibility as a twin problem. This description is adequate as the compatibility problem arises as a direct consequence of issue complexity in the European public sphere. If citizens indeed draw on national knowledge to render complex issues intelligible, this could impede the functioning of transnational communication, thus raising a serious problem for the EU's legitimacy. Why compatibility is so important in a transnational public sphere and how this compatibility can be assessed is the subject of the following sections.

1.3.1 Concepts: The European Public Sphere as Transnational and Top-down

Over the past years, an academic consensus seems to have emerged which conceptualizes the European public sphere as transnational rather than supranational. That is, European issues need not be debated in a supranational public space or from an exclusively European perspective. Rather, the communication and interaction between national public spheres can be seen as sufficient. Hence, the European public sphere would be **transnational**: it demands the Europeanization of national public spheres rather than the development of a new supranational communicative space (Hepp et al., 2016, p. 15; Risse, 2014a, 2014b; Statham, 2010; Trenz, 2005).

There are criteria by which we can assess whether debates in national public spheres qualify as European (Kantner, 2014, p. 410; Risse, 2014a, 2014b; Statham, 2010). First, multiple national public spheres must discuss the same issues at the same time. That is, a certain visibility and salience of European issues must be given. Second, fellow Europeans must be present as speakers or audiences of such debates, and their contributions must be viewed as legitimate. Finally, the framing of political problems must be compatible.

Past studies have found the European public sphere to meet the first and the second criterion. The first criterion – the need for synchronous national debates – is mainly met because the European public sphere often operates in a top-down manner, with a European event or statement triggering the national debates (see Figure 1.1). This is not uncommon as most modern mass public rather function in a top-down fashion (Crouch, 2004, pp. 5–19; Gerhards, 1998, p. 271; Habermas, 1982 [1962], pp. 217–233). In the European context, the top-down structure is enhanced by the fact that media reporting tends to focus on specific events (e.g., summits or legislative decisions) which necessarily put similar issues on the media agenda in the same moment (Eder &

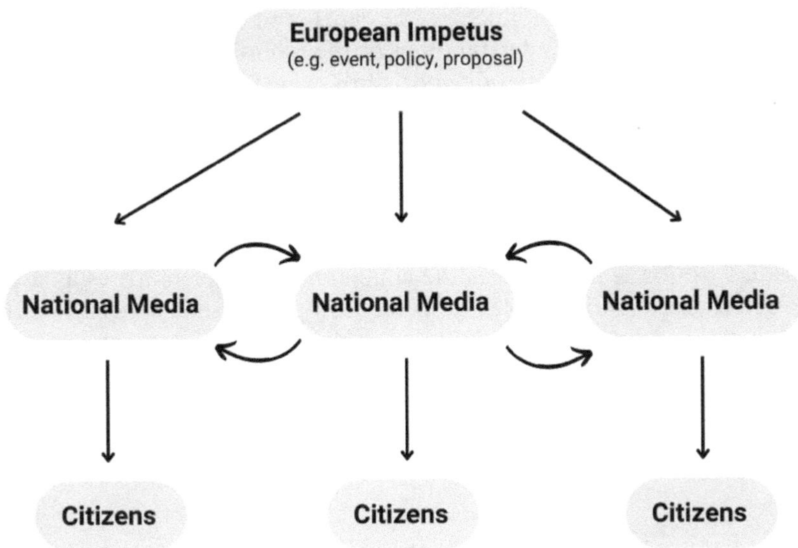

Figure 1.1 Transnational mode of functioning of European public sphere with citizens receiving information in top-down manner and with little horizontal interaction among citizens of different nations.

Kantner, 2000). It is thus no surprise that most European debates happen synchronously in national public spheres. The studies assessing this criterion also confirm that media coverage of these EU-related issues guarantees the necessary degree of visibility to speak of a European public sphere (Kantner, 2014; Koopmans, 2014; Risse, 2014a).

Similarly, the second criterion seems to be fulfilled as speakers from other European countries regularly feature in media reporting and seem to be presented as legitimate participants in the debates. National media do not only report on events on the European level but also cover statements and debates occurring in other national public spheres (Koopmans, 2014, pp. 79–81). In Table 1.2, these flows of communication are marked by the horizontal arrows connecting the national media outlets in separate public spheres. Thus, voices from other nations seem to be heard and represented in the European public sphere. Although the structures of claims-making are somewhat different than in national publics, foreign opinions seem to be generally accepted as legitimate (Koopmans, 2014; Risse, 2014a).

Regarding the third criterion (the compatibility of frames of reference), further research is needed. The available studies (e.g., Kantner, 2014; Trenz, 2000) find that differences in media reporting do not produce incommensurabilities in the European public sphere. Yet, these studies have two important shortcomings. First, they focus mainly on media representation. While we can be sure that media reporting happens in a reasonably compatible manner, this must not imply that citizens' interpretations are compatible too (for a diagnosis of the same research gap see Hepp & Wessler, 2009; an exception to this is Lingenberg, 2010). Referring back to Table 1.2, the studies only focused on the second layer labelled 'national media' and would have little to say about the bottom layer labelled 'citizens'. Yet, the position of citizens in the public sphere is arguably quite different from that of the media. Most citizens in Europe follow national media and mainly discuss politics (if at all) with national peers. After all, less than 3% of Europeans ever lived abroad (Schroedter et al., 2015, p. 182) and a large majority relies on national media for information (Hepp et al., 2016, pp. 160–187). Horizontal links on the level of individual citizens, therefore, are much weaker and there is a greater of danger of national incompatibilities to arise.[5] Hence, in order to reach a final verdict on the compatibility criterion, an analysis of citizens' representations is needed. In order to conduct such an analysis, however, a second shortcoming of the literature needs to be addressed: the absence of clear compatibility criteria. Although some studies develop important insights in this regard, a systematic discussion of compatibility requirements in democratic theory is still missing. It is precisely this latter shortcoming which the following section is supposed to remedy.

1.3.2 Operationalization: Three Criteria for Compatibility

In a public sphere, citizens are supposed to acquire information and, potentially, to exchange their views on the subject matter (Hepp et al , 2016, p. 14; Statham & Trenz, 2015, p. 291). In order for this to be possible, arguments and information need to be understood in a compatible manner. The emphasis here is on understanding: citizens need not agree but simply to understand the lines of argument they are confronted with. If understanding of arguments implies compatibility, inversely we can say that **misunderstandings imply incompatibility**. If citizens misunderstand the arguments in the European public sphere, the latter does not function well. I will therefore rely on the concept of a misunderstanding to formulate compatibility criteria. Rather than spelling out all the possible situations in which communication functions, I will develop an operationalizable definition of misunderstandings. This definition of misunderstandings then can serve as a yardstick for the assessment of compatibility (see Chapter 6).

What does it mean, then, for arguments to be misunderstood? How can we distinguish misunderstanding from disagreement? And what does this mean in the specific context of the European public sphere? I rely on the concepts provided by social representation theory in my attempt to answer these questions.

1.3.2.1 Criterion 1: Differences in Representation

The most basic criterion for a misunderstanding can be derived from the text–context distinction. This distinction is frequently used in social representation theory as well as other, related disciplines (for media studies see

Hepp & Wessler, 2009, p. 186; for discourse analysis see Wodak, 2009, p. 3). Accordingly, a statement (text) always acquires its meaning by reference to a set of background assumptions (context) which the audience is supposed to share (Jovchelovitch, 2012, pp. 118–120). A misunderstanding could be said to occur if a text is transferred to a context different from the one intended by the author and if the text thus acquires a new meaning. A similar definition has been used in discussions of the changing meaning of literary works (Bourdieu, 1998) or of pieces of art (Zabel, 2004, p. 286) from one national context to another.

Within the European public sphere, the texts of course are not works of literature but the arguments presented in European debates. The context into which these arguments are transferred is the variety of knowledge authorities in modern societies. In the words of social representation theory, the context is constituted, first, by the social group the argument is presented to and, second, by the anchoring domain it has access too. If an argument is connected to different anchoring domains by different social groups, the result will be different representations of that same argument. The argument would have acquired a different meaning for each group. It is this change of meaning that the first criterion for a misunderstanding needs to capture:

> Criterion 1. There is a difference in the representation of an argument which results from anchoring in different bodies of knowledge.

This criterion, however, is insufficient to define a misunderstanding because it cannot differentiate between a misunderstanding and a disagreement. Arguably, disagreements also result from a difference in anchoring domains. Mobilizing liberal ideology, for example, to understand an argument about state expenditure will yield very different results than an anchoring in socialist thought. Yet, the difference between liberals and socialists is commonly accepted as a normal disagreement happening in most democratic societies. Few people would see it as an indicator of a malfunctioning public sphere. In order to conceptualize incompatibility in the European public sphere, then, we need a criterion that allows us to differentiate disagreements from misunderstandings.

1.3.2.2 Criterion 2: Absence of Alternative Representations

In order to distinguish misunderstandings from disagreement, most of the existing literature seems to propose an awareness of the opposing position as the central criterion. Within social representation theory, Jovchelovitch (2012, p. 119) cites an awareness of different perspectives as a precondition for the functioning of modern public spheres. Within the literature on the European public sphere, Risse (2014b, p. 9) argues that differences in frames are compatible when they imply an understanding of diverging positions. Trenz (2000, pp. 347–349) uses a similar argument when distinguishing "incommensurability" from challenges to alternative arguments. Returning to the example, then, this allows us to explain why the difference between the liberal and the socialist would not qualify as a misunderstanding. Both groups arguably would be aware that there is an opposing political camp whose stance on the matter is different. Despite the different anchoring domains mobilized, their case would be a disagreement.

Social representation theory provides a useful concept to theorize this awareness of diverging positions: alternative representations. An alternative representation can be defined as a "representation of a potentially competing representation from within a social representation" (Gillespie, 2008, pp. 380–381). Confusing as it may sound, this definition captures the three central aspects of alternative representations. A "representation of a potentially competing representation" implies an awareness, first, of the group that entertains different ideas and, second, of the content of these ideas. This knowledge of a social group and their opinions, third, need not be perfect; it comes "from within a social representation", that is, it is shaped by the worldview of the person who entertains it. An alternative representation thus is a simplified version of others' ideas. In his original study of the public understanding of psychoanalysis, for example, Moscovici (Moscovici, 2004 [1961]) noted that communist newspapers depicted psychoanalysis as a subversive strategy of the class enemy. By individualizing problems, workers' class consciousness was to be undermined. This example contains both a vision of the social group (the capitalist class) and the content of their thought, while at the same time clearly being formulated from the standpoint of communist ideology. In a similar vein, the socialist in the example cited before probably entertains an (unfriendly) vision of liberal ideology and of the kind of people likely to subscribe to it.

Based on this definition of alternative representations, the second criterion can be formulated. Together with criterion 1, it forms a sufficient condition to identify misunderstandings.

> Criterion 2. The difference in representation is not covered by an alternative representation.

Alternative representations are not only useful to theorize awareness, they also help to establish how contested social representations are (Gillespie, 2008, p. 382). An alternative representation contains a diverging vision of reality – its presence or absence thus may reveal how widely an idea is accepted within a community. Social representation theory mainly distinguishes three types of social representations, depending on how stable they are (Duveen, 2007, pp. 547–548, 2008, pp. 370–372; Höijer, 2011, p. 5; Sammut & Gaskell, 2010, pp. 48–58). Hegemonic representations are the most stable. They are taken for granted within their community, resembling what anthropologists call tacit knowledge (Strauss, 2005, p. 203). Hegemonic representations thus come without alternative representations. The matter is different for emancipated representations which are stable but only pertain to a sub-section of society. The same is true of the final category, polemic representations. Both emancipated and polemic representations allow for the existence of alternative representations, with polemic representation engendering a more distorted vision of the opposing group. Moscovici's example of the communists and their vision of the class enemy falls into this latter category.

Assessing the strength of social representations is important when assessing compatibility in the European public sphere. Although the criteria established so far suffice to identify misunderstandings, within the European public sphere a comparison between different social groups is needed before we can speak of incompatibility. Due to the specific nature of the European Union, a third criterion is needed.

1.3.2.3 Criterion 3: National Standard of Comparison

In European studies, it has repeatedly been argued that questions of EU legitimacy need to be assessed by reference to a realistic national standard of comparison (e.g., Checkel, 2014; Koopmans, 2014). Using ideal conceptions of democratic theory as a yardstick for legitimacy, even national political systems would frequently be found wanting. Yet, nation-states are rarely diagnosed with a democratic deficit. Shortcomings within national systems are rather accepted as imperfections, which naturally occur when reality is compared to theory. In the context of the EU, however, such concessions are rarely made, and some aspects of the EU's perceived democratic deficit might be the result of the application of higher standards. Taking this imbalance into account, it seems insufficient to rely on purely theoretical criteria in the assessment of EU legitimacy. Rather, a realistic national standard of comparison needs to be crafted for every investigation.

In order to formulate a national standard of comparison for the compatibility question, we need to ask to what extent misunderstandings might occur in national public spheres. As pointed out when discussing criterion one, modern public spheres in general function under conditions of knowledge diversity (Chernilo, 2006; Jovchelovitch, 2006, pp. 91–97). Social representation theory was even developed to conceptualize such differences in understanding within the French public sphere (Moscovici, 2004 [1961]). The existence of different anchoring domains poses a challenge to national publics as much as it does to the transnational domain. We therefore might expect similar interpretive difficulties to appear in both cases. There is one notable exception, however: differences arising from national anchoring domains. As I have argued in the introduction, in national public spheres most participants are supposed to share national knowledge as an anchoring domain. Misunderstandings between people with access to different national anchoring domains, then, may be particularly frequent in the European public sphere. Applying a national standard of comparison, then, means that these specifically European misunderstandings need to be stronger than the hermeneutic difficulties encountered in national publics.

> Criterion 3. Inter-national incompatibilities need to be more pronounced than intra-national incompatibilities.

Assessing criterion three necessarily requires a comparison between different social groups. We need to assess the incompatibilities between members of different nations and compare them to incompatibilities appearing between social groups present within the nation. In this section, I have outlined some hypotheses with regard to the complexity problem. These hypotheses described social groups and the anchoring domains they have access to. As the compatibility criteria require precisely a comparison of such social groups, the same hypotheses can serve to generate predictions for the compatibility problem.

1.3.3 Hypotheses Regarding the Compatibility Problem

Having developed precise criteria for compatibility in the European public sphere, let us now see what kind of predictions our hypotheses would make regarding compatibility. Again, the complexity and the compatibility problem are tightly interlinked. The compatibility of arguments depends on the anchoring domains mobilized to render them intelligible. That is why the hypotheses developed for the complexity problem are also used to investigate the compatibility problem. From each hypothesis, we can derive a prediction for each of the compatibility criteria. That is, each hypothesis already contains a prediction regarding differences in representations (criterion 1) and a vision of what alternative representations would look like (criterion 2). Moreover, each hypothesis can already be assigned a role in the construction of a national standard of comparison (criterion 3). An overview of the hypotheses' predictions regarding the compatibility problem is presented in Table 1.2.

Let us begin with the **market experience** hypothesis. This hypothesis predicted that citizens would make an inference from market experiences to economic processes. This inference is supposed to be correct in the sense that the resulting representations of economic processes should be akin to economic theory. Thus, citizens' representations of economic processes should be similar irrespective of national context. While their assessments (the opinions) might differ, such differences are only due to different distributions of costs and benefits. A shared representation of the effects of given economic phenomenon is still presupposed: citizens share an understanding of how the costs and benefits are distributed among social groups while their positions within this shared distributional scheme differ. With regard to criterion 1, then, the market experience hypothesis predicts a **uniformity of representations**. Potential differences in opinion simply result from differences in economic positions

Table 1.2 Hypotheses regarding compatibility problem in the European public sphere (EPS)

	Criterion 1: Differences in representation of economic processes?	Criterion 2: What could alternative representations look like?	Criterion 3. Role in constructing national standard of comparison
Market experience (null hypothesis: no compatibilityproblem as representations are uniform)	• *Uniformity* of representations	• "We see the same economic process but judge it differently due to our positions in the economy"	• *No differences* in representation (no problem for EPS)
Economic theory	• Differences between *experts and laypeople*	• "people with economic training are more positive about market outcomes"	• *Intra-national* difference (if strongest, no problem for EPS)
State of the Nation	• Differences based on *placement of national economy* in economic hierarchy of states	• "We see the same process but judge it differently due to our nation's position in the global economic order"	• *Inter-national* difference (if strongest, problem for EPS)
National Culture	• Differences based on history, *language and national academic cultures*	• "In this country, people would disagree with us because they have a memory/ a term/a way of thinking that is not popular over here"	• *Inter-national* difference (if strongest, problem for EPS)

and should be covered by alternative representations as the distributional consequences of economic processes are known (criterion 2).

Like for the complexity problem, the market experience hypothesis thus functions as a null hypothesis for the compatibility problem. That is, it predicts that there might be no problematic relationship after all. If all lay representations are reasonably similar to those maintained in economics, there might be little need to worry about inter-national incompatibilities. Accordingly, the construction of a national standard of comparison would be unnecessary (criterion 3). National publics and the European public sphere alike would not face a complexity or a compatibility problem.

Let us turn to the **economic theory** hypothesis. This hypothesis describes how knowledge of economic theory is passed on through education, resulting in a **difference between lay and expert representations**. Regarding criterion 1, then, the hypothesis predicts people with and without access to economic training to entertain different representations of economic processes. More precisely even, the hypothesis implies that citizens who have had economic training might be more prone to construct representations of the market mechanism as mutually beneficial. An alternative representation (criterion 2) would require an awareness of this difference in representation. It might take the form of citizens thinking that "economists have very positive opinions about the free market" or, contrarily, that "non-economists don't know about the efficiency gains produced by the market". If we find differences in lay and expert representations, but no alternative representation thereof, we would have to speak of a misunderstanding.

Depending on the empirical results regarding criteria 1 and 2, the economic theory hypothesis could provide an example of **intra-national differences**. Misunderstandings between people with and without economic training would certainly also occur in national public spheres. If we are to construct a national standard of comparison (criterion 3), intra-national differences would be needed to have a fair standard of comparison for the problems arising in transnational communication. Thus, we could employ the incompatibilities between experts and laypeople as a yardstick to assess the gravity of incompatibilities in the European public sphere. Should lay–expert differences prove to be more pronounced than inter-national differences, we could assume the European public sphere to function relatively well.

Having established one hypothesis predicting intra-national misunderstandings to occur, let us now turn to the hypotheses that predict **inter-national differences**. The worth of nations and national culture hypotheses foresee incompatibilities between inhabitants of different nations, although they do so for different reasons. Both hypotheses provide examples of inter-national differences. For the construction of a national standard of comparison (criterion 3), these differences would need to be compared to the intra-national differences diagnosed by the economic theory hypothesis. If this comparison results in inter-national differences being stronger, a malfunctioning of the European public sphere would have to be attested. Should intra-national differences be stronger, it would be exaggerated to diagnose a legitimacy problem to the EU.

The **worth of nations** hypothesis postulates that differences in representations might arise from anchoring in the strengths and weaknesses of the national economy (criterion 1). According to this hypothesis, citizens perceive the well-being of their national economy as the central normative reference point. The assessment of a given policy, therefore, would depend on the characteristics of the national economy and on its position in the global economic order. As most citizens are mainly knowledgeable about their own national economy, representations and assessments of economic processes would differ. For such differences to be covered by alternative representations (criterion 2), citizens would be expected to cite some characteristics of foreign economies (e.g., "Germany produces a lot of cars"). Such diagnoses of different national economic interests would then have to be transferred to the citizens (e.g., "Germans might favor the abolition of tariffs and the free circulation of goods"). Anchoring in the state of the nation can be unproblematic in terms of incompatibility if it is accompanied by knowledge of the characteristics of foreign economies. If such knowledge is absent, misunderstandings might occur.

The final hypothesis to be discussed here is **national culture**. National culture comprises language, history and national academic cultures all of which might cause differences in representations when used as an anchoring domain in the European public sphere. Empirical studies have in fact already shown that such different representations exist. Assessments of the market mechanism, for example, differ significantly among (European) countries. French citizens mobilize stronger anti-market arguments than citizens of the United States (Thévenot et al., 2000) or of the UK (Duchesne, 2013; Duchesne & Ingelgom, 2008). Such differences have been attributed to different historical and linguistic meanings attached to concepts within the national context (Marková et al., 1998). Economic arguments circulating in the European public sphere, then, might trigger different collective memories or might evoke different meanings in the respective national languages. Social representations of economics generated through anchoring in national culture, therefore, might differ significantly among citizens of different European countries (criterion 1).

Interestingly, the danger of inter-nationally different representations might grow with the education level of the relevant social group. As the discussion of social hierarchies generated by national culture has shown (see section Chapter 1.2.3.4) in particular social groups with high status or education are prone to mobilize national culture in debates (for similar assessments of the stratification of access to national knowledge, see Haffert et al., 2019; Hepp et al., 2016, p. 30). Somewhat counter-intuitively, then, inter-national differences most probably occur among particularly educated social groups.

What would alternative representations of national culture look like (criterion 2)? Imagining such alternative representations is already harder than for the previous hypotheses. They would require citizens to state that their counterparts in a different country have different collective memories or specific linguistic expressions, or that they might be influenced by a unique academic culture. While reflecting on historical differences might be to some extent imaginable (e.g., reflecting on different national experiences of communism or fascism), awareness of linguistic or academic differences seems to require quite a bit of knowledge about foreign countries. In any case, different representations rooted in national cultures must not be problematic per se. If covered by the relevant alternative representations, they would not pose a challenge to the European public sphere.

Thus, having outlined the predictions of all four hypotheses with regard to the compatibility problem, the theoretical part of the chapter is complete. We have encountered the relevant theories and concepts that will be applied to both the complexity and the compatibility problem. Moreover, we have also seen how these concepts can be operationalized, resulting in a strategy for the identification of anchoring domains and social groups, and in the establishment of three criteria for compatibility in the European public sphere. Finally, I have established a number of hypotheses and have differentiated their predictions regarding each of the research questions. With these predictions at hand, let us proceed to the research design.

1.4 Research Design: A Worst-case Scenario for the European Public Sphere

Before elaborating the details of the research design, let us recall the aim of this study: **an analysis of the compatibility of social representations under the condition of issue complexity**. Section 1.3 has been concerned with detailing three criteria by which compatibility can be assessed: a difference in representation, the absence of alternative representations and a national standard of comparison. The research design needs to allow an assessment of these criteria. The following sections show how this can be achieved, first, by using focus group methodology (allowing for the observation of anchoring processes happening in the European public sphere) and, second, by means of sample selection (allowing for a comparison between social groups). Criteria one and two (anchoring and alternative representations) thus are mainly addressed in the following section on focus group design. Criterion three (comparison of intra-national and inter-national differences) and the hypotheses mainly inform the section about participant selection. Concerns about external validity of the study are taken up in a final section, which also discusses the selection of countries and interview locations. Together, these considerations should make clear why I consider this research design a **worst-case scenario**, that is, a simulation of transnational debates trying to maximize the potential for inter-national incompatibilities.

1.4.1 Focus Group Design

The first two criteria for compatibility in the European public sphere require an assessment of social representations and alternative representations, both of which are **intersubjective meaning structures**. The research design thus needs to generate data allowing for the observations of such shared patterns of meaning.

Focus groups have repeatedly been suggested as an adequate method for the study of intersubjective meaning structures (e.g., Gamson, 1992; Haegel, 2005, p.24; Krzyzanowski, 2008, p. 169). Focus groups, moreover, are a prominent method of research in those areas of the social sciences relevant to this book: social representation theory and European studies. Social representation theory embraces focus group methodology as it can highlight how individuals creatively adapt knowledge at their disposal to understand unknown phenomena (Elcheroth et al., 2011, pp. 745–746; Gillespie & Cornish, 2010, pp. 33–35; Moscovici, 1984, p. 67). In focus group discussions, anchoring processes become visible: individuals confronted with unknown concepts try to render them intelligible through collective deliberation. European studies, too, have seen an increasing usage of this methodology, although rather modestly so. Focus groups have been used to study public understanding of the EU as such (Duchesne et al., 2013), of shared perceptions of history (Gerhards et al., 2017) or of the role played by the EU in everyday political debates (White, 2011). Even EU institutions themselves have started employing this method, as the rise of qualitative Eurobarometer surveys indicates (Eurobarometer, 2009, 2011, 2014). These examples from European studies all focus on citizen perspectives, that is, the social representations of the political order they hold. This book, then, employs focus group methodology due to its capacity of uncovering intersubjective meaning structures.

Rather than observing patterns of meaning in general, however, this study requires an analysis of those social representations generated specifically in the European public sphere. The focus group design thus needs to simulate the structure of transnational debates. As I have pointed out in Section 1.3.1, the transnational public sphere mainly emerges when the same issues are discussed at the same time in separate national public spheres. Frequently, then, there is a kind of top-down process of communication with a European impetus triggering debates on the national level. By employing the same focus group design in different national contexts, the research design thus can mirror this mechanism of the European public sphere. Accordingly, the focus group design confronts citizens in different countries with the same trigger arguments drawn from the European level (see Figure 1.2). The focus groups bring together citizens of the same nation as this reflects the empirical reality of the European public sphere. Most citizens do not participate in transnational discussion groups, but rather discuss politics (if at all) with national peers. The material for such discussion is most commonly provided by national media, which in the research design is represented by the trigger arguments. The research design thus mirrors the European public sphere by having a (nationally mediated) European impetus triggering debates among fellow nationals.[6]

The focus groups, then, were organized in the following way: participants received a short introductory statement, presenting the general topic of discussion (trade or unemployment). This introduction included an explicit reference to the European dimension of the discussion (e.g., the aggregate level of employment within the EU or the reference to CETA as a trade deal recently negotiated by the Commission). As a first task, participants were handed nine little cards containing propositions on how to deal with the issue under question. In an initial task, participants were asked to select three propositions they liked while in a later round they were supposed to

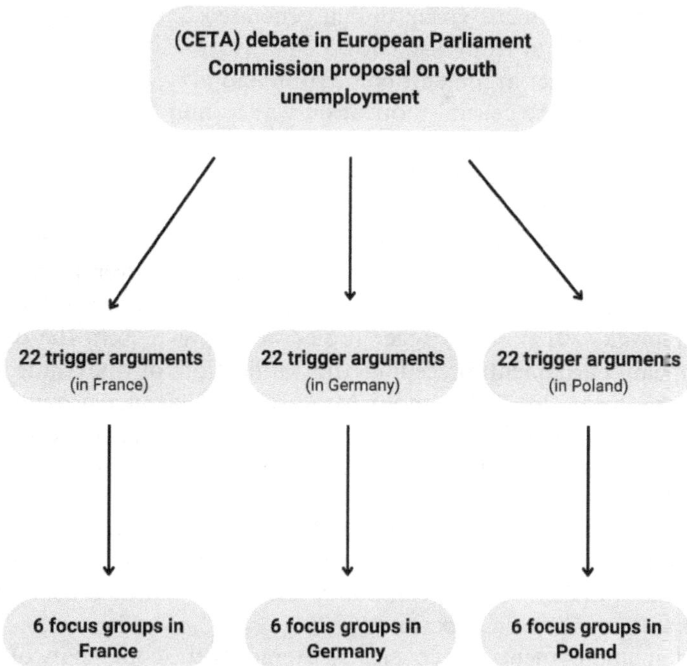

Figure 1.2 Research design mirroring transnational mode of functioning of European public sphere.

choose two they disliked. Participants gave brief justifications of their choice and the most frequently chosen propositions were discussed at greater length. A shorter, second task tackled larger questions of the relationship between the state and the economy. In the employment discussion, this part dealt with privatization, whereas in the trade groups it was concerned with the harmonization of regulations. For this task, citizens were confronted with three or four statements summarizing the opposing positions of different political camps. Participants were asked for their assessment of these statements. The complete focus group protocols can be found in Appendix 2.

This focus group design generated the possibility of a comparative analysis as participants would discuss the same propositions in each country. At the same time, it left some room for topic selection to participants as they only had to comment five out of nine propositions in the first task and were free to discuss the statements they considered most salient in the second task. Nevertheless, the focus groups mirrored the European public sphere as I understand it; the same European arguments triggered debates in different national contexts. Most segments of the discussion revolved around the same issues and had been triggered by the same argument. I will consequently refer to the statements that triggered such segments of the discussion as **trigger arguments**. In total, this focus group design generated 22 trigger arguments (18 from task one and four from task two).

Where did these trigger arguments come from and how were the topics of debate chosen? Again, the central motivation was to find topics that mirror discussions present in the European public sphere. The trigger topics thus were chosen from real debates that happened on the European level in issue areas in which the EU has been particularly active in recent years.[7] Trade, first, is a policy domain in which the EU commands significant competences. The mobilization around the trade deal with Canada, moreover, proves that issues of trade policy are salient in the European public sphere (Działo & Gawrońska-Nowak, 2017). The trigger topics were drawn from the debate in the European parliament preceding the ratification of the trade deal (European Parliament, 2017). Unemployment, second, has increasingly been featured in the EU agenda since the euro crisis, as the increasing concern with youth unemployment at the time might exemplify. Accordingly, trigger topics were chosen from a Commission proposal on the establishment of a youth guarantee (European Commission, 2012). With both trade and unemployment thus being salient in the European public sphere, the focus group design thus mirrors the transfer of European policy issues into national contexts as it might happen in real-world debates.

Trade and unemployment, moreover, also exemplify the complexity of economic issues discussed in the European public sphere. Both topics complement each other because the former mainly targets issues of international economics while the latter touches on many questions of economic policy within the EU. Together, then, trade and unemployment are issues allowing for the discussion of a wide range of economic phenomena. Covering this large range of economic phenomena rather than focusing on smaller debates implies acknowledging the complexity of economic debates often happening on EU level. In order to maintain this complexity, the formulations taken from real-world documents were not simplified. The trigger topics in both cases included expert terminology (e.g., foreign investment, non-wage labor costs, international competitiveness). The trigger topics thus were clearly instances of alien concepts to be rendered intelligible through anchoring by the participants. The choice of trigger topics, then, mirrors functioning of transnational communication under conditions of issue complexity. Confronting citizens in different countries with the same European trigger topics allows an observation of the differences in social representations formed in the different national contexts.

Apart from exhibiting the social representations formed in the European public sphere, the focus group design also needs to uncover a second form intersubjective meaning: alternative representations. Studying alternative representations thus essentially implies asking focus group participants reflexive questions. Such questions were asked in a short final part of the discussions. They were posed once in general, and once with an emphasis on inter-national differences ("which social group might have a different opinion than you? Do you think that there are national differences?"; see Appendix 2). The responses to these questions are crucial to the assessment of criterion two. Participants' awareness of diverging representations determines if interpretive differences constitute simple disagreements or problematic misunderstandings. While the first part of the focus groups, then, was designed to trace differences in social representations, the final part illuminates if citizens hold alternative representations covering these differences.

The focus groups thus were designed to allow for an observation of social representation and alternative representations in a realistic simulation of the European public sphere. The focus group design thus allows for analysis of criteria one and two for compatibility in the European public sphere. In order to assess the third criterion (the national standard of comparison) closer attention needs to be paid to the identification of the social groups having access to specific anchoring domains.

1.4.2 Participant Selection

The central concern in the selection of participants is to allow an observation of the anchoring domains described in the hypotheses Participants should belong to social groups having privileged access to the anchoring domains presented in Section 1.2.3. Ultimately, the participants for the focus groups were recruited among high school teachers, among estate agents and among members of amateur soccer teams. Although this selection might seem random, there is a multitude of reasons why they constitute a sample having access to the various anchoring domains described in the hypotheses. As I had limited resources in the collection of the empirical material, it was not possible to choose one group specifically corresponding to each of the anchoring domains. Each group chosen thus had to fulfill multiple functions in the research design, that is, each group had to cover multiple hypotheses. Teachers, agents and soccer players were chosen precisely because they might have access to multiple anchoring domains. In the following section, I review each of the anchoring domains presented in the hypotheses sections and I point out why teachers, agents and soccer players are a suitable sample to assess these hypotheses.

For the economic theory hypothesis, it has been noted that the central transmission mechanism is education. Economics or business is a subject of study in most universities and in some countries in high school. An assumption driving sample selection was thus that the higher the level of education, the greater the chance of including participants who had been economically trained at an institution of higher education. This reasoning pertained to teachers and to some extent to estate agents (who in most countries are not required to have formal education but were still assumed to have a high number of economically trained members among their ranks). This selection strategy proved successful: out of 64 participants, 12 were found to have had economic training.[8] This amounts to 19% all of participants. Participants with economic training were reasonably evenly spread across groups (three teachers, three soccer players and six agents) and across countries (five Polish, five French, two German). The sample thus allows the analysis of economic theory as an anchoring domain.

The market experience hypothesis stated that individuals conduct a self-interested cost–benefit analysis to anchor economic processes. Individuals assess the effect of trade deals on factors of production and the expected utility of unemployment benefits based on their situation in the economy. Such anchoring in costs and benefits might be particularly well observable in focus groups whose members have a similar position in the economy and thus a similar economic interest. This is true of teachers and estate agents who should, consequently, be prone to collectively develop this form of anchoring. In the soccer groups, contrarily, the identification of economic interests should be more contested as the members of soccer teams might hold different positions in the economy. Apart from this, the sample selection covers both the public (teachers) and the private sector (estate agents). This variety of perspectives is complimented by the soccer teams who tend to be more diverse in terms of occupational status. The soccer teams mainly consisted of white- and blue-collar workers who often brought in labor market or union experiences neither estate agents nor teachers were likely to make. The sample thus covers a wide range of different occupational sectors and economic experiences. Finally, estate agents are a particularly interesting group to observe the mobilization of market experience as an anchoring domain. Estate agents indeed have first-hand market experience – they are intimately concerned with questions of supply and demand on the housing market, and their salaries are frequently linked to their sales, thus being dependent on market processes. At the same time, estate agents are not required to have economic training and indeed in the sample two-thirds of them did not have any (twelve versus six). Estate agents are thus a perfect group to study how inferences from market experiences to larger economic processes are made. The sample thus allows an observation of how specific job groups draw inferences from their personal economic situation and of how they judge them based on their personal gains.

For both the state of the nation and national culture, the most important transmitting institutions are public education and, to a lesser extent, the public sphere. For both hypotheses, it has been argued that they constitute authoritative bodies of knowledge within nations and thus structure social hierarchies. It thus seemed reasonable to recruit participants commanding high degrees of symbolic capital in the respective domains. High school teachers seem to be a group particularly prone to command such national repertoires of meaning. It has been pointed out that in contemporary societies, national identity formation takes place in schools. Teachers thus tend to be social groups characterized by access to national reservoirs of knowledge as they play a central role in its transmission (for a similar argument see

Jaskulowski & Surmiak, 2017). Another group which might be prone to use these forms of national knowledge as an anchoring domain are soccer teams. As team members lack a common occupation as a shared anchoring domain, they might be more prone to mobilize national reservoirs of meaning – a layer of identity the groups shared. In absence of agreement about the distribution of individual benefits, soccer teams might be more likely to mobilize benefits to the national economy as such and derive a shared position from this anchoring point. In particular, teachers and soccer teams, then, were assumed to employ the state of the nation or national culture as an anchoring domain.

To conclude, the sample assembled social groups which do not only have access to the relevant anchoring domains, but in many cases were also very likely to draw on them. All the teachers, agents and soccer teams have been brought up in the educational institutions of the respective nation-states and they all participate in the respective national market. A significant amount even had economic training. The sample thus includes individuals who have made the relevant experiences and have access to the relevant anchoring domains. This sample thus allows for the identification of different social groups needed for the establishment of a national standard of comparison (criterion three). At the same time, with an overall size of 64 participants, the sample might be large for a qualitative study – by statistical standards it remains rather humble. This, of course, raises a question of external validity, that is, how to make inferences to the European public sphere at large from a sample this small.

1.4.3 Country Selection, Interview Locations and External Validity

A promising way of addressing concerns of external validity in small-*n*-studies is sometimes referred to as the "Sinatra condition" (Leuffen, 2007, pp. 152–153). The central idea of a Sinatra condition is to design a worst-case scenario. If a theory holds under the most unfavorable conditions, it is likely to hold under other conditions too. Based on Sinatra's famous line, if the theory makes it here it can make it anywhere. Designing a worst-case scenario thus allows for an inference from a limited number of hard cases to the validity of a theory under a much wider range of conditions. For the European public sphere, this means that if we test compatibility under the most unfavorable conditions and still do not find significant misunderstandings, we could assume the European public sphere to function in most other cases, too.

Under which conditions, then, are misunderstandings most likely to happen in the European public sphere? When discussing the hypotheses, I have described two anchoring domains which might produce internationally different social representations of economics. Arguably, the risk of incompatibility is highest in the European public sphere, first, when citizens are most likely to mobilize these anchoring domains. As the previous section has pointed out, participants were chosen based on their likeliness to employ the anchoring domains presented in the hypotheses section. We, therefore, already have a sample of participants which are highly likely to mobilize internationally different bodies of knowledge. In order to maximize such international differences, second, we also need to make sure that the differences between the national anchoring domains are as large as possible. The nations to be studied should differ in terms of the characteristics of their national economy and of the elements of their national culture potentially relevant to economic discussions. In other words, very **dissimilar cases** in the EU should be selected.

In a Union of 26 member states, a variety of cases could qualify as most dissimilar. I have opted for France, Germany and Poland because they constitute the largest representatives of three rather clearly identifiable economic blocks. As such, they represent different varieties of capitalism and these different characteristics of the national economies should result in divergent representations of the worth of nations. In the varieties of capitalism literature, France, Germany and Poland constitute the ideal types of different varieties of capitalism (Farkas, 2011; Nölke & Vliegenthart, 2009; V. Schmidt, 2003). Interestingly, studies on voting behavior in the council suggest that these three countries also represent the most prominent coalitions of states emerging for economic issues. Over questions of regulation, Northern countries, led by Germany, frequently oppose a Southern block spearheaded by France (Mattila, 2009). For questions of state sovereignty, including issues of legislative harmonization, the cleavage rather divides East and West with Poland lending its voice powerfully to the new member states (Copsey & Haughton, 2009; Thomson, 2009, p. 773). Therefore, each of the countries can be seen as to some extent representative of an economic block within the EU. Representing different economic interests rooted in differences between the respective economic systems, we might assume the systemic experiences and the state of the national economies of these countries to differ significantly. The 'Weimar triangle', then, does not only cover around 40% of the EU's population, but it also represents some of the most contentious economic cleavages within the EU.

Apart from these differences in the worth of nations, France, Germany and Poland also differ significantly with regard to the national culture hypothesis. Arguably, all three countries have widely different collective memories of economic events. I have highlighted, for example, the prominence of ordoliberal thought in Germany and its capacity to impact the perceptions of economic history (e.g., Müller, 2005). For France, the 'dirigiste' tradition and the specificities of the national concours system have previously been pointed out (Vail, 2020, p. 113). Finally, for Poland, the prominence of memories of communism (Gerhards et al., 2017) and the specific thought structures engendered during the transition to capitalism have been cited (Zarycki, 2014, 2015). In order to still aggravate these differences, for each country a specific historically loaded trigger topic was included in the focus group design. Targeting the German collective representation of hyperinflation as a root cause of Hitler's rise to power, the trigger topic 'inflation' was introduced (V. A. Schmidt, 2014). Aiming to trigger the specific historical relevance of meritocracy in the French context, a 'merit' topic was included as well. For Poland, a trigger demanding a 'right to work' was introduced, targeting potentially negative associations with the socialist past (Marková et al., 1998, pp. 821–823; Moodie et al., 2016, pp. 415–420). The research design thus also aimed to maximize differences in the national culture.

While the research design thus attempts to maximize the potential for inter-national differences through the choice of countries (exhibiting dissimilar national knowledges) and participants (having privileged access to this knowledge), it also must try to randomize the impact of other factors on the content of the focus groups. Qualitative small-*n*-studies cannot control for the impact of variables the same way quantitative studies do. By including participants with widely different characteristics (e.g., in terms of age, gender or political orientation), however, an over-determination of the results can be avoided. The hope is that the effects of uncontrolled variables can be eliminated if similar results are obtained among different groups of people (Gamson, 1992, pp. 189–190; Quinn, 2005, pp. 45–47). In the context of this study, this means that we can be more confident about social representations to be rooted in national anchoring domains if the people entertaining them do not share any characteristics except their nationality.

While the choice of countries, then, was motivated by the desire to increase inter-national differences, the interviewing locations within the nations were chosen in order to include a wide range of sociological backgrounds and of political orientations. I already pointed out in the section on participant selection that the choice of estate agents, teachers and amateur soccer players guarantees the presence of a wide range of positions in the economy. The choice of interviewing locations was motivated by an attempt to diversify political positions, too. The interviews were conducted in suburban areas of Paris, Berlin and Warsaw in which electoral results closely corresponded to the overall national results. While a focus on capital cities was necessary for logistical reasons, the choice of **politically representative suburban areas** helped to avoid tapping into non-representative urban milieus or subcultures. This was achieved, for example, by choosing Reinickendorf and not Prenzlauer Berg, Ursus and not Mokotov or Meaux instead of the 16ième. Unfortunately, I could not uphold the criterion for the agent groups as they were notoriously difficult to recruit. The sample, nevertheless, represents a diversity of age groups, political positions and employment situations, and it is somewhat balanced with regard to gender. A full overview of participants and a description of the recruitment process can be found in Appendix 3. For now, let me conclude that the diversity of perspectives included leads me to the assumption that the sample represents a rather typical cross-section of the respective national populations. While not being representative in the strict statistical sense, there is no reason to assume that the sample is fundamentally flawed.

Importantly, the implications for external validity of the research design differ with regard to compatibility and complexity. As argued above, maximizing the potential for inter-national differences while avoiding significant biases amounts to a worst-case scenario for compatibility in the European public sphere. Should no misunderstandings occur under these extremely unfavorable conditions, optimism for other situations is warranted. The selection of countries (very dissimilar cases) and interviewing locations (politically representative suburban areas) should strengthen the confidence in the possibility to make inferences from the empirical material. Despite the limited sample size, the research design should provide a **high degree of external validity for the compatibility question**.

The matter is somewhat different for the complexity problem. As participants were selected based on their privileged access to the anchoring domains in question, the research should be viewed as a **qualitative exploration of the various hypotheses**. The results with regard to the complexity problem thus should be mainly taken as evidence that certain mechanisms of complexity reduction are available to the population. Citizens can make sense of economic issues by anchoring them in more familiar bodies of knowledge. As a bottom line, however, the research design can only testify to the existence of such anchoring mechanisms – it cannot be taken as evidence of their distribution. Having outlined the research design and its implications for external validity, we know how the data for the present study was collected. The final section, then, describes how this data was analyzed.

1.5 Method of Analysis

1.5.1 Coding Process: Representations, Language and Experience

The empirical material of this book consists of 18 focus group discussions (around 300 pages of transcripts). In order to identify social representations from this material, I employed a three-step process of coding and restructuring the interview content. For each trigger topic, first, a discussion network linking independent causal units was formed using atlas.ti. These networks helped to visualize recurring patterns of meaning, which were aggregated into social representations in a second step. Finally, representations were linked to anchoring domains. This latter step was achieved partly by paying attention to the mobilization of personal experience and of specific language markers, which serve as indicators of specific anchoring domains in later chapters.

The first step of analysis consisted of bringing the interviews into a standardized form in order to simplify the identification of recurring patterns of meaning. One of the main concerns scholars have faced when analyzing focus groups is that arguments and assumptions are less structured in group interviews than they are in official sources or expert interviews. Well-formed reasoning might take a structure like proposition–evidence–conclusion. In focus groups, however, such perfectly structured arguments are the exception rather than the rule (Quinn, 2005, pp. 63–71; White, 2011, pp. 137–139). This is not to say that the arguments of focus group participants are inferior or less developed – they are just more difficult to spot. Reasoning as it happens in focus groups is fragmented and dispersed. Arguments might be picked up and developed at different moments during the interview, and shared assumptions might remain implicit.

In order to visualize these fragmented structures of argument, I created **discussion networks** using atlas.ti. The discussion networks effectively tried to visualize the process of discussion starting from a trigger argument. As can be seen in Figure 1.3, the network organizes a discussion segment into a number of horizontal layers. On the very top, we see the trigger topic (in this case 'innovation'). Linked to the trigger topic are the discussion segments which it sparked (on the left a German teachers' group and on the right a German soccer group, both discussing trade). The discussion segment's name already gives a broad overview of the central arguments it contains ('innovation as ambiguous concept' and 'new products stimulate innovation') In the layer below the discussion segments are the first associations participants had with the trigger topic. Discussions often covered multiple issues in parallel and the first associations show the different directions into which participants took a trigger topic. The two horizontal layers below the first associations contain a summary of the arguments and judgments brought up in the discussion. On the left part of Figure 1.3 we see, for example, that positive associations with innovation are linked to a vision of economic progress generating jobs (starting from 'competition'), whereas in the central argument a more critical stance is taken, weighing the costs and effects of innovation in different sectors (starting from 'product variety in wrong domains'). The bottom layer presents the examples given, for example, with the innovation-critical line of argument pointing to 'ten different kinds of toilet paper' as a pointless effect of product innovation. In total, in this process of organizing the dispersed structures of arguments, 2,525 citations were coded and linked to generate 78 discussion networks.[9]

For the identification of social representations, however, the focus had to be on the totality of the material rather than on individual trigger topics. In a second step of analysis, therefore, **patterns of argument were aggregated** from the entirety of the material. In multiple steps of dissembling and re-assembling, shared perceptions of the participants were identified. Specific attention was paid to social representations of actors, causal processes and normative reference points or to descriptions of the economic space. The discussion segment presented in Figure 1.3, for example, contains information with regard to all of these dimensions. Regarding actors, for example, big firms are depicted as profiting from a monopoly position – a fact contributing to the formation of the representation of *big firms* (throughout this book, the names of specific representations are written in Italics). Causally, we see that lower prices are linked to lower wages or job loss, a connection which later generated the representation of *wages as exploitation*. Normatively, we

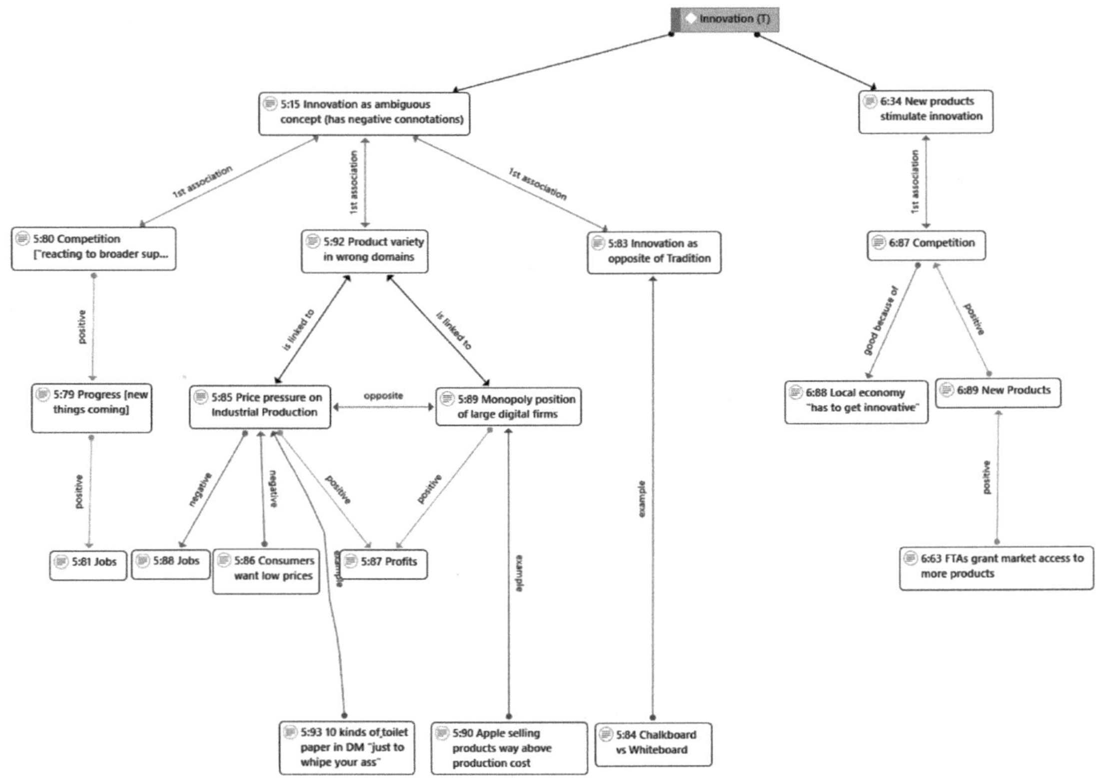

Figure 1.3 Discussion network for trigger topic 'innovation' as discussed by German teachers (to the left; citations start with a five) and German soccer players (to the right; citations start with a six).

see strongly diverging representations of economic progress, with innovation either being seen as inherently good or being put in the context of capitalist profit-making. Finally, we see some evidence concerning the structure of the economic space with innovative digital firms being located in the United States. The second step of analysis thus consisted of inductively identifying frequent patterns of meaning from the totality of the material.

The social representations thus identified had to be present in multiple groups to be considered in the analysis, that is, they had to appear with a minimum frequency. In the rest of the book, I only discuss social representations if they reach a minimum frequency of two, implying that they appeared in at least two separate focus groups. Although this seems to be a rather low standard, I wish to point out that similar operationalizations are common for small-*n*-studies of intersubjective meaning structures (e.g., Gamson 1992, p. 128 using agreement or disagreement of two participants as operationalization of a frame). When different people mobilize similar patterns of meaning in different contexts, this can already be seen as evidence for an underlying shared meaning structure (Quinn, 2005, pp. 45–47). Moreover, in the context of my study a higher minimum requirement would be extremely demanding if we are to study inter-group differences. There were, for example, only three groups in the same nation discussing the same trigger topics. Accordingly, already a minimum requirement of three would demand all national groups to mobilize exactly the same representations in order for the representation to be counted. A minimum requirement of two thus still allows for the observation of topic- and group-specific social representations while guaranteeing that the representation is social (e.g., intersubjectively shared) to a minimal extent.

The social representations thus formed were purposefully conceived as a relatively **small and combinable unit of analysis**. A representation, as I operationalized it here, is a vision of a single aspect of reality which can be combined in various ways to form larger units. This allowed to disentangle fragmented and dispersed lines of reasoning and to disaggregate them into small semantic units. I believe that other concepts frequently employed by qualitative researchers, such as frames, discourses, narratives or orders of worth, are much larger units of analysis, in the sense that they consist of multiple semantic units combined into a bigger picture. While it would have been possible to construct such bigger semantic complexes from the material, the focus on social representations preserves the flexibility and ambivalence of these visions of reality. They could be integrated into a variety of frames or might be included into the political arguments of widely different (and sometimes even opposing) political camps (see Chapter 7).

The final step of the analysis consisted in aggregating the rather small representations into the bigger picture. This implied **linking the social representations to anchoring domains and trigger topics**. Representations were linked to anchoring domains via the characteristics of the participant voicing them (access to the relevant anchoring domain) or via the analysis of the experiences or linguistic expressions mobilized. To show that a given social representation is based on a specific anchoring domain, the social representation should predominantly be mobilized by those participants that have access to the anchoring domain in question. With these patterns established, it became possible to find systematic differences in the understanding of trigger topics based on the mobilization of different anchoring domains. Participants with access to different anchoring domains would understand the same trigger arguments differently. The same argument, when presented to different groups, should trigger different representations. It is mainly this final step of the analysis that will be discussed in the following empirical chapters (Chapters 2, 3, 4, 5 and 7). In each of these chapters, I will first identify the groups of participants with access to a particular anchoring domain. After this, the focus will shift to analyzing how these groups produced different representations of the same trigger topics. Throughout the chapters, I will mainly present quotes starting from the same trigger topic, but revealing different understandings of that topic due to access to different anchoring domains. Readers interested in a review of the social representations before they were aggregated into this larger structure of arguments should consider browsing through Appendix 1.

Beyond the inductive three-step process of identifying social representations, I also coded potential indicators of anchoring domains. I have argued in the hypotheses' sections that in particular language and experience play a crucial role in some of the supposed anchoring domains. The market experience hypotheses supposes, for example, that access to the respective anchoring domain is transmitted via experience. The state of the nation, national culture and the economic theory hypotheses, on the other hand, postulate that participants with access to these anchoring domains should be prone to use specific ways of speaking drawn from the respective body of knowledge. Apart from inductively identifying social representations, then, I also used a standard coding scheme to mark language particularities and incidences of personal experience in the transcripts.

For experiences, the coding scheme was rather simple. The relevant text passages in which participants refer to lived experience of them or of someone they know were easy to spot. Participants frequently highlighted that what follows would be real-world experience, most probably to boost the credibility of the story. Text passages containing personal experiences or stories thereof were marked with a specific code denoting the source of the experience (e.g., workplace, consumption, family). In the discussion networks introduced before, such incidences of personal experience appear in the example-layer on the very bottom. In Figure 1.3 we see, for example, that consumption experience is mobilized with one of the teachers referring to the selection of toilet paper in a specific German drugstore.

The coding of language specificities was slightly more nuanced. I coded three forms of language usage: specific vocabulary, metaphors and personal pronouns. In terms of vocabulary, I mainly coded nationally specific expressions (e.g., terms specific to the respective national language, names of specific policies, popular sayings) and vocabulary drawn from economic theory (e.g., supply, demand, nightwatchman state, the invisible hand). Just like these specific jargons, metaphors also allow for inferences to the anchoring domains participants employ. A metaphor, in fact, can be understood as the transfer of meaning from one domain to another. Metaphors of ranking and race thus can be helpful in identifying representations of the international arena as a competition of states (as described in the worth of nations hypothesis) while machine metaphors point toward a representation of the economy as a complex apparatus in need of careful engineering (economic theory hypothesis). Finally, personal pronouns and in particular those of the first person plural help to assess group identifications. This is useful to analyze the impact of self-interested calculations (expecting the usage of 'we' as a reference to employment groups sharing similar economic interests) or of knowledge about the state of the nation (where 'we' would refer to the nation as a knowable economic agent). Including language specificities and incidences of experience in the analysis, then, is of help in the consequent chapters when the mobilization of different anchoring domains is assessed.

1.5.2 Internal Validity and Presentation of Results

How to lend credibility to the results of this inductive method of identifying social representations? A disadvantage of such inductively formed categories of analysis is that they make reliability tests rather difficult. The social representations I identified are the result of a six-month in-depth engagement with the material and they capture nuances of the argument that would be difficult to describe in a formalized codebook. An inter-coder agreement test, moreover, proved difficult to organize due to the language skills required to code the material. Rather than on formal inter-coder agreement tests, then, I rely on other mechanisms used in qualitative research to guarantee confidence in the results (e.g., Gaskell & Bauer, 2000).

I wish to stress three strategies I employ to render my results plausible. I have, first, already tried to describe the process of analysis in detail. Beyond this transparency of method, I attempt to back up all claims derived from the empirical material with appropriate verbatim evidence. For each social representation identified, I will provide at least two quotes. The fact that those quotes will be drawn from different groups is supposed to show that the meaning conveyed in them is in fact intersubjective. If participants of different age, occupation or nationality – people who have never met and will probably never meet – employ similar a vision of reality, this is an indicator that the representation is indeed social to some extent. The reader thus is asked to take a step a back and to wonder how it is possible that different people exhibit such strikingly similar thoughts. Obviously however, I cannot provide all relevant citations from the material as this would exceed the scope of any book. To remedy this lack of space, third and finally, I provide indicators of frequency and context for each social representation. That is, for each social representation discussed in the following sections I indicate how often and where it appeared in the material. This implies stating how many focus groups developed a similar representation and for how many different trigger topics they used it. I hope that this transparency of method, the usage of quotes from different groups and the precise indication of frequency and of location of the representations will provide my empirical findings with a degree credibility appropriate for qualitative research.

Apart from these conventional methods, I also provide a descriptive overview of my empirical material in Appendix 1. This overview is supposed to allow an in-depth verification of my results for those truly interested in the details of popular representations of the economy. In the preparation of this study, similar overviews of focus group material and of qualitative interviews have been a major help to me in formulating my hypotheses and in acquiring a sense of where the research might go. I hope to be able to be of similar help to those interested in pursuing tangential research. Yet, of course, an entirely neutral presentation of data is certainly difficult to achieve. Appendix 1 mainly presents those social representations which are relevant to the hypotheses and claims advanced in this book; leaving out some peripheral social representations was necessary for the sake of brevity and coherence. The overview is organized around four thematic fields: the economic world map (representations of progress, economic sector orderings and representations of world regions), representations of actors and causal processes in various markets (product, capital and labor market), representations of state functions (investor, re-distributor, competitor, regulator) and representations of ideologies (Keynesianism, liberalism, capitalism, socialism). Providing this neutral overview of my data thus is the final step I take to prove the internal validity of my findings, hopefully allowing the reader to find in-depth confirmation of my arguments.

When citing the focus group material further on in the analysis, I will use abbreviations to refer to the trigger topics and the focus groups. For the trigger topics, the central term of the propositions is used (e.g., the trigger card "boost innovation in the economy" is referred to as 'innovation'). For the focus groups, I use three-letter-abbreviations stating (in that order) the country, the group and the topic of discussion. For countries, 'F' refers to France, 'G' to Germany and 'P' to Poland. For the groups, 'A' indicates an agent, 'L' a teacher and 'S' a soccer group. For the topics, 'U' refers to unemployment and 'T' to trade (which is why teachers are not referred to by a 'T' but rather by the initial letter of the German translation *Lehrer*). FAT thus refers to a French group of agents discussing trade, whereas PSU is the group of Polish soccer players discussing unemployment. A full overview of group abbreviations is given in Appendix 2. Individual participants are referred to by their group name, a gender indicator (man, woman or nonbinary) and a participant number (e.g., GLUW1 is a female German teacher discussing unemployment). The moderator is abbreviated as 'DA', standing for Dorian Alt.

With these methodological clarifications at hand, let us now look at the empirical findings thus generated. The next part of the book presents the most important mechanism found in the focus group discussions: national anchoring.

Notes

1 It is important to note that experience does not exist in a vacuum. Experiences are subject to interpretation based on the social meaning structures available for such situations. In social representation theory, this process of projecting social representations into reality is called objectification. Social representations can have world-making features, that is, they shape experience as much as they might be shaped by it (Elcheroth et al., 2011, pp. 739–741; Höijer, 2011, pp. 7–13; Moscovici, 1984, pp. 38–43; Wagner et al., 1999, pp. 99–100). Experiences, then, are only partly features of individual agents; they always bear the mark of social meaning structures too.

2 Like for experience, this does not imply that language is a passive medium which simply guarantees a 'correct' designation of objects. Rather, languages and specific jargons perpetuate social meaning structures which *sedimented* into them over time (Billig, 1995, p. 18; White, 2009, p. 104, 2011, pp. 39–42). The vocabulary available to an individual thus significantly impacts how an idea can be anchored and how it will be further understood. While language thus perceived is a social structure shaping individual thought, individuals maintain agency due to the multitude of vocabularies that can be drawn on.

3 Viewing nationalism as an ontology helps to explain why I disregard branches of the literature that equate nationalism with a form of extremism. Nationalism in the present conception is a thin ideology that combines with other branches of thought rather than constituting a clearly identifiable political program (Billig, 1995, pp. 6–7; Calhoun, 1997, p. 4; Freeden, 1998; for the economic branch of this argument see Crane, 1998; Pickel, 2005, pp. 1–2).

4 The deep ontological status of nationalism has most famously been highlighted by Michael Billig (1995) who coined the term banal nationalism. According to this thesis, nationalism is at the same time fundamental and naturalized in our perception of the world – it has become banal and thus its impact frequently goes unnoticed.

5 The intensity of transnational linkages between individuals, of course, might rise with the increased usage of social media. Yet, also on social media such links still face significant language barriers or would probably still rely on some form of mediation via English language accounts.

6 By choosing the design, the study also meets the methodological demands in the recent literature on nationalism. In particular, studies of everyday nationhood emphasize the importance of a wait and listen approach (Duchesne, 2018, p. 845; Fox & Miller-Idriss, 2008, p. 556). Rather than asking people directly for their stance toward the nation, the research design leaves it to participants if they bring in national reference points. It thus allows for the observation of the relevance of nationhood in everyday talk.

7 A minor part of the trigger topics was included to trigger specific national meaning structures and thus to contribute to the construction of a worst case scenario. The reasons for the choice of these triggers are therefore elaborated in the last section dealing with country selection.
8 After each focus group discussion, participants were handed a short questionnaire, demanding educational and occupational information, a left–right placement and their last vote in a national election. Most information given in this study is drawn from the questionaires. However, more detailed information about participants' economic and personal situation often came up in the discussions.
9 Preferably, only one network was created per nation and trigger topic. Yet, for extensive discussion segments networks had to be made for single groups.

Bibliography

Anderson, B. R. O. (1991). *Imagined Communities: Reflections on the Origin and Spread of Nationalism*. Verso.

Armingeon, K., & Ceka, B. (2014). The loss of trust in the European Union during the great recession since 2007: The role of heuristics from the national political system. *European Union Politics*, *15*(1), 82–107. https://doi.org/10.1177/1465116513495595

Baxandall, P. (2004). *Constructing Unemployment: The Politics of Joblessness in East and West*. Ashgate.

Beattie, N. (1996). Interview and Concours: Teacher appointment procedures in England and Wales and France, and What They Mean. *Assessment in Education: Principles, Policy & Practice*, *3*(1), 9–28. https://doi.org/10.1080/0969594960030102

Beck, U. (2007). The Cosmopolitan Condition: Why Methodological Nationalism Fails. *Theory, Culture & Society*. https://doi.org/10.1177/02632764070240072505

Billig, M. (1995). *Banal Nationalism*. SAGE.

Blekesaune, M. (2007). Economic Conditions and Public Attitudes to Welfare Policies. *European Sociological Review*, *23*(3), 393–403. https://doi.org/10.1093/esr/jcm012

Bonikowski, B. (2017). Nationhood as Cultural Repertoire: Collective Identities and Political Attitudes in France and Germany. In M. Skey & M. Antonsich (Eds.), *Everyday Nationhood: Theorising Culture, Identity and Belonging after Banal Nationalism* (pp. 147–174). Palgrave Macmillan UK. https://doi.org/10.1057/978-1-137-57098-7_8

Bourdieu, P. (1998). The Social Conditions of the International Circulation of Ideas. In R. Shusterman (Ed.), *Bourdieu: A Critical Reader* (pp. 220–228). Blackwell.

Brinegar, A. P., & Jolly, S. K. (2005). Location, Location, Location: National Contextual Factors and Public Support for European Integration. *European Union Politics*, *6*(2), 155–180. https://doi.org/10.1177/1465116505051981

Brue, S., & Grant, R. (2007). *The Evolution of Economic Thought*. Cengage Learning.

Calhoun, C. J. (1997). *Nationalism*. University of Minnesota Press.

Carter, J. R., & Irons, M. D. (1991). Are Economists Different, and If So, Why? *Journal of Economic Perspectives*, *5*(2), 171–177. https://doi.org/10.1257/jep.5.2.171

Checkel, J. T. (2014). Identity, Europe, and the World Beyond Public Spheres. In T. Risse (Ed.), *European Public Spheres: Politics Is Back* (pp. 227–246). Cambridge University Press. https://doi.org/10.1017/CBO9781139963343.013

Chernilo, D. (2006). Social Theory's Methodological Nationalism: Myth and Reality. *European Journal of Social Theory*. https://doi.org/10.1177/1368431006060460

Collins, J. (2009). Social Reproduction in Classrooms and Schools. *Annual Review of Anthropology*, *38*(1), 33–48. https://doi.org/10.1146/annurev.anthro.37.081407.085242

Copsey, N., & Haughton, T. (2009). The Choices for Europe: National Preferences in New and Old Member States. *JCMS: Journal of Common Market Studies*, *47*(2), 263–286. https://doi.org/10.1111/j.1468-5965.2009.00804.x

Crane, G. T. (1998). Economic Nationalism: Bringing the Nation Back In: *Millennium*. https://doi.org/10.1177/03058298980270011001

Crouch, C. (2004). Why Post-Democracy? In *Post-Democracy* (pp. 1–31). Wiley.

Darriet, E., & Bourgeois-Gironde, S. (2015). Why Lay Social Representations of the Economy Should Count in Economics. *Mind & Society*, *14*(2), 245–258. https://doi.org/10.1007/s11299-015-0177-9

Delanty, G., Hutchinson, J., Kaufmann, E., Özkirimli, U. & Wimmer, A (2008). Debate on John Hutchinson's Nations as Zones of Conflict. *Nations and Nationalism*, *14*(1), 1–28. https://doi.org/10.1111/j.1469-8129.2008.00306.x

Díez Medrano, J., & Gray, E. (2010). *Framing the European Union in National Public Spheres* (pp. 195–222). https://doi.org/10.1017/CBO9780511761010.009

Duchesne, S. (2013). Social Gap: The Double Meaning of 'Overlooking.' In S. Duchesne, E. Frazer, F. Haegel & V. Van Ingelgom (Eds.), *Citizens' Reactions to European Integration Compared: Overlooking Europe* (pp. 65–95). Palgrave Macmillan UK. https://doi.org/10.1057/9781137297266_4

Duchesne, S. (2018). Who's Afraid of Banal Nationalism? *Nations and Nationalism*, *24*(4), 841–856. https://doi.org/10.1111/nana.12457

Duchesne, S., & Ingelgom, V. V. (2008). Comment les discussions deviennent politiques lorsque les francais, anglais et belges parlent d'Europe. *Politique europeenne*, *n°* *24*(1), 145–149.

Duchesne, S., Ingelgom, V. V., Frazer, E., Haegel, F., & Van Ingelgom, V. (2013). *Citizens' Reactions to European Integration Compared: Overlooking Europe* (2013 edition). Palgrave Macmillan.

Duveen, G. (2007). Culture and Social Representations. In *The Cambridge Handbook of Sociocultural Psychology* (pp. 543–559). Cambridge University Press. https://doi.org/10.1017/CBO9780511611162.029

Duveen, G. (2008). Social Actors and Social Groups: A Return to Heterogeneity in Social Psychology. *Journal for the Theory of Social Behaviour*, *38*(4), 369–374. https://doi.org/10.1111/j.1468-5914.2008.00385.x

Działo, J., & Gawrońska-Nowak, B. (2017). Social Expectations Concerning Free Trade Agreements. *Studia Polityczne*, *45*(3), 179–200.

Eder, K., & Kantner, C. (2000). Transnationale Resonanzstrukturen in Europa. In M. Bach (Ed.), *Die Europäisierung nationaler Gesellchaften. Sonderheft 40 der Kölner Zeitschrift für Soziologie und Sozialpsychologie* (pp. 306–331). https://doi.org/10.1007/978-3-322-80390-0_13

Ehrlich, S. D. (2010). Who Supports Compensation? Individual Preferences for Trade-Related Unemployment Insurance. *Business and Politics*, *12*(1), 1–22. https://doi.org/10.2202/1469-3569.1289

Elcheroth, G., Doise, W., & Reicher, S. (2011). *On the Knowledge of Politics and the Politics of Knowledge: How a Social Representations Approach Helps Us Rethink the*

Subject of Political Psychology. *Political Psychology*, *32*(5), 729–758. https://doi.org/10.1111/j.1467-9221.2011.00834.x

Eurobarometer. (2009). *Internal Market: Awareness – Perceptions – Impacts* https://ec.europa.eu/commfrontoffice/publicopinion/archives/quali_en.htm

Eurobarometer. (2011). *Internal Market: Awareness, Perceptions and Impacts*. https://ec.europa.eu/commfrontoffice/publicopinion/archives/quali/5983_awareness_en.pdf

Eurobarometer. (2014). *Coping with the Crisis*. https://ec.europa.eu/commfrontoffice/publicopinion/archives/quali/ql_6342_crisis_en.pdf

European Commission. (2012). *EUR-Lex—52012PC0729—EN* [Text/html; charset=UTF-8]. https://eur-lex.europa.eu/LexUriServ/LexUriServ.do?uri=COM:2012:0729:FIN:EN:HTML

European Parliament. (2017). *Debates – EU–Canada Comprehensive Economic and Trade Agreement—Conclusion of the EU–Canada CETA – EU-Canada Strategic Partnership Agreement (debate) – Wednesday, 15 February 2017*. www.europarl.europa.eu/doceo/document/CRE-8-2017-02-15-ITM-004_EN.html

Farkas, B. (2011). The Central and Eastern European Model of Capitalism. *Post-Communist Economies*, *23*(1), 15–34. https://doi.org/10.1080/14631377.2011.546972

Farr, R. M. (1993). Common Sense, Science and Social Representations. *Public Understanding of Science*. https://journals.sagepub.com/doi/10.1088/0963-6625/2/3/001

Foucault, M. (2006a). *Geschichte der Gouvernementalität. 2. Die Geburt der Biopolitik: Vorlesung am Collège de France 1978 – 1979*. Suhrkamp.

Foucault, M. (2006b). *Sicherheit, Territorium, Bevölkerung: Vorlesung am Collège de France; 1977 – 1978*. Suhrkamp.

Fougner, T. (2008). Neoliberal Governance of States: The Role of Competitiveness Indexing and Country Benchmarking. *Millennium*, *37*(2), 303–326. https://doi.org/10.1177/0305829808097642

Fourcade-Gourinchas, M. (2001). Politics, Institutional Structures, and the Rise of Economics: A Comparative Study. *Theory and Society*, *30*(3), 397–447. JSTOR.

Fox, J. E., & Miller-Idriss, C. (2008). Everyday Nationhood. *Ethnicities*, *8*(4), 536–563. https://doi.org/10.1177/1468796808088925

Fraile, M., & Ferrer, M. (2005). Explaining the Determinants of Public Support for Cuts in Unemployment Benefits Spending across OECD Countries. *International Sociology*, *20*(4), 459–481. https://doi.org/10.1177/0268580905058327

Freeden, M. (1998). Is Nationalism a Distinct Ideology? *Political Studies*, *46*(4), 748–765. https://doi.org/10.1111/1467-9248.00165

Gabel, M. J. (1998). *Interests and Integration: Market Liberalization, Public Opinion, and European Union*. University of Michigan Press.

Gal, S. (1989). Language and Political Economy. *Annual Review of Anthropology*, *18*(1), 345–367. https://doi.org/10.1146/annurev.an.18.100189.002021

Gamson, G., & William, A. (1992). *Talking Politics*. Cambridge University Press.

Gaskell, G., & Bauer, M. (2000). Towards Public Accountability beyond Sampling, Reliability and Validity. In P. Atkinson, M. W. Bauer, & G. Gaskell (Eds.), *Qualitative Researching with Text, Image and Sound: A Practical Handbook for Social Research* (pp. 336–350). SAGE.

Geertz, C. (2000). The World in Pieces. Culture and Politics at the End of the Century. In *Available Light: Anthropological Reflections on Philosophical Topics* (pp. 218–263). Princeton University Press.

Gerhards, J. (1998). Öffentlichkeit. In O. Jarren, U. Sarcinelli, & U. Saxer (Eds.), *Politische Kommunikation in der demokratischen Gesellschaft: Ein Handbuch mit Lexikonteil* (pp. 268–274). VS Verlag für Sozialwissenschaften. https://doi.org/10.1007/978-3-322-80348-1_14

Gerhards, J., Breuer, L. & Delius, A. (2017). *Kollektive Erinnerungen der europäischen Bürger im Kontext von Transnationalisierungsprozessen: Deutschland, Großbritannien, Polen und Spanien im Vergleich*. VS Verlag für Sozialwissenschaften. https://doi.org/10.1007/978-3-658-13402-0

Gillespie, A. (2008). Social Representations, Alternative Representations and Semantic Barriers. *Journal for the Theory of Social Behaviour*, *38*(4), 375–391. https://doi.org/10.1111/j.1468-5914.2008.00376.x

Gillespie, A., & Cornish, F. (2010). Intersubjectivity: Towards a Dialogical Analysis. *Journal for the Theory of Social Behaviour*, *40*, 19–46. https://doi.org/10.1111/j.1468-5914.2009.00419.x

Greenfeld, L. (1995). The Worth of Nations: Some Economic Implications of Nationalism. *Critical Review*, *9*(4), 555–584. https://doi.org/10.1080/08913819508443403

Habermas, J. (1982). *Strukturwandel der Öffentlichkeit: Untersuchungen zu einer Kategorie der bürgerlichen Gesellschaft*. Luchterhand.

Haegel, F. (2005). Réflexion sur les usages de l'entretien collectif. *Recherche en soins infirmiers*, *N° 83*(4), 23–27.

Haegel, F. (2013). National Frames: Reactions to a Multi-Level World. In S. Duchesne, E. Frazer, F. Haegel, & V. Van Ingelgom (Eds.), *Citizens' Reactions to European Integration Compared: Overlooking Europe* (pp. 34–64). Palgrave Macmillan UK. https://doi.org/10.1057/9781137297266_3

Haffert, L., Redeker, N., & Rommel, T. (2019). Hyperinflation, the Great Depression, and German Collective Economic Memory. Unpublished Working Paper, 37.

Hearn, J. (2006). *Rethinking Nationalism: A Critical Introduction*. Palgrave Macmillan.

Hepp, A., & Wessler, H. (2009). Politische Diskurskulturen – Überlegungen zur empirischen Erklärung segmentierter europäischer Öffentlichkeit. *Medien & Kommunikationswissenschaft*, *57*(2), 174–197. https://doi.org/10.5771/1615-634x-2009-2-174

Hepp, A., Elsler, M., Lingenberg, S., Mollen, A., Möller, J., Offerhaus, A., Sword, K., & Pospielovsky, D. V. (2016). *The Communicative Construction of Europe: Cultures of Political Discourse, Public Sphere, and the Euro Crisis*. Palgrave Macmillan UK. https://doi.org/10.1057/9781137453136

Hobolt, S. B., & de Vries, C. E. (2016). Public Support for European Integration. *Annual Review of Political Science*, *19*(1), 413–432. https://doi.org/10.1146/annurev-polisci-042214-044157

Hobsbawm, E., & Ranger, T. (1992). *The Invention of Tradition*. Cambridge University Press.

Höijer, B. (2011). Social Representations Theory: A New Theory for Media Research. *Nordicom Review*, *32*(2), 3–16. https://doi.org/10.1515/nor-2017-0109

Jaskulowski, K., & Surmiak, A. (2017). Teaching History, Teaching Nationalism: A Qualitative Study of History Teachers in a Polish Post-industrial Town. *Critical Studies in Education*, *58*(1), 36–51. https://doi.org/10.1080/17508487.2015.1117006

Jovchelovitch, S. (2006). *Knowledge in Context: Representations, Community and Culture*. Routledge. https://doi.org/10.4324/9781315173368

Jovchelovitch, S. (2012). Narrative, Memory and Social Representations: A Conversation between History and Social Psychology. *Integrative Psychological and Behavioral Science*, *46*(4), 440–456. https://doi.org/10.1007/s12124-012-9217-8

Kaneva, N. (2006). Memories of Everyday Life in Communist Bulgaria: Negotiating Identity in Immigrant Narratives. *Colorado Research in Linguistics*.

Kangas, A. (2013). Market Civilisation Meets Economic Nationalism: The Discourse of Nation in Russia's Modernisation. *Nations and Nationalism*, *19*(3), 572–591. https://doi.org/10.1111/nana.12023

Kantner, C. (2014). The European Public Sphere and the Debate about Humanitarian Military Interventions. *European Security*, *23*(4), 409–429. https://doi.org/10.1080/09662839.2014.890595

Killingsworth, M., Klatt, G., & Auer, S. (2010). Where Does Poland Fit in Europe? How Political Memory Influences Polish MEPs' Perceptions of Poland's place in Europe. *Perspectives on European Politics and Society*, *11*, 358–375. https://doi.org/10.1080/15705854.2010.524408

Koopmans, R. (2014). How Advanced is the Europeanization of Public Spheres? Comparing German and European Structures of Political Communication. In T. Risse (Ed.), *European Public Spheres: Politics Is Back* (pp. 63–96). Cambridge University Press. https://doi.org/10.1017/CBO9781139963343.005

Krzyzanowski, M. (2008). Analyzing Focus Group Discussions. In R. Wodak & M. Krzyzanowski (Eds.), *Qualitative Discourse Analysis in the Social Sciences* (pp. 273–306) Palgrave Macmillan.

Lamont, M., & Molnár, V. (2002). The Study of Boundaries in the Social Sciences. *Annual Review of Sociology*, *28*(1), 167–195. https://doi.org/10.1146/annurev.soc.28.110601.141107

Lamont, M., & Thévenot, L. (2000). Introduction: Toward a Renewed Comparative Cultural Sociology. In L. Thévenot & M. Lamont (Eds.), *Rethinking Comparative Cultural Sociology: Repertoires of Evaluation in France and the United States* (pp. 1–22). Cambridge University Press. https://doi.org/10.1017/CBO9780511628108.001

Leiser, D., Bourgeois-Gironde, S., & Benita, R. (2010). Human Foibles or Systemic Failure—Lay Perceptions of the 2008–2009 Financial Crisis. *The Journal of Socio-Economics*, *39*(2), 132–141. https://doi.org/10.1016/j.socec.2010.02.013

Leuffen, D. (2007). Case Selection and Selection Bias in Small-*n* Research. In T. Gschwend & F. Schimmelfennig (Eds.), *Research Design in Political Science: How to Practice What They Preach* (pp. 145–160). Palgrave Macmillan UK. https://doi.org/10.1057/9780230598881_8

Lingenberg, S. (2010). Fallstudien zur europäischen Verfassungsdebatte. In S. Lingenberg (Ed.), *Europäische Publikumsöffentlichkeiten: Ein pragmatischer Ansatz* (pp. 183–226). VS Verlag für Sozialwissenschaften. https://doi.org/10.1007/978-3-531-92120-4_5

Mackenzie, D. (2008). *An Engine, Not a Camera: How Financial Models Shape Markets*. MIT Press.

Marková, I., Moodie, E., Farr, R. M., Drozda-Senkowska, E., Erös, F., Plichtová, J., Gervais, M.-C., Hoffmannová, J., & Mullerová, O. (1998). Social Representations of the Individual: A Post-Communist Perspective. *European Journal of Social Psychology*, *28*(5), 797–829. https://doi.org/10.1002/(SICI)1099-0992(199809/10)28:5<797::AID-EJSP896>3.0.CO;2-6

Mattila, M. (2009). Roll Call Analysis of Voting in the European Union Council of Ministers After the 2004 Enlargement. *European Journal of Political Research*, *48*(6), 840–857. https://doi.org/10.1111/j.1475-6765.2009.01850.x

Mau, S. (2005). Europe from the Bottom: Assessing Personal Gains and Losses and its Effects on EU Support. *Journal of Public Policy*, *25*(3), 289–311. https://doi.org/10.1017/S0143814X05000346

Mérand, F. (2006). Social Representations in the European Security and Defence Policy. *Cooperation and Conflict*, *41*(2), 131–152. https://doi.org/10.1177/0010836706063659

Mitchell, T. (1998). Fixing the Economy. *Cultural Studies*, *12*(1), 82–101. https://doi.org/10.1080/095023898335627

Moodie, E., Markova, I. & Plichtova, J. (2016). Lay Representations of Democracy: A Study in Two Cultures: *Culture & Psychology*. https://doi.org/10.1177/1354067X9514002

Moody, M. & Thévenot, L. (2000). Comparing Models of Strategy, Interests, and the Public Good in French and American Environmental Disputes. In L. Thévenot & M. Lamont (Eds.), *Rethinking Comparative Cultural Sociology: Repertoires of Evaluation in France and the United States* (pp. 273–306). Cambridge University Press. https://doi.org/10.1017/CBO9780511628108.010

Moscovici, S. (1984). The Phenomenon of Social Representations. In R. M. Farr & S. Moscovici (Eds.), *Social Representations* (pp. 1–67). TPB.

Moscovici, S. (2004). *La psychanalyse, son image et son public*. Presses Universitaires de France. https://doi.org/10.3917/puf.mosco.2004.01

Müller, K. (2005). Nationalist Undercurrents in German Economic Liberalism. In E. Helleiner & A. Pickel (Eds.), *Economic Nationalism in a Globalizing World* (pp. 141–164). Cornell University Press.

Nakano, T. (2004). Theorising Economic Nationalism*. *Nations and Nationalism*, *10*(3), 211–229. https://doi.org/10.1111/j.1354-5078.2004.00164.x

Nassehi, A. (2019). *Muster: Theorie der digitalen Gesellschaft*. C.H.Beck.

Nölke, A., & Vliegenthart, A. (2009). Enlarging the Varieties of Capitalism: The Emergence of Dependent Market Economies in East Central Europe. *World Politics*, *61*(4), 670–702. https://doi.org/10.1017/S0043887109990098

Norval, A. J. (2000). Review Article: The Things We Do with Words – Contemporary Approaches to the Analysis of Ideology. *British Journal of Political Science*, *30*(2), 313–346. https://doi.org/10.1017/S0007123400000144

Offe, C. (2005). The European Model of 'Social' Capitalism. Can It Survive European Integration? In M. Miller (Ed.), *Worlds of Capitalism: Institutions, Economic Performance and Governance in the Era of Globalization* (pp. 141–172). Routledge.

O'Rourke, K. H., Sinnott, R., Richardson, J. D., & Rodrik, D. (2001). The Determinants of Individual Trade Policy Preferences: International Survey Evidence [with Comments and Discussion]. *Brookings Trade Forum*, 157–206. JSTOR.

O'Toole, G. (2003). A New Nationalism for a New Era: The Political Ideology of Mexican Neoliberalism. *Bulletin of Latin American Research*, *22*(3), 269–290. https://doi.org/10.1111/1470-9856.00078

Özkirimli, U. (2005). *Contemporary Debates on Nationalism: A Critical Engagement*. Macmillan Education UK.

Peet, R. (2002). Ideology, Discourse, and the Geography of Hegemony: From Socialist to Neoliberal Development in Postapartheid South Africa. *Antipode*, *34*(1), 54–84. https://doi.org/10.1111/1467-8330.00226

Pettit, P. (1995). The Virtual Reality of "Homo Economicus." *The Monist*, *78*(3), 308–329. JSTOR.

Pfetsch, B. (2014). Blind Spots in the Analysis of the Media-Politics Relationship in Europe. In B. Pfetsch (Ed.), *Political Communication Cultures in Western*

Europe: Attitudes of Political Actors and Journalists in Nine Countries (pp. 1–12). Palgrave Macmillan.

Pickel, A. (2005). Introduction: False Oppositions. Reconceptualizing Economic Nationalism in a Globalizing World. In E. Helleiner & A. Pickel (Eds.), *Economic Nationalism in a Globalizing World* (pp. 1–18). Cornell University Press.

Prior, M. (2007). *Post-Broadcast Democracy: How Media Choice Increases Inequality in Political Involvement and Polarizes Elections*. Cambridge University Press.

Provencher, C. (2011). Towards A Better Understanding of Cognitive Polyphasia. *Journal for the Theory of Social Behaviour*, *41*(4), 377–395. https://doi.org/10.1111/j.1468-5914.2011.00468.x

Quinn, N. (2005). How to Reconstruct Schemas People Share, From What They Say. In N. Quinn (Ed.), *Finding Culture in Talk: A Collection of Methods* (pp. 35–81). Palgrave Macmillan US. https://doi.org/10.1007/978-1-137-05871-3_2

Rehm, P. (2011). Social Policy by Popular Demand. *World Politics*, *63*(2), 271–299. https://doi.org/10.1017/S0043887111000037

Rehm, P. (2016). *Risk Inequality and Welfare States: Social Policy Preferences, Development, and Dynamics*. Cambridge University Press.

Risse, T. (2014a). No Demos? Identities and Public Spheres in the Euro Crisis. *JCMS: Journal of Common Market Studies*, *52*(6), 1207–1215. https://doi.org/10.1111/jcms.12189

Risse, T. (2014b, November). *Introduction*. In T. Risse (Ed.), *European Public Spheres: Politics Is Back* (pp. 1–26). Cambridge University Press. https://doi.org/10.1017/CBO9781139963343.005

Rosamond, B. (2002). Imagining the European Economy: "Competitiveness" and the Social Construction of "Europe" as an Economic Space. *New Political Economy*, *7*(2), 157–177. https://doi.org/10.1080/13563460220138826

Sammut, G., & Gaskell, G. (2010). Points of View, Social Positioning and Intercultural Relations. *Journal for the Theory of Social Behaviour*, *40*(1), 47–64. https://doi.org/10.1111/j.1468-5914.2009.00422.x

Schmidt, V. (2003). French Capitalism – Transformed, Yet Still a Third Variety of Capitalism. *Economy and Society*, *32*(4), 526–554. https://doi.org/10.1080/0308514032000141693

Schmidt, V. A. (2014). Speaking to the Markets or to the People? A Discursive Institutionalist Analysis of the EU's Sovereign Debt Crisis. *The British Journal of Politics and International Relations*, *16*(1), 188–209. https://doi.org/10.1111/1467-856X.12023

Schroedter, J. H., De Winter, T. & Koelet, S. (2015). Beyond l'Auberge Espagnole: The Effect of Individual Mobility on the Formation of Intra-European Couples. *European Journal of Population*, *31*(2), 181–206. https://doi.org/10.1007/s10680-015-9343-3

Smith, A. D. (1998). Invention and Imagination. In *Nationalism and Modernism: A Critical Survey of Recent Theories of Nations and Nationalism* (pp. 117–142). Routledge.

SPIEGEL, D. (2020, January 20). *"Bloomberg" führt Deutschland erstmals als innovativste Nation der Welt—DER SPIEGEL – Wirtschaft*. www.spiegel.de/wirtschaft/unternehmen/deutschland-als-innovativste-nation-der-welt-eingestuft-a-a09f9e5a-6fad-4d8a-b58b-0172c29cbf39

Statham, P. (2010). Europe's Search for a Public. In R. Koopmans and P. Statham (Eds.), *The Making of a European Public Sphere: Media Discourse and Political Contention* (pp. 1–11). Cambridge University Press.

Statham, P., & Trenz, H.-J. (2015). Understanding the Mechanisms of EU Politicization: Lessons from the Eurozone Crisis. *Comparative European Politics*, *13*(3), 287–306. https://doi.org/10.1057/cep.2013.30

Stoker, G., Hay, C., & Barr, M. (2016). Fast Thinking: Implications for Democratic Politics. *European Journal of Political Research*, *55*(1), 3–21. https://doi.org/10.1111/1475-6765.12113

Strauss, C. (2005). Analyzing Discourse for Cultural Complexity. In N. Quinn (Ed.), *Finding Culture in Talk: A Collection of Methods* (pp. 203–242). Palgrave Macmillan US. https://doi.org/10.1007/978-1-137-05871-3_6

Swidler, A. (1986). Culture in Action: Symbols and Strategies. *American Sociological Review*, *51*(2), 273–286. JSTOR. https://doi.org/10.2307/2095521

Thévenot, L., Moody, M., & Lafaye, C. (2000). Forms of Valuing Nature: Arguments and Modes of Justification in French and American Environmental Disputes. In M. Lamont & L. Thévenot (Eds.), *Rethinking Comparative Cultural Sociology: Repertoires of Evaluation in France and the United States* (pp. 229–273). Cambridge University Press. https://doi.org/10.1017/CBO9780511628108.009

Thomson, R. (2009). Actor Alignments in the European Union Before and After Enlargement. *European Journal of Political Research*, *48*(6), 756–781. https://doi.org/10.1111/j.1475-6765.2009.00848.x

Trenz, H.-J. (2000). Korruption und politischer Skandal in der EU. Auf dem Weg zu einer europäischen politischen Öffentlichkeit? *KZfSS Kölner Zeitschrift Für Soziologie Und Sozialpsychologie, Sonderheft*, *29*, 332–359.

Trenz, H.-J. (2005). The European Public Sphere: Contradictory Findings in a Diverse Research Field. *European Political Science*, *4*(4), 407–420. https://doi.org/10.1057/palgrave.eps.2210051

Vail, M. I. (2020). National Liberalisms in a Neoliberal Age: Ideas and Economic Adjustment in Contemporary France and Germany. *Comparative European Politics*, *18*(2), 109–127. https://doi.org/10.1057/s41295-019-00155-3

van Bavel, R., & Gaskell, G. (2004). Narrative and Systemic Modes of Economic Thinking. *Culture & Psychology*, *10*(4), 417–439. https://doi.org/10.1177/1354067X04042892

Voelklein, C., & Howarth, C. (2005). A Review of Controversies about Social Representations Theory: A British Debate. *Culture and Psychology 11*. https://doi.org/10.1177/1354067X05058586

Wagner, W., Farr, R., Jovchelovitch, S., Lorenzi-Cioldi, F., Markova, I., Duveen, G., & Rose, D. (1999). Theory and Method of Social Representations. *Asian Journal of Social Psychology*, *2*. https://doi.org/10.1111/1467-839X.00028

Waks, L. J. (2006). Globalization, State Transformation, and Educational Restructuring: Why Postmodern Diversity Will Prevail Over Standardization. *Studies in Philosophy and Education*, *25*(5), 403–424. https://doi.org/10.1007/s11217-006-9014-2

Weber, E. (1976). *Peasants Into Frenchmen: The Modernization of Rural France, 1870-1914*. Stanford University Press.

White, J. (2009). The Social Theory of Mass Politics. *The Journal of Politics*, *71*. https://doi.org/10.1017/S0022381608090075

White, J. (2011). *Political Allegiance After European Integration*. Palgrave Macmillan. www.palgrave.com/gp/book/9780230279780

White, J. (2019). *Politics of Last Resort: Governing by Emergency in the European Union*. Oxford University Press.

Wodak, R. (2009). *Discursive Construction of National Identity*. Edinburgh University Press.

Zabel, I. (2004). The (Former) East and its Identity. In Hlavajova, M & Winder, J. (Eds.) *Who If Not We Should at Least Try to Imagine the Future of All This*. pp. 283–288. Artimo.

Zarycki, T. (2014). Innowacjonizm jako legitymizacja. Dyskursy innowacji, gospodarki opartej na wiedzy, społeczeństwa informacyjnego i pokrewne w perspektywie krytycznej. *Zarządzanie Publiczne*, *27*, 5–19. https://doi.org/10.7366/1898352912702

Zarycki, T. (2015). Modernizacja kulturowa i psychologiczna jako ideologia inteligenckiej hegemonii. *Przegląd Socjologiczny*, *64*(2), 45–68.

Part I

National Anchoring

2 National Culture and Past Politicization

2.1 Introduction

How do citizens understand the incredibly complex political issues which form the subject of most debates in the European public sphere? What happens if we ask a French teacher for her opinion on international mobility of capital? How does an estate agent in Warsaw react when you ask him about the effect of state spending on unemployment rates? How does a member of an amateur soccer team in Berlin conceptualize the effect of trade on state sovereignty? All the people cited above are European citizens. As such, they form part of the European public sphere: through mediation of national media, they will be confronted with European arguments of similar complexity on a regular basis. Apart from the economic examples cited above, similarly complex questions arise with regard to climate change, concerning internet governance or in the context of the global COVID-19 pandemic. Issue **complexity** is a characteristic feature of the European public sphere and of international politics more generally.

This chapter discusses one solution to the complexity problem: **national anchoring**. Citizens can use national knowledge to render complex issues intelligible. If citizens are confronted with complex economic questions in the European public sphere, they mobilize their knowledge of past national politics to generate nationally specific social representations of the phenomenon in question. Frequently, national debates coin specific linguistic expressions, which make it easier for citizens to recall the complex arguments they became familiar with in the past. A French teacher might mobilize politically loaded vocabulary from past national debates (*délocalisation*) to understand the effects of the free movement of capital. The Polish estate agent might draw on his assessment of the Polish governments' recent family support program (*500+*) to judge potential spending programs on EU level. And the German midfielder might recall the inefficiency of German federalism (*Kleinstaaterei*) to make an argument for international trade cooperation. In all cases, knowledge about national politics is mobilized to render complex European arguments intelligible.

DOI: 10.4324/9781003335610-4

The novelty of the concept of national anchoring lies in its insistence on memories of past politics as a principal source of political knowledge. This finding corresponds to the predictions of the national culture hypothesis presented in Chapter 1. In this hypothesis, the term culture refers to the symbols and meaning patterns which are temporarily de-contested within national societies. There are various elements of national culture that can be used for anchoring: apart from memories of past politics, the empirical material also shows that economics can be anchored in memories of grand history or in discourses popularized through national academic cultures. Yet, importantly these elements seem to be known to the population mainly because they were mobilized in recent political debates as prominent reference points. If elements of national history and national academic cultures appeared in the focus groups, they had mostly been linked to recent policy debates (e.g, memories of socialism to *500+* in Poland or ordoliberal thought to the criticism of the ECB in Germany). What popularizes national meaning structures, then, is their politicization in the national public sphere and their sedimentation into national languages. **Ideal-typically, national anchoring is the process of anchoring complex issues in memories of past politics**. This mechanism explains both the success of the national culture hypothesis (this chapter) and of the worth of the nation hypothesis (Chapter 3). Highlighting the impact of relatively banal national policy debates on citizens' political imagination is the major contribution of the concept.

National anchoring – somewhat obviously – causes inter-national differences in citizens' understanding of economics. Yet, these differences are not exclusive, meaning there are no social representations that pertain exclusively to the members of one nation. The effect of national anchoring is to facilitate the making of certain arguments for citizens socialized in a specific national context. Importantly, this means that it is harder, but not impossible, for citizens without access to these national anchoring domains to make the same arguments. Nationally loaded vocabulary is a prime example of this mechanism: its availability often allows to summarize a complex causality in a short expression. This expression, in turn, will resonate with fellow nationals who have the same anchoring point in mind, thus facilitating communication and often generating support. The argument thus becomes more persuasive (and more frequent, as more people will dare making it). The French teacher cited above will easily convince her peers once she cites the politically loaded French expression regarding international mobility. It will prove much more difficult for a German teacher to present the same argument as an adequate expression for it is missing in her national language. Throughout the chapter, then, I will show how some representations are very easily mobilized in some national contexts, while citizens from other nations form the same representations only rarely and with great difficulty. Inter-national differences appear as differences in the **frequency and persuasiveness of arguments**.

The chapter proceeds in accordance with the two-step process outlined in the theory chapter. In the next section (Section 2.2), I will identify the **social**

groups with access to the relevant anchoring domains. Concretely, this implies establishing which focus group participants have access to the forms national knowledge identified in the hypotheses. Having established which participants qualify as having access to national culture, the following sections then analyze if national culture was mobilized as an anchoring domain. In the focus groups, all participants were presented with the same trigger arguments drawn from the European level. If the elements of national culture were employed to render these issues intelligible, we should observe **differences in the representation of trigger arguments.** The largest of these sections (2.3.1) is dedicated to anchoring in memories of past politics. Two briefer sections address less frequently mobilized elements of national culture (national academic culture in Section 2.3.2 and grand history in Section 2.3.3). In the conclusion, I explain why the prominence of past politicization as an anchor should crucially amend our understanding of the relationship between nationhood and public perceptions. National anchoring feeds on memories of somewhat banal day-to-day politics, rather than on pompous conceptions of grand history or national identity.

2.2 Identification of Social Group

The first step in analyzing the impact of an anchoring domain is to identify those citizens who have access to it. In the hypotheses section, I have highlighted a number of mechanisms which can serve to transmit specific forms of knowledge to groups of people and which can thus serve as indicators for access to an anchoring domain. For the national culture hypothesis, school education and the public sphere are the decisive transmission mechanisms. The focus groups brought together participants who, first, had completed their school education in the respective country, and second, had lived in the respective country for the longest part of their lives.[1] In each country, then, the assembled participants had been exposed to school education and to the national public sphere for a long period of time. In particular, teachers should be prone to command the relevant national forms of knowledge as they perform a crucial role in transmitting them (remember that the school is considered the school of the nation). The participants in each country, then, did have access to the form of national knowledge described in the national culture hypothesis.

Practically, this means that I operationalize access to national knowledge via the participants' nationality. All of the focus group participants had spent the major part of their lives in their country of origin – nationality thus is a proper indicator for exposure to the national public sphere and to the national education system. For the rest of the book, then, I treat the participants of different nationality as the social groups which have access to specific national anchoring domains and thus might generate inter-nationally different representations of complex arguments (see Figure 1.2). In total, the six focus groups per country assembled 22 French, 21 German and 21 Polish participants. The differences in their representation of the trigger arguments will be the subject of the following sections.

2.3 Representation of Arguments: Anchoring in National Culture

In the empirical material, participants mobilized the elements of national culture as an anchoring domain for complex European issues. Anchoring in national culture produced differences in the representation of the trigger arguments 'mobility', 'workers' rights' 'expenditure', 'entrepreneurship', 'sovereignty', 'interest' and 'right to work'. Of all the hypothesis, then, national culture was the most frequently employed anchoring domain.

2.3.1 Past Politics Sedimented into National Languages: Concurrence déloyale, 500+, Kleinstaaterei

The most frequent element of national culture employed as an anchoring point is national vocabulary coined in past political debates. The way national vocabulary impacts the frequency and persuasiveness of representations is most clearly visible for the trigger topic 'mobility'. In the unemployment discussions, participants were asked the question 'how can the unemployment rate in the EU be lowered' and were handed a card reading 'boost international mobility of labor' as a potential answer. As we will see in the next chapter, Polish and German participants employed different anchoring domains to render this argument intelligible. While Polish participants frequently mobilized systemic experiences of mobility, German participants anchored the argument in knowledge about the characteristics of their national economy. Accordingly, the Polish groups mainly ended up forming a representation of *migration as a personal prospect* whereas the Germans saw *migration as talent* (for details on these representations of migration see Appendix 1, Section A1.4). In the French groups, yet another vision of migration dominated. Migration was most frequently described as a *race to the bottom* using specific national vocabulary.

> FAUW2: "I have something similar. In the sense that … With respect to the domain of work, we see, for example, foreign doctors that come to France and are under-paid. And we, our doctors, have to go abroad because they don't have the salaries, the salaries they deserve. It would be with respect to this, to firms that are delocalized [délocalisés], that go abroad."
>
> – French agents discussing 'mobility'

> FLUM1: "Yes, that's what I understood. Delocalization [délocalisation]. [FLUW1: Yes]. And that can create problems for a country's development. If unemployment follows."
>
> – French teachers discussing 'mobility'

Several things should be noted about the quotes. First, the statements are made by relatively inactive participants. Both FAUW2 and FLUM1 were not particularly vocal during the discussions and in particular FLUM1 seemed to be rather timid throughout. Second, in both statements a complex economic causality (*migration as a race to the bottom*) is expressed using specific national vocabulary (*délocalisation*). Third, because of the usage of this specialized terminology the statements remain relatively short. And despite this brevity, finally, the participants (at least in the case of FLUM1) get support from their peers. The availability of specific national vocabulary seems to facilitate the ease of making some complex arguments and increases the likelihood of being understood by fellow nationals. Let us now see what happens if the respective vocabulary is not available.

> GSUM1: "'International Mobility of Labor' – of course. Eh [pause] we have that actually or it should be like that. Ehm it would also be nice, and that is not mentioned here, if the competitiveness of law ... So there would need to be the same law everywhere, the same taxes, et cetera ... Because like this they wander, it is just moving around like in a board game [*Mensch-ärgere-dich-nicht*]. Then off they go to the next country, because they say: 'Ah, here things are cheaper.' And off they go. Then you got some new employees over there, but you lose them in the original country. Well? That doesn't make sense. So, the law should be the same everywhere. In the end, this will take a couple of years, but in the end, it has to be the aim."
>
> – German soccer players discussing 'mobility'

In several ways, the quote by a German soccer player is the mirror image of the previous ones. First, GSUM1 is a very vocal and eloquent participant. As a member of a trade union, he is knowledgeable about many economic issues and dominates large segments of his focus group. Yet, in the quote above he clearly struggles to bring his point across. The quote's beginning is characterized by disfluency: GSUM1 pauses and struggles to find the right words. The expression he finds ("the competitiveness of law") is a spontaneous and rather awkward creation which doesn't resonate with his peers. GSUM1, then, must go into detail explaining the process he criticizes. He does so by likening international factor mobility to a board game and by spelling out the firms' reasoning. In other words, GSUM1 has to mobilize quite a bit of rhetorical skill to make a point the French participants could make using few words. His quote is much longer and does not get any support from the peers in his group. GSUM1's difficulty in evoking the representation of *migration as a race to the bottom* contrasts sharply with the ease of French participants who had national vocabulary at their disposal. It seems logical, then, that the representation of migration as a race to the bottom was most frequent in France while participants in Germany and Poland mostly relied on different representations.

The trigger topic of 'mobility' thus provides evidence of inter-national differences resulting in the mobilization of national culture as an anchoring domain. Arguably, the inter-national thus generated are differences in the **frequency and persuasiveness** of arguments. What does this specifically mean? Regarding frequency, the central point is that reference points in national culture – and particularly specific linguistic expressions – make it much easier to voice specific arguments. It is much easier to briefly allude to *délocalisation* than to come up with your own expression for it and make up a fictive scenario in which a firm decides to move abroad. As further examples will show throughout the chapter, the fact that an argument is easier to make seems to increase the number of participants willing to make it. If specific national vocabulary is available, shy and rather silent participants will suddenly step forward and make arguments that are only voiced by the most vocal and informed participants in other nations. At the same time, the fact that the specific references to national culture are known to other participants boosts the chances of obtaining support for the argument. In particular, the arguments contained in specific linguistic expressions have a good chance of being recognized as legitimate by the other participants. Arguments that can be anchored in national culture thus are not only more frequent in the respective national context they are also accepted as more persuasive. How anchoring in national culture boosts the frequency and persuasiveness of arguments can also be observed for the trigger topic 'worker's rights'.

> FLTM3: "And the protection of workers' rights, what we have seen with the agreement between Canada and the United States where this was the main problem. It produced unfair competition [*concurrence déloyale*]."
>
> FLTM2: "Bravo."
>
> – French teachers discussing 'workers' rights'

> FSTM6: "Look, with regard to the workers here, they are called posted workers [*travailleur détaché*]. What is a posted worker? People that come from Romania to work in France. Only that they do the same work but are paid two times less than a French worker."
>
> FSTM1: "Yes, yes!"
>
> – French soccer players discussing 'workers' rights'

> PSTM4: "I would approach this from a different perspective. Not simply production-wise, but rather ... This defense of workers' rights, what was already mentioned earlier, that the country should take care of that. And I would actually approach the matter in such a way that a strong inflow of foreign firms, of foreign capital, that [...] from the state's perspective a domestic firm ... Big companies start dictating their conditions to the state. If they focus on the rights of their workers and say: 'Well. Listen up! Something.' I don't know. 'We will

do this, this and this. You got to do as we say, for if not, we'll fuck off.' Right?"

PSTM5: "But it is already like that! And that's a huge problem. Mercedes comes in and says that they want to open an engine factory in Lower Silesia. So they come and say: 'Ok, make your offer! What can you give us?' Well and Poland, that is Mr. Morawiecki, is fucking shivering and starts straight away to think something up ... 'Cool, thanks guys. Good idea, but wait, we'll just go to Slovakia first. [PSTM1: To Slovakia! Do you know what they offered us there?] And do you know what the Hungarians said? We will get back to you eventually!' And then they stay silent for some fucking time. And Morawiecki is sitting there with his guys: 'Ok, we promised on TV that Mercedes will invest here. Have to offer them something good, so they come here.'"

– Polish soccer players discussing 'investment'

In the first two quotes, we see how French participants employ specifically loaded national vocabulary to describe complex economic processes (*concurrence déloyale* and *travailleur détaché*). Again, the statements are quite short but get explicit support from other participants. On the trigger topic 'workers' rights', again, French participants mobilize representations of a global race to the bottom, and they do so with great ease, simply by employing specific expressions which will resonate with their peers. PSTM4's attempt to evoke a representation of a *race to the bottom of firms* seems to be much more difficult (for details on this representation, see Appendix 1, Section A1.3.7). His statement is marked by disfluency and by a spectacular sequence of imprecisions ("'Well. Listen up! Something.' I don't know. 'We will do this, this and this."). Luckily, PSTM5 comes to his aid, having a concrete example of this process in mind. Both PSTM4 and PSTM5 are highly vocal and economically trained participants and thus they manage to get their point across. Nevertheless, the amount of direct speech and position-taking and the sheer length of the statement show how much rhetorical effort is needed to describe a race to the bottom in the absence of a suitable national vocabulary. These difficulties might explain why in response to the trigger topic 'workers' rights' race to the bottom representations were only used in one German and one Polish group, while they dominated in all of the French groups. The availability of specific national vocabulary made it easier for the French participants to mobilize these representations and thus increased their frequency and persuasiveness in the respective national context.

Where does such specific national vocabulary come from? How do words acquire specific meaning within national cultures? For *travailleur détaché*, *concurrence déloyale* or *delocalization*, and, in fact, for most examples of national vocabulary in the empirical material the answer is the same. Specific terms in the respective national languages often acquire their meaning in salient political debates. In periods of intense contestation of political issues, terms such as *travailleur détaché*, *concurrence déloyale* or *delocalization* become buzzwords, often comprising complex arguments in a single expression. National vocabulary thus performs a shortcut function. It squeezes a lot of discursive baggage into a few words. The above mentioned examples from France, for example, acquired salience during the 2005 referendum on the European constitutional treaty (Hutter & Kerscher, 2014, pp. 271–272; Lingenberg, 2010, p. 211; Schmidt, 2007, pp. 1005–1007; Skrodzka-Bates, 2011; Sternberg, 2018, pp. 157–158). They are specifically national not because they are unique to the French language, but because they carry specific meaning within France. Even though terms such as *travailleur détaché* are translatable, the expressions *'entsendeter Arbeiter'* or *'pracownik delegowany'* are largely unknown in Germany and Poland. The specificity of national vocabulary lies in its currency within the national population and in the specific memories of past political debates it evokes.

The examples of national vocabulary given above, in other words, are examples of anchoring in national culture. National culture can serve as an anchoring domain rendering complex European arguments intelligible, providing **memories of past politics sedimented into language**. To sum up, for the trigger topics 'mobility' and 'workers' rights', we see differences between the French participants and their counterparts, which result from anchoring in national culture.

Memories of past politics sedimented into the national language also function as an anchoring point in some of the Polish groups. To be more precise, Polish participants tend to anchor the trigger arguments 'expenditure' and 'entrepreneurship' in knowledge about a recent government spending program called *500+*. In both cases, anchoring in national culture produces inter-national differences in the understanding of the trigger arguments. To begin with, the trigger argument 'expenditure' was handed to participants in the unemployment discussions. It proposed to 'increase state expenditure to stimulate demand'. In the following quotes, we see the different reactions of French and Polish participants to this trigger argument.

FAUM1: "For me it was 'increase state expenditure'. I don't think that's a good strategy. How to explain that? It's complicated. But I think in terms of spending, France is there already. I think in terms of debt, France is already running a deficit."

– French agents discussing 'expenditure'

FSUW1: "'Increase state expenditure to stimulate demand'."

FSUM1: "Yes. I agree."

DA: "Could you explain a bit?"

FSUW1: "Well, I think the state has already passed the … How to say that? The maximum percentage. And in addition, there will be the debt of the SNCF. That will be another five or six billion of debt."

– French soccer players 'expenditure'

PSUM2: "In Poland for example something good we have in that direction is *500+* because that creates jobs. I would say it increases domestic demand because one knows that this money goes into consumption."

– Polish soccer players discussing 'expenditure'

PLUW4: "'Increase state expenditure'. If it was increased in such a way that there would be for example something like public work projects. Like we make, I don't know, for example we build new streets or something else and from then on things start spinning. If it was like that. And certainly not like: 'Just get yourself 500 złoty'."

PLUW3: "Yes!"

PLUW2: "This outgivery [*rozdawnictwo*] is blossoming. It just blossoms at the moment."

– Polish teachers discussing 'expenditure'

The quotes above show that French and Polish participants employed different anchoring domains for the trigger topic 'expenditure' and that they, consequently, form different representations of the causalities implied by the trigger argument. The French seem to mobilize a representation of the characteristics of their national economy, stressing in particular the pressure on the state to lower its deficits (frequently implying pressure to lower the high social standards, which cause the high levels of state spending). The trigger argument 'expenditure', consequently, is mainly chosen as a negative card in the French groups.

Contrasting sharply with this negative view of state spending are the representations mobilized by the Polish participants. In both quotes, quite explicit and surprisingly detailed representations of *Keynesianism* are mobilized (see also Appendix 1, Section A1.6.1). The use of vocabulary drawn from economic theory (e.g., "domestic demand") and machine metaphors (e.g., "things start spinning") reveal proximity to Keynesian economic thought. Where French participants see the threat of an increased state deficit, Polish participants form quite elaborate representations of multiplier effects. Representations of Keynesianism appeared occasionally in German and French groups (mainly among the economically trained), but they were surprisingly frequent among non-trained Polish participants. When made in the Polish groups, finally, the arguments also enjoyed a high degree of persuasiveness as the supportive reactions by PLUW3 and PLUW2 in the final quote show.

The fact that such sophisticated representations of economic theory are entertained by participants who never enjoyed formal economic training in their life is astonishing. How can the high frequency of Keynesian arguments in Poland be explained? Arguably, the key to understanding lies in the national vocabulary used for anchoring: *500+*. *500+* is a family support program introduced by the PiS government in 2016, granting 500 złoty to each household with more than two children. It was fiercely opposed by the opposition and remained a controversial issue regularly discussed in the public sphere

(Gdula et al., 2017, pp. 13–14), even up to the 2019 European and national elections. Keynesian arguments were frequently mobilized in defense of *500+*. In the focus group material, then, we see that Polish participants reproduce representations of Keynesianism with astonishing regularity when they talk about *500+*. The public discussions surrounding *500+*, apparently, popularized Keynesian arguments. Where the term *500+* is mobilized as an anchoring point, memories of the debate surrounding this policy come up as well. Moreover, we see that it doesn't even matter which side of the debate the participants were on. PSUM2 is a convinced PiS supporter while all teachers in PLU sympathize with left-wing or liberal opposition parties. The teachers, in fact, denounce *500+* as *rozdawnictwo*, a term which might be best translated as "targetless outgivery" and which was used repeatedly by the opposition to criticize the program (e.g., TVN24, 2016; TVP info, 2018). *500+* thus is a perfect example of anchoring in national culture. A contentious public debate spread specific representations of economic theory to the population, and memories of this debate are then mobilized as an anchoring domain for complex European issues. Mobilizing knowledge of past national politics helps to understand complex economic arguments, but it also creates inter-national differences.

The inter-national differences thus created are differences in the **frequency and persuasiveness** of arguments. Anchoring in *500+* does not generate representations which are exclusively used by Polish participants. The representation of *Keynesianism*, in fact, was employed in Germany and France as well, in particular by participants with economic training (see Chapter 5). The availability of national vocabulary, however, seems to facilitate the making of some arguments. Knowledge of *500+* made it easier for Polish participants to make Keynesian arguments and it ensured that these arguments were understood by their peers. While representations of *Keynesianism* resonate well with Polish participants (thus being surprisingly frequent among them), they do appear in other countries too (yet almost exclusively among the economically trained). Again, then, inter-national differences are differences in frequency and persuasiveness.

Anchoring in *500+* was also crucial for the understanding of the trigger topic 'entrepreneurship'. This trigger argument proposed to 'advance citizens' entrepreneurial spirit' in order to lower unemployment in the EU. This trigger topic was particularly salient in the German groups, and, to a lesser extent, in the Polish ones. In opposition to the idea of entrepreneurship, in both countries, representations of *the classical employee* were formed. Laziness and unwillingness to show initiative were identified as the indicators of such an employee mentality (see also Appendix 1, Section A1.4.2). The employee mentality can hence be used to explain why people do not find a job, thus creating a representation of *the unemployed as lazy*. In both the Polish and the German groups, this pejorative representation of the unemployed was formed through anchoring in national policies. German participants employed memories of the liberal reform programs in the early 2000 (*Ich-AG* and *Hartz-IV*), while

Polish participants frequently mobilized *500+* to depict citizens who rely on state aid. Again, memories of past politics served as an anchoring domain, and these memories found expression in the respective national languages (as the names of specific policies are remembered).

This anchoring in elements of national political culture produced differences in the representation of the trigger argument 'entrepreneurship'. While the representation of *the unemployed as lazy* seemed similar at first sight, when looking closer, it becomes apparent that these representations reflect very specific national cleavage structures and memories of past debates. In the German groups, Hartz-IV recipients are depicted as male and unwilling to work because they can make almost the same amount of money living off state aid. This representation clearly reflects the public debate in Germany since the early 2000s, which increasingly spread the idea of individual responsibility as the cause of economic success, and thus constructed an image of the unemployed as unwilling and lazy (Chassé, 2010, pp. 14–15; Nachtwey, 2016, p. 95; Vail, 2020, pp. 120–121). The German discussions, consequently, tend to center on the question if recipients of unemployment benefits should be sanctioned, that is, if benefits should be cut in case an unwillingness to work is diagnosed. Anchoring in Hartz-IV thus does not only produce a vision of the unemployed which reflects specific national cleavages, it also triggers questions and debates which used to be salient in the respective national public.

Anchoring in *500+* produces a slightly different vision of the *unemployed as lazy*. This vision seems to blend criticism of *500+* with a discourse of the homo sovieticus. In this view, communism is presented as a mentality which shapes a national character until today:

> PLUW2: "I think that the generation of my mom – above 80 – remembers the times when things were just given to them. [..] the government provided a lot of things: vacation, summer camps, trips, and flats, right? And today nobody gives anything to anybody anymore [PLUW1: Yeah]. You have to take a credit yourself and you have to earn money to repay it. And back in the days, things were just given to you. You were entitled to them – end of story. Therefore, the older generation, let's say … Today we have a government which starts working in a similar fashion. It just hands out things. Well, and some people like that."
>
> – Polish teachers discussing alternative representations

PAUW1: "I think today everybody who wants to work will find a job."

PAUM1: "Yeah but jobs are somewhere out there on the market, right? Have to find them first. Thus, the question is if …"

PAUW2: "There are also those who do not want to work … '

PAUW1: "Today, there is *500+*, so for some parents it doesn't pay off to work anymore [PAUW2: They don't work]. They say that unemployment among mothers rose. Because they rather sit at home with their children and get 500 złoty than to go to work. In those poorer areas ..."

PAUW2: "And frequently they have more than one child, right?"

– Polish agents discussing 'state expenditure'

PSTM4: "So I would say it also depends on someone's current material situation. Because if you simply receive a lot of welfare payments and generally you sit ... Well, three children, one of the parents works, the other sits at home. They will have a very different opinion about free trade because innovativeness doesn't really concern them."

– Polish soccer players discussing alternative representations

In the quotes, a vision of the homo sovieticus seems to blend with the cleavage structure of current Polish society, with urban liberals criticizing rural conservatives as dependent on state aid and lacking a feeling of individual responsibility. In the first quote, the mentality of socialist times is directly linked to the government's current welfare policies. And at least some of these complaints about a communist mentality seem to be picked up in the later quotes, which exclusively focus on *500+*. The typical *500+* recipient is depicted as a woman, a mother to many children often living in rural areas of Poland. It is hard to believe that these characteristics are randomly chosen by the participants; rather, they seem to reflect specific national cleavages. The *500+* mother seems to be a proxy for a typical PiS voter. The role as a housewife, the fact that the family has many children and its localization in the (often eastern) countryside seem to imply that the family is conservative, Catholic and hence most probably PiS voting. At the same time, the representations of the *500+* mother play on a notion of backwardness, a failure to integrate into the new capitalist age. By staying at home and relying on state support, the *500+* recipient is depicted as a homo sovieticus who has not listened to the wind of change (Zarycki, 2014, 2015). Again, in the nuances of the Polish representation of the unemployed, we find traces of past debates (in this case concerning the transformation to capitalism) and a mobilization of national cleavages. The representation of the *500+* mother bears resemblance to constructions such as the "welfare queen", a gendered representation of the unemployed observed in the United States (Gilman, 2013; Hancock, 2003). While the welfare queen is projected on racial divisions, representations of *500+* recipients seem to reflect specifically Polish religious, cultural and regional cleavages. While the German and Polish representations of the unemployed are not too different, then, it should be noted that anchoring in past politics reproduces national debates and cleavages. Names of specific policies (*500+*, *Hartz-IV*, *Ich-AG*) carry significant discursive baggage and thus might produce international differences in the representation of complex arguments although for the trigger topic 'entrepreneurship' these differences remained minor.

Finally, memories of past politics sedimented into national languages also serve as an anchoring point for the trigger topic 'sovereignty'. In the trade groups, participants were presented with several arguments concerning the state's capacity to regulate the economy after the conclusion of free trade deals. One of the propositions read 'it is bad to limit national sovereignty on economic matters'. In particular, Polish and German participants developed quite different representations of this trigger topic, with the former hailing it as a means to limit the influence of transnational firms while the latter associated it with memories of federalist inefficiency.

> PLTW3: "I thought about the last proposition. 'It is bad to limit national sovereignty on economic matters'. I think that the state should have more control of what happens. [PLTW1: Yes, yes!] In order to defend us."
>
> – Polish teachers discussing 'sovereignty'

> PATM2: "Here we have for example 'attract foreign firms/investment'. Theoretically this should be something really good. It would pump capital into the country. There would be more investment. People could get employed. Economic success. But it depends on your political or economic world view. Such a take-over of the market by foreign firms could not be good for a country if it loses its sovereignty or its own means for economic development."
>
> [...]
>
> PATM3: "So I think that last proposition is most convincing. As it was already said: it is not good for a state to be overly dependent on foreign capital. That the capital is invested here, but that it can be easily withdrawn from the country. To me that's the most important."
>
> – Polish agents discussing 'sovereignty' and 'investment'

> GATM1: "We will not solve the problems of the earth as single states. The aim has to be not only to create a Europe, but to create a world. But of course we already see with Europe how difficult this is. In the background that should be the main aim though. Because just in terms of climate – if we want to talk about it but of course it is a very urgent topic – we will not solve these problems if there is someone somewhere who says: 'I am not joining in'. [. . .] That's why I think the sovereignty of a single nation is rather [pause] lame. Look at Bavaria. That's also a separate nation and, small as they are, they think they can stop the whole world with their issues. And that's simply nonsense."
>
> – German agents discussing 'sovereignty'

> GSTM2: "Well, but you see what happens with too much *Kleinstaaterei*: nothing works anymore in the EU. You should rather unify things, so you can speak with one voice. And if everyone just minds their own business, this doesn't help anyone either, if you have a patchwork of

> different customs regulations. So you have to cede sovereignty somewhere because the world is increasingly globalized. And to increase customs and to say: 'Everyone on their own!' is simply the wrong approach."
>
> – German soccer players discussing 'sovereignty'

For the Polish participants, the term 'national sovereignty' seems to have positive connotations. In the quotes above, representations of *Poland as an economy in development* seem to be mobilized (see Chapter 3). PATM2 stresses the importance of sovereignty for economic development before the trigger topic 'sovereignty' was even introduced to the participants. PATM3 later echoes his positive assessment, thus showing that the sovereignty argument enjoys a high degree of persuasiveness. Similarly, PLTW3's rather vague demand that the state should be in control receives immediate support. In the Polish groups, then, national sovereignty was often viewed as a means to reduce the dependence on foreign capital in the process of economic development. The trigger argument was thus mainly seen as positive.

In the German groups, on the contrary, the trigger topic 'sovereignty' was viewed negatively. This negative assessment, arguably, resulted from anchoring in memories inefficient federalism. In the first quote, GATM1 cites Bavaria (one of the most powerful federal states in Germany) as an example of the harmful egoism of small states. In the second quote, GSTM2 mobilizes national vocabulary to express a similar concern. "*Kleinstaaterei*" (best translated as little-statism) is a term coined by German nationalists in the 19th century to decry the division of Germany into small sovereign territories (Wagner, 1974, p. 516). The term, however, remains current to this day in public debates about the division of competences between the federal and regional governments[2] and in German pro-EU discourses (Bücker, 2008, pp. 2220–2222). Again, we find that memories of past politics sedimented into national languages are used as anchoring point for European arguments. Due to the availability of specific national vocabulary, German participants generated representation of 'sovereignty' different from their Polish counterparts.

This difference in the representation of 'sovereignty' is, yet again, a difference in **frequency and persuasiveness**. The arguments advanced by German and Polish participants are known to the other side, but they are mobilized more rarely. German participants, for example, expressed concerns about firms from China investing in Germany at some point in the discussions. The representation of the EU as a response to global challenges, on the other hand, is sometimes also employed by Polish participants. Like for 'mobility', 'workers' rights' and 'expenditure', differences in national culture facilitated the mobilization of some representations with regard to 'sovereignty', too. This, however, did only affect the frequency and persuasiveness of the representations and did not create representation that are nationally unique. Anchoring in past politics impacted the frequency of specific arguments, rather than generating representations that are exclusive to the citizens of one country.

2.3.2 National Academic Cultures: German Ordo-liberalism

Memories of relatively recent national debates thus function as an important anchoring point for complex European arguments. A similar process can be observed for the trigger argument 'interest', although here the differences partly seem to result from different academic cultures in the field of economics. In particular, German ordo-liberalism seems to have quite an impact on public debates in Germany and thus popularized certain representations that are less frequent in other national contexts.

How did this form of national anchoring play out in the empirical material? In the unemployment groups, participants were asked how unemployment in the EU could be lowered and they were presented with a card reading 'ensure low interest rates to facilitate investment'. A quite specific form of national anchoring of this trigger topic could be observed in the German groups. In the two German groups, which discussed the topic, a representation of the *EU as an investor* was mobilized (see also Appendix 1, Section A1.5.7). The ECB is cited as the institution determining interest rates and Mario Draghi is named as its head.

GSUM4: "Well, that's not my favorite. I think interest rates are low enough. [...]

GSUM2: "Of course. I mean Mr. Draghi is living that at the moment."

GSUM4: "I don't think we have to tackle that at the moment. That's why I did not pick the card." [...]

GSUM2: "Well in the moment it's working well [GSUM4: Well ... (skeptical)]. As things stand Mr. Draghi is living the opposite. You permanently hear the interest screw should go up again at some point [GSUM4: Yes]. That is also linked to inflation. But uhm a little push is always good because – be it for a startup or something else – if you want to build something you need capital. If you don't have it, if you have courage, if you have the entrepreneurial spirit but you don't have cash ... [...] And then, of course, it makes sense to work with low interest rates."

– German soccer players discussing 'interest"

GAUM1: "Concerning low interest rates for example – well it is also about investment. But it is the ECB's task – if you consider a whole different level, not Berlin, not the federal level, but the EU-level – it is partly the task of the EU, of the ECB, that inflation remains constant. Or that it remains low. And that they control the development of interest rates. So, on the one hand, of course it is positive to control that and so on. On the other hand, of course it is difficult for investors who

> need to park their money, it is difficult for them to find something which promises decent return."
>
> – German agents discussing 'interest'

The quotes are striking as they reveal detailed knowledge about the ECB's mandate for price stability and because the representation of the *state as investor* is attributed to an EU institution. Despite this appreciation for facilitated investment, both quotes convey a rather reserved attitude toward the ECB's policy of low interest rates. In the first quote, GSUM2 expresses some unease with Mr. Draghi's policy, while GSUM4 is straightforwardly opposing it. In the second quote, "investors who need to park their money" become a normative reference point. Both quotes make somewhat vague references to inflation, implying a certain degree of unease with the policy at stake. Yet, what is striking about the quotes beyond this critical position is the detailed knowledge about the functioning of the ECB. Mr. Draghi is the only political figure from an EU institution ever to be named in the focus groups – a fact which underlines that such detailed knowledge of EU institutions is infrequent. Both quotes, moreover, testify to an awareness of the ECB's mandate to keep inflation constant. In other words, the German participants seem to command knowledge about the EU, which was largely absent among the participants from other countries. Their representations of the trigger argument 'interest' differed from those of Polish and French participants, as the trigger was anchored in the ECB's low interest rate policy.

This difference in the representation of the trigger topic 'interest' seems to be a consequence of past debates in the German public sphere, impacted in turn by a specific national academic culture. German public discourse surrounding the euro-crisis was heavily influenced by ordo-liberal thought (Bulmer, 2014; Crespy & Schmidt, 2014). Ordo-liberalism is a school of economic thought originating in Freiburg. While it has been a major influence on the Chicago school, it remains a separate body of thought (e.g., assigning a stronger role to the state), being salient mainly in German academia. It thus constitutes an example of a national academic culture – a body of thought mainly maintained within the academic institutions of a specific country. One of the main tenets of ordo-liberalism is price stability and thus constant inflation rates. Accordingly, ordo-liberal economists were very critical of the low interest rates established by the ECB in response to the euro-crisis. Due to its dominance in German academia, arguments stressing the negative impact of low interest rates acquired a high degree of salience in the German public sphere. Arguably, the German participants' awareness of ECB's policy mirrors the salience of ordo-liberal considerations in the German public. Specificities of national academic culture can be popularized via public debates and thus cause inter-national differences in the understanding of complex European arguments.

This inter-national difference in the representation of the trigger topic 'interest' is a difference in frequency and persuasiveness. The representation of the ECB as an investor was brought up in one non-German group, a group of French estate agents who had all enjoyed economic training. The argument thus was not entirely unknown to participants outside Germany, but it required a significant degree of expert knowledge to make it. Again, we see that anchoring in national culture facilitates the making of specific arguments. As was observed already for *500+* and Keynesianism, salient political debates can spread quite specific forms of expert knowledge to a wide audience.[3] The German participants thus could draw on knowledge of ordo-liberal arguments from the time of the euro-crisis and they could expect their peers to be aware of these arguments, too. The criticism of the ECB's interest rate policy, then, was more frequent and more persuasive in the German groups but it was not an exclusively German representation.

The spread of ordo-liberal arguments seems to support the claim that memories of recent politics are more important as an anchoring point than grand history. Ordo-liberal ideas do not seem to form a collective historical memory, but rather were activated in recent political debate about concrete policies. This becomes apparent when considering the reactions to the trigger argument 'inflation'. German inflation *angst*, often depicted as a result of 1923 hyperinflation, supposedly was responsible for the rejection of the ECB's interest rate policy by much of the German public. Yet, in opposition to earlier studies (e.g., Haffert et al., 2019; Schmidt, 2014, pp. 191–194), I do not find a specifically German fear of inflation. Even though there was a trigger argument specifically designed to test this expectation, no collective memories of hyperinflation were mobilized in the German groups. I take this as further evidence that it is not grand history that is most frequently mobilized as an anchoring point but rather recent political debates that happened in the respective national public sphere. In fact, almost all historical events or debates mobilized in the focus groups happened during the respective participants' lifetime. The only exception to this are young Polish participants who entertain quite explicit representations of socialist times. These collective memories of socialism are the last aspect of national culture to be discussed in this chapter.

2.3.3 Memories of Grand History: PRL and DDR

History is one of the most important domains of national knowledge production. The construction of national history was at the core of the national project. To this day, history as taught in most high schools remains largely national in focus. Inter-national differences in the perception of historical events are well documented (e.g., Gerhards et al., 2017; Toth, 2019, p. 1032). Yet, to what extent are these collective memories of grand history mobilized as an anchoring domain?

Arguably, in the empirical material, grand history plays a minor role as an anchoring point. The only notable exception to this are memories of socialist dictatorship and the resulting representations of the ideology of *socialism* (see

Appendix 1, Section A1.6.4). Socialist rule is the only historical period recalled by participants who did not live at the time. At the same time, the representation of socialism served as an anchoring point. In particular, the trigger argument 'right to work' was very frequently anchored in collective memories of the socialist system. This trigger topic appeared in the unemployment groups. The card suggested to "establish a right to work for all citizens" in order to fight unemployment in the EU.

GSUM2: "'A right to work for all citizens'. Well, if that's supposed to work like in the *DDR*, that's going to be difficult. It's not just rumors, but what you heard everywhere: three people doing the work of one – unemployment rate zero. But efficiency also zero."

– German soccer players discussing 'right to work'

GLUM2: "Just like in the *DDR*, right? You didn't only have a right but also ... [...] So if I am, I don't know what, a cook or a train conductor. So I would also have the right to work as a cook or as a train conductor. And it can be implemented because some agency will say: 'Alright, just go into this firm. Ey you guys, now you have an additional cook!' End of story."

GLUM3: "Exactly. And then you get to throw away everything you cooked."

– German teachers discussing 'right to work'

DA: "Ok. And you also chose 'establish a right to work' as a negative card ..."

PAUW1: "I have that as well."

PAUM1: "Well, that smells a bit of that saying we have in Poland. 'If you sleep, if you stand – 2000 złoty in your hand'. Did I get that right, PAUW2? Like it was back in the days. [PAUW2: [laughing] Yes, that's how it was. I remember.] Everyone was forcefully squeezed into some job. I don't say it was bad to have jobs for these people. But it is such an artificial creation of jobs which are neither effective nor do they generate any profit. It really doesn't make sense."

– Polish agents discussing 'right to work'

PLUW2: "'Establish a right to work for all citizens' – we had that already. [PLUW3: Yes; PLUW4: Yes, yes, yes!] We went through that in Poland. Was it even a right? It was a duty! An assignment. It was like that in Poland. [PLUW4: Yes.] You got a little card and went to *Pcimie dolne*[4] in the middle of nowhere and you had to work there. It was like that."

PLUW4: "To cite a classic: 'Who doesn't work, doesn't eat.'"

PLUW2: "Right. And I think it should not be like that. That's why I think it's negative."

– Polish teachers discussing 'right to work'

The quotes above show how memories of socialist dictatorship are mobilized to create a negative representation of the trigger topic 'right to work'. Socialism is remembered as a ridiculously inefficient system. The examples of a cook throwing away his food or of getting paid for sleeping serve to depict the proposed 'right to work' as a ridiculous and unrealistic idea. The rejection of the proposal is even stronger in the final quote in which older Polish participants remember the obligation to work as a form of oppression. In the quotes, moreover, national vocabulary (often the names of the respective regimes, *DDR* in Germany and *PRL* in Poland) or popular sayings (PLUW4's Lenin quote and PAUM1's proverb) seem to carry the historical memories. In all cases, references to socialism make it immediately clear that the trigger argument is pointless and even potentially dangerous. Anchoring in memories of socialist dictatorship thus produced strongly negative assessments among the German and Polish participants. As such memories were absent in the French groups, their representations of the trigger argument 'right to work' are more ambivalent and sometimes even positive.

> FSUW1: "So: 'Establish a right to work for all'. I assume that we have all had the chance to work, to be able to use your hands. And so there would be a lot more resources ... Well, the state could profit and so we could ... Well, how to say this? [...] If I, for example, or someone who is unemployed since a week, a year maybe, if he woke up one morning and said: 'I really want to work instead of resting on my achievements.' The state should give him work so he could contribute."
>
> FSUM1: "But that is a question of personal motivation!"
>
> – French soccer players discussing 'right to work'

> FLUW2: "Well ok, we agree it's a bit problematic. The state cannot hire everyone. The state cannot do everything, it cannot create this number of jobs. [...] But there are still some needs. I don't know. If you look at the motorways, if you look at the public trash cans everywhere. I would like it if there were people to take care of that!"
>
> FLUW1: "But it is too expensive!"
>
> – French teachers discussing 'right to work'

For the French groups, the trigger topic 'right to work' caused controversial discussions, with some participants opposing the idea and others defending it. Both quotes are extracts from such contentious discussions. In both cases, a participant is initially making a statement in favor of a 'right to work' before being opposed by a peer. While thus not being uniform in their reactions, at least for some French participants, the trigger argument 'right to work' had positive connotations. The absence of memories of socialist dictatorship thus causes more positive evaluations of arguments frequently associated with socialist ideology. This in line with the findings of previous studies

(Marková et al., 1998; for a positive assessment of socialism in France see Duchesne, 2013, pp. 76–80; Duchesne & Ingelgom, 2008). For economic issues, then, memories of socialism can serve as an anchoring domain. The availability or absence of such memories creates inter-national differences in the understanding of some complex arguments.

Again, the inter-national difference observed for the trigger argument 'right to work' is a difference in the **frequency and persuasiveness** of representations. In the German and Polish groups, it seemed very easy to discredit the trigger topic right to work. A negative representation of socialism seems to be quite strong and rather far spread. A reference to the past socialist state (*DDR* or *PRL*) or a commonly known proverb sufficed to create consensus in the German and Polish discussion groups. In the quotes above, we can see that the speakers often get support in their anti-socialist statements, frequently even by multiple participants. The arguments, thus, could easily be made by a wide range of participants and, moreover, were greeted with support when they were advanced (i.e., they were persuasive). Contrary to this, French participants did not have negative memories of socialism at their disposal. It was thus more difficult for them to convince their peers that a 'right to work' was negative. Negative associations with the trigger topic thus were less frequent in France. Ultimately, the reaction in all Polish and two out of three German groups were exclusively negative while all French groups remained ambivalent. Associations of inefficiency appeared in France as well, but in absence of historical references they remained less frequent and not very persuasive.

2.4 Conclusion

This chapter has explored a mechanism allowing citizens to make sense of complex economic arguments: **national anchoring**. When citizens are confronted with complex economic arguments in the public sphere, they can mobilize elements of national culture to render these issues intelligible. Among all the potential bodies of knowledge national cultures provide, one stood out as a particularly frequent anchoring point: knowledge of past politics. In the focus groups, participants frequently mobilize memories of past political debates or of salient policies implemented by their national governments. This form of anchoring was visible for the trigger 'mobility', 'workers' rights' 'expenditure' and 'sovereignty', and more indirectly also 'interest' and 'right to work'.

National anchoring has a strong linguistic dimension. Recent political struggles often have left traces in the respective national languages. Contested policies or laws are given specific names; public debates load some expressions in the national language with specific meaning or they popularize scientific terminology which remains widely unknown in other nations. National vocabulary such as *Fachkräftemangel, travailleur détaché, délocalisation, Kleinstaaterei* or *rozdawnictwo* was shown to transport specifically national meaning structures. **Memories of past politics, sedimented in national languages**, are the most frequent form of national anchoring.

National anchoring produces differences in the **frequency and persuasiveness** of representations. This mechanism is particularly well observable where the elements of national culture find expression in national vocabulary. The availability of specific national terms seems to facilitate the description of some causalities. Instead of describing complex argumentative chains, participants simply mention the salient national term and can be sure to be understood by their fellow nationals. Within the given national context, then, the argument is more frequent (as more people dare making it) and it is more persuasive (more participants agree with it). Throughout the chapter, we saw that quite complex economic arguments are made by less eloquent participants that command the fitting national vocabulary while very outspoken participants in other countries fail to bring the same point across. While the latter frequently struggle with disfluency and lack of resonance, the former frequently get support for just dropping a single, nationally loaded expression. The ease of making a specific argument translates into inter-national differences in the frequency and persuasiveness of representations.

The finding that memories of past politics are one of the most prominent anchoring point in the material is surprising. Much on the literature investigating the impact of national meaning structures on citizens' perceptions of complex issues is dedicated to the influence of grand discourses about history and identity (Haegel, 2013; Müller, 2005; Pickel, 2005; Thévenot et al., 2000). The finding that memories of socialism play a role in the understanding of economics, for example, has been well documented (Marková et al., 1998). While I do find evidence underlining the influence of these factors, they are used much less frequently for anchoring than memories of past politics. Moreover, memories of grand history often appear simply because they were standard in the context of recent policy debates (e.g., accusations of *500+* being a return to socialism was a staple of opposition rhetoric in Poland). The kind of memories that seem to influence national perceptions of complex issues thus seem to be relatively banal. Not grand historical struggles, golden ages or economic miracles dominate the citizens' perceptions. Rather, it is relatively small nation-contained policy debates which create significant path dependencies for the understanding of future questions. In this sense, the concept of national anchoring is a contribution to the growing body of literature focusing on **banal nationalism** (Billig, 1995; Duchesne, 2018; Fox & Miller-Idriss, 2008). National idiosyncrasies seem to come into existence when citizens are exposed to the day-to-day banalities of national politics. It is not the grand waves of history but the daily tickle of news, scandals and party politics that end up shaping the popular imagination.

We will see a similar argument about the impact of past politicization playing out in the next chapter. Discourses about the strength and weaknesses of the national economy seem to be popularized through national politicization and national vocabulary as much as the elements of national culture are.

Notes

1 Only four participants reported to have lived abroad: PSTM1 (Argentina), GAUM2 (France), GLUW1 (France) and FLUW2 (Spain).
2 The corona crisis provided ample evidence of this usage (for references to both Kleinstaaterei and a "patchwork of regulations" see, for example, Werner, 2020)
3 The spread of expert knowledge through salient national debates foreshadows a claim I will defend in the chapter. We cannot assume expert knowledge to be present in the citizenry – rather, we have to prove the existence of a functioning transmission mechanism to show how it got there. Let's consider the example of inflation. In a study assessing public opinion on economic integration, Brinegar et al. (2004, p. 65) make the following assumption about citizens' knowledge: "our second specific premise is that citizens know that European integration institutes an independent central bank regime capable of punishing inflationary wage policies". In light of my empirical findings, I argue that such an assumption is a massive overgeneralization. There might be some citizens who hold the relevant knowledge, but these would either be those with economic training or those confronted with public debates on ECB policies. For the rest of the population, it seems vastly exaggerated to assume an awareness of the ECB's mandate for price stability.
4 Pcimie dolne seems to be a stereotypical name of some far-away fictive village. At least I have not found a village of this name on any map.

Bibliography

Billig, M. (1995). *Banal Nationalism*. SAGE.

Brinegar, A. P., Jolly, S. K., & Kitschelt, H. (2004). Varieties of Capitalism and Political Divides Over European Integration. In G. Marks & M. R. Steenbergen (Eds.), *European Integration and Political Conflict* (1st ed., pp. 62–90). Cambridge University Press. https://doi.org/10.1017/CBO9780511492013.006

Bücker, N. (2008). EU heißt-was? Historische und aktuelle'frames' in polnischen und deutschen Europa-Diskursen. In K.-S. Rehberg (Ed.), *Kongress" Die Natur der Gesellschaft"* (pp. 2215–2227). Campus Verlag.

Bulmer, S. (2014). Germany and the Eurozone Crisis: Between Hegemony and Domestic Politics. *West European Politics*, *37*(6), 1244–1263. https://doi.org/10.1080/01402382.2014.929333

Chassé, K. A. (2010). *Unterschichten in Deutschland: Materialien zu einer kritischen Debatte*. VS Verlag für Sozialwissenschaften. https://doi.org/10.1007/978-3-531-92140-2_2

Crespy, A., & Schmidt, V. (2014). The Clash of Titans: France, Germany and the Discursive Double Game of EMU Reform. *Journal of European Public Policy*, *21*(8), 1085–1101. https://doi.org/10.1080/13501763.2014.914629

Duchesne, S. (2013). Social Gap: The Double Meaning of 'Overlooking.' In S. Duchesne, E. Frazer, F. Haegel, & V. Van Ingelgom (Eds.), *Citizens' Reactions to European Integration Compared: Overlooking Europe* (pp. 65–95). Palgrave Macmillan UK. https://doi.org/10.1057/9781137297266_4

Duchesne, S. (2018). Who's Afraid of Banal Nationalism? *Nations and Nationalism*, *24*(4), 841–856. https://doi.org/10.1111/nana.12457

Duchesne, S., & Ingelgom, V. V. (2008). Comment les discussions deviennent politiques lorsque les francais, anglais et belges parlent d'Europe. *Politique europeenne, n° 24*(1), 145–149.

Fox, J. E., & Miller-Idriss, C. (2008). Everyday Nationhood. *Ethnicities*, *8*(4), 536–563. https://doi.org/10.1177/1468796808088925

Gdula, M., Dębskiej, K., & Trebki, K. (2017). *Dobra Zmiana w Miastku. Neoautrytaryzm w Polskiej Politycy z Perspektywy Małego Miasta*. Krytyka Polityczna. http://krytykapolityczna.pl/file/sites/4/2017/10/Dobra-zmiana-w-Miastku.pdf

Gerhards, J., Breuer, L. & Delius, A. (2017). *Kollektive Erinnerungen der europäischen Bürger im Kontext von Transnationalisierungsprozessen: Deutschland, Großbritannien, Polen und Spanien im Vergleich*. VS Verlag für Sozialwissenschaften. https://doi.org/10.1007/978-3-658-13402-0

Gilman, M. E. (2013). The Return of the Welfare Queen. *American University Journal of Gender, Social Policy & the Law*, *22*, 247.

Haegel, F. (2013). National Frames: Reactions to a Multi-Level World. In S. Duchesne, E. Frazer, F. Haegel, & V. Van Ingelgom (Eds.), *Citizens' Reactions to European Integration Compared: Overlooking Europe* (pp. 34–64). Palgrave Macmillan UK. https://doi.org/10.1057/9781137297266_3

Haffert, L., Redeker, N. & Rommel, T. (2019). Hyperinflation, the Great Depression, and German Collective Economic Memory. Unpublished Working Paper, 37.

Hancock, A.-M. (2003). Contemporary Welfare Reform and the Public Identity of the 'Welfare Queen.' *Race, Gender & Class*, *10*(1), 31–59. JSTOR.

Hutter, S. & Kerscher, A. (2014). Politicizing Europe in Hard Times: Conflicts over Europe in France in a Long-term Perspective, 1974–2012. *Journal of European Integration*, *36*(3), 267–282. https://doi.org/10.1080/07036337.2014 885752

Lingenberg, S. (2010). Fallstudien zur europäischen Verfassungsdebatte. In S. Lingenberg (Ed.), *Europäische Publikumsöffentlichkeiten: Ein pragmatischer Ansatz* (pp. 183–226). VS Verlag für Sozialwissenschaften. https://doi.org/10.1007/978-3-531-92120-4_5

Marková, I., Moodie, E., Farr, R. M., Drozda-Senkowska, E., Erös, F., Plichtová, J., Gervais, M.-C., Hoffmannová, J. & Mullerová, O. (1998). Social Representations of the Individual: A Post-Communist Perspective. *European Journal of Social Psychology*, *28*(5), 797–829. https://doi.org/10.1002/(SICI)1099-0992(199809/10)28:5<797::AID-EJSP896>3.0.CO;2-6

Müller, K. (2005). Nationalist Undercurrents in German Economic Liberalism. In E. Helleiner & A. Pickel (Eds.), *Economic Nationalism in a Globalizing World* (pp. 141–164). Cornell University Press.

Nachtwey, O. (2016). *Die Abstiegsgesellschaft: Über das Aufbegehren in der regressiven Moderne*. Suhrkamp Verlag.

Pickel, A. (2005). Introduction: False Oppositions. Reconceptualizing Economic Nationalism in a Globalizing World. In E. Helleiner & A. Pickel (Eds.), *Economic Nationalism in a Globalizing World* (pp. 1–18). Cornell University Press.

Schmidt, V. A. (2007). Trapped by Their Ideas: French Élites' Discourses of European Integration and Globalization. *Journal of European Public Policy*, *14*(7), 992–1009. https://doi.org/10.1080/13501760701576494

Schmidt, V. A. (2014). Speaking to the Markets or to the People? A Discursive Institutionalist Analysis of the EU's Sovereign Debt Crisis. *The British Journal of Politics and International Relations*, *16*(1), 188–209. https://doi.org/10.1111/1467-856X.12023

Skrodzka-Bates, A. (2011). Clandestine Human and Cinematic Passages in the United Europe: The Polish Plumber and Kieślowski's Hairdresser. *Studies in Eastern European Cinema*, *2*(1), 75–90. https://doi.org/10.1386/seec.2.1.75_1

Sternberg, C. (2018). What Were the French Telling Us by Voting Down the 'EU Constitution'? A Case for Interpretive Research on Referendum Debates. *Comparative European Politics*, *16*(2), 145–170. https://doi.org/10.1057/cep.2015.21

Thévenot, L., Moody, M. & Lafaye, C. (2000). Forms of Valuing Nature: Arguments and Modes of Justification in French and American Environmental Disputes. In M. Lamont & L. Thévenot (Eds.), *Rethinking Comparative Cultural Sociology: Repertoires of Evaluation in France and the United States* (pp. 229–273). Cambridge University Press. https://doi.org/10.1017/CBO9780511628108.009

Toth, M. (2019). Challenging the Notion of the East–West Memory Divide. *JCMS: Journal of Common Market Studies*, *57*(5), 1031–1050. https://doi.org/10.1111/jcms.12870

TVN24. (2016, July 2). *Spór o 500 zł na dziecko. "Oszustwo i rozdawnictwo" vs. "PO miała osiem lat i nie zrobiła nic."* TVN24 Biznes. https://tvn24.pl/biznes/pieniadze/program-500-plus-w-ogniu-krytyki-ra617290-4465734

TVP info. (2018, October 7). *Opozycja: Program 500+ to rozdawnictwo, zniechęca kobiety do pracy*. www.tvp.info/38022192/opozycja-program-500-to-rozdawnictwo-zniecheca-kobiety-do-pracy

Vail, M. I. (2020). National Liberalisms in a Neoliberal Age: Ideas and Economic Adjustment in Contemporary France and Germany. *Comparative European Politics*, *18*(2), 109–127. https://doi.org/10.1057/s41295-019-00155-8

Wagner, K. (1974). Das 19. Jahrhundert. In F. Maurer, F. Stroh, & H. Rupp (Eds.), *Deutsche Wortgeschichte* (pp. 493–524). De Gruyter.

Werner, J. (2020, April 15). Reaktionen auf Berliner Beschlüsse: „Nicht die Zeit für Kleinstaaterei und einen Corona-Flickenteppich". *DIE WELT*. www.welt.de/regionales/hamburg/article207290223/Reaktionen-auf-Berliner-Beschluesse-Nicht-die-Zeit-fuer-Kleinstaaterei-und-einen-Corona-Flickenteppich.html

Zarycki, T. (2014). Innowacjonizm jako legitymizacja. Dyskursy innowacji, gospodarki opartej na wiedzy, społeczeństwa informacyjnego i pokrewne w perspektywie krytycznej. *Zarządzanie Publiczne*, *27*, 5–19. https://doi.org/10.7366/1898352912702

Zarycki, T. (2015). Modernizacja kulturowa i psychologiczna jako ideologia inteligenckiej hegemonii. *Przegląd Socjologiczny*, *64*(2), 45–68.

3 Neoliberalism and the Worth of Nations

3.1 Introduction

When citizens discuss economics, things often get emotional. Far from being a cold-blooded discussion of monetary costs and benefits, economic arguments trigger feelings of pride and inferiority, optimism and depression. One of the most common ways these feelings are expressed is through an identification with the fate of the national economy. Citizens exhibit quite detailed amounts of knowledge about the strengths and weaknesses of their national economy and they cheer for its success as much as they seem to regret its failures. The performance of the national economy turns citizens into 'nobodies' or 'world champions', it might give them the feeling of 'being all the way up front' or 'falling behind'. And while the strengths and weaknesses of each national economy differ, the criteria for economic success are surprisingly similar across borders. No matter where, national economies are either ranked based on their innovativeness or based on their success of regulating the economy. Citizens seem to have in their heads an economic world map, a vision of the global economy as a hierarchy of states based on different matrixes of assessment. The global economic arena thus determines not only the wealth but also the **worth of nations** (Greenfeld, 1995).

This chapter shows how citizens mobilize knowledge of the worth of nations to render complex economic issues intelligible. Knowledge about the characteristics of the national economy and about its performance vis-à-vis other nations can serve as an anchor helping to understand a range of complex economic questions. Assessing the worth of nations thus is the **second form of national anchoring** frequently found in the empirical material. The chapter will also address the question of how this knowledge is made available to citizens. On the one hand, past politicization – again – plays an important role popularizing certain conceptions of the national economy. Just as discussed in the previous chapter, the worth of nations is often assessed using specific national vocabulary coined in salient past debates (e.g., *Exportweltmeister*, *Fachkräftemangel*). On the other hand, the cross-national similarity of the criteria on which the rankings are based points to the influence of transnationally available discourses. More specifically, one of the evaluative matrixes

DOI: 10.4324/9781003335610-5

seems to be based on neoliberal discourses, with innovative progress as the central criterion. An alternative hierarchy seems to draw on social-ecological discourses. Given this co-existence of national specificities within larger transnational discourses, it seems that knowledge of the worth of nations is spread when transnational economic discourses are applied to national realities and then incorporated into salient national debates. The worth of nation is an anchoring domain disseminated through the **politicization of transnational discourses in the national arena.**

The chapter proceeds as the previous one. In Section 3.2, the **social group** with access to knowledge of the worth of nations needs to be established. This section shows that the worth of nations is a transnationally coherent body of knowledge. Access to these transnational discourses is provided mainly through politicization in the national public sphere. In Section 3.3, I show that access to knowledge of the worth of nations causes **differences in the representation of trigger topics**. Again, arguments differ in their frequency and persuasiveness depending on how well they can be anchored in the features of the respective national economy. I conclude with a discussion of the external validity of the findings, in particular with regard to the generalizability of the concept of national anchoring.

3.2 Identification of Social Group: How to Know the Features of the National Economy?

The hypothesis I test in this chapter is the worth of nations hypothesis. This hypothesis is partly derived from the literature on methodological nationalism, and it postulates that the nation has become a naturalized object of analysis in most social sciences, including economics. Accordingly, economics produces knowledge about the national economic system; it constitutes the **national economy as a knowable object** (Foucault, 2006 [1978], pp. 400–402; 449–513; Foucault, 2006 [1979], pp. 13–40; Mitchell, 1998). It is thus possible to describe the characteristics of the national economy to know its strengths and weaknesses. Knowledge production about national economies, moreover, has increasingly acquired an international dimension. Viewing the nation as the natural unit of analysis has produced a tendency to depict the international arena as a competition of states. A multitude of organizations benchmark and rank nations according to economic criteria (e.g., competitiveness, innovativeness, GDP, exports, etc.). What emerges is a symbolic hierarchy of nations based on their economic worth (e.g., Fougner, 2008; Greenfeld, 1995, p. 555; J. White, 2019, pp. 69–73). The worth of nations hypothesis relies on the public sphere and – to a lesser extent – education as the transition mechanism, as indicators such as innovativeness or competitiveness can hardly be experienced on an individual level.

As argued in the theory chapter, the first step in investigating how complex issues are anchored is to establish which social groups have access to which bodies of knowledge. We need to know which people have access to an anchoring domain before we can argue that anchoring in this domain produced differences in understanding. In the previous chapter, I have already shown which participants in my focus group have access to specifically national sources of knowledge, either through experience, education or exposure to the public sphere. With the worth of nation relying mainly on the public sphere for transmission, this operationalization remains valid. Participants who have visited school and continuously lived in a country are considered to have access to the relevant national forms of knowledge, including to specific knowledge about the features of the national economy.

With the way participants can access knowledge of the worth of nations being thus already established, this section focuses on a different matter. Rather than on the transmission of knowledge, it focuses on the knowledge itself, trying to establish that the worth of nations is indeed a coherent discourse that needs to be treated as a separate anchoring domain. The point of this section is to show that descriptions of national economic strengths and weaknesses are not idiosyncratic but rely on transnationally shared logics of assessment.

3.2.1 The Economic World Map: National Characteristics, Transnational Criteria

Participants' knowledge of the characteristics of their national economy does not exist in a vacuum. Rather, it is embedded in a set of normative representations that depict the global economic arena as a hierarchy of states. This bundle of representations based on which the worth of nations is assessed is what I call the economic world map. On this map, each world region is assigned specific economic characteristics. States and regions are assessed based on two logics of evaluation: one based on a vision of progress as innovation and one based on a social-ecological vision of progress. Based on these visions of progress, different hierarchies of economic sectors are formed, which in turn allow for the ranking of countries with regard to the value of their exports or the quality of their regulation (see Table 3.1).

Progress is one of the most important normative reference points in the empirical material. A frequent observation participants make is that they live in an ever-changing world. This diagnosis of permanent change is mostly expressed by metaphors of movement, of direction. Countries, firms, individuals or even humanity as such can be described as advancing, as moving forward or backward. While this diagnosis is widely shared, it quickly becomes apparent that the judgment of the perceived changes differs fundamentally. Are the new products we see truly useful? Does digitalization truly help individuals? Participants provide different answers to the question whether the world is moving in the right direction. The first vision of progress that can be discerned in the material depicts *progress as innovation* (see Appendix 1, Section A1.1.1). In this representation, the changes produced by the current economic order are embraced and celebrated. The dynamism of the modern

Table 3.1 Ranking of sectors and regions based on different representations of progress

	Innovation-centered vision of progress	Social vision of progress
Criterion for sector ordering	• Advancement in **economic development**	• Centrality to **human flourishing**/basic needs
Typical sector ordering	• Digital > industrial > agricultural	• Agriculture > housing > consumer goods
Criterion to judge nations	• **Strength of exports** in most valued sector	• **Quality of regulation** in most valued sector
Typical ranking of regions	• United States > China/ Western Europe > Southern Europe	• Northern Europe > Southern Europe > United States/China
Typical objects	• Silicon Valley vs Greek olive oil	• Local ecological apple vs cheap Chinese toy

economy and the pressure it puts on individuals, countries and firms are interpreted as advancement. Innovative pressures thus should be supported and further enhanced. Creative destruction (in particular through digitalization) is viewed as ultimately beneficial.

> FATW1: "We are in a world which changes, which moves, and we have to stimulate that innovation."
>
> – French agents discussing 'innovation'

> GSUM4: "[reading out trigger topic]: "Ensuring that wages reflect merit" [...] If people do not perform well, they should not be paid well. If people perform, they should be paid well. There has to be a certain performance pressure. Otherwise, we are not advancing."
>
> – German soccer players discussing 'merit'

> GSTM3: "Welcome to the world of video-streaming. It's the same. For us it is super comfortable. For the old video-shops it's the end."
>
> – German soccer players discussing 'investment'

The social representation of progress as innovation thus embraces the omnipresent economic changes of a globalizing world. Pressure on individuals, firms and countries is viewed as positive as it helps to overcome old products and services with newer, superior ones. These quotes (like most quotes referring to any vision of progress) contain metaphors of movement and direction ("a world which changes, which moves", "Otherwise, we are not advancing"). They essentially express an embracement of the dynamism of the modern economy. The usage of the pronoun we (all quotes) and the work-place analogy in quote two show that innovativeness can be a principle of assessment for individuals, nations or even humanity. The principle of innovativeness is also applied to firms in quote three with new products being positively judged as useful innovation raising the standard of living ("for us it is super comfortable"). The enthusiasm for creative destruction is repeatedly voiced with regard to digitalization, as the upheaval the arrival of digital firms is causing is viewed as ultimately beneficial. Performance and adaptation pressure for individuals, countries and firms thus is embraced in the name of collective progress.

An orthogonally opposed perspective is articulated in the representation of *social progress* (see Appendix 1, Section A1.1.2). This latter vision shares the diagnosis of permanent change articulated in *progress as innovation* but judges it negatively. Permanent economic change and performance pressure are depicted as harmful; progress is viewed as currently going into the wrong direction. This representation of progress again affects multiple levels, pointing to the negative effects of performance pressure on individuals, denouncing the inutility of many products celebrated as innovative, and sketching more socially beneficial steps of development.

PAUW2: "The world moves forward, but our wages don't."
– Polish agents discussing 'merit'

FLUN1: "[reads out the trigger topics] 'Ensure that wages reflect merit'... That is to say meritocracy and I think that we already live in a pretty stressful society where people get depressions every two seconds. [...] The people get depressed because there is this disgusting pressure being put on everything we have to do."
– French teachers discussing 'merit'

GLTM1: "Well, innovation is a rather positive term, right? But it can also be seen negatively. Innovation and tradition are often viewed as an opposition and tradition can also be something beautiful. [GLTW3: Yeah, I miss our chalkboards; GLTW2 loughs; GLTW1: Definitely!] Yes! The question is if our innovative whiteboards are better [GLTW3: Exactly; GLTW1: hm (approving)]."
– German teachers discussing 'innovation'

The quotes share a diagnosis of a fast-moving world but see predominantly negative consequences arising from the permanent pressure to perform and adapt. While the first citation decries that the permanent stress of adaptation is not properly compensated, the second sees the acceleration of change mirrored by an accelerating rate of depressions. In particular, the latter quote is the precise opposite of GSUM4's statement on performance pressure before – a fact which is all the more evident as both start off with the same trigger topic. The almost orthogonal opposition of social progress to the innovative vision is also very evident when digitalization is at stake (quote three). Participants mobilizing the social vision often question the benefit of innovation and refuse to celebrate products because they are new. Progress as it happens presently in society thus does not produce desirable results. This implies that progress should rather take other more socially beneficial routes, which often means that economic efforts should be focused on sectors truly central to human flourishing.

Based on these competing visions of progress, the importance of economic sectors can be assessed. A sector's worth is dependent on its contribution to the respective form of progress. The *innovation-based sector ordering* (see also Appendix 1, Section A1.1.3) hierarchizes economic sectors based on a vision of economic development. The first step in this development is agricultural production, followed by industrialization and cumulating in the emergence of a digital economy. Accordingly, agricultural products are valued less than industrial products, and industrial production is viewed as less advanced than the digital economy.

> GAUM2: "A country which already implemented this well is Ireland. Ireland, to the disadvantage of other European countries of course, has extremely low taxes for companies. That's why Google is there, Facebook, all settled there. Because what does Ireland have to offer? Apart from sheep and agriculture there wasn't much. Fisheries maybe. But they do not have heavy industry. That's why they got themselves a new sector. By adapting to the digital firms."
>
> – German agents discussing 'non-wage labor costs'

> GATW1: "We are lacking a lot of things here. Seriously, I think if you go to America or to London, there are really … Concerning innovative ideas they are always a step ahead of us! I am not travelling there all the time, but sometimes I like to go to London or New York. And once I am there, I always think: Crazy, we are backward somehow. […] Uber, for example! Nobody, or very few people, are taking taxis these days in other countries. There is only Uber. Airbnb is prohibited here and so on. […] I think all of that … it's pretty great. Everybody can make money with that. And the hotels survive anyway because they have a different target group. Maybe not as many as before, but ok, then we have a couple of hotels less."
>
> – German agents discussing 'investment'

The first quote is supposed to contain a success story. Hosting digital firms is clearly viewed as a good sign for the Irish economy, indicating that Ireland has reached the final step of development. Moreover, the usage of the word 'already' in the first sentence shows that this sequence of sectors is assumed to be the natural course of development to be imitated by others. The second quote connects the innovation-based sector ordering back to the vision of progress as innovation. Germany's industry-based economy is described as "backward somehow" and creative destruction brought on by the digital sector is embraced. Both quotes also testify to the fact that the innovation-based sector ordering is heavily used in the judgment of countries. In particular, agricultural products are frequently judged as inferior to others and employed as metaphors of low worth (e.g., a French soccer player complaining that France would only export "garlic" to Canada).[1] The hierarchization of digital products and firms over industry and far over agriculture thus is a prominent tool to judge a country's exports and its general advancement.

Opposed to this vision is the *social ordering of sectors* (see also Appendix 1, Section A1.1.4). This representation hierarchizes sectors based on their centrality to human flourishing. It is mainly employed when the desired degree of state intervention in specific sectors is discussed. In this hierarchy, agriculture is on top followed by other sectors necessary for subsistence (housing, electricity, transport, education). All these sectors – while not having to be state-run – should at least be tightly regulated. On the bottom of the hierarchy are "brainless" consumer products, which are viewed as inessential to human development and can be left to market forces.

> GSUM1: "Well so all these costs, rent, electricity and so on. If the state would regulate that and if it would say: 'The rents are staying constant, constant for a relatively long time.' Of course, that's against entrepreneurship [GSUM4: Hmhm (approving)], but you do not need entrepreneurship in every area."
>
> – German soccer players discussing 'merit'

> GSTM1: "I would like to know how much tax Amazon is paying in Germany. […] If I can register in Luxemburg in order to avoid paying taxes … [GSTM2 loughs]. That's my favorite example. […] Attracting foreign firms is not a bad thing in itself, but I'd already be happy if all firms would pay taxes. […] If that would work, that would be a true step forward."
>
> – German soccer players discussing 'SMEs' & 'investment'

In the social hierarchy, sectors are ordered by their centrality to human flourishing, and accordingly, demands for state regulation are advanced. In the first quote, this is done for electricity and housing, two sectors often qualified as basic needs. The second quote shows that this sector ordering is linked to the social vision of progress. Digital advancement is viewed skeptically because it undermines the state's capacity to generate revenue and regulate economic sectors. True social progress ("a true step forward") are not new digital services, but taxes being paid to the state to allow for the safeguarding of basic human needs. The social sector ordering thus is intimately linked to the social vision of progress. A similar ranking of sectors has been observed by other qualitative studies, for example, when stricter criteria for public procurement are demanded depending on the sector (Eurobarometer, 2009, pp. 75–81).

Taken together, the two competing visions of progress and the respective sector orderings form the economic world map. Each vision of progress entails a logic of assessment based on which countries are ranked. In the innovation-based vision, a country can be assessed based on the sector in which its exports are most renowned. In the social-ecological vision, the quality of regulation in the most important sectors is assessed (see Table 3.1). Based on this matrix of ranking, different world regions can be qualified (for representations of the West, the Far East, Eastern Europe, Northern Europe and Southern Europe; see Appendix 1, Sections A1.1.5–A1.1.7). Yet, the most detailed rankings are presented for the participants' respective countries. We will see these representations of the characteristics of the national economy in the following section. Importantly, however, these descriptions of the national economy are based on the matrixes of assessment found in the economic world map. Knowledge of the worth of nations, therefore, is rooted in transnational discourses. The innovation-centered or the social-ecological criteria of assessment are available across nations.

3.2.2 Placing France, Germany and Poland on the Economic World Map

Participants in the focus groups place their own countries on the economic world map and they do so in great detail. In addition to the two orderings of economic sectors, participants use migration flows as an indicator of a country's economic attractivity (see Table 3.2). What emerges is specific social representations of Poland (as an economy in development), Germany (as an industry-based exporting economy) and France (as an economy characterized by high standards). Interestingly, the European Union is also sometimes placed on the economic world map, mainly when it is compared to the United States in terms of social and product standards (see Chapter 7).

Table 3.2 Placement of participants' own nations on the economic world map

	Strengths of exports	Quality of regulation	Migration flows
France	• Weakness of industry due to high prices/ quality	• High quality (in particular agriculture)	• Destination
Germany	• Exports in industry (in particular cars)		• Destination
Poland	• Provider of labor for foreign industry	• Rising level of wages/of labor market regulation	• Origin and destination
EU	• No 'European industry'/ 'European firms'	• High European standards	• No 'European economy'

Poland is most frequently represented as an *economy in development* (see Appendix 1, Section A1.1.8). I use the term development not in order to refer to a concrete definition of developing nations, but for two reasons related to the empirical material. First, Polish participants frequently use the term development themselves when they speak about the characteristics of the national economy. Second, when placing their nation on the economic world map, they frequently view Poland in an intermediate position. In terms of sectors of the economy, Poland is viewed as a provider of skilled labor for transnational firms, thus having a rather well-established industrial base while still struggling to achieve higher levels of innovativeness. In terms of migration, Poland might be a traditional country from which migration originates, but it is increasingly depicted as a destination of migration, too.

Many descriptions of the Polish economy start with a diagnosis of poverty, lack of money or low wages.

> PLTW2: "With us in Poland it is mostly like that: there is no cash."
> – Polish teachers discussing 'investment'

This diagnosis has consequences for the assessment of migration flows and for the identification of the sectors of the economy in which the Polish economy is strong. In the following quote, both indicators are connected. We see how low wages and the perceived lack of means for investment cause Poland to be stuck in an intermediary position on the economic world map, struggling to reach higher levels of development.

> PSTM5: "We are only tools … That is, technological firms come here, and they don't care about us. The only thing that matters is that someone stands by the robe or in the storage room or such simple tasks. Which means that this doesn't really stimulate the Polish economy to a high degree. Innovativeness. Because, on the other hand, I don't know, can you imagine such a situation, let's say, in Korea? Korea is one of these economic tigers, one of the big ones, where you have firms like Samsung and so on. Can you imagine that a German firm goes there, and the Koreans only do the work with robes and hammers? [PSTM1: Rather no]. Over there they develop and organize things themselves. Same in Japan which is also such a technological country."
>
> PSTM1: "Yeah but we don't have anyone to compare to, you know, because we are nobody. We are not powerful. We don't produce anything."
>
> PSTM4: "Well, but actually we have pretty good technological development. At the polytechnical schools or somewhere. We have very good researchers."
>
> PSTM1: "Only stupid that we do not have money to invest in this [PSTM4: Yes]. Polish researchers just go abroad and work for some foreign

consortium. Right? [PSTM4: Selling their technology …] Well, if you earn 3000 złoty here and there you can earn 3000 euros."

– Polish soccer players discussing 'investment'

A number of typical assessments can be observed in this quote. In the beginning we see a typical application of the progressive ordering of sectors, placing Poland in behind nations that are more advanced in digital innovation. Poland's industry is described essentially as the provision of manual labor for foreign firms. The very low placement in the global economic hierarchy ("We are nobody"), however, is contradicted. Poland has the potential for innovation but lacks money in order to promote it. This diagnosis of not being able to profit from innovative potentials and thus relying on foreign investment is widely shared in the Polish groups.

Similarly, Poland is also in an intermediary position with regard to migration. In the quote above, we see a perfect example of how the low wage level in Poland is viewed as the main cause of migration. Examples in which Polish participants complain about a brain drain are abundant; apart from research, other professions tempted to leave westward are English teachers or doctors. Yet, Poland is not exclusively viewed as a country of origin but increasingly also as a destination of migration. Participants stress in particular the arrival of workers from Ukraine, thus granting an intermediary position to Poland in the overall European course of westward migration. Becoming a destination of migration is partly viewed as a sign of growing economic attractiveness, thus confirming the overall representation of Poland as an economy in development.

PAUW1: "Well look, we were for example in Austria because Austria lacks engineers. That's why we could work there."

PAUW2: "There we could do it. But we were just rented out as cheap labor, right? In Austria …"

PAUM1: "Exactly! It is a bit like …"

PAUW2: "It was always a bit like that …"

PAUW1: "… that we went to the West."

PAUW2: "… that in Poland … Yeah! Like I think … People just earn more, right? It simply is like that. Wages here are lower. That's why it's easier to like rent someone out, right? Under someone's command [PAUW1: Yeah, because they needed us], because back then we were working as leased labor, right? [loughs] We had nothing to say, we just had to do what they wanted."

– Polish agents discussing 'mobility'

PSTM1: "I live by the border with Germany, same height as Berlin. Most people simply no longer want to work there [in the Special economic area]. Because they still pay the lowest wages. You know what, the majority of workers there are now Ukrainians. Do you get that?

Ukrainians move to the West of Poland, not far from the German border only to work there in such a tax-free area."

– Polish soccer players discussing 'investment'

Germany is mainly represented as an industry-based exporting economy. This self-assessment frequently comes with a high degree of pride in the achievements of the national economy. Germany, in other words, is described as the *export world champion*. In terms of sectors, this perceived leadership role regarding industry implies a certain backwardness in terms of digitalization, thus not placing Germany at the very top of the global hierarchy. In terms of migration flows, Germany is clearly viewed as a destination country. The representation of the German economy frequently finds expression in very specific national terms such as *Fachkräftemangel* and, of course, *Exportweltmeister*.

GATM2: "Germany is the export world champion in the automobile industry and so on. So where there is demand we can satisfy that demand, and we can create jobs by producing here and by exporting."

– German agents discussing 'work'

GATW1: "Concerning innovation, I do not think that we are up front in Germany. Although I would like that. [...] Uber for example! Nobody, or very few people, are taking taxis these days in other countries. There is only Uber. Airbnb is prohibited here and so on."

– German agents discussing 'investment'

The quotes below illustrate Germany's placement in the global economic hierarchy with regard to the sectors of the economy. In the first citation, industry is clearly named as the sector on which the strength of the German economy is based. The competitiveness of industrial goods is symbolized by cars – a representation spread enough to be mobilized by non-German participants as well. The strength of German industry seems to be the source of considerable pride – note, for example, the triumphant usage of metaphors of ranking, with Germany being described as the "champion". While some German participants celebrate these achievements in the industrial sector, other participants take a more skeptical stance toward the German position in the global order, often decrying the lack of digital innovation in the German economy. In the second quote, GATW1 employs a metaphor of ranking ("we are not up front") to decry Germany's lack of digital innovation.

While Germany's position according to the worth of its exporting sectors is thus somewhat contested, with regards to the migration indicator most participants agree. Germany is a destination of migration. Again, there is a specific national expression to describe Germany's position as a destination of migration. *Fachkräftemangel* refers to the lack of qualified employees supposedly haunting the German economy (see next section). While lagging behind in the digital sector, the representations of the German economy are still largely optimistic, featuring a booming industry in need of international talent.

Although France is, according to official rankings, also among the world's leading industrial nations, the social representations of the French economy differ from those of Germany. French participants rather entertain a vision of their economy as characterized by *high standards*, in terms of both product quality and labor regulation. These assessments thus rather seem to be based on the social ordering of sectors, with concerns about the quality of agricultural production and about pressure on wages being frequently voiced.

The French economy is most frequently represented by high-quality agricultural products and other luxury goods. High-quality meat or cheese and high-end fashion items are most frequently cited as characteristics products. French wine is probably the most telling example in this context, as it can be mobilized as a symbol of high-quality traditional agriculture and as an example of luxury products, being sold for several thousand euros a bottle. Whether the high quality of French products constitutes as competitive advantage is contested.

> FATM1: "Tourism is an interesting sector too. In France, we are profiting a lot from this. [FATW1: Yeah, we are relying a lot on tourism]. And I think Paris is the most visited city on earth! [...] That is also due to a specific image. All these Asians, for example, come to buy their handbags in the Galerie Lafayette."
>
> – French agents discussing 'investment'

> FSUM3: "In France, we have a reputation for product quality. The only problem we have is that we struggle to export it."
>
> – French soccer players discussing 'exports'

In the first quote we do not only see a metaphor of ranking characteristic of such placements on the economic world map ("the most visited city"). The quote also constitutes an example of an optimistic assessment of the French position in the global economic hierarchy. In the second quote, we see a more skeptical vision, voicing concerns about high-quality French production being eliminated by cheaper foreign products (see also the quote about genetically modified organisms (GMOs) later in this section). France is thus depicted as a high-standard economy whose position in the global order is under pressure.

A similarly contested representation can be identified with regard to migration flows. On the one hand, France is clearly viewed as a destination of migration due to high wage levels and good social security standards. On the other hand, these high labor market standards are perceived as threatened by migration.

FAUW2: "I mean with regard to the world of work where you see for example that there are doctors who come to France from other countries in order to work here, and they are being under-paid. And we, our doctors, have been forced to go abroad because they no longer earn the salaries they deserve! That's what I mean, I mean the firms that are *délocalisés*."

– French agents discussing 'mobility'

Like in the German case, we see that specifically national terminology is used to describe the threat posed to labor standards by the free movement of people. *Délocalisation* normally refers to the movement of firms to countries with lower standards. Other terms French citizens frequently mobilize in this context are *travailleur détaché* (posted worker) or *concurrence déloyale* (unfair competition). Both in terms of sectors and in terms of migration flows, then, French citizens depict their economy as a space of high standards which are increasingly under pressure.

It has been the purpose of this section to show that representations of the strength and weaknesses of national economies are rooted in overarching transnational discourses. Representations of the national economy can be based on innovative or social-ecological sector orderings or it can be a function of migration flows. The fact that these indicators are similarly employed by participants from all countries seems to underline the claim that these representations of national economy are linked to transnational discourses. This finding is supported by other studies who found similar representations of economic regions among citizens from the entire EU. In particular, representations of the East and the West seem widespread (e.g., with regard to the quality of professional qualifications, Eurobarometer, 2009, pp. 57–62, or with regard to lower capacity of firms to deliver high-quality results, Eurbarometer, 2011, pp. 41–46). Similarly, other focus group studies have found Europeans to use migration flows as an indicator of economic attractivity (Eurobarometer, 2014, p. 54). What is striking, moreover, is that these social representations of the national economy seem to evolve significantly over time. Qualitative studies conducted in the 2000s repeatedly found Western Europeans to be concerned with the inflow of cheap labor from Poland, frequently mobilizing a representation of the Polish plumber (Lingenberg, 2010, pp. 214–216; J. White, 2011, pp. 143–145). White's participants, moreover, also described the German economy as the "tail-light" of Europe (ibid., p. 187). Fifteen years later, we find some Germans boasting about their economy's strength while the countries from which cheap labor is coming have moved further east, and Poland itself has become the destination of work migration (A. White, 2018, p. 8). Poland's and Germany's placement on the economic world map seem to have changed. The Polish plumber, apparently, hasn't survived the economic crisis. While representations of the national economy thus can be updated over time, the transnational criteria that underpin knowledge of the worth of nations seem to be transnationally shared and stable.

Which are the transnational discourses the worth of nation is based on then? As the title of this chapter suggests, I believe neoliberal discourses are an important inspiration for the worth of nations. Following a definition of neoliberalism as the application of economic principles to areas beyond economics, I find that the worth of nation provides two examples of such an extension of economic imperatives. First, there seems to be an analogy between the firm and the state, suggesting that the state should act like an economic agent. The focus on exports suggests that the state is to pay less for its inputs than for its outputs. It often comes together with a vision of the *state as an investor* (see Appendix 1, Section A1.5.2), clearly advocating that the state – like a start-up – should seek to invest in promising areas of innovation. At the very least, the state should act as a *competitor* (see Appendix 1, Section A1.5.4), attracting firms that might do the investing and innovating for it. The export indicator thus seems to be based on an application of the economic imperatives governing firms to the state. Second, the migration indicator seems to be based on a vision of migrants as human capital. The concept of human capital is central to neoliberal thought, as it allows the extension of economic rationalities to individual actors (Foucault, 2006, pp. 311–312). Notions such as *Fachkräftemangel* or the brain drain decried in some Polish groups clearly show that migrants are simply considered a factor of production needed in specific sectors of the economy. Taken together, the innovation-centered logic and the migration indicator seem to combine into a representation of the international order as a neoliberal competition of states. States, like firms, are to compete for workers, capital and sales.

3.3 Representation of Arguments: Anchoring in the Worth of Nations

Having established the origin and content of knowledge of the worth of nations, let us now explore how this anchoring domain can help citizens to render complex issues intelligible. In the focus groups, participants used representations of the national economy as an anchoring domain to understand the trigger arguments. Arguably, this was the case for three of the 22 trigger arguments. Little surprisingly, the trigger arguments in question mainly targeted the international arena. In the trade discussions, 'work' and 'exports' were frequently anchored in the perceived strengths and weaknesses of the national economy. The same is true of the trigger topic 'international competitiveness', which came up in the unemployment discussions. I will now consider the inter-national differences in the representations of these trigger topics in turn.

For the trigger topics 'work' and 'exports', anchoring in knowledge about the worth of nations produced particularly strong differences between German and French participants. In the relevant focus groups, participants were asked "which should be the aims of a good free trade agreement?" and they were handed cards reading "create jobs" and "increase exports" as potential answers. In a later task, participants were handed the same cards, but now the question was reversed ("which of these arguments have negative connotations for you?"). Participants could thus choose the cards either as something negative or as something positive. Interestingly, the trigger arguments 'work' and 'exports' were chosen as positive predominantly by German participants and as negative predominantly by French participants, while Polish participants remained rather ambiguous. Arguably, this difference resulted from anchoring the trigger argument in knowledge about the respective national economies.

> GATM2: "Germany is the export world champion in the automobile industry and so on. So where there is demand we can satisfy that demand, and we can create jobs by producing here and by exporting."
>
> – German agents discussing 'work'

> GSTM2: "So I thought 'Increase exports' is an obvious choice. Eliminate customs, so you can sell stuff abroad. And logically that increases exports. So if you have another market because you sell stuff abroad, you have to increase production, and thus you also need more workers. That's why 'create jobs'. I also thought that was logical."
>
> – German soccer players discussing exports

In the German groups, the trigger topics 'exports' and 'work' were viewed as closely linked. The causal connection between exports and jobs seemed obvious to most of the participants. This certitude is given verbal expression in the second quote where GSTM2 describes the link as "obvious" and "logical". Arguably, the perception of this causal connection results from anchoring in the specific characteristics of the German economy. Commonly perceived as strong in the industrial sector (note references to "the automobile industry", "production" and "workers" in both quotes), an opening of markets through free trade thus is interpreted as an impetus for additional job creation. The term "export world champion" is not an invention of GATM2 but a commonly used expression popularized both by German economists and national newspapers (e.g., *Exportweltmeister – Deutschland hängt China ab*, 2017; Sinn, 2005; for the fortification of this self-perception during the euro crisis, see Mylonas, 2012). When anchored in the perceptions of industrial strength, the trigger arguments 'work' and 'exports' thus acquire a positive connotation for the German participants.

> FSTM3: "In France, we have a reputation for product quality. The only problem we have is that we struggle to export it." […]
>
> FSTM1: "But why would French producers not profit from this? Why would they not sell their stuff abroad?"

FSTM6: "Well because ... For several reasons. The first one is that 15 years ago we entered the European community. They call that globalization. That is to say there are no more customs between European countries [FSTM1: Yes, that's Schengen]. That means that there is meat from Spain and other products from Rumania. Same for the workers that come here, they are called *travailleur détaché*. What is a *travailleur détaché*? People that come from Rumania in order to work in France. The only difference is that they do the same work, but they are paid two times less than a French employee."

– French soccer players discussing 'exports'

FATM1: "But free trade can also be bad, for example for the labor market. Because it creates unemployment. If you look at Europe, you ... Here in France, you have social security payments and so on. For someone on minimum wage, an employer still pays 2000, maybe even more. And next door, in Rumania, you can make people work for two, three, four times less than that."

– French soccer players discussing 'work'

Where French participants mobilize the characteristics of their national economy as an anchoring domain, their representations of the trigger arguments 'work' and 'exports' are negative. The citations above exhibit some typical aspects of the representation of France as a *high-standard economy*. In the first quote, agriculture (or rather "meat") is cited as an example of a sector in which high-quality French production is undercut by competitors from low-standard regions (Eastern and Southern Europe). This causes France to "struggle to export". Apart from the circulation of goods, the circulation of labor also indicates that France is a high standard economy. France's high work standards might make her a destination of migration, but the inflow of labor undercuts the original standards. Specifically loaded national vocabulary ("*travailleur détaché*") is mobilized to explain this process. In the second quote, a similar process is described, also mobilizing Rumania as an example of lower labor regulations. French participants, then, understood the trigger topics 'work' and 'exports' to imply a loss of exports and a loss of jobs. In opposition to their German counterparts, anchoring in the characteristics of the national economy produced negative representations of the trigger arguments.

The reactions of Polish participants are more ambiguous and fall somewhat in between the German and the French representations. To begin with, the Polish groups assign lower salience to these arguments – the trigger topic 'work' is barely discussed. On the trigger topic exports, however, some typical features of the representation of Poland as an economy in development are employed as an anchoring point. Like the French and German participants, some Polish groups mobilize knowledge of the characteristics of their national economy as anchoring domain.

PLTW2: "Take technological firms. Programmers for example can work in foreign firms which sit I don't know where, in France, Belgium or Germany. Right? [PLTW3: hmhm (approving)]. And at the same time, they live here in Poland, right? [...] We have a lot of educated people here in Poland. And this kind of treaty also makes things easier for them. Because it must not always be export of products, we can also export services, right? [...] So we can earn in euro but live in Poland." [PLTW1 laughs]

– Polish teachers discussing 'exports'

In the quote, Poland appears as the provider of a competitive and educated labor force. Labor is both treated as an exported good ("services") and serves as an indicator for international migration flows. Poland is clearly placed in the economic hierarchy behind the West (symbolized by "France, Belgium or Germany"). At the same time, a potential to catch up is stressed ("we have a lot of educated people here"). The trigger topic 'exports' thus produces an ambivalent reaction, triggering both a perception of backwardness and a possibility of development. Like in the previous quotes, the nation is referred to with the pronoun 'we' and a global hierarchy of states is evoked. Anchoring in knowledge of the worth of nations produced inter-nationally different representations of the trigger topics 'exports' and 'work'.

A similar pattern of differences appears for the trigger argument 'international competitiveness'. This trigger topic was presented to a different set of participants – those discussing unemployment. In these groups, participants were asked how the unemployment rate in the EU could be lowered. As a potential response, they were handed a card reading 'increase international competitiveness'. In response to this trigger argument, participants mobilized the representations of their national economy and reached similar conclusions as for 'exports' and 'work'. Consequently, the same pattern of interpretation emerges, with German participants picking the card as positive and French participants viewing it as a danger, while Polish participants showed ambivalent reactions.

GSUM3: "[reads out trigger topic] 'Increase competitiveness'. For Germany in the EU, that is already the standard. We are all the way up front."

– German soccer players discussing 'competitiveness'

GLUW1: "[reads out trigger topic] 'Increase international competitiveness'. As I understand it that would be similar. That could work via tax cuts or via the free movement of ehm – how do you call that? – top-qualified employees. If we say we want to attract IT-specialists from India, for example. And not only that ... How do you call that? Work migration, right? [...] Sorry, Fachkräftemangel, that's the term."

GLUM3: "Fachkräftemangel! For example, if in Germany more care workers are needed – maybe this isn't really fair – but if there is free movement of people, then people will come from Eastern Europe and take these positions."

– German teachers discussing 'competitiveness' and 'mobility'

In the quotes, we see how a representation of the German economy and its placement on an economic world map are used as anchoring points. The participants depict Germany's economy as booming and, thus, in need of foreign employees. Linguistically, we see that national vocabulary is available to describe Germany's status as a destination of migration ("Fachkräftemangel"). Furthermore, metaphors of ranking ("we are all the way up front") and frequent references to Germany as "we" convey the impression of pride in the acknowledgment of Germany's privileged economic position. The country is placed higher in the economic hierarchy than other countries "in the EU" or in comparison with "Eastern Europe". Based on this representation of the national economy, the trigger argument 'international competitiveness' is assigned positive value.

FLUW3: " 'Increase International competitiveness' – the problem is that we are already hyper globalized. So the little guy who grows his tomatoes over here as he can … If there are hectares of tomato fields in Spain and Portugal, he just cannot have the same production costs."

– French teachers discussing 'competitiveness'

FAUW1: "Alright, let's go. So with 'increase international competitiveness' I am not too sure … Maybe I didn't understand it correctly, but it means that the other countries can sell more over here. So it will cost jobs over here in France. Because we know that French enterprises are not particularly competitive internationally [loughs]. So I think this could cause trouble."

– French agents discussing 'competitiveness'

The French groups reach a different assessment of the trigger topic 'international competitiveness' than their German counterparts. In both quotes, French enterprises are depicted as losers in the international competition. The first quote diagnoses this lack of competitiveness in the agricultural sector – a sector typically cited as an example of French high-quality production. In the second quote, international competition is anchored in the fear of job loss. Just like for 'exports' and 'work', the trigger argument 'international competitiveness' produces negative representations among the French participants. No gain, but a loss is feared from international competition.

PLUW2: "Yes, yes! That's what I thought about. Why did I choose it? I think it results from the fact that … Well, I have a certain impression, a feeling that Poles always feel a bit inferior and so they never go abroad with their products."

PLUW1: "Yeah, we have a kind of complex." […]
PLUW2: "I know that we have good things. We would have good things to sell …"
PLUW3: "We just don't know how to sell them." […]
PLUW4: "The blue laser at the Politechnika in Warsaw, I think someone got a patent for it."
PLUW3: "Well exactly."

– Polish teachers discussing 'competitiveness'

PSTM1: "Yeah but we don't have anyone to compare to, you know, because we are nobody. We are not powerful. We don't produce anything."
PSTM4: "Well, but actually we have pretty good technological development. At the polytechnical schools or somewhere. We have very good researchers."
PSTM1: "Only stupid that we do not have money to invest in this [PSTM4: Yes]. Polish researchers just go abroad and work for some foreign consortium. Right? [PSTM4: Selling their technology …] Well, if you earn 3000 złoty here and there you can earn 3000 euros."
[…]
PSTM1: "Yeah, it was the same with this blue laser which was created by Poles."
PSTM4: "A lot of things were invented by Polish people."
PSTM1: "They sold it, man! For a million euros or so. Well, great!"

– Polish soccer players discussing 'investment'

Polish participants also mobilize a representation of their national economy in response to the trigger topic. And, of course, this specific representation of the national economy causes them to form yet another different representation of the argument. In the first quote, PLUW2 diagnoses a feeling of inferiority ("a kind of complex"), which she criticizes as unjustified in light of the innovativeness of Polish researchers. Like for 'exports', the talent and education of the Polish population is cited as an economic strength. The second quote is derived from a different trigger topic, but it is worthwhile considering it in this context because it mirrors the first one in a remarkable way. In its beginning, PSTM1 seems to exhibit precisely the feeling of inferiority discussed by PLUW2 ("we are nobody"). The feeling of inferiority is contradicted citing the exact same innovation generated by Polish researchers ("the blue laser"). Yet most importantly, the quote also gives an explanation why this innovativeness fails to increase the status of the Polish economy: a lack of investment causes the innovations to be sold to foreign companies or the researchers to go abroad. Together, the quotes provide a perfect illustration of the representation of Poland as an *economy in development*. In this representation, Poland's qualified labor force is depicted as its main asset, promising future development while implying present dependence on and even exploitation by foreign firms. Anchoring the trigger topic 'international competitiveness' in this representation of the national economy triggers mixed feelings for Polish participants. Their reaction thus differs yet again from those of their German and French counterparts.

Three conclusions should be drawn from the analysis of the trigger topics 'exports', 'work' and 'international competitiveness'. First, knowledge of the worth of the national economy can serve as anchoring domain for complex economic issues. Citizens have specific knowledge about the characteristics of their national economy, and they use this knowledge to render complex economic issues intelligible. This, in turn, means that citizens' representations of complex economic arguments differ depending on their representation of the national economy.

Second, these inter-national differences in the representation of complex arguments are differences in the **frequency and persuasiveness** of specific representations. While participants entertain very specific and nationally different representations of their national economy, they share a representation of the *economic world map* (see Section 3.2.1). Thus, while some assessments are more frequent in some countries, the criteria of evaluation are shared beyond national borders. With regard to 'exports' and 'work', for example, we saw that German participants most frequently took up the trigger argument as positive, while French participants mainly saw it as negative. Yet, this does not mean that the relevant representations of economic causalities are unique to the respective nations. German participants do use the argument that greater competition can lower standards (see Section 3.3) – but they connect it to fewer trigger topics and thus end up employing it less frequently. Inversely, a representation such as *migration as talent* might be particularly strong within the German groups (as it links up with the needs of the national exporting industry), but it is used in the French groups as well, albeit more rarely. Anchoring in the worth of nations thus increases the frequency of representations in the respective national context and it boosts the persuasiveness of the resulting evaluation of economic processes. The resulting representations, however, are not exclusive to the respective nations.

Third and finally, knowledge of the worth of nations seems to be spread by past **politicization**. Like the differences in national culture discussed in Chapter 2, different representations of the national economy find expression-specific national vocabulary. In the German and the French cases, terms such as *Fachkräftemangel* or *travailleur détaché* were employed to describe specific characteristics of the national economy. Inter-national differences thus often have a strong linguistic dimension. The existence of such nation-specific vocabulary is the result of salient national debates, which spread certain expressions to the point of grounding them in the respective national language. This finding clearly supports the assumption that knowledge of the worth of nations is spread via the national public sphere. While based on transnational discourses, these discourses need to be activated and popularized through national debates.

3.4 Conclusion

This chapter has explored how citizens render complex issues intelligible by anchoring them in knowledge of the worth of nations. In this form of national anchoring, citizens employ knowledge about the strengths and weaknesses of their national economy to form an opinion on economic questions. Participants exhibit striking similarities in the criteria they use to determine and rank the attractivity of their own national economies. A nation's place in the global economic hierarchy can be assessed according to neoliberal discourses of innovative progress and attractivity for human capital, but economies can also be judged using social-ecological discourses with a focus on the quality of regulation. The fact that these criteria of assessment are similar in all three countries underlines that the worth of nation is a transnationally available body of knowledge. This finding is further supported by the similar linguistic features which references to the worth of nations exhibit: participants employ the pronoun 'we' to refer to their national economies and they use metaphors of ranking and race to describe the global economic hierarchy. Placing the nation in the global hierarchy thus can convey feelings of pride or inferiority. Knowledge about the national economy engenders a specific way of referring to the nation as unified actor facing equals in an international competition. Employing knowledge of the worth of nations as an anchoring domain helps citizens make sense of the complex economic processes making up the international order.

Anchoring in the worth of nations is similar to anchoring in national culture (discussed in the previous chapter) in two important ways. First, while the worth of nations is a transnationally available body of knowledge, it is adapted to local circumstances and spread via national public spheres. Like national culture, the knowledge of the worth of nations is spread particularly through **politicization in the national arena**. References to specific linguistic expressions coined in such salient debates (e.g., *travailleur détaché*, *Fachkräftemangel*) testify to this link. Second, anchoring in the worth of the nation creates inter-national differences in the frequency and persuasiveness of arguments. Representations of economic processes appear more frequently and command more support if they seem relevant to the national economy – but in the empirical material they are never unique to a single nation.

Given these similarities, let us review both forms of national anchoring together. How frequent was it in the empirical material overall and what is the external validity of these findings? In my focus group discussions, participants in France, Germany and Poland were presented with the same arguments drawn from EU-level debates. Of these 22 trigger arguments, for nine national anchoring produced significant inter-national differences (anchoring in the worth of nations for 'international competitiveness', 'work' and 'exports'; anchoring in national culture for 'mobility', 'workers' rights' 'expenditure', 'sovereignty', 'interest', and 'right to work'). In my focus groups, then, for 40% of all topics discussed, significant inter-national differences were found.

In the empirical material, therefore, national anchoring is a crucial factor illuminating how citizens make sense of the economic order around them. National anchoring seems to be an important mechanism determining citizens' perceptions of European economic issues.

Care, however, is warranted in generalizing these results. For the complexity question, this study was not designed to maximize external validity but rather to allow a specific exploration of national anchoring domains. Participant selection was based on access to national culture and the worth of nations – the participants, therefore, are particularly likely to employ national anchoring. Beyond this sample, national anchoring may be less frequent. That being said, however, it seems highly unlikely that the phenomenon would disappear entirely. While the frequency of national anchoring beyond the sample can be contested, its existence should not. Given the coherence of the phenomenon across all three nations studied in this book, moreover, it is my suspicion that national anchoring operates in issue areas other than economics and in countries other than France, Germany and Poland. In the conclusion, I will spell out some of these potential avenues for future research in greater detail. But for now, the simple fact that national anchoring exists already has important implications for the complexity and for the compatibility problem. The next two parts of the book will spell out the implications of national anchoring for each of these debates.

Note

1 For more examples of the kind, it is fruitful to review German newspaper coverage of the euro crisis in which Greece, for example, was often depicted as a country exporting nothing but Feta and olive oil.

Petersdorff, W. von. (2011, June 26). Ausweg aus der Schuldenkrise: Was die Griechen können. *FAZ.NET*. https://www.faz.net/1.2723

Bibliography

Eurobarometer (2009). *Internal Market: Awareness, Perceptions and Impacts* (p. 133). https://ec.europa.eu/commfrontoffice/publicopinion/archives/quali_en.htm

Eurobarometer (2011). *Internal Market: Awareness, Perceptions and Impacts*. https://ec.europa.eu/commfrontoffice/publicopinion/archives/quali/5983_awareness_en.pdf

Eurobarometer (2014). *Coping with the Crisis*. https://ec.europa.eu/commfrontoffice/publicopinion/archives/quali/ql_6342_crisis_en.pdf

Exportweltmeister – Deutschland hängt China ab. (2017). bild.de. www.bild.de/geld/wirtschaft/export/eilmeldung-exportweltmeister-50026446.bild.html

Foucault, M. (2006). *Geschichte der Gouvernementalität. 2. Die Geburt der Biopolitik: Vorlesung am Collège de France 1978 – 1979*. Suhrkamp.

Fougner, T. (2008). Neoliberal Governance of States: The Role of Competitiveness Indexing and Country Benchmarking. *Millennium*, *37*(2), 303–326. https://doi.org/10.1177/0305829808097642

Greenfeld, L. (1995). The Worth of Nations: Some Economic Implications of Nationalism. *Critical Review*, *9*(4), 555–584. https://doi.org/10.1080/08913819508443403

Lingenberg, S. (2010). Fallstudien zur europäischen Verfassungsdebatte. In S. Lingenberg (Ed.), *Europäische Publikumsöffentlichkeiten: Ein pragmatischer Ansatz* (pp. 183–226). VS Verlag für Sozialwissenschaften. https://doi.org/10.1007/978-3-531-92120-4_5

Mylonas, Y. (2012). Media and the Economic Crisis of the EU: The 'Culturalization' of a Systemic Crisis and Bild-Zeitung's Framing of Greece. *TripleC: Communication, Capitalism & Critique. Open Access Journal for a Global Sustainable Information Society*, *10*(2), 646–671. https://doi.org/10.31269/triplec.v10i2.380

Petersdorff, W. von. (2011, June 26). Ausweg aus der Schuldenkrise: Was die Griechen können. *FAZ.NET*. www.faz.net/1.2723

Sinn, H.-W. (2005). Basar-Ökonomie Deutschland – Exportweltmeister oder Schusslicht? *ifo Schnelldienst*, *58*(6), 3–42.

White, A. (2018). How Are Countries Affected by Migration? An "Inside-out" Approach to Change in Sending and Receiving Countries. In A. White, I. Grabowska, P. Kaczmarczyk & K. Slany (Eds.), *The Impact of Migration on Poland: EU Mobility and Social Change* (pp. 1–10). UCL Press. https://library.oapen.org/handle/20.500.12657/28334

White, J. (2011). *Political Allegiance after European Integration*. Palgrave Macmillan. www.palgrave.com/gp/book/9780230279780

White, J. (2019). *Politics of Last Resort: Governing by Emergency in the European Union*. Oxford University Press.

Part II

The Complexity Problem

4 Diverse Understandings

Market Experiences and the Rational Choice Model

4.1 Introduction

For the beginning of this chapter, I wish to quote some claims made in papers studying public opinion on trade:

> "Those who believe they will be harmed by increased trade will support compensation [for the effects of trade]."
>
> (Ehrlich, 2010, p. 6)

> "Individuals in export-oriented sectors feel the pressure of imports and thus their attitudes to trade are intermediate: they do not favor trade as much as individuals in non-traded sectors, but neither are they as protectionist as individuals in import-competing sectors."
>
> (Mayda & Rodrik, 2005, p. 3)

> "Trade liberalization raises the prices of a country's exportable goods while lowering those of its imported goods. As a result, workers that heavily consume their country's exportable goods experience price increases for their consumption bundles relative to workers that more heavily consume imported and import-competing goods."
>
> (Baker, 2005, p. 925)

I find these quotes fascinating for two reasons. First, they seem to be quite normal statements to be found in academic papers. Reading them for the first time, one might notice nothing unusual. What could be more normal than people losing from trade opposing it? I believe the familiarity with this line of argument illustrates well how widespread the assumptions expressed in these quotes are in much of public opinion research. Yet, second, rather than containing common-sense wisdom, these quotes make a far-fetched empirical claim: they assume knowledge of economic theory to be present in the minds of citizens. For the predictions above to be true, all citizens must be aware of the consequences of complex economic processes as they are described in economics. Whether it is the effects of trade on the exporting industry or on the

DOI: 10.4324/9781003335610-7

price of import-competing goods – citizens are supposed to know the causal effect of trade. Under the banality of these common-place quotes, therefore, we find a far-reaching assumption: the assumption that the public is perfectly informed.

The quotes above are perfect examples of the **market experience hypothesis** (see Table 1.1, Chapter 1). The market experience hypothesis stipulates that all citizens alike assess economic processes based on their material interests. Citizens without economic training should be able 'adequately' represent economic processes based on an inference from personal economic experiences. Representations of causal processes thus are uniform and differences in judgment result from different positions in the economy. These assumptions are mirrored in the quotes, which assume citizens to be affected differently by trade while their understanding of the effects of trade should be the same. This uniform knowledge of the effects of trade in turn results from anchoring in personal experiences (e.g., of the development of wages and prices). The prediction that lay representations will uniformly correspond to economic theory implies a very optimistic conclusion for the complexity problem: If lay representations of complex issues were the same as those entertained by experts, the public is perfectly informed. Regarding the complexity problem, therefore, the market experience hypothesis is a kind of null hypothesis: it claims that there is no problem after all.

This chapter tests the market experience hypothesis by asking if social representations of economic processes are indeed uniform, or alternatively, if lay and expert representations differ. Thus, it will answer the question if the European public sphere indeed faces a complexity problem. I show that the market experience hypothesis fails for two reasons. First, anchoring economic issues in personal experience does not guarantee an inference to economic theory. Personal experiences of wage development, consumption and tax paying feed into a morally loaded **discourse of the normal people**, rather than providing an anchoring point for economic theory. Second, and more importantly, social representations of economics are **not uniform, but highly diverse**. After discussing national anchoring in the previous chapters, the discourse of the common people provides another example of an anchoring domain creating social representations that differ widely from economic theory.

These findings have important implications for public opinion research. In many branches of the literature, there is a tendency of tacitly imputing expert knowledge into the minds of the population. The prominence of the market experience hypothesis is a prime example of this tendency as it simply assumes citizens to hold the same level of objective economic information available to economists. Yet also beyond economics, the same tendency of projecting expert knowledge into lay minds can be found. Political scientists, for example, attribute elaborate accountability calculations to the electorate when it is unlikely that citizens hold the same kind of knowledge of the relevant policies and institutional responsibilities (Henceroth & Oganesyan, 2019). Legal scholars assume citizens to worry about details of the constitution, which – outside the scholarly community – are probably very little known (Ackerman, 2019). Some European studies scholars see Euroskepticism as a function of the single market's distributional effects, when many citizens have only a vague idea about what the EU is in the first place (Gabel, 1998; Hakhverdian et al., 2013). All these approaches fail to appreciate the fact that laypeople think differently than experts. Rather than simply imputing patterns of thought familiar from the academic community to the larger population, we need to acknowledge that the **study of lay representations is a prerequisite to any study of public opinion on complex issues**. Without an investigation into the diversity of lay representations, claims about public opinion on complex issues need to be taken with a mountain of salt. This is what it means to acknowledge the existence of a complexity problem in the European public sphere.

This chapter proceeds in two steps. Section 4.2 identifies the social groups that have access to the relevant anchoring domain (market experiences). It assesses the role of economic experiences as an anchoring domain and shows why these experiences combine into a discourse of the common people rather than into generalized representations of a homo economicus. The final section, then, shows how anchoring in economic experiences affects the interpretation of complex economic arguments. Lay representations are shown to be diverse and, on average, much more negative in their depiction of market forces than economic theory would suggest. I conclude by elaborating on the implications of the findings for public opinion research.

4.2 Identification of Social Group: the Homo Economicus or the Common People?

Let us consider first the social group which the market experience hypothesis targets. The market experience hypothesis is based on a vision of the homo economicus. According to this vision, individuals are mainly driven by material self-interest. The expected costs and benefits of a policy determine individuals' assessment of it. All rational individuals are capable of performing this kind of cost–benefit calculation based on their personal economic experiences. Market experience is an anchoring domain and **everyone having experiences in the respective markets has access** to it. In the focus group material, then, we should expect participants to identify the effects of a given policy on their personal economic situation first.

Let us now consider if the empirical material indeed confirms these expectations. In the focus group discussions, participants seem to draw on their material interest in a variety of ways. The most straightforward expression of self-interest are statements that explicitly refer to *individual* costs and gains.[1] Some participants hailed lower taxes or lower prices because they would financially profit from such developments. Others saw the arrival of foreign firms as an improvement of their personal career opportunities. With a frequency of five, however, such direct references to personal material gains remain extremely rare. Mobilizing one's personal gains and losses does not seem to be the main avenue of expression for self-interest.

This rarity of statements about individual gains, however, should not be taken as evidence for the overall irrelevance of self-interested considerations. Proponents of rational choice theory might rightly object that the context of a group discussion is not particularly conducive to the highlighting of personal gains. If asked anonymously, the participants might have been more willing to disclose underlying material motivations. In group discussions, and particularly among members that know each other, revealing one's personal financial situation might simply seem out of place. On a number of occasions, the participants' statements about individual gains seem to be made with an apologetic, almost ironic undertone. Participants laugh nervously or change their voices while making these statements, as if they were apologizing in advance for an inappropriate comment. This unease of expression seems to support the conclusion that individual interests are not straightforwardly announced in the group discussions.

What alternative strategies might there be, then, for individuals to voice their self-interest in a group discussion? A potential answer is provided by the literature on the sociology of justification, which has long been concerned with explaining participants' behavior in focus groups. According to this literature, participants in a discussion attempt to generalize their claims in order to convince their peers (e.g., Boltanski & Thévenot, 1991, p. 19; Michèle Lamont, 2012, pp. 208–210). If participants wanted to voice personal grievances or material interests, then, they would attempt to formulate their point as the concern of a larger group. Rather than explicit references to participants' individual economic situations, we should expect to find references to the interest groups of which they are part. Personal interests might be assigned to generalized groups of people.

Which references to groups of people can be found in the focus group material, then? Do participants construct their individual concerns as **collective interests**? Arguably, a primary locus of identification should be job groups. Most of the focus groups (those with teachers and those with estate agents) assembled participants who work in the same domain. For these groups, then, it should be a rather simple task to depict their economic interests as collective ones, as they should at least be shared among the members of the discussion group. Yet, again we find relatively little empirical evidence of this mechanism. Some teacher groups collectively complain about their wage level and some agent groups show signs of identification with the firm they work for. Overall, however, with a frequency of seven, references to participants' *job groups*[2] remain the exception rather than the rule.

Do we observe other forms of generalization of individual material interests? How else are participants' economic situations depicted as collective concerns? Arguably, the most frequent kind of group representation takes the form of a **generalized normal person**. As can be seen in detail in Appendix 1 (sections A1.2–A1.4, starting p. 200), individuals construct representations of standardized actors in the various markets. There are representations of generalized actors such as *the consumer, the taxpayer* or *the working people*, which constitute important normative and causal reference points. What is more, these representations are very frequently based on personal experiences. Participants seem to mobilize their personal experiences in the market (e.g., consumption experiences) to construct groups of actors (e.g., consumers) who share an interest (e.g., low prices). Representations of 'normal people' thus might be the result of an attempted generalization of individual interests and this generalization of individual interest might be proof of the homo economicus model. Rather than pointing to their individual situation, participants seem to mobilize the fate of interest groups they form part of. They thus seem to behave according to the model of the homo economicus, rationally calculating the effects of a given policy on their personal economic situation.

Viewing the group representations discussed above as proof for the homo economicus model, however, remains only one possible interpretation. The representations of 'normal people' might be self-interest in disguise, but they also lend themselves to a different explanation. Previous focus group studies have repeatedly pointed to the salience of a discourse of **the little people** in political debates. Beginning with studies of class consciousness among workers in the 1980s, political sociologists found a self-representation as 'the little man' to be an important point of political identification (Halle, 1984; J. White, 2011, pp. 88–90). Later studies showed that a similar representation of the common people appears in political discussions far beyond the working classes (e.g., Gamson, 1992, p. 108; O'Connor, 2012, pp. 462–467). These representations of the common people can be mobilized to explain political phenomena. The imagined fate of the common people is a potential anchoring domain.

Two features have commonly been noted about the representation of the little people. First, it is based on shared experiences (Gamson, 1992, p. 108). The little people are defined as those that have a realistic outlook on life – their problems are real and they are the essence of everyday life struggle. Working hard, providing for a family or paying bills feature prominently in this list of struggles of common people. While these experiences would be compatible with the expectations of the market experience hypothesis, a second aspect in the representation of the little people clearly distinguishes it from purely self-interested calculations. The common people are **constructed in opposition to other social groups**. On the one hand, these are elite groups such as managers or politicians. These elites are said to inhabit an unreal world of numbers and figures and to be ignorant of the troubles of everyday life (J. White, 2011, pp. 92–108). On the other hand, the little people can be constructed via a downward distinction, for example, from those who are dependent on state aid (ibid.) or from refugees (Gdula, 2017, pp. 34–38). In both cases, the distinction is based on the supposed absence of a shared experience (the experience of hard work). The representations of the common people, then, are not based on a generalization of self-interest but rather on the distinction from other social groups which are viewed as morally corrupt. While being anchored in similar experiences of economic struggle, the common person is not simply a self-interested homo economicus but a **moral category**.

Appreciating the difference between the homo economicus and the representation of the common people is important for the assessment of the market experience hypothesis. The hypothesis demands that individuals anchor complex questions in an assessment of individual gains. In the empirical material, we have found some representations of interest groups, which might confirm this assumption. Figures such as *the working people*, *the consumer* or *the taxpayer* might be the expression of participants' material interests. The representation of the little people, however, would provide a competing explanation. Rather than resulting from anchoring in material interests, these representations can be understood as moral categories. In this understanding, *the working people*, for example, are a positive reference point because they do honest work (in opposition to the elites who are dishonest and in opposition to the unemployed who do not work). In the understanding of the market experience hypothesis, on the contrary, the working people would be a positive reference point because they represent an interest group the participants are part of. In the latter case, their fate matters because it represents the participants' material gains, in the former it matters because it is morally right.

In the empirical material, there is significant evidence that the representations of actors are moral categories rather than an expression of self-interest. The representations of actors are often normatively ambiguous; the assessment of their actions depends on whether they behave in a morally acceptable way. This seems to support the idea that the representations of interest groups are not solely based on material interest. If only material gains would matter, we would expect participants to promote gains for these interest groups regardless of the effect of their actions. An ideal-typical homo economicus would defend his interest without reference to ulterior moral criteria. In the next sections, I will go through the relevant representations of actors, explaining how the market experience hypothesis would explain the appearance of these representations and then arguing that the representation is more likely an expression of the discourse of the common people. This can be done for the product market (*the consumer*), the labor market (*the working people*) and for state–market relationships (*the taxpayer*). The role of capital market (*the investor*) is negligible.

4.2.1 The Investor

The focus group discussions were centered on two topics: trade and unemployment. In the hypotheses section (Chapter 1, Section 1.1.4), I have sketched the way both trade and unemployment discussions could be anchored in material self-interest. Concerning trade, it has been argued that participants should identify with the affected factors of production. The Heckscher–Ohlin model is designed to predict the outcomes for two factors of production: capital and labor. Accordingly, participants should identify either as labor or as capital holders. The effect on the respective factor then could be interpreted as the effect on their personal situation. Indeed, we see such an identification on both the labor and capital market, albeit to a varying extent.

On the capital market, the representation of *the investor* is rather weak. An identification with investors only happens briefly in two German groups when discussing the ECB's low interest rates (for empirical examples, see Chapter 2). Additionally, in two Polish groups the housing market is cited as an example of personal investments. Overall, however, the participants do not view themselves as capital holders all too frequently, and rising or falling returns to capital are almost never considered a relevant normative reference point. The representations of the capital market thus do not provide evidence sufficient to support the market experience hypothesis.

4.2.2 The Working People

Identification with the relevant factor of production is more frequent on the labor market. The representation of *the working people* is strongly based on a generalization of economic situations, for example, of the experiences of working hard, feeding a family, and paying bills (Appendix 1, Section A1.4.4). At the same time, representations of the working people are often based on a distinction from an elite managerial class and they often draw on the experience of the bad working conditions in big firms.

> FSUM1: "Today, in Carrefour, the employees get a share of the profits amounting to 50 euros for this year. Back in the days they got the equivalent of a car, around 10,000 euros. 10,000 euros back then, 50 euros today. Just because a law was passed by the president and by the national assembly which unfortunately today … Bah here you go, 50 bucks and you shut up and you're quiet. And the bosses get billions. It's the stock market bosses of the CAC40."
>
> – French soccer players discussing 'merit'

> GSUM1: "In normal enterprises it is like this: If the boss is well, I am well. [GSUM4: Yes exactly]. Ok. And you saw really well in the big firms, they make two billions of profit, they are doing well, and they fire you anyway. And that's where the scissors are spreading, and you lose faith that the people in theory think of … They just think about themselves. The upper levels are earning a lot, the lower level a bit less but the bottom level – 'ha, we can do without it! We'll find new ones!'"
>
> – German soccer players discussing 'entrepreneurship'

Both quotes exhibit striking similarities. Both center around the wages paid in big firms. Both, moreover, contain explicit references to a management elite ("the stock market bosses" and "the upper levels"). Finally, both contain a negative vision of profits, which are unfairly distributed while being obscenely high (amounting to "billions" in both cases). Firms' profits only benefit a small and coherent management elite (note how GSUM1 lets the managers refer to themselves as "we"). The normal employees in Carrefour or "the bottom level" do not receive a share of the firms' economic success. The working people thus constitute the normative reference point – their losses are being decried. This moral dimension of the representation of the normal people is highlighted by mobilizing the negatively connotated representations of *the manager* and *big firms* (see Appendix 1, Sections A1.3.3 and A1.3.4 for detail). Apart from this upward distinction, the working people can also be defined in opposition to groups who stand below them in the social hierarchy. Importantly, the working people are honest and willing to work and thus need to be distinguished from those unwilling to contribute.

> GSUM4: "I rather mean this style of thought of classical employees, this extreme employee mentality. Right? 'Employers are always shit'. [GSUM1: Yes] It is such a general attitude that people complain about their employer and they forget that they are being paid by him and that this can only function if you perform. […] 'Ugh, my boss is stupid' [laughs]."
>
> – German soccer players discussing 'entrepreneurship'

> GLUM1: [reads out card] " 'Advance citizens' entrepreneurial spirit' – well so they don't just subordinate themselves. [change of voice: whiny] 'Well I applied here and there. Oh no, nobody wants me'. So they think themselves: 'Ok, I want to work. There is something I am good at, something I can do. I want to work, I want to make money.' "
>
> – German teachers discussing 'entrepreneurship'

In the quotes, a social representation of *the classical employee* is advanced. This classical employee is distinguished, on the one hand, from *the entrepreneur*, and on the other hand from *the working people* (see also Appendix 1, Sections A1.4.1 and A1.4.4). The entrepreneur is a poster-child of economic behavior, being driven to excellent economic performance by her inspiration and passion for her job. The working people are not motivated by inspiration, but rather by the wages they need to earn. But they still work hard to earn these wages, driven by their need to pay their bills and feed their families. The classical employee does not share the experience of hard work. She is depicted as whiny, reliant on social security and quick to give up. The classical employee is an immoral person, free riding on the shoulders of others. Again, it becomes clear that the representation of the working people has a strong moral dimension. A willingness to contribute is required in order to be accepted as normal. In turn, this means that the representation of the working people is not simply an extension of personal interest. Rather than simply promoting the interests of employees (which would be rational as almost all participants are employees themselves), participants' support for the working people is conditional on their willingness to work hard and to contribute.

The fact that a willingness to contribute and work hard lies at the core of the representation of the normal people means that this representation can be extended to other areas. The working people, for example, can occasionally be unemployed, as long as they apply their work ethic to their job search or if the reasons for their unemployment are viewed as systemic rather than individual (see representation of *the precarious*, Appendix 1, Section A1.4.5). More importantly in this context, however, the working people – driven by a legitimate desire for higher wages – can also migrate. When discussing the effects of migration, then, the focus group participants are often very sympathetic to the concerns and well-being of economic migrants. In the context of the trade discussions, for example, the representation of *migration as a race to the bottom* emerges. In this representation, working people move abroad for a higher salary in the destination country (see Appendix 1, Section A1.4.9). This representation shows how the economic situation of the working people in different countries can be imagined in order to judge economic processes. In particular, French groups use this representation of *migration as a race to the bottom* to decry low wages resulting from labor mobility. Polish groups, on the other hand, frequently stress the wage gains associated with working in a Western country or firm. The representation of *migration as a personal prospect* is, as the name indicates, based on personal experience (see Appendix 1, Section A1.4.10). The representation is most frequently mobilized to weigh the material gains of migration (mostly wage rises) against personal costs (mostly leaving behind family and doing more unqualified labor). As predicted by the market experience hypothesis, then, participants seem to identify with the factor of production they belong to, and they seem to mobilize these group interests in order to assess trade deals.

Yet, the representation of *migration as a personal prospect* is also not exclusively based on material considerations. While the expectation of higher wages plays a prominent part in this representation, there are strong moral components, too. Participants use their personal prospects of migration to raise non-economic concerns, for example, about the dignity of labor. Experiences of material gains from migration are intimately connected to questions of justice. I will discuss this representation of the labor market in greater detail later in this chapter when assessing the anchoring of trigger arguments. Let us maintain for now though that representations of migration do not seem to be simple extensions of self-interest. On the labor market, more generally, representations of actors have a strong moral dimension rather than being the expressions of the amoral calculations of a homo economicus.

4.2.3 The Consumer

On the product market, the actor most likely to be the result of the generalization of material self-interest is *the consumer* (see Appendix 1, Section A1.2.1). Both in political as well as scientific discourse, consumers are expected to approve of trade if they profit from lower prices (e.g., Baker, 2005, pp. 925–926; European Parliament, 2017). This assumption seems to be confirmed by the focus group material as the consumer is represented as an actor primarily driven by a consideration for price. The representation of the consumer, moreover, is frequently underpinned by personal experiences (e.g., shopping and other consumption decisions).

> FSUM1: "That is to say if a box of chocolate was only two euros, we would eat it every day. If the baguette was only ten cents and not a euro like today, you would eat it everyday day. If the beef steak was at three euros, I would eat meat every day. Do you see what I mean? If you do that you re-launch consumption."
>
> – French soccer players discussing 'non-wage labor costs'

> PLTW2: "In Lidl you now have these little chocolates with peanut butter, right? [PLTW1: Yeah, I know, I know!] Re … Ree …"
>
> DA: "Reese's."
>
> PLTW2: "Yes."
>
> PLTW1: "They are delicious."
>
> PLTW2: "But for those, for those … One of these little chocolates costs five złoty. That's half of our hourly wage. You have to work half an hour for such a little waffle."
>
> – Polish teachers discussing 'variety'

Both quotes clearly show that the decision to consume is driven by a consideration for the price of goods. In both cases, moreover, the participants seem to identify with a vision of a poor consumer for whom lower prices would help to improve her standard of living. The benefits attributed to the generalized figure of the consumer, then, might in fact mirror the individual cost–benefit calculations of the participants. For the product market, participants might have anchored their representations in their interest in low prices, as the market experience hypothesis would predict.

Yet, the degree of legitimacy assigned to consumption behavior is contested. While some participants (as in the quotes above) clearly see lower prices and increased potential for consumption as their personal interest, most participants seem to have reservations about the act of consumption. The consumer is not viewed as a positive figure per se; rather, other normative considerations come into play when consumption behavior is judged. The following quotes, for example, show how the social ordering of sectors is mobilized in order to determine whether consumption behavior is legitimate:

> GLTM1: "So particularly with things that are coming from nature prices can't get any lower [GLTW3: Yes]. I can understand everybody who doesn't have money and who buys the cheapest stuff, but I feel obliged ... Let's say with our income you can afford ecological products which are only ten cents more."
>
> – German teachers discussing 'prices'

> FSTM3: "We go to Carrefour, we try at least to pay attention to quality [FSTM6: Yes]. You take European brands, you pay attention. Of course the people try to consume French stuff, but those are the people that have the means. The people that buy ecological goods are those who have the means."
>
> – French soccer players discussing 'standards'

> FSTW1: "Brand image, for example. Take apple which buys their raw materials super cheap but sells phones for 1000+. It's all in the minds of consumers. If you start selling foie gras for two euros today, who can be sure it will be bought? The people know quality. They might think that it's not good. [...] It's like that. The consumer is an idiot."
>
> – French soccer players discussing 'non-wage labor costs'

The consumer thus emerges as a moral category whose actions are assessed with regard to ulterior criteria (e.g., her personal financial resources or the sector of the economy from which she is buying). The consumer is not solely a representation of participants' desire to profit from lower prices, but she also becomes the object of criticism if she buys stupid consumerist items or if she is ignorant of the impact low prices have on production conditions. Low income goes some way in excusing a desire for cheaper products, but the overall representation of the consumer stresses a responsibility to buy the right products (based on the representations of different *sectors of the economy*; see Appendix 1, Sections A1.1.3 and A1.1.4). The representation of the consumer thus oscillates between a rational citizen looking for deals and a consumerist imbecile, manipulated by marketing and causing harm in other parts of the world. In any case, the consumer is clearly not a simple extension of individual material interest. An interest in low prices is only viewed as legitimate under certain conditions. The consumer thus appears as a moral category in the quotes, as a normal person distinguished from consumerist "idiots" who only pay attention to prices. The normal "people try to consume French stuff" (i.e., they pay attention to standards) if they have the means for it. The consumer thus is an ideal typical case of a representation that could be based on the generalization of individual interest, but which more probably is derived from the moral category of the common people.

4.2.4 The Taxpayer

In parallel to these self-interested calculations of the effects of trade on the product and on the labor market, the market experience hypothesis also predicts attitudes toward unemployment to be a function of material self-interest. More specifically, participants are expected to view unemployment benefits as a form of insurance paid for by tax money. Accordingly, taxes and other contributions should be viewed as a form of investment, an advance payment for future services. While no such claims were made on an individual level, the focus group discussions nevertheless featured a social representation that came close to such an understanding of taxes as investments. The representation of *the taxpayer* was prominent in particular in the unemployment discussions (see Appendix 1, Section A1.5.1). Like the other representations of interest groups in this section, representations of the taxpayer are frequently anchored in personal experience. Complaints about high tax rates and bills recently paid were commonly mobilized for its support. The taxpayer seems to be another representation of an interest group, which is based on personal experiences.

Yet also the representation of *the taxpayer* does not seem to be exclusively based on self-interest. Rather, the taxpayer is constructed as a moral counterpart to economic and state elites. To begin with, the taxpayer is not necessarily mobilized to call for a lowering of taxes. Paying taxes is viewed as a moral obligation and those who escape this obligation (e.g., *big firms* and *the manager*) are depicted as immoral actors (see Appendix 1, Sections A1.3.3 and A1.3.4). Furthermore, the taxpayer mainly appears when state expenditure is discussed (that is, mainly in the context of the representations of the *state as an investor* or as a *re-distributor*). The representation of the taxpayer is used to address the destination rather than the amount of state spending (see Appendix 1, Sections, A1.5.1–A1.5.3). Again, the taxpayer does not necessarily require a lowering of taxes but demands her money to be spent prudently. The representation of the taxpayer thus serves to question the spending decisions of state elites. The representation of the taxpayer also seems to be anchored in a notion of the common people, rather than in a concern for personal financial gains.

In conclusion, then, it seems that the representations of actors in the empirical material could result from anchoring in both – material self-interest or a moral discourse of the common people. While I believe the evidence strongly suggests the latter, I acknowledge that the empirical material provides valid arguments for both interpretations. Participants might anchor questions of trade policy in their material interest and they might express these interests by attributing them to larger groups such as consumers or the working people. Similarly, participants might assess questions of unemployment mainly by assessing the costs they bear as taxpayers. Yet, these representations could just as well be the result of a self-identification as the morally superior common people.[3] Ultimately deciding which anchoring mechanism was at work is tricky based on the empirical material available – self-interest is simply too elusive a concept and it could be argued to be buried somewhere in most of these representations. Borrowing an expression from statistics, the representations of actors are 'overdetermined' in the sense that they could have possibly been produced through anchoring in different domains (see left two columns in Table 4.1 at the end of Section 4.3.3).

What does this mean for market experience hypothesis? Do the focus group participants argue like homines economici who anchor complex arguments in their personal economic situation? While I doubt that we can explain the representations of actors discussed above by reference to material interest alone, the first element of the market experience hypothesis is not falsified. It remains a viable possibility that the focus group participants are primarily driven by material interests when judging complex economic phenomena. My criticism of the market experience hypothesis, therefore, will focus on its second element: the inference from personal experience to economic processes. While self-interest might motivate participants' arguments, it certainly does not guarantee a uniform understanding of economic causalities (let alone a correct inference to the explanations provided by economic theory). Even if participants see representations such as the consumer or the working people as an extension of their personal interests, they still perceive the impact of economic policies on these interest groups differently. While potentially united by similar interests and experiences, participants generate very different representations of the trigger arguments in the focus group discussions. The market experience hypothesis does not necessarily fail due to a lack of self-interest; but it definitely fails in predicting citizens' understandings of complex economic arguments.

4.3 Representations of Arguments: The Problem of Inference

I have argued before that the market experience hypothesis predicts representations of economic processes to be uniform across social groups. Individuals are supposed to make an inference from their personal situation to macro-economic processes. This inference is to be 'correct' in the sense that it mirrors the explanation economic theories would provide for the experience. Concerning the representation of trigger topics, then, the market experience hypothesis predicts **representations to be uniform**. While subsequent judgments of these economic phenomena might vary with participants' economic interests, the representations of the economic causalities producing the phenomena should be reasonably similar. Assessments of outcomes might differ depending on an individual's economic position, but representations of the processes producing these outcomes should be uniform across the various interest groups.

In the hypotheses section, I have identified three examples of macroeconomic causalities of which citizens should have relatively uniform representations. First, citizens are supposed to infer the effect of free trade from the development of product prices. Second, citizens are supposed to grasp the effect of migration on wage levels in their country. Finally, citizens should be able to assess macro-economic risks to calculate the expected utility from unemployment benefits. For the focus group discussions, then, the market experience hypothesis predicts participants to produce similar representations where the respective issues are triggered.

In the following section, I test if participants indeed develop similar representations of the macro-economic causalities covered by the market experience hypothesis. I will focus on three trigger topics in particular: 'prices', 'mobility' and 'entrepreneurship'. I argue that for each of these trigger topics we find a variety of different representations, although the market experience hypothesis would predict a uniformity of visions. In particular, where personal experiences are mobilized, representations differ greatly from the explanations of economic theory. This is what I call the **problem of inference**: there is no functioning inference mechanism from market experiences to economic theory. The market experience hypothesis is therefore falsified.

4.3.1 The Product Market: Diverse Representations of the Price Mechanism

The first representation of economic causalities participants are supposed to share concerns the effect of free trade on product prices. According to some applications of the Heckscher–Ohlin model, citizens are in favor of trade deals if these agreements cause product prices to fall (e.g., Baker, 2005, pp. 925–926). The Heckscher–Ohlin model predicts that trade liberalization will lower overall product prices due to a more efficient allocation of factors of production. The rational consumer thus would see her material interest advanced if she had to spend less on shopping, so the argument. We have seen in the previous section that a representation of the consumer is mobilized in the focus groups and that this representation is potentially an expression of participants' self-interest. Now the question is whether participants do also perceive the causal link between free trade deals, greater efficiency in the allocation of factors of production and lower prices.

Representations of this causal mechanism should have been triggered by the trigger topic 'prices'. Participants were asked the question "What should a good free trade deal achieve?" and were handed a card reading "lower prices for consumers" as a potential answer. According to the market experience hypothesis, we would expect participants to make an inference from their consumption experiences and to notice that prices of goods fell after the conclusion of free trade deals. As a reason for this lowering of prices, we would expect them to cite a more efficient allocation of resources resulting from factor and product mobility. Indeed, there seems to be a representation of the price mechanism that comes reasonably close to this vision: *price (efficiency)* (see Appendix 1, Section A1.2.2). In this representation, participants pointed at specialization and a more efficient division of labor as the main reason for lower prices. In its focus on the efficiency of the free market, this representation could be taken mirror the causal process described in the Heckscher–Ohlin model.

Does this representation of the price mechanism confirm the market experience hypothesis then? I do not think so for two reasons. First, the representation *price (efficiency)* is not anchored in experiences. Rather, it is often advanced using specific jargon from economic theory, thus suggesting that it results from anchoring in pre-existing theoretical knowledge. Rather than inferring the theory from experience, participants seemed to know about the theory beforehand. Second, and more importantly, *price (efficiency)* was neither the only nor the most frequent representation of the price mechanism. It was only mobilized six times in all focus group discussions. Competing representations of the price mechanism, for example, *price (quality)* with a frequency of 16 or *price (factors of production)* with a frequency of 22, were much more common (see Appendix 1, Sections A1.2.3 and A1.2.4). Both these latter representations describe the price mechanism in a way that would not allow to draw the conclusions foreseen by the Heckscher–Ohlin model. If lower prices are viewed as the result of lower quality, for example, consumers would face a trade-off (a zero-sum game) rather than certain material gains. Hence, it would not be obvious why consumers should be enthusiastic about trade deals. *Price (quality)*, moreover, is a representation that is firmly anchored in market experiences. Participants make explicit references to consumption situations when developing this representation, thus indicating that an inference from their personal experience to a larger economic process was made. Yet, this inference from market experience does not produce the representations expected by the market experience hypothesis. Consumption experiences did not suggest efficiency gains but a price–quality trade-off.

As I will make a similar argument for the other representations discussed in this section, let me dwell on this in some more detail. Let's have a look at two citations starting from the trigger topic prices and ending up producing a representation of prices as quality.

DA: "Another card read "a lower price level". Is that something everyone can agree on?"

FLTW1: "It depends on whether the norms are respected. If products are cheaper, if we will attract more cheap products which are not necessarily French and which are based on lower norms than ours … […]"

FLTW3: "Yeah, I have the impression that people nowadays start to appreciate products of higher quality instead of idiotic gadgets." [support from group]

– French teachers discussing 'prices'

GATW1: "But it's all subsidized anyway, the whole agriculture. [GATM2: Yes, yes!] But that's it. That's why there is a problem if you now start importing all the milk from Poland … What happens with the subsidized stuff?"

GATMM2: "There we go. What kind of milk is arriving there? Is that milk complying with our standards? Or is it just: let's cover milk supply, check. But maybe it's dirty stuff."

– German agents discussing 'prices'

Both quotes provide examples of how participants explain the development of product prices after the conclusion of a free trade deal. In both cases, consumption experiences are mobilized as an anchoring domain. While the first quote seems to address consumption decisions regarding products in general,[4] the second quote explicitly refers to food (milk). Yet, the prospect of lower consumption prices in these domains does not produce an inference to the increased efficiency of markets after free trade (as the market experience hypothesis would have it). Rather, lower prices are explained by lower product quality. Mobilizing elements of the economic world map, non-French or Polish standards are perceived as lower, thus engendering simultaneously lower prices and lower product quality. We can conclude, then, that anchoring in consumption experiences does not always produce representations such as *price (efficiency)*, but that it can result in various representations of the price mechanism, including *price (quality)*. Low prices do not necessarily cause enthusiasm about free trade, but more frequently entail skepticism regarding product quality. Representations of the trigger topic 'prices' thus were not uniform but diverse. Moreover, where market experiences were used as an anchoring domain, the resulting representations did not necessarily correspond to the predictions of the Heckscher–Ohlin model. Representations of the product market do not provide evidence for the inference mechanism foreseen by the market experience hypothesis.

4.3.2 The International Labor Market: Diverse Representations of Migration

Is the market experience hypothesis more successful regarding the other causalities it expected to observe? The second causal mechanism citizens are supposed to infer from their personal economic situation is the effect of factor mobility on wages. The Heckscher–Ohlin model predicts an equalization of factor prices after liberalization, with abundant factors gaining profitability. Accordingly, capital owners in capital-abundant countries profit because they can move their capital abroad to profit from higher interest rates. Similarly, workers from low-wage countries can move to high-wage countries to profit from higher wages. This inflow of new workers will increase labor supply in high-wage countries and thus lower wages. Workers in high-wage countries, therefore, should oppose liberalization out of fear for lower wages, while workers in low-wage countries should embrace it. These judgments imply that capital owners and workers entertain the same representation of the causal process at work (their representations are uniform). In both cases, a representation of factor–price equalization as the result of factor mobility is required. It is the existence of this shared representation that needs to be investigated. We have seen in the previous section that participants indeed employ a representation of the working people, which might be an expression of their material interest in high wages.[5] Now we need to investigate whether participants perceive the effect of labor mobility on wages to be as the Heckscher–Ohlin model predicted.

In order to assess participants' understanding of the effect of factor mobility on wages, let us have a look at the representations formed in response to the trigger argument 'mobility'. The Heckscher–Ohlin model predicts attitudes toward labor mobility to vary with location, implying that citizens in low-wage countries should be enthusiastic about future pay rises while citizens in high-wage countries should fear an undercutting of their wages. In the focus group discussions, then, we would expect French and German groups to be somewhat more skeptical than Polish groups about the trigger argument 'mobility'. At the same time, all groups should perceive the same causal mechanism at work, that is, the equalization of factor prices through liberalization. According to the market experience hypothesis, the knowledge of factor–price equalization should result from inference from personal experiences, for example, from the development of wages.

These predictions of the market experience hypothesis, however, are not confirmed for the same reasons we already saw for the trigger topic 'prices'. First, there is a multitude of representations of migration, rather than a single causal mechanism identified by all participants. In the German groups, for example, the most frequent representation is that of *migration as talent* (see Appendix 1, Section A1.4.8). This representation of migration focuses on a causal process which is absent in the Heckscher–Ohlin model: the inflow of human capital into the national economy. Due to this difference in the representation of the macro-economic causality, the German participants (mostly employees in a high wage country) end up arguing largely in favor of migration – a result contrary to the expectations generated by the market experience hypothesis. Rather than anchoring the argument in the needs of the national economy, the market experience hypothesis would have expected German employees to perceive a lowering of the wage level as the effect of labor mobility. While such representations occasionally appear (see discussion of *migration as race to the bottom* in next paragraph), they are only one representation of migration among many others. Representations of migration were diverse rather than uniform.

Second, no inference from market experience to economic theory can be observed. The representation that comes closest to the causality of the Heckscher–Ohlin model is that of *migration as a race to the bottom* (see Appendix 1, Section A1.4.9). This representation is most common among French participants, thus potentially confirming that employees in high-wage countries might fear lower wages resulting from labor mobility. Yet, it is questionable whether this representation is based on market experiences. The French groups mobilize very specific national vocabulary, which has been politically loaded in public debates over the past years (e.g., *travailleur détaché, délocalisation, concurrence déloyale*). Rather than in market experiences, the representation of *migration as a race to the bottom* seems to be anchored in national knowledge (see Chapter 2).

Personal experiences with regard to migration are almost exclusively mobilized by the Polish participants. Yet, representations of *migration as a personal prospect* result in very ambiguous assessments of migration dynamics, rather than in straightforward enthusiasm as the market experience hypothesis would predict.[6] While Polish participants appreciate the higher wages they might gain abroad, they are also aware of the personal costs of migration (e.g., performing less-skilled labor or abandoning their friends and family). Arguably, on average the Polish participants' visions of migration tend to be the most negative, sometimes cumulating in a representation of migration as a pointless replacement.

> PLUW4: "[reads out card] 'Encourage international mobility of workers'. We were always mobile. Where aren't we? Where are there no Poles abroad?
>
> PLUW3: "Generally they are at the dishwashers. [laughs] [PLUW2 & PLUW3: Exactly!]"
>
> PLUW2: "There is a problem with that. I chose the same card, only before. I think it should be like that that we are able to move. But I want to work according to my qualifications! But if I go to Germany and – excuse me – what will I be there? I will take care of old people [PLUW3: Yes; PLUW4: Nothing else]. […] Actually, I could only change pampers."
>
> – Polish teachers discussing 'mobility'

> PAUW1: "Ok. I chose 'Encourage international mobility of workers'. And I dislike it because I think that everybody would leave. [PAUW2: Yes] My colleagues in the housing sector left and they were replaced by Ukrainians [PAUW2: Yes]. It is such a … This one guy left for Norway, and now he comes back to Poland every two months and he has three children. Well, that's just … [makes a suffering sound]. And he was replaced by Ukrainians and in Ukraine the situation is exactly the same as here. They have kids and family there but have to sit here and work. The problem just carries on ..."
>
> – Polish agents discussing 'mobility'

In the quotes, we see what happens when Polish participants anchor the trigger topic 'mobility' in their personal experiences. Both quotes are based on personal experiences of the participants themselves or of their friends and family. Contrary to the expectations of the market experience hypothesis, the personal prospect of migration does not trigger enthusiasm for international mobility. The prospect of higher wages is acknowledged, but it is heavily outweighed by the personal costs and indignities associated with working below qualification in a different country (most strongly expressed by the pampers and dishwasher metaphors in the second quote). While these Polish participants clearly seem to make a realistic cost–benefit calculation, high wages are clearly not the most important factor for assessing migration. Personal experiences of labor mobility thus do not guarantee an inference to the causal mechanism described by the Heckscher–Ohlin model. Like representations of the price mechanism, representations of migration vary with the anchoring domain mobilized in their creation. Participants in the focus groups do not share a uniform vision of the effect of migration on wages, as the market experience hypothesis would have it.

4.3.3 The Domestic Labor Market: Diverse Representations of Social Security Payments

The last economic mechanism described by the market experience hypothesis concerns unemployment rather than factor mobility. The market experience hypothesis predicts participants to make a self-interested calculation with regard to unemployment benefits. In this vision, taxes are viewed as an investment paying for unemployment insurance and the risk of being unemployment determines the expected utility from this investment. We have already seen in the previous section that participants construct a representation of *the taxpayer*, which is mainly mobilized to judge destinations of state expenditure. It could be argued that this representation of the taxpayer reveals an understanding of taxes as a payment for expected social services. What would be missing to complete the self-interested calculation predicted by the market experience hypothesis, then, is an assessment of the risk of being unemployed. For the unemployment discussions, macro-economic risk is the causal mechanism participants are supposed to infer from their job experiences, just like factor–price equalization was the mechanism to identified for factor mobility in the trade discussions.

Is there a uniform representation of economic processes at least for the issue of unemployment then? Arguably, participants do not identify macro-economic risks as the reason for unemployment. The overall state of the economy is rarely cited as an explanation for joblessness. Rather, participants rely on an individualized explanation. Not macro-economic risk, but individual behavior is identified as the main reason for being unemployed. This explanation is particularly well visible for a trigger topic such as 'entrepreneurship'. In unemployment discussions, participants were asked the question 'How can unemployment be lowered?' and confronted with the trigger argument 'advance citizens' entrepreneurial spirit'. In response to this trigger argument, participants frequently mobilized representations such as *the entrepreneur* and *the classical employee*. I have already discussed these representations above when pointing out the moral undertones of the representation of the working people (Section 4.2.2). Yet, these representations are also mobilized to explain unemployment: someone with an employee mentality (i.e., lacking motivation and not taking initiative) obviously struggles to find work. The resulting representation of *the unemployed as lazy* shows well that unemployment is represented mainly as a moral problem. Unemployment benefits are judged based on a notion of deservingness rather than based on a self-interested calculation (see also van Oorschot, 2010). Again, then, the market experience hypothesis fails to predict how participants understand economic causalities as it is the individual attitude of the unemployed and not macroeconomic risk that determines the success of a job search. This failure of the market experience hypothesis is further highlighted by the fact that representations of the classical employee and the unemployed as lazy are based on experiences of the participants themselves in the job world. Workplace inferences to the causes of unemployment thus produce representations of mentality and not of economic risk. The market experience hypothesis also fails with regard unemployment.

We can conclude, then, that lay representations of economic processes are by no means uniform and they certainly do not always correspond to the predictions of the relevant economic theories (shown in the two columns on the right in Table 4.1). The market experience hypotheses expected all participants to infer the same economic causalities from their economic experiences. Yet, as we have seen for the trigger topics ‘prices’, ‘mobility’ and ‘entrepreneurship’, no such inference to economic theory happens. Instead of *uniform* representations of factor–price equalization or of economic risk, participants entertained a **variety of different representations** depending on the anchoring domain mobilized. Moreover, where market experiences were mobilized as an anchoring domain, the resulting representations of economic processes did not correspond to economic theory. There does not seem to be a functioning inference mechanism from experience to economic theory.

4.4 Conclusion

In this chapter, I have shown that the complexity problem in the European public sphere is to be taken seriously. I have tested the market experience hypothesis and argued that it fails for two reasons. First, it seems unlikely that representations of economic actors are simply generalizations of personal interest. Rather than conveying a vision of the homo economicus, the actor representations seemed to be based on a **discourse of the common people**. While some form of self-interest might still be underlying these representations, the common-people explanation seems much more plausible, given the strong moral connotations of these representations and their construction in opposition to elite social groups. Second, representations of causal processes in the economy are **diverse and not uniform**. Accordingly, lay representations differ widely from the expectations of experts. This is particularly true where economic issues are anchored in personal experiences: rather than allowing for an inference to economic theory, market experiences serve to underpin

Table 4.1 Falsification of market experience hypothesis

	Social Group		**Representation of trigger topics**	
	Understood as *generalization of interest* (expected by hypothesis)	**Understood as derivative of *'common people'* (contradicting hypothesis)**	***Uniform* representations (expected by hypothesis)**	***Diversity of representations* actually present (contradicting hypothesis)**
Product market	• Consumers seeking low prices	• *Consumer* as moral agents • Caring about standards • Distinguished from "consumerist idiots"	• *Price (efficiency)*	• *Price (quality)* [experience based] • *Price (factors of production)*
Labor market (domestic)	• Taxpayers seeing taxes as investments/ insurance	• *Taxpayer* as moral agent • Caring about taxes being spent prudently • Distinguished from *big firms* and *manager*	• Representations of macroeconomic risk (absent)	• Representations of individual responsibility (e.g., *the entrepreneur*)
Labor market (inter-national)	• Working people seeking high wages	• *Working people* as moral category • "Willing to contribute" • Distinguished from *classical employee* and *the lazy unemployed*	• Representations of factor-price equalization (e.g., *migration as race to the bottom*)	• *Migration (personal prospect)* [experience based] • *Migration (talent)*

a negative vision of the market, feeding into the discourse of the common people cheated by an economic elite. This latter argument is crucial for the falsification of the market experience hypothesis. While the influence of self-interest as a basis for judgment is difficult to ultimately disprove, I can show that citizens' representations simply do not align with the predictions of the market experience hypothesis.

My criticism of the market experience hypothesis thus is mainly focused on its assumptions of the knowledge citizens hold. Representations of economic processes are diverse and mostly do not correspond to economic theory (for examples of studies assuming citizens to hold near perfect information about economic causalities see Brinegar & Jolly, 2005; Ehrlich, 2010; Fraile & Ferrer, 2005; O'Rourke et al., 2001; Rehm, 2011, 2016). The diversity of representations implies that an insistence on a rational-choice or self-interest-based model of public opinion becomes a somewhat empty proposition. Without knowing the causality on which the self-interested calculation is based, knowing that people behave like a homo economicus does us little good. If we want to salvage the market experience hypothesis, it needs to be amended by an understanding of lay representations of the economy. We need to know which sources of knowledge people employ to anchor economic causalities to understand how their cost–benefit calculations will play out. Without such a close analysis of the anchoring domains citizens employ, researchers run the danger of simply imputing their own assumptions into the minds of everybody else. The market experience hypothesis fails because it is exactly based on such an imputation of economic expert knowledge into the minds of ordinary citizens.

What is the external the external validity of these findings, given that my study is based on a sample of 64? I would argue that my findings are likely to be **generalizable beyond the sample** for two reasons. First, the results are extremely univocal. There is literally not a single case in which an inference from personal experience leads a participant to perceive economic processes as prescribed by economic theory. Those citizens who see economic processes as predicted by the market experience hypothesis do so only as the result of education (see Chapter 5) or because national politicization might have popularized specific representations (see Chapter 2). But even these exceptions are rare. Even participants with economic training were not forming representations of macro-economic risk, for example. And national politicization only created the representations needed by the market experience hypothesis in one out of three countries, causing only participants in France to sometimes reason according to the hypothesis while it failed entirely for Poland and Germany. If the market experience hypothesis works for some individuals, this is only because they have access to specific anchoring domains. The social groups with access to these anchoring domains, second, are over-represented in the sample. Around 16% of my participants had access to economic training and most of them were selected to have privileged access to national anchoring domains. In reality, therefore, it is likely that the market experience hypothesis will hold in far less cases than it did in my sample.

The larger takeaway from this chapter, therefore, is that **studying social representations is a prerequisite to studying public opinion**. This diagnosis is in alignment with a growing body of sociologists who highlight the importance of the subjective dimension of knowledge for the study of public opinion (e.g., Mau, 2005). With regard to the economy, we need to stop focusing on objective knowledge to determine popular assessments and rather turn to understand the idiosyncrasies of the popular imagination. It will be subjective representations more than scientific realities that will help us understand why some economic slogans, projects and arguments actually resonate with the citizenry. It has been argued, for example, that these "folk economics" have been crucial to the success of Donald Trump (Swedberg, 2018). Arguably, it will also be subjective perceptions of the single market that determine attitudes toward European integration, rather than the elaborate economic models of political economists that determine objective winners and losers (Alt et al., 2020; see also chapter 7). As I will argue in the conclusion of this book, this finding is applicable beyond economics, too. Generally speaking, we need to know how someone understands a phenomenon before we ask her opinion about it. Citizens' understanding of complex questions depends on the pre-existing stocks of knowledge (the anchoring domains) they have access to. Without a close analysis of these anchoring domains and of the representations they engender, we should refrain from making generalizations about public opinion on complex issues.

Given this disjuncture between citizens' perceptions and expert knowledge, it should thus be accepted that the European public sphere faces a complexity problem. To what extent this complexity problem prevents the European public from fulfilling its democratic role will be the question of the subsequent chapter. While this chapter has dealt with the assumption that citizens hold near perfect information of economic causalities, the next chapter will assess the opposite assumption, namely that citizens are uninformed and do not sufficiently understand economic processes to meaningfully debate them in a public sphere.

Notes

1 Frequency 5; exports (PLT), non-wage labor costs (PSU), investment (GAT, PLT, PST); for ironic undertone: 2; expenditure (GLU), interest (FLU).

2 Expenditure (GLU), Inflation (FLU), Merit (GAU, GSU, PAU, PLU), variety (PLT).

3 It is interesting to observe that representations of the 'common people' are found in most of the focus groups, relatively independent of the social status of participants. That is why I speak of the 'common' or 'normal people' rather than of the 'little people' as previous studies have done (e.g., J. White, 2011). Finding representation which pitch normal people against elites among middle class citizens (e.g., teachers)

is an interesting result. It could be taken to imply that discourses appealing to the common people might resonate with a wide range of social strata. I will discuss further implications of this finding in Chapter 7.

4 The opposition of "products of higher quality" to "idiotic gadgets" seems to suggest a mobilization of the social sector ordering (see Appendix 1, Section A1.1.4). Idiotic gadgets being a prime example of consumerist objects, the products of high quality referred to might well be food.

5 The representation of *the investor* is extremely infrequent and effects of capital mobility on interest rates are barely discussed in the focus groups. The analysis therefore only focuses on labor as a factor of production and disregards capital.

6 The Polish representations of migration are the only representations in the material based on specifically national economic experiences. In Poland, 12% of the population have the experience of working abroad (among 25- to 34-year-olds, the number even raises to 27%; A. White, 2018, p. 2). Polish citizens thus are very likely to experience international labor mobility or to witness examples thereof in their personal surroundings. They are also prone to experience specific forms of discrimination and injustice to which Western Europeans are not subject (Favell, 2009, pp. 178–183). This explains why representations of migration are more personal, ambivalent, and complex in the Polish groups.

Bibliography

Ackerman, B. A. (2019). *Revolutionary Constitutions: Charismatic Leadership and the Rule of Law*. The Belknap Press of Harvard University Press.

Alt, D., Brandes, E. & Nonhoff, D. (2020). Can the European Parliament Satisfy the People? Voter Mandates and Accountability Links in the European Elections 2019. In M. Kaeding, M. Müller, & J. Schmälter (Eds.), *Die Europawahl 2019: Ringen um die Zukunft Europas* (pp. 365–375). Springer Fachmedien. https://doi.org/10.1007/978-3-658-29277-5_30

Baker, A. (2005). Who Wants to Globalize? Consumer Tastes and Labor Markets in a Theory of Trade Policy Beliefs. *American Journal of Political Science*, *49*(4), 924–938. https://doi.org/10.1111/j.1540-5907.2005.00164.x

Boltanski, L. & Thévenot, L. (1991). *De la Justification: Économies de la Grandeur*. Gallimard.

Brinegar, A. P. & Jolly, S. K. (2005). Location, Location, Location: National Contextual Factors and Public Support for European Integration. *European Union Politics*, *6*(2), 155–180. https://doi.org/10.1177/1465116505051981

Ehrlich, S. D. (2010). Who Supports Compensation? Individual Preferences for Trade-Related Unemployment Insurance. *Business and Politics*, *12*(1), 1–22. https://doi.org/10.2202/1469-3569.1289

European Parliament (2017). *Debates—EU-Canada Comprehensive Economic and Trade Agreement—Conclusion of the EU–Canada CETA – EU–Canada Strategic Partnership Agreement (debate)—Wednesday, 15 February* 2017. www.europarl.europa.eu/doceo/document/CRE-8-2017-02-15-ITM-004_EN.html

Favell, A. (2009). Immigration, Migration and the Free Movement of People in the Making of Europe. In J. T. Checkel & P. J. Katzenstein (Eds.), *European Identity* (pp. 167–189). Cambridge University Press.

Fraile, M., & Ferrer, M. (2005). Explaining the Determinants of Public Support for Cuts in Unemployment Benefits Spending across OECD Countries. *International Sociology*, *20*(4), 459–481. https://doi.org/10.1177/0268580905058327

Gabel, M. J. (1998). *Interests and Integration: Market Liberalization, Public Opinion, and European Union*. University of Michigan Press.

Gamson, G., and William, A. (1992). *Talking Politics*. Cambridge University Press.

Hakhverdian, A., van Elsas, E., van der Brug, W. & Kuhn, T. (2013). Euroscepticism and Education: A Longitudinal Study of 12 EU Member States, 1973–2010. *European Union Politics*, *14*(4), 522–541. https://doi.org/10.1177/1465116513489779

Halle, D. (1984). *America's Working Man: Work, Home, and Politics among Blue Collar Property Owners*. University of Chicago Press.

Henceroth, N. & Oganesyan, R. (2019). The Effect that Structural and Investment Funds Have on Voter Behaviour in European Parliamentary Elections. *JCMS: Journal of Common Market Studies*, *57*(3), 599–615. https://doi.org/10.1111/jcms.12837

Lamont, M. (2012). Toward a Comparative Sociology of Valuation and Evaluation. *Annual Review of Sociology*, *38*(1), 201–221. https://doi.org/10.1146/annurev-soc-070308-120022

Mau, S. (2005). Europe from the Bottom: Assessing Personal Gains and Losses and its Effects on EU Support. *Journal of Public Policy*, *25*(3), 289–311 https://doi.org/10.1017/S0143814X05000346

Mayda, A. M. & Rodrik, D. (2005). Why Are Some People (and Counturo More Protectionist than Others? *European Economic Review*, *49*(6), 1393–1430. https://doi.org/10.1016/j.euroecorev.2004.01.002

O'Connor, C. (2012). Using Social Representations Theory to Examine Lay Explanation of Contemporary Social Crises: The Case of Ireland's Recession. *Journal of Community & Applied Social Psychology*, *22*(6), 453–469. https://doi.org/10.1002/casp.1125

O'Rourke, K. H., Sinnott, R., Richardson, J. D. & Rodrik, D. (2001). The Determinants of Individual Trade Policy Preferences: International Survey Evidence [with Comments and Discussion]. *Brookings Trade Forum*, 157–206. JSTOR.

Rehm, P. (2011). Social Policy by Popular Demand. *World Politics*, *63*(2), 271–299. https://doi.org/10.1017/S0043887111000037

Rehm, P. (2016). *Risk Inequality and Welfare States: Social Policy Preferences, Development, and Dynamics*. Cambridge University Press.

Swedberg, R. (2018). Folk Economics and Its Role in Trump's Presidential Campaign: An Exploratory Study. *Theory and Society*, *47*(1), 1–36 https://doi.org/10.1007/s11186-018-9308-8

van Oorschot, W. (2010). Public Perceptions of the Economic, Moral, Social and Migration Consequences of the Welfare State: An Empirical Analysis of Welfare State Legitimacy. *Journal of European Social Policy*, *20*(1), 19–31 https://doi.org/10.1177/0958928709352538

White, A. (2018). How Are Countries Affected by Migration? An 'Inside-out' Approach to Change in Sending and Receiving Countries. In A. White, I. Grabowska, P. Kaczmarczyk, & K. Slany (Eds.), *The Impact of Migration on Poland: EU Mobility and Social Change* (pp. 1–10). UCL Press. https://library.oapen.org/handle/20.500.12657/28334

White, J. (2011). *Political Allegiance After European Integration*. Palgrave Macmillan. www.palgrave.com/gp/book/9780230279780

5 Informed Understandings

Economic Theory and the Deficit Model

5.1 Introduction

Citing the malfunctioning of the European public sphere as part of the EU's democratic deficit has long been a truism. It may sometimes seem that the very concept of the European public sphere has been invented mainly to be able to deny its existence or criticize its mode of functioning. Given the skeptic attitude of much of the scholarly community, it is somewhat surprising that a major argument against its functioning has rarely been explored: **the deficit model**. Usually, the deficit model is understood to capture a range of studies arguing that citizens are uniformed and incoherent in their opinions (Caplan, 2011; Flynn et al., 2017; Luskin & Bullock, 2011). The deficit model has been around at least since the 1950s and – in memory of its early proponents – it is sometimes referred to as the Arnold–Lippman consensus. Its central tenet has remained relatively constant since then: Citizens do not possess the level of knowledge that would be desirable in a democracy (Cortassa, 2016). This deficit of knowledge puts into question the functioning of the public sphere: how is rational deliberation supposed to take place with most people not understanding the basic arguments (see, for example, Gunn, 2014)? Given this impediment to the functioning of the public sphere, the deficit model is a crucial challenge to the democratic legitimacy of any political system.

The deficit model seems to **apply a forteriori to the European level**. This is mainly the case because the European public sphere is strongest in areas in which the EU commands significant competences (Koopmans, 2014). EU competences, alas, tend to cover highly complex issue areas. Arguably, some of the most salient and complex domains in which the EU is active are economic – including interest rate policy, trade policy and various forms of market regulation. Publicly debating such issues seems to require high levels of economic expert knowledge, which most citizens seem unlikely to hold. In fact, as we have seen in the previous chapter, European citizens' understandings of economics are very diverse and often differ largely from economic orthodoxy. Given the level of issue complexity in the European public sphere, then, we should expect the deficit model to be applicable. This would significantly

DOI: 10.4324/9781003335610-8

diminish the quality of transnational deliberation on European policy issues, thus further undermining EU legitimacy.

In this chapter, I argue that there is good reason to be much more optimistic than the deficit model suggests. I present three arguments to show that **European citizens' understandings of economics are informed.** To begin with, a part of the citizenry has had economic training and uses this knowledge to anchor economic issues (education argument). While this group is certainly not a majority, it is larger than one might assume, given that even citizens with brief experience of economics classes in high school are capable of reproducing basic tenets of economic theory. Yet even the arguments of citizens without economic training, second, should largely be considered informed, even if they are at odds with orthodox economic theory. Many of the representations advanced by citizens without economic training still correspond to positions held by political actors or heterodox economists – simply rejecting them as uninformed or incorrect thus seems to be overly restrictive. Lay–expert differences might partly be grounded in different normative commitments rather than in deficits of understanding (normativity argument). Finally, the fact that citizens employ various anchoring strategies generally testifies to their capacity to creatively bridge knowledge gaps and process new information. Arguably, much of the literature on the deficit model oversees this fact due to its strict focus on knowledge of facts. While citizens might not have the latest economic statistics at hand, they are still capable of spelling out highly complex causal relationships (causality argument).

The chapter will be organized along the lines of these three arguments. Section 5.2 deals with citizens with economic training. It does so by testing the economic theory hypothesis developed in Chapter 1, identifying first which participants have access to the relevant anchoring domain and then showing how anchoring in economic theory changed these participants' understanding of specific trigger topics. In Section 5.3, then, I argue that the representations of non-trained participants should also be considered informed and well thought through. The section presents both the normativity argument (the claim that representations deviating from orthodox economic theory are not necessarily uninformed) and the causality argument (the claim that ignorance of economic statistics and facts might be outweighed by an understanding of economic causalities). In the conclusion, I reflect on the external validity of these findings for the European public sphere and place them in the larger context of the scholarly debate surrounding the deficit model. While the generalizability of the results is limited, they warrant optimism regarding European citizens' capacity to understand and discuss complex economic issues.

5.2 Testing the Economic Theory Hypothesis

In the previous chapter, we have seen that the European public sphere indeed faces a complexity problem. Social representations of economics are so diverse that in most cases they do not correspond to economic theory. Yet, in some cases they do and this section will explore why this is the case. How do citizens acquire knowledge of economic theory? Which domain of knowledge do they employ for anchoring and how has this knowledge been transmitted to them? Which part of citizenry can be considered perfectly informed in the sense of having access to expert knowledge?

In the theory section, we have explored two competing hypotheses trying to explain how knowledge of economic theory spreads in the populace. Chapter 4 has already falsified the highly optimistic assumptions of the market experience hypothesis, which claimed that citizens would make inferences to economic theory from their personal experiences. In opposition to the market experience hypothesis, the **economic theory hypothesis** predicts that access to economic theory is transmitted through education, not experience. Participants with access to economic training are supposed to mobilize their knowledge of economic theory as an anchoring domain, thus frequently forming representations of the market as mutually beneficial. Participants who never have been subjected to economic training, on the other hand, need to rely on alternative anchoring domains, thus more frequently generating representations of the market as a zero-sum or negative sum game. The economic theory hypothesis, moreover, predicts differences in language usage. The mobilization of economic theory by economically trained participants should be accompanied by the usage of **specific vocabulary and typical metaphors**. Concepts that have a specific economic definition might mean entirely different things to economically trained and non-economically trained participants. The economic theory hypothesis, then, expects expert and lay participants to differ in their representation of the market and it predicts these differences to find linguistic expression.

In order to test the economic theory hypothesis, we again need to focus on two aspects. First, we need to identify the participants with access to this anchoring domain. Second, we need to investigate whether those participants with access to economic training exhibited a different understanding of the trigger arguments. Each of these steps will be the subject of one of the following subsections.

5.2.1 Identification of Social Group: Education or Public Sphere?

Economics is a well-known academic discipline. It should be undisputable that the ideas and theories comprising this body of knowledge can be used as an anchoring domain. It is more difficult, however, to identify those who have access to this anchoring domain. How do we know that somebody else knows about economic theory? How can we single out the participants with access to this anchoring domain in the focus group discussions?

In Chapter 1, I have described two potential avenues for the spread of knowledge about economic theory. The first, and more easily identifiable, transmission mechanism is education. Economic knowledge is passed on through educational institutions. It is taught in university classes and, in some countries, forms part of high school curricula, too. Tracing back which of the participants have participated in economics classes in the past, then, is a promising way of establishing if the participants have access to this anchoring domain. I have spoken a lot so far about 'participants with economic training' – practically, this refers to those participants who have taken economics classes in high school or university.

In the focus groups, participants were handed a small questionnaire after the discussions, asking some personal information, including the level of education and if they had ever participated in economics classes. Eleven out of 64 participants stated that they had been subject to such training.[1] For ten of these participants, training happened at the university or job education level, while only one participant took economics classes in high school. For most participants, these classes happened years or even decades ago. Thus, they might not be experts in a strict sense of the word. Having had access to economic training might not allow for a perfect reproduction of complex economic arguments. Having been confronted in depth with economic theory at some point of your life, however, might cause a certain familiarity with certain patterns of thought and it might enable participants to use a specific vocabulary. In short, I assume that participants might not remember the content of economic theory in detail, but they might maintain a memory of some basic tenets. For the economic theory hypothesis, then, I operationalize access to this anchoring domain via participation in economics classes.

Apart from education, the second transmission mechanism identified in Chapter 1 is the public sphere. Arguments drawn from economic theory might appear in newspaper articles, TV news or Twitter posts. Tenets of economic theory are present in mainstream media, in particular in times of salient economic events (e.g., crises or reforms). Apart from mainstream media, moreover, there are of course specialized news outlets which deal intensively with economic issues all around the year. Participation in such expert publics might result in similar levels of economic knowledge as courses in higher education do. Participants in the focus groups, then, might have acquired economic knowledge through the public sphere, by following expert media or by paying attention to salient debates on economic issues.

The impact of the public sphere as a transmission mechanism, however, seems negligible in the focus group material. The social representations that seem to mirror ideas from economic theory are mainly employed by the 11 participants who had access to economics courses in the past. Even though these economically trained participants only account for one sixth of all participants, they are responsible for more than half of the mentions of economic theory representations in the material. Some of these representations are even exclusively used by participants who had access to economics courses in the past. When I speak of experts or participants with economic training then, I refer to the 11 participants who studied economics at some point of their lives.

Being aware of the public sphere mechanism, nevertheless, is important to explain those (few) mentions of economic theory that are not caused by economically trained participants. The frequency of one representation in particular would otherwise be hard to explain: *Keynesianism*. The representation of Keynesianism, as the name indicates, closely mirrors an economic theory. Where it is mobilized, moreover, economic jargon is abundant, with participants frequently employing machine metaphors to explain how the economy would 'spin again' or how it would be 're-launched' (see Appendix 1, Section A1.6.1). Yet, more than half of these elaborate references to Keynesian economic theory are made by participants who never set foot in an economics classroom. Rather, we see from the discussion context in which the statements are made that they are drawn from salient debates that took place in the respective national public spheres. All mentions of Keynesianism in the Polish groups, for example, happen in the context of discussions about the government spending program *500+* (for an elaborate discussion of this mechanism, see Chapter 2). Salient national debates, therefore, can sometimes serve as a transmission mechanism for economic knowledge. For the rest of this chapter, it is thus important to be aware that references to economic theory can be made by participants who did not have economic training, albeit much more rarely. This explains why the social representations discussed in the following section are mainly, but sometimes not exclusively, used by participants with formal economic training.

5.2.2 Representations of Arguments: The Market as Mutually Beneficial

Having established which participants have access to economic theory as an anchoring domain, let us investigate if this anchoring domain is mobilized for the understanding of complex arguments. Do participants who have had economic training entertain representations of the economy different from their non-trained counterparts?

The economic theory hypothesis provides a clear answer to this question. According to this hypothesis, arguments that depict the market as mutually beneficial lie at the core of standard economic theory. We have seen in the hypothesis section that such arguments have been developed for the theory of free trade as much as for the labor market. The free exchange of goods (and capital) between countries is supposed to generate benefits for all parties involved just like the free interplay of supply and demand on the labor market is supposed to generate overall welfare gains. If participants mobilize their knowledge of economic theory as an anchoring point, then, we should expect these participants to construct social representations of the market as mutually beneficial. Inversely, participants without economic training should rely on zero-sum or negative sum representations of the market in the same situations.

Do we find such representations of the market in the empirical material? To answer this question, it makes sense to categorize social representations of market processes in a way that makes them comparable to economic

Table 5.1 Social representations of the market predominantly used by economically trained participants

	Product market	**Capital market**	**Labor market**
Mechanism	Price	Investment	Wage
Central Actors	*The consumer*	*Big firms* and *the manager*	*The working people* *the entrepreneur* *The classical employee*
Positive sum game	***Price (efficiency)*** *Exchange (products)*	***Profits (re-investment)*** *Exchange (ideas & capital)*	***Migration (efficiency)*** *Wage (exchange)*
Zero-sum game	*Price (quality)*	*Profits (exploitation)*	*Wage (exploitation)* *Migration (talent)* *race to the bottom (migration)*
Negative sum game	*Race to the bottom (products)*	*Race to the bottom (firms)*	*Migration (pointless replacement)*

theory. To do so, representations of economic causalities were ascribed either to the product, the capital or the labor market (see Table 5.1). Each market was organized around a central mechanism (prices, investment and wages). Different representations of this mechanism produce different benefit distributions (e.g., *price as efficiency* being a positive sum game, while *price as quality* is zero-sum; for a detailed overview of the various representations see Appendix 1, Sections A1.2–A1.4). There are four representations of causal mechanisms that appear on different markets. First, positive sum games can be the result of **efficiency** arguments, which postulate that markets allocate resources in a manner that doesn't create losers. **Exchange** arguments entail positive sum games too. Here two parties exchange goods, money or capacities and both are better off after the exchange. Third, zero-sum games are frequently based on representations of **exploitation** in which an elite benefits at the expense of the people. Finally, on all markets, a **race to the bottom** is construed. Due to the international mobility of products, firms and workers, states are forced to lower standards, thus generating significant harm to local workers, consumers or the environment. This harm is somewhat balanced in the case of migration, where migrants are viewed as legitimate recipients of benefits. This is not the case for the product and the capital market in which big firms are the winners of this process. The assessment of economic questions thus depends on the social representations of causal processes in different markets and on the distribution of benefits these representations imply.

What is striking about the four recurrent causal mechanisms is that one of them, efficiency, is exclusively used by participants with economic training. In other words, participants with economic training have a way of representing the market as mutually beneficial, which is alien to non-trained participants. When non-trained participants construct representations of the market as mutually beneficial, they rely on notions of exchange. In these 'exchange' representations, the market appears as a positive sum game because both parties involved in a voluntary exchange gain something they desired (e.g., an employer an employee and the employee her wage). Efficiency representations go beyond the description of mutually beneficial deals. Rather, the market is depicted as a virtuous cycle that continuously generates benefits by allocating resources in the best possible manner. Through specialization and an optimal allocation of work and capital, benefits are generated without producing losers.

Let us now see how these different representations of the market are mobilized in the focus group discussions. In the rest of the section, I will go through examples of lay–expert differences for each of the three markets, discussing the trigger topics 'prices', 'variety', 'investment', 'innovation', 'state versus market' and 'mobility'. For each of these trigger topics, I have chosen citations that start with one of the participants explicitly citing one of the trigger topics, thus showing that the discussion segments started from the exact same trigger. I will then contrast the course of the discussion in a group with an economically trained participant with a discussion group in which no expert was present. For reasons of brevity, I will limit myself to two or three citations for each of the trigger topics although, of course, there would be an abundance of alternative examples in particular for lay representations.

5.2.2.1 Prices as Efficiency

The representations of the product market constitute an ideal typical example of lay–expert differences. On the product market, the central causal mechanism is the price mechanism. Different versions of the price mechanism were spelled out in particular in the focus groups which centered on trade, and more specifically, for the trigger topics 'prices' and 'variety'. In this part of the discussions, participants were asked the question "which should be the aims of a good free trade agreement?" and they were handed cards reading "low prices for consumers" and "greater product variety" as potential answers. In response to these triggers, economically trained participants tended to form the representation *price (efficiency)*. This representation describes lower prices as the result of a more efficient division of labor, and it hails free trade agreements for their potential to increase international specialization (see Appendix 1, Section A1.2.2). Accordingly, the trigger arguments 'prices' and 'variety' had positive connotations for most economically trained participants. Participants without economic training, on the contrary, more frequently mobilized representations such as *price (quality)* or *price (factors of production)*, which stress negative side effects of low prices. To most of these lay participants, then, the trigger arguments 'prices' and 'variety' came with rather negative associations. Let us consider the example of 'prices' first:

FLTM3: "I chose the same card: 'low prices for consumers'. If you specialize in one good or a specific way of production, you will necessarily produce more, and prices will fall."

– French teachers discussing 'prices'

DA: "Another card that was chosen was 'a lower price level'. Is everybody agreeing that this is a good thing?"

FLTW1: "It depends on whether the norms are respected or not. If products are less expensive, if we are going to attract more products which are cheaper, but which aren't necessarily French and which thus adhere to standards that are less good than ours. [FLTM1: That's not necessarily good.] Yes, with regard to our market, that can make things collapse." – French teachers discussing 'prices'

The quotations above come from different moments in a group discussion of French teachers on trade (FLT). In the first quote, FLTM3, the only economically trained participant in the group, presents his initial choice of trigger cards. He presents a number of stringent causal relationships (more specialization causes more output, which causes lower prices), which bear close resemblance to the causal chains we would expect to find in economic textbooks. Confronted with a trigger argument drawn from an EU-level debate, FLTM3 anchored the idea of a lower price level in a conception of specialization he most probably learned about in an economics class. Anchoring in economic theory produced a mutual benefit representation of the market and a positive assessment of the trigger topic 'prices'.

The second quote is from a later section of the same group discussion. After the moderator re-draws attention to the trigger argument 'prices', FLTW1 presents her understanding of the of the trigger card and gets support for her opinion by FLTM1. FLTW1 seems to mobilize two adjacent representations of the price mechanism: *price (quality)* and *price (factors of production)*. Product quality standards are identified as a factor of production and low prices are consequently associated with low quality. Rather than mutually beneficial specialization, the lay participants in this group take low prices to result from lower quality. Without access to economic theory as an anchoring domain, the market thus appears as a zero-sum game in which there is a trade-off between price and quality. The absence of economic theory as an anchoring domain resulted in a significantly more negative representation of the trigger topic 'prices'. A similar process can be discerned for the trigger topic 'variety'.

PATM2: "'Greater product variety'. It seems to me that let's say ... If we talk about free trade, about deals between countries, the aim should be to make the largest possible range of products accessible to consumers or to facilitate the exchange of products. Because one country can specialize in one good and the second in another and both will be available in both countries on a high level, that is in good quality."

– Polish agents discussing 'variety'

PLTW1: "Well 'Low prices for consumers' – yeah, it's important. But here it is somewhat less important. It's important but maybe not too much. Because if there is high quality, then the price is like information. Right? This is a high-quality product. That's why the price is high."

– Polish teachers discussing 'prices'

PLTW1: "I can go first. Ok. In opposition to my colleagues, I chose 'larger product variety' as a negative card. Because if there are really going to be too many of these products, I am afraid that we will be flooded with low-quality products. And that could be ... well. [PLTW3: I also thought about this ...] That could really be something bad that would follow from this proposition."

– Polish teachers discussing 'variety'

The quotes above are drawn from a Polish agent and a Polish teacher group, both discussing trade. In the first quote, PATM2, an economically trained participant, makes an argument, which is remarkably similar to the point made by FLTM3 in the quotation before. Anchoring the trigger argument 'variety' in an idea of international specialization, PATM2 depicts the market as mutually beneficial. The trigger argument 'variety' is taken to imply higher product quality achieved through free trade. Contrary to this, the last two quotes bring together two statements by PLTW1. When discussing the trigger topic 'prices', PLTW1 forms an ideal typical representation of the price mechanism as quality. Drawing on this representation of *price (quality)*, the trigger topic 'variety' takes on a negative connotation for her, implying a danger of lower product quality. For the trigger argument 'variety' as well, then, we see a sharp difference between lay and expert representations. Economically trained participants tend to anchor the argument in notions of specialization and efficiency, thus forming a representation of the product market as mutually beneficial, while participants without access to economic training end up constructing more pessimistic representations of the market.

5.2.2.2 Migration (Efficiency)

A similar process can be seen on the labor market where participants with economic training are the only once to stress that work is a resource to be efficiently allocated by market forces. In the focus groups, this representation popped up for the trigger topic 'mobility'. In the following quotes, participants had been asked how unemployment could be lowered and they were handed a card reading "boost international mobility of labor" as a proposition. The first two quotes feature participants with economic training, while in the latter quotes participants without such training are speaking.

GAUM1: "In the EU, the opportunity to go elsewhere exists already [GAUW1: Yes]. Free movement of labor."

GAUM2: "I think that is why you say labor market. Because it is a market. I mean, of course people aren't a commodity. But the more mobile, the easier the mobility … It is like free trade in the sense that if goods or in this case workers can move more freely, if this this enhanced, then they can be better employed or can earn more [GAUM1: Yes]. Because they can say: "I can also – I don't know – work in Italy or in England or whatever. But my labor, my capacities are needed there and for my … So instead of being unemployed at home, I go where there is work [GAUW1: Yes]."

– German agents discussing 'mobility'

GLUM3: "This 'international mobility' could also be helpful. I mean that's what already happens when there is high unemployment in Italy or Spain and people are needed in Germany, that people have the opportunity to change to another country. To facilitate this is a good strategy in my opinion."

– German teachers discussing 'mobility'

PAUW1: "Well, we got kind of dried out in my opinion. Of course, I understand that people leave. But let's say we train a doctor, we pay for his schooling a shitload of money, and then we pay him badly, so he leaves [PAUM1: Yes]. So we don't have a doctor, but we invested in his training [PAUW2: And we already don't have money [laughs]]. And another country then employs him, gives him an income but doesn't bear the cost of education. It's a form of stealing."

– Polish agents discussing 'mobility'

PLUW4: "[reads out card] 'Encourage international mobility of workers'. We were always mobile. Where aren't we? Where are there no Poles abroad?"

PLUW3: "Generally they are at the dishwashers. [loughs] [PLUW2 & PLUW3: Exactly!]"

PLUW2: "There is a problem with that. I chose the same card, only before. I think it should be like that that we are able to move. But I want to work according to my qualifications! But if I go to Germany and – excuse me – what will I be there? I will take care of old people [PLUW3: Yes; PLUW4: Nothing else]. […] Actually, I could only change pampers."

– Polish teachers discussing 'mobility'

In the first quote, GAUM2 stresses that the market mechanism engenders mutual benefits. Workers "can be better employed or can earn more", implying that there are benefits for both employees and employers and that the overall system promises efficiency. Analogies with the free movement of goods reveal a proximity of thought to representations such as *price (efficiency)*. Like in this latter case, the free market is depicted as a positive sum game, benefitting all parties involved. Similarly, the second quote depicts migrants and the country to which they are migrating as winners of free movement. Free movement of labor thus helps to reduce unemployment as labor is moved where it is most needed. Just as on the product market, the market is depicted as the guarantor of efficiency, allocating resources in the best way possible. This representation of migration (efficiency) was exclusively used by economically trained participants.

It is thus no surprise that the non-economically trained participants we hear in the latter quotes advance different visions. In the first quote, PAUW1 mobilizes a representation of *migration as talent*, stressing the negative consequences of a brain drain on her country (see also Appendix 1, Section A1.4.8). In the second, PLUW4 forcefully highlights personal indignities associated with the prospect of migrating and performing less qualified labor (note the metaphors of "pampers" and "dishwashers" to stress these negative aspects of work migration). In both cases, then, the untrained participants construct more negative visions of international migration, seeing it as a form of zero-sum game in which the balance of benefits might well tip toward the negative. Participants' reactions to the trigger topic 'migration' then seem to confirm the economic education hypothesis. Participants with economic training use economic theory as an anchoring domain, producing representations of the market that are more positive than those of their peers.

5.2.2.3 Profits as Re-investment

Similar observations can be made on the capital market, albeit with a more linguistic dimension. Different representations of the capital market mainly result from different definitions of the concept of profits. Economically trained participants were the only ones to define profits as a form of re-investment. When this representation of *profits as re-investment* was employed as an anchoring point, the capital market could be depicted as a virtuous circle (see Appendix 1, Section A1.3.2). For participants without economic training, however, profits seemed to have more negative connotations. Most frequently, they were represented as the result of unfair business practices employed by big firms and managers. This representation of *profits as exploitation* paints an image of the market as a negative sum or, at best, a zero-sum game in which a small elite harvests the benefits at the expense of normal people (see also Appendix 1, Section A1.3.5). Lay–expert differences in the representation of the capital market, then, are in part linguistically driven: they result from entirely different usages of the term 'profits'. These differences were particularly strong on the trigger topics 'investment' and 'innovation'.

> PSTM4: "Look, the truth is that through this start-up culture firms develop. Through this start-up culture which exists – I don't know – for ten years. The firms themselves already cut back their R&D because they do not need to look for new technologies and new paths of development because they can buy that from start-ups. For 100,000, for a 1,000,000, for 10,000,000 dollars. And that's a situation which is good for the little guy who sits at home and thinks of something. 'Good. I have a great idea. I start doing it. I need …' But you don't have a business, right? You need 10,000,000 quid. For you 10,000,000 quid – wow. For him 10,000,000 – nothing. And you know: You sell it, you earn. You are happy because someone bought your product [PSTM1: And the investor is making millions and is also happy]."
>
> – Polish soccer players discussing 'investment'

> GATM1: "Win–win doesn't exist."
> GATM2: "Of course it does. If you get something in exchange …"
> GATM1: "Win-win was invented by those who know what they are talking about because they won."
>
> – German agents discussing 'investment'

These two quotes exhibit some striking similarities. First, they employ the same vocabulary when talking about the internal mechanism of firms, which engenders innovation. In the first quote, the positive associations with profits clearly stem from references to economic theory as the use of relevant vocabulary ("R&D") implies. Profits are depicted as a mutually beneficent exchange where one side pitches in its creativity and the other its money, and both profit, though somewhat unevenly. Profits thus are seen as indicators of positive sum games, causing all parties to gain. This notion is strongly contradicted in the second quote by a participant without economic training. Referring to representations of big business and their unfair advantage in negotiations, "win–win" is decried as a lie serving to hide the system's flawed premises working in favor of the strong. This difference in the understanding of profits becomes even more apparent in the take-up of the trigger topic 'innovation'.

> FLTM3: "The treaty works toward a number of objectives, it will create jobs, it will create value, and product prices will fall. So forcibly you'll have larger profits for the enterprises. And logically, a part of these profits will be channeled toward innovation, toward research and development and so it will increase … [pause]. Yeah, it helps to have done economics in high school."
>
> – French teachers discussing 'innovation'

GLTM1: "That's why I did not chose the innovation card. Because it is [pause] ambiguous. It can be advantageous, or it can backfire. So, for example, I don't really think free trade can create jobs in our society today. I don't think there is more potential for jobs in industrial production processes. Definitely not if everything is to remain cheap and affordable and so on. Let's just look at where people do their shopping: it's not the luxury shops, the majority of the population goes to Lidl, Aldi, Netto. And this might create profits, but it doesn't create jobs and it doesn't create product diversity. It creates an enormous price pressure for producers. And in other areas product diversity is impeded by brand rights or technological knowledge. So I think in the Internet domain, for example, we have a monopoly market, and we would need greater product diversity. [GLTW1, GLTW2 and GLTW3: hm (approving)]. Apple can sell its products at any price regardless of the actual production costs because it has a monopoly position."

– German teachers discussing 'innovation'

The trigger argument 'innovation' was also handed to participants in the trade discussions when the overarching question was: "which should be the aims of a good free trade agreement?" The trigger card proposed to "boost innovation in the economy" as a potential aim. Above we see the reactions of a French teacher with economic training (FLTM3) and a German teacher without access to this anchoring domain (GLTM1). FLTM3 clearly creates a representation of the capital market as a virtuous circle in which profits form the basis for future innovation, which, in turn, increases future profits. This representation of profits as re-investment clearly results from anchoring in economic theory, as FLTM3's final reference to his economics class in school indicates. Note also that FLTM3 uses the same vocabulary drawn from economic theory ("R&D" and "research and development") as PSTM4 in the previous quote.

While anchoring in economic theory thus produces a mutual benefit representation of the market, the trigger card 'innovation' has a very different effect on GLTM1, a participant without economic training. Like FLTM3, GLTM1 is convinced that innovation will create profits. Yet, for GLTM1 these profits result from the squeezing of employees in the industrial sector and from the abuse of patent rights by monopolistic firms in the digital sector. Profits imply exploitation; innovation ("brand rights and technological knowledge") is but a means to perpetuate this unfair profit-making ("a monopoly position"). The representations of the capital market thus show once more that economically trained participants entertain more positive visions of the market, and they show that these visions can be driven by specific linguistic expressions available to the respective groups. Interpretive differences between experts and laypeople can go to a point where single words (in this case 'profits') have fundamentally different meanings to both groups.

To highlight the specific strength of this kind of interpretive difference, I will refer to it as a **semantic difference**. Semantic differences appear when the same term has opposing meanings for different groups. Semantic differences will play a crucial role in my argument down the road when international differences are compared to intra-national ones. The power of such semantic differences is also evident beyond the capital market and the understanding of profits. They appear in particular for trigger topic 'state vs market', where vocabulary drawn from the ideology of liberalism is employed to construct a positive vision of the free market.

5.2.2.4 Liberalism versus Capitalism

On the trigger topic 'state vs market', participants were confronted with four arguments at the same time. One of these arguments read: "Too much regulation impedes commercial activity". In the following citations, we see the discussion of this proposition in three different groups, with the first two being comprised of participants with economic training.

> DA: "So which of these arguments convince you?"
> FATM1: "So concretely: Liberal economy or not, right?"
> DA: "Well, which of these arguments seem convincing?"
> FATM1: "Well, there is a grain of truth in everything."
> [...]
> DA: "Can you give an example of what's good and what's bad?"
> FATM1: "It is right that too much regulation at a given moment can kill the economy, right?"
> FATW1: "But you still have to regulate".
> FATM1: "You still have to regulate but I want to say that at a given moment if your product has to be like exactly like this or like that – that imposes limitations on the producer. And again, this gives an advantage to those with greater means of investment because it is easier for them to adapt to regulation."
>
> – French agents discussing 'state vs market'

> PATM1: "I think … The second argument is like the closest to my opinion. Like I think where it comes to economic issues the state shouldn't be an obstacle for entrepreneurship. One knows: the invisible hand of the market and so on [laughs]. So the state should be a kind of watchman and not someone who determines the frame. So I have a rather capitalist approach [laughs] to this question."
> PATM2: "Well, I agree that too much regulation harms entrepreneurship. In my opinion this point is more important than the others. Because I was also educated in the spirit of the free market and of all these things. And so I agree."
>
> – Polish agents discussing 'state vs market'

> DA: "Ok. Another argument was: 'Too much regulation impedes entrepreneurship'.
> GSTM1: "Well, from the enterprises perspective ..."
> DA: "From the enterprises perspective?"
> GSTM2: "Well, yeah. Every enterprise says that."
> GSTM1: "Exactly. But for us it is better if we have less toys that cause cancer. Right? Well, ok, we regulated, and we limited entrepreneurship, but we limited it for the sake of the population."
> – German soccer players discussing 'state vs. market'

In the first two quotes, we see how economically trained participants employ vocabulary drawn from economic theory to construct positive visions of the market. FATM1's first reaction to the argument is to anchor it in a representation of *liberalism* ("liberal economy or not, right?"; see Appendix 1, Sections A1.6.2 and A1.6.3). In the second quote, PATM1 mobilizes the Smithian metaphor of the invisible hand and the concept of the nightwatchman state, before PATM2 cites his economic education as the reason for his support of the free market. I find these examples instructive because they show how specific terms or concepts can serve as anchoring points that render an argument intelligible. Connecting the 'state vs market' argument to concepts drawn from economic theory helped the economically trained participants to form a positive assessment of the trigger argument.

Contrary to the representation of *liberalism* mobilized by the economically trained participants in the first two quotes, the non-trained participants in the final quote seem to mobilize a vision of *capitalism*. Two specific representations seem to be evoked in this quote. First, a representation of *big firms* is employed to construct an opposition between business interests and the interests of the population (see Appendix 1, Section A1.3.3). Second, by choosing poisonous toys as an example, the participants contrast pointless consumerism with legitimate health concerns (evoking the *social ordering of sectors;* see Appendix 1, Sections A1.1.4). Without references to the vocabulary of liberalism, the free market thus is depicted in a rather somber manner, setting flawed priorities and profiting the few at the expense of the many. Like in the representation of profits, in the representations of *liberalism* and *capitalism* encapsulate a semantic difference, with concepts having fundamentally different meanings for experts and laypeople. The trigger topic 'state vs market' thus confirms once more that economically trained participants entertain more positive representations of the market, and that these representations are frequently created through anchoring in specific terminology.

To sum up, the empirical material seems to confirm the economic theory hypothesis. Participants who have had economics classes in high school or university form more positive representations of the market mechanism than their non-trained counterparts. A number of mutual benefit representations of the market are even exclusively used by economically trained participants.

Importantly, economically trained participants frequently seem to mobilize specific terms or concepts drawn from economic theory as anchoring points. If these terms or concepts are unknown to untrained participants or if they have different meanings, I have proposed to call the resulting difference in the interpretation a **semantic difference**. Semantic differences between experts and laypeople resulted from different understandings of terms such as profits or liberalism. Experts and laypeople, then, seem to produce very different representations of complex arguments. Differences between the economically trained and those without access to economic training can reach a level where the same word means different things to them.

5.2.3 Implications for the Deficit Model: The Education Argument

At first sight, the implications of the economic theory hypothesis for the European public sphere seem to be somber. Only citizens with access to economic training seem to have access to expert knowledge. Most social representations of economics differ strongly from economic orthodoxy, mostly in being more pessimistic about the outcomes produced by free markets. In testifying to this difference between trained and not-trained citizens, the economic theory hypothesis contrasts sharply with the market experience hypothesis, which was falsified in the previous chapter. Economic knowledge is transmitted to the citizenry **through education, not by inference from experience**. While the market experience hypothesis falsely assumed citizens to be almost perfectly informed about the outcomes of economic processes, the economic theory hypothesis leaves us with the uncomfortable conclusion that expert knowledge is only available to a small part of citizens.

Yet, while the group of economically trained participants is certainly small, it might not be as small as one might think. That is to say, the sample revealed a variety of ways in which participants had been subjected to economic training over the course of their lives. This means that university education was a frequent but by far not the only way to learn the basic tenets of economic theory. Other participants picked up their knowledge during high school (FLTM3) or vocational training (FATM1, FATW1 and FATW2). To retain the basic gospel of the free market one year of high school education seems to suffice – a fact that largely broadens the group of people that are considered economically trained. While the group of people with access to economic expert knowledge thus might be smaller than in my sample, it might still be a sizable percentage of the overall population.

The economic education argument, however, is clearly insufficient to refute the deficit model. The largest part of the population still does not hold the same ideas as economic experts. The rest of the chapter is therefore dedicated to arguing why I – nevertheless – do not believe that this majority of untrained citizens suffers from a knowledge deficit. Economic laypeople might hold more negative representations of the markets, but these views are not uninformed.

5.3 Challenging the Deficit Model: Why Lay Representations Are Informed

Many scholars – economists at the forefront – have argued that citizens are insufficiently informed about economics (e.g., Bartels, 2005). As a consequence, it has often been deduced that the blessings of the free market are not sufficiently appreciated by the citizenry – leading to all kinds of inefficiencies as voters demand harmful regulation and other policies producing deadweight losses to society (Bennett & Friedman, 2008; Caplan, 2011; Somin, 2015). The differences found between economically trained and non-trained participants in my sample seem to confirm that laypeople might suffer from an anti-market bias: they fail to see the mutual benefits a free market generates. I believe, however, that such a reading of the results would be mistaken. At least in this most rigid form – as an insistence on orthodox economic theory as the only permissible standard of public rationality – the economic version of the deficit model is untenable.

5.3.1 The Normativity Argument

The first reason why I believe the deficit model is overly pessimistic is because I believe it to be overly restrictive in its normative assumptions. When dealing with the problem of citizen competence, one of the most difficult questions lurking in the background is that of truth. How do we define what is correct and what is incorrect? Is there a univocal scientific definition of truth we can rely on? How do we address the concerns of postmodern scholarship that insists on the validity of local forms of knowledge? And in balancing these poles, how do we avoid slipping into a form of normative relativism (Norris, 2011, pp. 147–150)? These questions far exceed the scope of this book and they would probably exceed the oeuvre of the most learned philosophers. My argument, therefore, will not be an attempt to define a standard of economic truth. Nor is it supposed to be a call to treat all economic opinions as equally valid. Instead, I simply wish to voice the intuition that orthodox economic theory is too narrow a normative standard. It is, in fact, a standard that – while applied to citizens to depict them as unqualified – is neither upheld in the scholarly community nor applied in politics. Thus, I believe the diversity of representations exhibited by participants without economic training in my sample should not be seen as uninformed deviance from the scientific standard. Rather, I would understand these representations as the voicing of alternative normative commitments in a diverse discursive space. If voiced by political leaders, no one would think of disqualifying these arguments as stupid. Rejecting them because they are voiced by ordinary citizens seems normatively over-restrictive and, in some cases, would amount to hermeneutic injustice.

Let me spell this out in some more detail. The starting point of the argument should be the observation that economists themselves are much more divided over some basic principles than the deficit model seems to admit. Keynesianism preaches very different remedies than the Chicago school and both differ greatly from the original assumptions of neoclassical economics. Next to these standard theories, there is a wide range of heterodox economic approaches. In other words, it is unlikely that economists would agree among themselves which statements of my focus group participants need to be qualified as deviant from economic theory and which still fall into the realm of acceptable opinion. Take the different reaction to the trigger topic 'prices' discussed in Section 5.2.2.1. Is it acceptable to argue that lower prices might result from lower standards elsewhere or is this an expression of an irrational anti-market bias? I don't think all members of the economic scholarly community would agree on the latter. The common version of the deficit model thus simply overstates the coherence of economic doctrine (for a similar argument, see Lupia et al., 2007). Proponents of this vision seem to cloak their own ultra-liberal normative commitments in the mantle of ontology.

The inadequacy of such an ultra-orthodox normative standard becomes more obvious if we think about applying it to politics. Imagine a politician would argue against a trade deal on the basis that standards are unequal and that the deal would not constitute a level playing field. Few commentators and economists would denounce this politician as uninformed or, worse still, as someone willingly denouncing scientific truth. Yet, this is the judgment that scholars have passed on citizens for indulging in similar heresies. Just as we would not think of censoring the public sphere in the name of scientific economic truth, we should refrain from interpreting deviations form orthodox liberalism as evidence of a knowledge deficit.

The need to accept the diversity of lay representations mostly as legitimate opinions rather than disqualifying them as false facts is even more obvious when we turn to matters of personal experience. A small, but non-negligible reason for the diversity of lay representations is anchoring in personal experiences. The resulting representations are often the most fervently advanced and emotionally laden ones, indicating that they matter greatly to their proponents. Accepting the normative standard proposed in the deficit model implies denying the legitimacy of these positions. It would mean denouncing citizens as irrational if they question the superior efficiency of an international labor market, even if – as in the case of the Polish teachers in Section 5.2.2.3 of this chapter – the counter-argument would be made based on the personal costs and indignities associated with migration. It would also mean denouncing those that see profits as the result of exploitation even if their arguments are based on a lifetime of experience as an industrial worker (such as, for example, GSUM1 in my sample; see Chapter 4, Section 4.2.2). I believe such an imposition of normative standards would amount to nothing less than hermeneutic injustice (Fricker, 2006), once more underlying why the narrow normative focus of the economic deficit model is untenable.

5.3.2 The Causality Argument

Keeping in mind that the diversity of lay representation should be viewed as normatively admissible, I believe it is important to highlight a second, more methodological argument against the deficit model. This second argument targets the focus of many proponents of the deficit model on economic facts. I maintain that this focus on facts obscures many less tangible competences that enable citizens to make sense of economic questions. While few citizens have the latest economic statistics at hand, many are capable of spelling out rather complex economic processes and causalities. The various anchoring strategies we have encountered in the course of this book testify to this ability to creatively make sense of economic arguments. Many studies insisting on the deficit model simply are not based on the data necessary to uncover the causalities citizens see at work when making economic judgments. As a consequence, the studies often impute false causalities into the minds of citizens, obscuring the actual complexity that underpins citizens' reasoning. The deficit model thus is partly based on an overly narrow definition of knowledge coupled with insufficient data. If we adopt a broader understanding of competence and look at the intricacies of reasoning, a more nuanced and optimistic picture of citizen competence emerges.

Focusing on facts seems to be an obvious strategy of assessing political or economic knowledge. This definition of political knowledge is shared in particular by proponents of the deficit model. Somin (2016, p. 9), for example, defines political knowledge as "awareness of factual matters related to politics and public policy". Standard items employed to measure the extent of economic knowledge include, for example, asking for extent of state spending in different areas or for estimates of key economic indicators such unemployment rate (see, for example, Caplan, 2011). And indeed, I fully agree that it is advantageous to know these statistics; they can be considered an indicator of political knowledge. Yet, facts and statistics are not the only way to explain economic phenomena. Even without having a concrete idea of the statistics of the day, citizens might still know enough about general workings of economic processes. While not knowing how big state spending is, it is already good to know how raises and reductions of state spending affect the economy; instead of knowing the current unemployment rate, having an informed opinion on how unemployment comes about is also a form of knowledge. Again, this is not to say that facts do not matter. But citizens might be able navigate their way through the difficult waters of economic knowledge without much statistical knowledge at hand. In fact, this is what happened in my empirical material: there was a large diversity of different representations stressing different aspects of complex economic processes, but economic statistics were almost absent. My participants might have failed if their knowledge had been tested on a factual questionnaire. But given the opportunity to argue freely, they made their points convincingly.

To be fair, even proponents of the deficit model do not exclusively rely on factual knowledge. A second strategy employed to test economic knowledge relies on prompts spelling out causal relationships and asking respondents to signal agreement or disagreement. This strategy is clearly designed to test causal knowledge. Yet, again I would like to point out that this is insufficient to test competence. This is so because the reasons to agree or disagree with statements are rarely recorded by such surveys. Given the normative pluralism we should accept as the basis of most economic debates (which I defended in the previous section), such questions should rather be seen as recording differences in opinion, rather than differences in knowledge. What should be judged in order to assess competence is the quality of justification, rather than the opinion itself. Without such data at hand, we are left to speculate if citizens hold certain economic opinions for good reasons or if their reasoning is rather poor. Scholars promoting the deficit model often opt for the latter option and simply impute misguided reasoning or biases into the minds of subjects.

A perfect example of this is Caplan (2011) who first identifies a list of potential biases from the writings of Adam Smith and other economic philosophers and then proceeds to argue that these biases must be the reason for citizens' stubborn refusal to adopt orthodox liberal opinions. It goes without saying that Adam Smith's speculation about the opinions of his contemporaries is not the kind of data public opinion research should be based on. In an interesting way, some proponents of the deficit model mirror the authors that promoted the market experience hypothesis. Whereas the former impute biases into the minds of the population, the latter simply ascribed perfect information to them. In both cases, adequate micro-level data on citizens perceptions is missing. If we want to judge citizens' competence in debating economics, we need to know which causalities citizens see at work and how they formed their opinion on them.

While I am far from proposing my own model of assessing citizen competence, then, I believe my findings are aligned with studies that adopt a broader definition of the concept. In recent years, the literature on citizen competence has seen a shift away from factual knowledge and toward the assessment of the capacity for information processing, justification and argument (e.g., Cramer & Toff, 2017; Goren, 2012; Lupia, 2016). I believe the anchoring processes we have explored in the previous chapters do provide further evidence of the importance of such "soft skills" for the overall assessment of political competence. Anchoring complex economic processes in more familiar bodies of knowledge helps citizens to make sense of political questions even if they hold very little factual knowledge. The diversity of lay representations of the economy should be seen as evidence of the diversity of economic causalities citizens might see at work when forming their opinion. If we rely on data that obscures these processes of sense-making, we will arrive at unnecessarily pessimistic judgments of citizen competence.

5.4 Conclusion

In this chapter, I have expressed my doubts about the validity of the deficit model for the issue area of economics. As a first step, the **differences between participants with and without economic training** were assessed. Participants who had access to economic training at some point in their life were shown to use their knowledge of economic theory as an anchoring domain. These expert participants entertain more positive representations of the market than their lay counterparts. Economically trained participants frequently depict the market as mutually beneficial where non-trained participants view trade-offs or even mutually harmful processes. Lay–expert differences sometimes take the form of semantic differences, with different interpretations of complex arguments resulting from anchoring in specific vocabulary, which is available to one social group but not to the other. In short, expert and lay citizens seem to understand complex economic arguments in such a fundamentally different way that sometimes the same words no longer mean the same thing to them.

Despite these pronounced differences between experts and laypeople, I argue that **the deficit model is not confirmed** by my empirical results. This is so, first, because there is a significant share of people with access to economic expert knowledge, and it seems that as little as one year of high school education might suffice to internalize the basic tenets of economic theory. Yet while economically trained citizens still constitute a minority, I argue that the representations of my non-trained participants should also be considered informed. I pointed out, second, that orthodox economic theory is too narrow a normative focus to determine scientific truth. Arguments questioning the efficiency of the market cannot simply be dismissed as irrational bias or cunning populism, as is often done by proponents of the deficit model. The diverse social representations advanced by lay participants, in fact, mirror arguments employed by politicians and more heterodox economists; they should be viewed as legitimate contributions to a pluralistic public debate. Given this diversity of informed positions, third, I argued that many studies confirming the deficit model were methodologically ill-equipped to do so. A focus on facts and true-or-false statements obscures the complexities of citizens' reasoning. In line with recent approaches to citizen competence, I argued for a wider understanding of the term, encompassing not only factual knowledge, but also the capacity to process information and form reasoned justifications. In this understanding, national anchoring and other anchoring processes are new examples of citizens' capacity to creatively overcome knowledge deficits and form reasoned opinions.

While these empirical results thus lend little support to the deficit model, they also do not command the **external validity** to fully disprove it. Remember that participants for my focus group discussions were selected to have privileged access to the anchoring domains stipulated in the hypotheses. As a result, participants might have found it particularly easy to make sense of the trigger topics, given that most of them could mobilize national knowledge or economic theory to anchor these complex economic issues. Unfortunately, then, we cannot expect all citizens to be equally capable of making sense of complex arguments. Yet, while it should be relatively easy to determine the percentage of people with access to economic training, diagnosing the availability and quality of national anchoring across the population is more difficult. The task of future research should be to test the role of this phenomenon on more representative samples.

Despite these reservations with regard to external validity, I believe the findings of this book are still good news for the European public sphere. The simple fact that a mechanism such as national anchoring exists should increase our faith in citizens' capacity to informedly partake in public debates. The fact that issues in the European public sphere are extraordinarily complex must not reduce the quality of deliberation. At least in my sample, citizens' representations of economics were informed, in large parts due to national anchoring. If citizens are thus are able to cleverly make sense of the intricate policy issues decided at the European level, **the complexity problem in the European public sphere might be overcome**. This is good news for the functioning of the European public sphere and thus for EU legitimacy. Yet, while national anchoring might provide a solution to the European public sphere's alleged complexity problem, it might cause trouble in a different area. The more national anchoring impacts public perceptions, the greater the danger for inter-national incompatibilities becomes. The final part of the book, therefore, will address the European public sphere's compatibility problem.

Note

1 FATM1, FATW1, FATW2, FLTM3, PATM1, PATM2, PSTM1, PSTM4, PSTM5, GAUM2 and GLUM2.

Bibliography

Bartels, L. M. (2005). Homer Gets a Tax Cut: Inequality and Public Policy in the American Mind. *Perspectives on Politics*, *3*(1), 15–31. https://doi.org/10.1017/S1537592705050036

Bennett, S. E. & Friedman, J. (2008). The Irrelevance of Economic Theory to Understanding Economic Ignorance. *Critical Review*, *20*(3), 195–258. https://doi.org/10.1080/08913810802503418

Caplan, B. (2011). *The Myth of the Rational Voter*. Princeton University Press. www.degruyter.com/document/doi/10.1515/9781400828821/html

Cortassa, C. (2016). In Science Communication, Why Does the Idea of a Public Deficit Always Return? The Eternal Recurrence of the Public Deficit. *Public Understanding of Science*, *25*(4), 447–459. https://doi.org/10.1177/0963662516629745

Cramer, K. J. & Toff, B. (2017). The Fact of Experience: Rethinking Political Knowledge and Civic Competence. *Perspectives on Politics*, *15*(3), 754–770. https://doi.org/10.1017/S1537592717000949
Flynn, D. J., Nyhan, B. & Reifler, J. (2017). The Nature and Origins of Misperceptions: Understanding False and Unsupported Beliefs about Politics. *Political Psychology*, *38*(S1), 127–150. https://doi.org/10.1111/pops.12394
Fricker, M. (2006). Powerlessness and Social Interpretation. *Episteme*, *3*(1–2), 96–108. https://doi.org/10.3366/epi.2006.3.1-2.96
Goren, P. (2012). *On Voter Competence*. Oxford University Press.
Gunn, P. (2014). Democracy and Epistocracy. *Critical Review*, *26*(1–2), 59–79. https://doi.org/10.1080/08913811.2014.907041
Koopmans, R. (2014). How Advanced is the Europeanization of Public Spheres? Comparing German and European Structures of Political Communication. In T. Risse (Ed.), *European Public Spheres: Politics Is Back* (pp. 63–96). Cambridge University Press. https://doi.org/10.1017/CBO9781139963343.005
Lupia, A. (2016). *Uninformed: Why People Know So Little about Politics and What We Can Do about it*. Oxford University Press.
Lupia, A., Levine, A. S., Menning, J. O. & Sin, G. (2007). Were Bush Tax Cut Supporters 'Simply Ignorant'? A Second Look at Conservatives and Liberals in 'Homer Gets a Tax Cut.' *Perspectives on Politics*, *5*(4), 773–784. https://doi.org/10.1017/S1537592707072210
Luskin, R. C. & Bullock, J. G. (2011). "Don't Know" Means "Don't Know": DK Responses and the Public's Level of Political Knowledge. *The Journal of Politics*, *73*(2), 547–557. https://doi.org/10.1017/S0022381611000132
Norris, P. (2011). *Democratic Deficit: Critical Citizens Revisited*. Cambridge University Press. https://doi.org/10.1017/CBO9780511973383
Somin, I. (2015). The Ongoing Debate Over Political Ignorance: Reply to My Critics. *Critical Review*, *27*(3–4), 380–414. https://doi.org/10.1080/08913811.2015.1139283
Somin, I. (2016). Democracy and Political Ignorance: Why Smaller Government Is Smarter. In *Democracy and Political Ignorance*. Second Edition. Stanford University Press. https://doi.org/10.1515/9780804799355

Part III

The Compatibility Problem

6 Testing Compatibility

Three Criteria for the European Public Sphere

6.1 Introduction

On 4 March 2019, Emanuel Macron launched a proposal for reform of the European Union, which tells us a lot about the functioning of the European public sphere and its potential problems (Macron, 2019). The statement, addressed to the citizens of Europe, was published in one major national newspaper in each of the 28 member states. It was translated into the respective languages and sparked relatively independent debates in each national public sphere. Almost ideal-typically, this process shows the transnational nature of the then European public sphere: the same European issues were discussed at the same time in separate national publics (see Chapter 1). Moreover, Macron's statement covered issues of considerable complexity, including concerns as specific as trade policy, social security regulations, innovation policy or product standards. As characteristic as this may be of the European public sphere, issue complexity is problematic in a transnational public sphere. As we know from the previous chapters, the citizens of Europe (the addressee of Macron's declaration) employ national knowledge to render complex issues intelligible. Thus, Macron's declaration might have been understood differently by citizens in each of the 28 countries. How can we speak of a functioning public sphere given such a potential diversity of representations? How can the EU's future economic policy be meaningfully debated without causing inter-national misunderstandings? Put briefly, **in a transnational public sphere, national anchoring causes a compatibility problem**.

Why exactly is compatibility important? If understood as a transnational public sphere, the European public sphere needs to meet several criteria to fulfill the legitimizing functions assigned to it in democratic theory. One of these conditions for the functioning of the European public sphere is that arguments are understood in a compatible manner. Although debates do take place in the respective national publics, the arguments exchanged should be grasped by participants of all nationalities in a compatible fashion. Whether the European public sphere meets this compatibility requirement is one of the central questions of this book (RQ2).

DOI: 10.4324/9781003335610-10

To assess the compatibility problem in the European context, I have developed three criteria. These criteria should help to determine when we can assume that citizens understand each other's arguments or when we diagnose misunderstandings (see Chapter 1, Section 1.3.2). They are formulated using social representation theory:

> Criterion 1. There is a difference in the representation of an argument which results from anchoring in different bodies of knowledge.
>
> Criterion 2. The difference in representation is not covered by an alternative representation.
>
> Criterion 3. Inter-national incompatibilities need to be more pronounced than intra-national incompatibilities.

Each section of the following chapter is dedicated to one of the criteria. Concerning criterion one, we need to ask if differences in the representation of trigger topics were more pronounced between participants of different nationalities or between citizens within the same national public. This **comparison of differences in representation** is undertaken in Section 6.2. In this part of the chapter, I draw on empirical evidence from previous chapters, with economically trained and non-trained participants serving as examples of intra-national differences (Chapter 5) whereas the chapters on national anchoring provide the examples of inter-national differences (Chapters 2 and 3). For criterion two, we need to assess to what extent inter-national and intra-national differences were covered by **alternative representations**. Were participants aware of the differences in representation we uncovered in the previous chapters? This question is answered in Section 6.3, drawing on segments of the focus group material thus far not discussed. In the final section, I discuss the **external validity** of the empirical results in light of the research design.

Based on this assessment, I argue that **the European public sphere functions in terms of compatibility**. National anchoring causes some problems of understanding in the European public sphere, but these incompatibilities are less pronounced than the incompatibilities found in national publics. In my assessment of the criteria, I find that the intra-national differences I analyze are quite strong and that they are covered only by rather distorted and polemic alternative representations (see middle row in Table 6.1). In comparison to this, inter-national differences seem to be less pronounced, yet only partly covered by alternative representations (see lowest row in Table 6.1). While both forms of differences thus are problematic in their own way, they might not appear equally frequently in the European public sphere at large. As the research design was construed to maximize inter-national differences, we might expect these differences to be less pronounced in other circumstances (see column on the right in Table 6.1). In terms of the Sinatra condition, as the European public sphere has made it here, it might make it anywhere.

Table 6.1 Assessment of compatibility criteria using results of Chapters 2, 3 and 5

	Hypothesis/ anchoring domain	**Strength of interpretive differences (criterion 1)**	**Quality of alternative representations (criterion 2)**	**External validity beyond research design**
Intra-national differences	• Economic theory (experts vs laypeople)	• **Exclusive** usage of mutual benefit representations by experts	• **Distorted** representation of expert arguments (polemic representations)	• **Greater differences** to be expected in national public spheres
Inter-national differences	• Worth of nations • National culture	• Differences in **frequency and persuasiveness**	• **Accurate** representation of other nations' economic interest • **No representation** of other national cultures	• **Smaller differences** to be expected in European public sphere

6.2 Criterion 1: Different Representations of Arguments

The first criterion identifies differences in the representation of arguments as a necessary condition for misunderstandings. In my focus group discussions, I have simulated anchoring processes by confronting participants with complex economic statements, the so-called trigger arguments. Chapters 2, 3, 4 and 5 have shown how different representations of these trigger arguments result from anchoring in different anchoring domains. For the trigger topic 'mobility', for example, anchoring in economic theory produced a representation of *migration as efficiency* among the economically trained participants, whereas the mobilization of national culture resulted in a representation of *migration as a race to the bottom* in the French groups. Anchoring in different bodies of knowledge thus did produce different representations of complex arguments.

If we want to assess the consequences of such interpretive differences for the European public sphere, we need to apply a national standard of comparison. For criterion one, this implies comparing the differences between participants of different nationalities to those who were discerned among citizens within the same national public sphere (in this case, economically trained and non-trained participants). Does access to economic training cause more fundamental differences than the availability of national forms of knowledge? Were the differences in the representation of trigger topics in Chapter 5 more pronounced than those in Chapters 2 and 3?

Let us begin by assessing the strength of interpretive differences resulting from anchoring in economic theory. In Chapter 5, I have shown that anchoring in this body of knowledge produces significant differences in the representation of six trigger topics: 'prices', 'variety', 'investment', 'innovation', 'state vs market' and 'mobility'. What is striking about these interpretive differences between economically trained and non-trained participants is that many representations popular among the former are never used by the latter. In other words, there are some social representations in the empirical material which are **exclusively** used by participants with economic training. Economically trained participants, for example, were the only ones to represent the market as mutually beneficial due to its efficient allocation of resources. This was the case for trigger topics such as 'variety', 'price' or 'mobility'. Economically trained participants entertained representations of these trigger arguments which never crossed the minds of their non-trained counterparts (e.g., the representations of *migration as efficiency* or *price as efficiency*). Differences resulting from anchoring in economic theory, therefore, are quite pronounced, with many representations being entertained exclusively by participants with access to this anchoring domain.

The strength of these differences also finds linguistic expression. In Chapter 5, I have introduced the notion of **semantic differences**, pointing out that differences in social representations sometimes seem to be driven by differences in the vocabulary available to participants. For participants with and without economic training, such semantic differences again seem to be quite pronounced. Different representations of the trigger topics 'investment', 'innovation' and 'state vs market', for example, seem to result from differences in the usage of specific vocabulary. For 'investment' and 'innovation', many participants mobilize the notion of profits to form an assessment of the argument. Yet, profits seem to imply re-investment for the economically trained, whereas many non-trained participants view profits as the result of exploitation. The same word thus has different meanings for both groups. Again, some definitions are exclusive to the economically trained. Such fundamentally different definitions can be diagnosed for other terms as well, as the opposing representations of *capitalism* and *liberalism* illuminate. Semantic differences between participants with and without access to economic training, then, are also quite pronounced. Lay–expert representations differ to a point where even single words acquire fundamentally different meanings.

In comparison to this, differences between participants from different nations seem to be less pronounced. Rather than producing representations that pertain to one nation exclusively, national anchoring generates differences in the **frequency and persuasiveness** of representations. In Chapters 2 and 3, I have shown that national anchoring produces significant differences in the representation of nine trigger topics. For 'international competitiveness', 'work' and 'exports', these differences result from anchoring in knowledge about the worth of the national economy (see Chapter 3). Yet, while the current strengths and weaknesses of the national economy privilege certain representations over others, this does not mean that the same representations are absent in other national contexts. German participants, for example, are particularly vocal in pointing out the benefits of exports to their economy, but the causal link between exports and jobs is known to participants from other countries too.

Representations resulting from anchoring in national culture are not exclusive to single nations either (see Chapter 2). Anchoring in national culture produced differences for the trigger topics 'mobility', 'workers' rights', 'expenditure', 'sovereignty', 'interest' and 'right to work'. In particular, past political debates seem to have popularized some representations within the respective national contexts. Yet, the relevant representations still appear within the other nations, albeit less frequently. A good example of this was the anchoring of the trigger argument 'expenditure' in the Polish governments' family program *500+*. Memories of the debate surrounding *500+* made Keynesian arguments easily understandable to Polish participants while representations of Keynesianism still appeared occasionally in other groups as well. Inter-national differences thus remain differences in the frequency and persuasiveness of representations.

Again, this nature of inter-national differences is reflected by the kind of semantic differences that were observed. In Chapters 2 and 3, I argued that the availability of specific national vocabulary impacts the ease of making specific arguments. National vocabulary is often coined in salient political debates and thus can serve to transport complex causalities in simple expressions. Terms such as *travailleur détaché*, *500+* or *Kleinstaaterei* facilitate the mobilization of some representations within a national context, and they help to enlist support as the term is known to other participants, too. In other words, the availability of national vocabulary increases the frequency and persuasiveness of representations. These semantic differences are less pronounced than those observed for economic theory. While some economically trained participants defined some terms in a way that was entirely alien to non-trained participants, differences in national languages simply facilitated the expression of representations generally known beyond the national context. Rather than the same words acquiring different meaning, the same meaning was expressed using different words.

While the examples of both intra-national and inter-national differences in representation were discussed at length in the relevant chapters, let us consider another empirical example here. In the introduction, I have referenced the concrete case of Emmanuel Macron making several (partly economic) suggestions and transmitting them to national publics. In the text, Macron touches on a number of trigger arguments present in my focus groups:

> Our borders also need to guarantee fair competition. [...] Europe, where social security was created, needs to introduce a social shield for all workers, east to west and north to south, guaranteeing the same pay in the same workplace, and a minimum European wage appropriate to each country and discussed collectively every year.
>
> (Macron, 2019)

This proposal of Macron comes very close to at least two trigger arguments: 'workers' rights' and 'mobility'. Based on the empirical results presented in the previous chapters, we can assume that the quote above would have produced both inter-national and intra-national differences in interpretation.

To begin with, we have discerned significant inter-national differences for both 'workers' rights' and 'mobility' (see Chapter 2, Section 2.3.1). In both cases, these differences in representation resulted from anchoring in national culture and, more specifically, from the availability of politically loaded vocabulary in the French language. Hearing the quote by Macron, thus, French citizens are very likely to think of *concurrence déloyale* or *travailleurs détachés*, thus forming a representation of *migration as a race to the bottom*. Polish and German citizens might get a similar idea from the quote although most probably they would rather mobilize their own national knowledge (e.g., migration experiences or a concept such a *Fachkräftemangel*). In any case, even if a German or Polish citizen were to understand the Macron quote as an instance of *migration (race to the bottom)*, it would be much harder to put this idea into words. In Chapter 2, I have provided ample evidence of the difficulty of mobilizing such representations if the relevant anchoring points in national culture are lacking. Focus group participants in Germany and Poland exhibit disfluency when mobilizing *migration (race to the bottom)* and they do not get approval from other members of the discussion group; yet, they sometimes mobilize these representations nonetheless.

If we imagine the (arguably unlikely) case that a German citizen goes to the office on the morning of 4 March 2019 and gets into a discussion about the EU at lunch, it would be difficult for that citizen to get the message of the Macron quote across. As there is no politically loaded expression for *concurrence déloyale* in German, she would have to spell out the causal mechanism of a race to the bottom in detail and, probably, would get little or no positive reaction from her colleagues (just as focus group participants in Germany did not support this representation when it was mobilized). It is thus not impossible that a German citizen mobilizes this representation; it is just more difficult than it would be for her imaginary French counterpart. On average, we would expect the Macron quote to trigger a representation of *migration (race to the bottom)* very frequently in France, but a lot less frequently in Germany or Poland. The inter-national difference is a difference in frequency and persuasiveness.

Yet, Macron's quote is also certain to produce differences in representation intra-nationally, and arguably, these differences are more pronounced. Among economically trained participants, the trigger topic 'mobility' has been shown to produce a representation of the international labor market based on efficiency (see Chapter 5, Section 5.2.2.2). This representation of *migration as efficiency* depicts the free market as mutually beneficial and thus would see Macron's attempts to regulate the labor market as a deadweight loss. At the same time, my empirical findings suggest that it would be impossible (or at least extremely unlikely) to find a person without economic training articulating such a view. In other words, while we could still imagine Polish and German citizens to mobilize a predominantly 'French' representation of the Macron quote, I doubt that the same point could be made for lay–expert differences. Non-economically trained participants simply did not mobilize representations such as *migration (efficiency)*. The lay–expert differences in the understanding of the Macron quote thus probably would be exclusive differences, not simply differences of frequency and persuasiveness. Views of a French expert and a French layperson (intra-national) would differ more strongly than those between French laypeople and their German counterparts (inter-national).

Differences in the representation of complex arguments (and the semantic differences accompanying them) thus seem to be most pronounced between participants with economic training and their lay counterparts. Differences between nations mainly affect the frequency and persuasiveness of arguments, while experts employ representations and terminology largely alien to laypeople. As I have chosen the latter group as an example of incompatibilities present in national publics, we can conclude that **intra-national differences in the representation of trigger topics seem to be stronger than inter-national**

differences. Interpretive differences alone, however, are not yet problematic for the European public sphere. Rather, we need to know to what extent participants are aware of these differences to determine whether they constitute misunderstandings or disagreements.

6.3 Criterion 2: How to Identify Alternative Representations?

The second compatibility criterion establishes a distinction between misunderstandings and disagreements. This distinction is important as both are based on a difference in the representation of arguments. Yet, while disagreements are a necessary part of any democratic debate, misunderstandings impede the legitimizing function a public sphere is to play in a democracy. Arguably, misunderstandings are problematic because they imply ignorance of the opposing position. In case of a misunderstanding, participants in a debate cannot agree to hold different positions, they are unaware of the interpretive difference in the first place.

In social representation theory, an awareness of diverging opinions is called an alternative representation. Before we go into the exact operationalization, let me stress that alternative representations, to some extent, always remain caricatural. This means that they are not identical with the social representations they are meant to depict. In the context of criterion two, this implies that we should not expect citizens to know the exact content of diverging opinions. Rather, an awareness of the existence of people with another opinion and a vague idea of the direction of disagreement should be viewed as sufficient.

In the focus group discussions, I have attempted to uncover alternative representations by asking participants a series of reflexive questions (see Chapter 1, Section 1.4.1). At the end of the discussions, two questions were posed, one targeting alternative representations of intra-national differences ("Who/what people/which social group might have a different opinion than you?") and the other fishing for alternative representations of inter-national differences ("Do you think that there are national differences?"). The resulting discussion segments were subsequently analyzed using the same method I employed for the rest of the focus group material (see Chapter 1, Section 1.5). This seems adequate as alternative representations are also social representations – hence it seemed reasonable to employ the same method of analysis. Consequently, I also rely on the same strategy of presenting evidence, providing two exemplary quotes per relevant representation identified. Again, the fact that such quotes necessarily come from quite different groups is supposed to serve as evidence of the intersubjective or social nature of the representation presented.

6.3.1 Alternative Representations of Intra-national Differences

By assessing alternative representations, this section establishes if lay–expert differences in representation constitute misunderstandings or disagreements.

This will tell us to what extent national publics suffer from compatibility problems, thus establishing a national standard of comparison for the European public sphere. The point of the section, thus, is not to establish if alternative representations are shared across countries, but simply to explore an example of intra-national incompatibilities that might occur in any national public sphere.

Are there alternative representations in the empirical material, then, that cover lay–expert differences? The alternative representations of intra-national differences identified by the focus group participants can be roughly divided into two groups. The first and somewhat smaller group could be summarized under the label **political divisions**. This implies that participants used political indicators such as party names or ideologies to identify others with a different opinion. Four different types of political divisions could thus be distinguished although none of them was particularly frequent. The rarest representation was that of *people at the extremes*,[1] a reference to both the radical left and the radical right. Somewhat more frequently mobilized was the distinction between *the people and the elite*,[2] which depicted politicians as a coherent group holding different opinions than the people they represented. Equally frequent, but only employed in Polish groups, was a distinction between *government and opposition*,[3] which often came with quite elaborate descriptions of sociological characteristics of the supporters of each fraction. Yet, the most frequent political division mobilized was that between *the left and the right*.[4] This was at the same time the only representation of a political division that could have covered the differences between economically and non-economically trained participants. It included references to liberal parties which "rely on the free market" (GST). These references, however, remained rather vague, and, with a frequency of two, rather infrequent. What is more, none of the alternative representations of political divisions fully covered the differences in representation between experts and laypeople.

Does the second group of alternative representations fare better in this regard? This group of representations of intra-national differences centers on the idea of **material interest**. In these representations, the opinions of other people are viewed as a function of their material interest. This mechanism of judgment is common to all people while their economic position differs.[5] Identifying diverging opinions thus implies identifying the effects of economic processes on different social groups. A classic example of this kind of alternative representation is the representation of sector differences, that is, of different *employment groups*.[6] Farmers or state employees are often cited as such interest groups mainly considering potential benefits for their sector. Another social group which participants identify as sharing specific interests are *the poor*.[7] This representation mainly highlights lower income (and hence greater interest in immediate material benefits), but sometimes also comes with rather classist ideas about differences in education (e.g., resulting from the fact that poor people have to work a lot and thus have no time to be informed about politics).

Among these interest-based alternative representations, however, only one seems to cover the interpretive differences between people with and without access to economic training. The alternative representation of *the rich and big business*[8] is mobilized to explain why other people might be more enthusiastic about the free market. The explanation, in line with the other interest-based representations, is that the social group in favor of the unregulated market must profit from it. While the representation thus does not directly identify economic training as the origin of the interpretive difference, it comes surprisingly close to describing the lay–expert differences observed in Chapter 5. In the following quotes, we see how the interest of the rich in the free market is applied to the capital, the labor and the product market.

> GATM1: "The rich, to say it from the other side, they have exactly this opinion. They want to push through these things because they have an interest in it. They just think: 'How can I position myself even better, be the first firm worldwide and generate even greater market shares?' [GATM2: Yes]. And so these are the people who make the free trade agreements. And because there are only stock market firms today in which there are people who only want to make money and only think of their profit, all other criteria are neglected in these negotiations."
>
> – German agents discussing alternative representations

> PLTW1: "I would mention for example big businesses, these really huge ones. I don't necessarily mean businesses that deal with technology, with its development and so on, but rather those that deal with trade. I don't know. These big retailers … I don't know. It would be like, let's say they would have to introduce better workers' rights, then they would also have to mobilize greater financial resources [PLTW2: Ah! Yes!]. But their goal is to make money, and not to spend too much of it [PLTW2: Costs as low as possible!]. Right? It would be that way. These big businesses that don't invest in their people …"
>
> – Polish teachers discussing alternative representations

> FLUW2: "So for example what you said about the rich, they will not agree. Because they will say: 'I have capital. That's what matters!'"
>
> FLUB1: "They claim that they deserve our money."
>
> FLUW2: "Well, they have developed our society with a strategy that worked. So: 'My strategy, my capital!'"
>
> FLUB1: "Yeah. And my grand grand father …"
>
> FLUW2: "No wait, I put myself in their shoes. You see? And I think that is exactly what happens most of the time. So they tell themselves: 'I deserve the money I earned. So I have a right to it. And if you take it from me via taxes or other costs, I can just go elsewhere where they don't demand anything. Or less.'"
>
> – French teachers discussing alternative representations

In the first quote, the interest of the rich in the free circulation of products is explained. The rich are depicted as the group that pursues free trade agreements and designs them at their will. Their interest in the creation of the free market is to "generate even greater market shares" for the firms they control. Note, moreover, how the rich are essentially identified with big business. The representation of *big firms* is mobilized, as big firms are described as international, profit[9]-hungry stock market firms (see Appendix 1, Sections A1.3.3, A1.3.4 and A1.3.5). This representation of big firms is even more evident in the second quote in which big business is depicted as an opponent of labor market regulation. Again, a free market is depicted as a tool of profit-making for big firms. After the labor and the product market, then, the third quote describes the interest of the rich in the free movement of capital. Together, all three quotes form a decent representation of the interpretive differences observed in Chapter 5. Although the alternative representations do not contain the idea that the market is mutually beneficial, they testify to an awareness that other groups view the free market more positively.

Is it problematic, then, that the representations depict material interest rather than economic training as the origin of the interpretive difference? Can we speak of disagreement where the opposing position is caricatured as the egoism of a business elite? Arguably, the alternative representation of *the rich and big business* partly covers the interpretive differences between laypeople and experts as the latter are frequently viewed as part of the business elite. The representation of the rich might include people who have economic training. Throughout the empirical material, the rich, business leaders and managers are depicted as people who are close to the economy or who represent "the interests of the economy" (GLU, alternative representations). This might also imply being knowledgeable about economics. Arguably, it would not be absurd to assume that business leaders quite frequently have enjoyed economic training. This argument seems to be supported by the last alternative representation to be discussed in this section: the representation of *the economists*.[10] On the one hand, this rather infrequent representation explicitly cites economic training as the source of differences in the representation of complex arguments. On the other hand, the economists are identified among those people whose material interest would be advanced by a free market. In the following quotes, we see that economists and business elites might in fact constitute a single group in the minds of some participants.

> PATM2: "I would say differences in education. Levels of education. [...] Because not all things in the contemporary world are that obvious. They are a bit messy and heavily interconnected. That's why it takes an effort to understand them. At first sight they might look very different than after digging into them for longer. That's why I think differences in education or different profiles of education because we are ... [towards D] You chose people from the same sector. [to

PATM1] I understand that you're also in the housing sector, right? So what should we disagree about?" [laughter from the group]

– Polish agents discussing alternative representations

FLTW4: "Which other groups? Well, economists maybe. [someone points at FLTM3; laughter]. No, no, but seriously, I think they would have a different opinion. Because it's mainly rentability and profits and so on."

FLTM1: "Yeah, I think the higher the socio-professional category, the more people will be in favor of free trade [FLTW4: Yes]. If you have more people with higher income, you will have more positive opinions [FLTW4: Yes]. And if you ask more people with fragile jobs and with low levels of qualification, the more you'll find an opposition because there will be some kind of defensive reflex. 'Oh, that will create more competition so we will not have benefits but greater risks.' So the more privileged the socio-professional category, the greater the support. If you had the same discussion with bankers, brokers, and insurance traders, I think they'd really be in favor."

– French teachers discussing alternative representations

The two quotes are the clearest cases in which an awareness of the differences between citizens with and without economic training is expressed. In the first quote, PATM2 oscillates between a rather classist conception of some people simply being smarter than others ("levels of education", "it takes an effort to understand") and the idea that there are different kinds of education ("profiles of education", "people from the same sector"). In this latter understanding, the economically trained are also those who have a shared interest in the flourishing of their respective sector ("so what should we disagree about?"). The quote is drawn from a discussion of Polish estate agents in which a majority of participants had enjoyed economic training and had dominated the discussion. The "profile of education" dominant in their sector most probably refers to economic training. Similarly, the second quote is drawn from a discussion in which an economically trained participant (FLTM3) had been present. Here, the identification of economic experts with business elites is even more explicit. Like in earlier quotes, vocabulary drawn from economic theory is assigned negative meaning ("rentability and profits and so on"). A representation of *big firms* is clearly in the subtext, as "bankers, brokers and insurance traders" all work in the stock market. The enthusiasm for the free market thus is depicted as a characteristic of a small elite with economic training. In the minds of some participants, the rich and people with economic training apparently were collapsed into a single category.

Can we assume, then, that lay–expert differences are covered by alternative representations? Does the representation of economic theory as an ideology of the rich imply that this interpretive difference in national publics remains compatible? Arguably, the opinions of people with economic training are depicted in a very distorted manner. In the beginning of this section, I have pointed out that this is to some extent normal for alternative representations. Alternative representations always depict but a fraction of the diverging position they cover, and they often remain superficial. Yet, in the present case, the alternative representations seem to be distorted beyond this normal simplification. Rather than just shortening the alternative position, the arguments of the rich and the business elite are delegitimized by unveiling them as the material interest of the few. In the quotes we saw above, representations of *big firms* and of *the manager* are frequently mobilized (see Appendix 1, Sections A1.3.3 and A1.3.4). Both representations carry strong pejorative undertones, often depicting the business elite as morally corrupt. Viewing pro-market arguments as the expression of these actors' material interest thus is a form of delegitimizing these opinions.

In social representation theory, such heavily distorted visions of diverging opinions are called **polemic representations** (Duveen, 2007, pp. 547–548, 2008, pp. 370–372; Höijer, 2011, p. 5; Sammut & Gaskell, 2010, pp. 48–58; see also Chapter 1, Section 1.3.2.2). While polemic representations still testify to a degree of awareness of an opposing position, they do not provide a solid basis for democratic disagreements because they deform opposing opinions to the point of not being recognizable. The intra-national differences analyzed in this section, then, are only covered by quite polemic alternative representations. **National publics thus seem to have some trouble in fulfilling the compatibility criteria**, as they feature strong interpretive differences and only distorted representations thereof. Let us now see if the European public sphere fares even worse in this regard.

6.3.2 Alternative Representations of Inter-national Differences

In Chapters 2 and 3, I have shown that national anchoring can produce quite pronounced differences in the representation of complex arguments. Two anchoring domains were particularly frequent: knowledge about the worth of the national economy and national culture (in particular memories of past politics). Do these inter-national differences constitute misunderstandings? Or are European citizens aware of the different views their counterparts in other countries hold?

Like for intra-national differences, the most frequent representation of inter-national differences is based on a concern for material interests. At the end of each focus group discussion, participants were asked if citizens in other countries think differently. In 11 of the 18 groups, citizens of other countries were imagined to be guided by an interest in the economic well-being of their country.[11] Concretely, this alternative representation can be divided into three assumptions. First, people everywhere think in a similar manner, that is, they follow their material interest. Second, people employ the well-being of their national economy as a proxy for their own prosperity. Economic success of the nation promises economic success of the individual, and vice versa. This implies, third, that inter-national differences in opinion result from differences in the countries' economic situations. In other words, knowledge of the strength and weaknesses of the respective national economy determines how citizens in other countries will view a policy proposal.

To determine the different effects of a policy on different national economies, participants rely on the representation of the *economic world map*. The economic world map is a transnationally (surprisingly) similar representation, ordering countries by cardinal directions and placing them in a hierarchy according to different sets of economic criteria (see Chapter 3). The economic world map thus can provide information about a country's economic situation. If citizens are assumed to derive their opinions from the effects of a given policy on their national economy, the economic world map can be used to deduce the opinions of individuals in other countries. A good example of this mechanism can be observed in the following quote.

> PSTM5: "So for example Scandinavia and these countries like Sweden, Norway, Finland and so on, they are crazy about all environmental or quality standards. Right? […] The point is that if, for example, we had to throw all these countries in one pot and if we had to make common standards [PSTM4: Well, rather not] – well, then some will have very high demands while others – Greeks or Italians or these Southern societies – won't give a fuck [PSTM2 loughs; PSTM1: They pay attention to other questions]. So … Same if we look at, I don't know, Poland, Ukrainians, Belarussians. Well, for sure we are culturally similar in comparison with some other group. And we also wouldn't give a damn because for us only counts that things are cheap and that they function."
>
> [strong disagreement voiced by group]
>
> PSTM1: "No!"
>
> PSTM2: "No! I am sorry, that's simply false."
>
> PSTM4: "We are the most interesting country in this regard because we are entirely in between. We are in between the West – which means good quality – and on the other hand we are a poor country which has to look at costs and this kind of things."
>
> – Polish soccer players discussing alternative representations

In the quote, we can observe how the representations of the economic world map is used to imagine the opinions of other Europeans. To begin with, we find an almost complete representation of different regions on the economic world map, and of the characteristics typically assigned to them. The North ("Scandinavia and these countries like Sweden, Norway, Finland") supposedly has high standards, both for the environment and for product quality. "Southern societies", on the contrary, are depicted as less concerned with these questions. Eastern nations are described as poor, and hence more concerned with low prices than with quality standards. Finally, geographical proximity to the West is taken to imply "good quality", with Poland taking a position in between, highlighting its status as an *economy in development* (see Chapter 3 or Section A1.1). The cardinal directions thus are assigned economic characteristics. Yet, what is more, the opinions of citizens in the respective areas are derived from the state of the respective national economy. This becomes clear as nations are referred to using personal pronouns ("they pay attention to other questions"; "we also wouldn't give a damn"). Inter-national differences in the assessment of policies thus are derived from a country's economic situation, that is, its placement on the economic world map.

Arguably, deriving foreign opinions from the economic world map produces an alternative representation of the worth of nations hypothesis. The worth of nations hypothesis describes how citizens use knowledge of the strength and weaknesses of their national economy as an anchoring domain. In Chapter 3, we have seen that the employment of this anchoring domain created inter-national differences in the representation of the trigger arguments 'exports', 'work' and 'competitiveness'. In the following quotes, we see how participants use the economic world map to create surprisingly adequate alternative representations of these inter-national differences.

DA: "Ok. The last question is whether … Do you think that people in other countries have a different opinion regarding this?"
FATW1: "Yeees!"
FATM1: "Absolutely!"
FATW2: "Yes."
FATW1: "According to the situation in the country already! According to the situation in the country!"
[…]
FATM1: "After all, everyone is an egoist."
FATW1: "A Rumanian. I think a Rumanian will reason differently."
DA: "What would his reasoning be?"
FATW1: "Hmhm, maybe I'll rather take someone from Greece. A Greek will think … Well, he is really in the shit, isn't he?"
[…]
FATM1: "Maybe it is as we said earlier. Everything depends on the equilibrium of a country's trade balance [FATW1: Yes]. A country which exports a lot will want to boost exports even more. And a country which … Well, and the same for imports."

– French agents discussing alternative representations

GATW1: "I think a lot of people … Well, we are the big winners of the EU. Right? Germany is doing great [GATM2: Yes, yes.] And many other countries – Italy, France – are doing worse. A lot of countries in fact …"
[…]
GATM1: "Well, if you take Greece, what do they have to offer economically?"

GATM2: "Yeah, economically small countries, they will have significant differences."

– German agents discussing alternative representations

In the first quote, we find a precise representation of the inter-national differences observed for the trigger argument 'exports'. Just as we saw in Chapter 3, citizens who perceive their country's exports to be competitive form more positive opinions of this argument. Citizens of a country whose exports are not going well (in the discussion segment, Greece and Rumania are cited as examples) might be more negative. It is striking that the country examples provided are from Southern and Eastern Europe, two regions frequently placed in an inferior position in the economic hierarchy of states. The economic world map is mobilized in a similar way in the second quote. Here again, Southern European countries are described as "economically small". As they do not have a lot "to offer" (i.e., to export), their citizens will be less enthusiastic about the idea to open up markets to international competition. The quote therefore describes the inter-national differences in the representation of the trigger topics 'exports' and 'work' with astonishing precision. Inter-national differences resulting from anchoring in knowledge of the worth of the nation thus seem to be covered by alternative representations.

Apart from the circulation of goods, the economic world map also provides information about the circulation of labor. Representations of the economic world map thus can also be employed to imagine inter-national differences on questions of economic migration. In Chapters 2 and 3, we have seen that citizens in France, Germany and Poland generate very different representation the trigger topic 'mobility'. In the following quotes, we see that these inter-national differences might be covered by alternative representations.

GSTM2: "Well in countries which have been hard-hit by the euro-crisis. Portugal, Spain, Greece. I think it is doubtful whether they say: 'Hurray! Our enterprises will have more foreign competition!'"

GSTM3: "They have high unemployment rates particularly among the younger people [GSTM1: Yes]. I think they might be happy to first take care of the needs of their own economy and don't necessarily need a free trade agreement to open the doors to foreign enterprises and their products. They might be happy if they are able to work in their own country after finishing their education, rather than having to migrate."

– German soccer players discussing alternative representations

PLTW2: "Maybe others would be afraid of us coming. If we migrate there, they might fear that we would work for lower wages and that their labor market would suffer from this. Because Poles might agree to very low wages – which for us would be high – but for them they would be too low."

[...]

PLTW1: "Same with, let's say, people that come here from Ukraine and that work for very low wages, [PLTW2: Yes, yes, yes.]. Right? Because they mess up our market. That's why we weren't liked in England [PLTW2: Yes]. Over there, Poles were that nation."

– Polish teachers discussing alternative representations

Both quotes contain very rich references to the economic world map and to events of recent economic history, which made this ranking of states transparent. In the first quote, the historical reference point is the euro-crisis, which provides a vision of Southern Europe as economically weak. Again, these countries' position on the economic world map can be used to deduce the opinion of their citizens. Citizens supposedly are aware of the link between "the needs of their own economy" and their own material well-being. This desire to stay home despite the temptation of better employment opportunities abroad comes quite close to the representation of *migration as personal prospect*, which was predominantly used by Polish participants. Similarly, in the second quote a Polish group succeeds in constructing an adequate alternative representation of the inter-national differences regarding 'mobility'. Here again, a representation of the economic world map facilitates the position-taking. As both origin and destination, Poland is in an intermediate position regarding migration flows. Thus, an inference can be made from public opinion toward Ukrainian migrants to the opinions of other citizens on the inflow of Polish workers. Again, an event of recent economic history (the Brexit debate) seems to serve as a crystallizing point for a country's status in the migration hierarchy. The negative attitude toward migration attributed to citizens in destination countries, in fact, seems to reflect the inter-national differences in the representation of trigger argument 'mobility' with astonishing precision. In particular, the frequency of *migration (race to the bottom)* in France seems to be adequately covered by this alternative representation. For issues of international labor mobility, then, the economic world map thus seems to provide good alternative representations, too.

Other inter-national differences in the understanding of complex arguments, however, are not covered by alternative representations. While differences resulting from anchoring in the worth of nations could be deduced from the economic world map, no such mechanism seems to exist for differences resulting from anchoring in national culture. In the empirical material, we find occasional representations of *differences in mentality*,[12] but these references to different cultures or histories remain very vague and are never supported by actual examples of the substantive differences in opinion they supposedly produce. What is more, participants seem to be largely unaware of the political struggles and debates which are salient in other nations. The only exception to this is a vague perception of a *rise of nationalism*[13] in places as diverse as Poland, Hungary, Britain, the United States and Italy. Yet again this alternative representation does not cover any of the interpretive differences that were actually observed in the empirical material. While it is understandable, then, that citizens are most informed about domestic politics, this seems to be problematic for the European public sphere. In Chapter 2, I have shown that memories of past politics are very frequently employed for national anchoring. The inter-national differences this form of anchoring produces are not covered by alternative representations as citizens are simply unaware of the political debates which constitute salient anchoring points for their counterparts in other countries. Anchoring in national culture thus might produce misunderstandings in the European public sphere. Where citizens employ analogies with national politics to render complex European arguments intelligible, the European public sphere might face a significant compatibility problem.

Let us consider what this would mean for the Macron example discussed throughout this chapter. We have already seen in Section 6.2 that there might be different representations of Macron's argument, depending on whether economic theory or national culture is used as an anchoring domain. Where national culture is mobilized, inter-national differences in representation ensue, for example, with representations of *migration as race to the bottom* being more frequent and persuasive in France. I have constructed the thought experiment of a citizen discussing Macron's proposal with her colleagues over lunch. The central point of my argument was that a citizen in Germany would have greater difficulty convincing her peers than her imaginary French counterpart. *Migration (race to the bottom)* will be more frequent and persuasive in a French context.

What do alternative representations add to this example? The absence of alternative representations of national culture implies that the French and the German citizen mentioned above are unaware of each other's situation. The German citizens do not know what Macron's arguments mean to the French and that *migration (race to the bottom)* might be the most prominent and persuasive representation triggered. This is the kind of misunderstanding, then, that might happen specifically in the European public sphere. Arguments might resonate with specific meaning structures in national culture, thus privileging certain arguments in one national public sphere and leading to debate in a very different direction in others. As citizens are unaware of these inter-national differences in representation, the result is a misunderstanding, not a disagreement. Misunderstandings specific to the European public sphere result from differences in national culture not reflected by alternative representations.

The extent to which inter-national differences are covered by alternative representations thus varies strongly. While participants seem to be aware of the state of foreign economies, the politics of other nation-states remain largely unknown. Therefore, differences resulting from anchoring in the worth of nations are covered by quite adequate alternative representations. Anchoring in national culture, on the contrary, seems to produce a kind of international misunderstanding, an inter-national difference in the interpretation of complex arguments that citizens are unaware of. Thus, at least parts of the inter-national differences observed in Chapter 2 seem to inhibit the functioning of transnational communication. The European public sphere does not operate without hermeneutic difficulties. It will be the aim of the final section to ultimately determine if these differences are stronger than in national publics.

6.4 External Validity: Compatibility Problems beyond the Focus Group Material

In the previous section, we have seen that inter-national misunderstandings do appear in the European public sphere. Sometimes, complex arguments mean different things to citizens of different nations. Does this imply that that transnational communication in Europe does not function properly? Does the EU have a lack of democratic legitimacy due to a malfunctioning public sphere? Arguably, drawing such pessimistic conclusions would be exaggerated. Even though inter-national differences produce incompatibilities, these incompatibilities do not seem more pronounced than intra-national problems of communication. Moreover, if we consider that the research design was meant to maximize inter-national differences, it seems unlikely that these differences will be stronger beyond the empirical material. Compatibility problems in the European public sphere are probably no more pronounced than in national publics. If national publics set the standard of legitimacy, the EU does not have a problem regarding its public sphere.

I wish to make three arguments to support this conclusion. First, **aggregating the results from criterion one and two, inter-national and intra-national incompatibilities seem to be approximately equally strong**. Arguably, both kinds of incompatibilities are problematic in their own way and it seems difficult to decide on a ranking. Regarding criterion one, the intra-national differences in representation were stronger, entailing the exclusive use of some representations and an entirely contrary usage of vocabulary. Inter-national differences only caused a difference in the frequency and persuasiveness of arguments. For criterion two, the situation seems to be reversed to some extent. At first sight, intra-national differences seemed to be less problematic as they were quite extensively covered by alternative representations. Contrary to this, an important section of inter-national differences (those resulting from anchoring in national culture) were not covered. Yet, for those inter-national differences that were covered (those resulting from knowledge about the worth of nations), the alternative representations were of better quality. Thanks to quite uniform representations of the economic world map, these alternative representations were very adequate, while the representations of the intra-national differences remained polemic and quite distorted. With one kind of difference being stronger and having only polemic alternative representations, while the other is weaker and only partly covered, there is no reason to characterize either form of incompatibility as stronger than the other. The European public sphere and national public spheres fail the first two compatibility criteria in some (although differing) regards, and I see no reason to define one of these failures as graver than the other. In my empirical material, arguably, inter-national and intra-national incompatibilities are equally pronounced.

As much for the incompatibilities observed in my empirical material. But what might these results tell us for discussions beyond the focus group material? Will the finding that inter-national incompatibilities are no stronger than intra-national incompatibilities remain valid? Arguably, considering the external validity of these results reinforces the case for the functioning of the European public sphere. These considerations provide arguments two and three.

As the second argument, we should acknowledge that **intra-national differences are probably stronger than observed in the analysis**. Throughout this chapter, I have employed differences between participants with and without economic training as an example of intra-national differences. Yet, this hermeneutic difference is probably neither the only nor the strongest difference we should expect to find in a national public sphere. As I have pointed out in Chapter 1, modern national societies are characterized by a multitude of knowledge authorities. In the foundational study of social representation theory, strong interpretive differences were diagnosed, for example, between Catholics and communists (Moscovici, 2004, pp. 369–437). This salience of religious and socio-economic divisions has long been confirmed by cleavage theory (Rokkan & Lipset, 1967). Other political divisions that can result in interpretive differences in national publics are abundant, for example, between city and countryside, between generations or between citizens with different value orientations. Yet, all these potential sources of intra-national differences were not assessed in the present study. In reality, therefore, we should expect intra-national differences to be much more numerous and potentially stronger than those depicted in this book.

While intra-national differences thus are probably stronger, **inter-national differences should be less pronounced beyond the empirical material**. This is the third and probably most important argument indicating that the European public sphere does not have a compatibility problem. In Chapter 1, I have shown that the research design for this study was meant to create a worst-case scenario for the European public sphere. Through country (most dissimilar cases) and participant selection (citizens with privileged access to national anchoring domains) and through focus group design (including nationally loaded trigger arguments), the potential for national differences was consciously maximized. Yet, even under these very unfavorable conditions, inter-national differences did not seem to be more pronounced than intra-national differences. Under more favorable conditions (and arguably most debates in the European public sphere will happen under more favorable auspices), inter-national differences should be less frequent and less pronounced. While the empirical results thus already indicate that the European public sphere seems to function reasonably well, for cases beyond the focus group material we could be even more optimistic. Inter-national and intra-national differences are approximately equally strong in the empirical material and the scale probably tips toward the latter in most other cases. Incompatibilities in the European public sphere appear, but they are less pronounced than those we should expect to find in national publics.

6.5 Conclusion

The present chapter has provided an answer to the second central question of this book (do inter-national differences in social representations inhibit the functioning of the European public sphere?). In doing so, I believe it has closed one of the last important gaps in the literature on the functioning of the European public sphere: testing the **compatibility criterion at the citizen level**. As opposed to previous studies (Kantner, 2014; Risse, 2010, pp. 162–171; Trenz, 2000), I drew on focus group material rather than on media reporting to assess the compatibility problem in the European public sphere. Media outlets are very important transmission mechanisms for information in a functioning public sphere and thus analyses of the compatibility of news reporting is important. Yet, I believe that we ultimately need to assess how citizens understand the information and debates transmitted by the media if we are to reach a final verdict on the functioning of a public sphere. If we are to assess the European public sphere's legitimizing function, what matters in the end is the compatibility of citizens' understandings of arguments. I believe, therefore, that this chapter has shed light on an aspect of the European public sphere which thus far has received relatively little attention despite its importance for the EU's legitimacy.

In practice, testing the compatibility criterion on the citizen level meant assessing the three compatibility criteria developed in Chapter 1 by using the empirical results developed in Chapters 2, 3 and 5 (see Table 6.1). Having conducted these tests, I maintain that **the European public sphere seems to function despite the existence of inter-national differences**. The European public sphere does not have compatibility problems which go beyond the problems we should expect to find in national publics. Admittedly, inter-national differences exist, and they are only partly covered by alternative representations. Yet, these inter-national misunderstandings do not seem to be stronger than intra-national problems of communication. Most importantly, however, the research design was constructed to maximize inter-national differences, and it neglected a large variety of potential sources of intra-national misunderstandings. Thus, inter-national incompatibilities should be even less pronounced beyond the research design, while intra-national communication is likely to face even greater difficulties. In my opinion, the European public sphere thus has prevailed under very unfavorable conditions. In the spirit of the Sinatra condition, we could conclude that if the European public has made it here, it might make it anywhere.

One of the cases in which the European public sphere has shown its proper functioning, then, might be Macron's declaration cited in the beginning of the chapter. Macron's arguments might have been picked up differently in different countries. German citizens might have appreciated them for their focus on innovation and exports, while debate in Poland might have focused on the re-negotiation of the posted workers' directive. But Macron's arguments were probably understood in very different ways by his fellow nationals, too. At least those citizens living in France who have had economic training attached different meanings to the statement than most others. Before we accuse the European public sphere of a failure of communication, then, we should worry about the functioning of public communication in France. And, inversely, if we accept France's public sphere to function reasonably well, we should not worry about incompatibility in the European public sphere. As I believe few people diagnose a malfunctioning of the French public sphere, it seems fair to assume that the European public sphere fulfills its legitimizing function rather well. We can say, then, that Macron's statement was indeed understood by the citizens of Europe.

For a Union hosting such wide linguistic, historical, political and economic differences as the EU, this conclusion is no matter of course. Rather, the fact that communication can be successful across such apparent differences is a puzzle in itself. In other words, rather than investigating the effects of international differences, we might wonder about the extent of transnational similarities. In the final chapter of this book, I will sketch out a number of theories addressing this question of similarity among Europeans. These theories attempt to define what constitutes a European demos.

Notes

1 Frequency 2; alternative representations (FAT, GLT).
2 Frequency 3; alternative representation (FAU, FSU, PLU).
3 Frequency 3; alternative representations (PAU, PLU, PSU).
4 Frequency 4; alternative representations (FAT, GST, GAU, GLU); references to the German FDP in GST and GLU.
5 Ironically, this alternative representation seems to mirror the market experience hypothesis. Rather than providing confirmation for the hypothesis, however, I would argue that it simply testifies to its popularity even beyond academic circles.
6 Frequency 8; (FAT, FST, GAT, PAT, PLT, PST, FAU, PLU).
7 Frequency 10; alternative representations (FLT, FST, GAT, GLT, GST, PAT, PST, FSU, GLU, GSU).
8 Frequency 6; alternative representations (FLT, GAT, PLT, FLU, FSU, GSU).
9 The representation of profits used here seems to be that of profits as exploitation as the firms are described as neglecting "all other criteria". The fact that semantic differences appear in this representation might be taken as evidence that it indeed mirrors the differences between economically trained and non-trained participants.
10 Frequency 2; alternative representations (FLT, PAT).

11 Later on, I show that this is in fact an *alternative representation of the worth of nations hypothesis*. Frequency: 11; alternative representations (FAT, GAT, GST, PST, FAU, FSU, GAU, GLU, GSU, PAU, PLU)
12 Frequency: 3; alternative representations (FAT, GAT, GSU).
13 Frequency: 7; alternative representations (GAT, GLT, PAT, PLT, FST, PAU, PLU).

Bibliography

Duveen, G. (2007). Culture and Social Representations. In J. Valsiner & A. Rosa (Eds.), *The Cambridge Handbook of Sociocultural Psychology* (pp. 543–559). Cambridge University Press. https://doi.org/10.1017/CBO9780511611162.029

Duveen, G. (2008). Social Actors and Social Groups: A Return to Heterogeneity in Social Psychology. *Journal for the Theory of Social Behaviour*, *38*(4), 369–374. https://doi.org/10.1111/j.1468-5914.2008.00385.x

Höijer, B. (2011). Social Representations Theory: A New Theory for Media Research. *Nordicom Review*, *32*(2), 3–16. https://doi.org/10.1515/nor-2017-0109

Kantner, C. (2014). The European Public Sphere and the Debate about Humanitarian Military Interventions. *European Security*, *23*(4), 409–429. https://doi.org/10.1080/09662839.2014.890595

Macron, E. (2019). *Pour une Renaissance européenne*. elysee.fr. www.elysee.fr/emmanuel-macron/2019/03/04/pour-une-renaissance-europeenne

Moscovici, S. (2004). *La psychanalyse, son image et son public*. Presses Universitaires de France. https://doi.org/10.3917/puf.mosco.2004.01

Risse, T. (2010). *A Community of Europeans?: Transnational Identities and Public Spheres*. Cornell University Press.

Rokkan, S. & Lipset, S. M. (1967). *Cleavage Structures, Party Systems and Voter Alignment. An Introduction*. Free Press.

Sammut, G. & Gaskell, G. (2010). Points of View, Social Positioning and Intercultural Relations. *Journal for the Theory of Social Behaviour*, *40*(1), 47–64. https://doi.org/10.1111/j.1468-5914.2009.00422.x

Trenz, H.-J. (2000). Korruption und politischer Skandal in der EU. Auf dem Weg zu einer europäischen politischen Öffentlichkeit? *KZfSS Kölner Zeitschrift Für Soziologie Und Sozialpsychologie, Sonderheft*, *29*, 332–359

7 Explaining Compatibility

Economic Politicization and the European Demos

7.1 Introduction

> We need to protect European industries and European farmers and to support and protect our SMEs, start-ups, and exporters. We also need to protect and promote our service industries, innovation, and European IPR [intellectual property rights]. I believe that there is a broad consensus on this both inside and outside this House. […] Today that means approving CETA.
>
> – Iulu Winkler (EPP)

> The caricature according to which there are only two schools of international trade – the school of protectionism, advocated by populists, and the school of ultra-liberalism, shared by a large majority in this Parliament – is unbearable. I would even say that this bipolar conception is suicidal for Europe today. Europe is capable of doing better, Europe deserves better. […] [CETA is] an agreement which gives more rights to multinationals; an agreement that weakens public services, farmers, SMEs; an agreement that places investor rights above social and environmental rights; [...] That's why I'll be voting against it.
>
> – Maria Arena (S&D)

> I am not speaking to the useless exponents of the European Commission, who are deaf, but I am speaking to the Italian and European citizens who are following us. Today you are complicit in yet another gift to multinationals and finance. About 200,000 workers will lose their jobs in Europe: factory workers, farmers, small entrepreneurs. Today you choose to bring hormone meat and GMO wheat to our children's tables, perhaps treated with pesticides banned in Europe […]. So hurry up and give your little friends the last gifts, because the peoples are coming to get you.
>
> – Matteo Salvini (at the time ENF)

The quotes above are drawn from the European Parliament's debate preceding the ratification of CETA, a trade deal negotiated with Canada. Yet, what we

DOI: 10.4324/9781003335610-11

see in the quotes goes beyond mere politics. Rather than simply justifying an international agreement, the delegates sketch visions of a **European identity constructed around economic issues**. The first quote promotes the idea of a European economy whose innovativeness and strength in exports may become the substrate of national pride. Contrary to this, the second quote alludes to a European social model, a compromise between economic ideologies based on Europe's historical achievements in the area of social rights. The final quote borrows some of these references to a social Europe but articulates them with populist fury, calling on the people to overthrow the economic elite, which allegedly controls the EU. Whether identity stems from a shared interest in the success of the European economy, from a historically grown social model or from the desire of the common people to overthrow the corrupt elite, the quotes tell us something about the political community the orators seek to address. In the eyes of these members of the European Parliament, Europeans should understand themselves as an economic community.

Conceptions of political community are linked to the concept of a public sphere in a complex way. On the one hand, symbols and identities are constructed and permanently re-negotiated in the public sphere. Public debates can be drivers of identity formation (Anderson, 1991; Delanty et al., 2008, pp. 16–17; Eder & Kantner, 2000, pp. 314–315; Risse, 2010, pp. 6–8). On the other hand, shared symbols and meaning structures are frequently identified as a precondition for the functioning of a public sphere (Eder & Kantner, 2000, pp. 308–309; Habermas, 1992b, p. 453, 2002, p. 60, 2011, pp. 56–57 & 78; Hepp & Wessler, 2009, p. 190). Citizens need common anchoring domains to make sense of political debates. For national public spheres, it is nationalism that provides such shared bodies of knowledge. Nationalism thus understood is a discourse equipping all members of a political community with the interpretive means to participate in public debates (Calhoun, 1997, p. 4; Hearn, 2006, p. 12; Özkirimli, 2005, pp. 29–30). Strangely enough, then, nationalism both depends on and promotes the emergence of a public sphere (Calhoun, 1997, p. 99). **A public sphere is a pre-condition for a political community, and the other way around.**

This dialectical relationship between political communities and public spheres explains why the empirical results of this book culminate in questions about the European demos. Chapters 2 and 3 have investigated how national anchoring enables public debates. National meaning structures have been shown to enhance citizens' capacity to discuss complex political issues by providing shared anchoring domains. Chapter 6 has proceeded to argue that communication in the European public sphere seems to function as well as in national public spheres. This chapter investigates **why transnational communication was possible**. Empirically, the chapter mainly considers those social representations that were not discussed in the previous chapters (as it focuses on representations that were transnationally shared rather than on those that were inter-nationally different). In the empirical material, inter-national differences were only discerned for nine out of 22 trigger arguments. For the majority of topics, then, the representations entertained by the participants were remarkably similar. So, if the communication in the European public sphere seems to function, doesn't this mean that there must be some form of European political community already? If we accept that shared meaning structures are a precondition for public communication, doesn't the cross-national similarity of representations imply that there are some anchoring domains all Europeans have access to? Diagnosing the functioning of the European public sphere in terms of compatibility implies arguing for the existence of a European demos.

Admittedly, the argument I wish to make here only targets a fragment of a much larger debate on the EU's political community. I limit myself in two important regards. First, the only aspect of a demos I comment on here is the availability of shared bodies of knowledge (i.e., of shared anchoring domains). Arguably, there are other requirements for the existence of a demos (e.g., the degree of solidarity among strangers; Risse, 2014), which cannot be assessed using the empirical evidence available in this study. Second, I only consider bodies of knowledge related to economics as a potential substrate of the European demos. Since the early 2000s, nationalism studies have repeatedly highlighted the potential of economic discourses to form the basis of nation-building (Duina & Smith, 2019; Helleiner, 2002; Pickel, 2005). But, of course, economics is but one among many potential issue areas around which a European identity could be constructed. Assessing to what extent knowledge on economic matters is shared among European citizens thus makes an important, though not an all-encompassing contribution to the debate on the European demos.

Practically, this chapter tests two such economic and knowledge-based conceptions of the European demos. Both are derivatives of the hypotheses developed for national knowledge in Chapter 1 (see Table 7.1). On the one hand, just as knowledge about the national economy can be collected to assess the worth of the nation, the EU can be defined as an economic space with measurable characteristics, too. Two definitions of the **worth of the Union** can be discerned: one neoliberal in orientation (the EU as an actor in a global competition of states) and one based on the idea of a European social model (the EU as a space of compromise between economic systems). On the other hand, just as debates in national public spheres create memories of past politics, the same process in the European public might generate elements of a **European political culture**. This is the diagnosis (and hope) of scholars stressing the importance of politicization for the emergence of a demos.

The test of these hypotheses strongly highlights the importance of politicization for community building on the European level. A process of European anchoring – analogous to national anchoring – can be observed, as citizens employ transnationally shared memories of recent European politics to make sense of economic issues. I show that two anchoring domains indeed seem to be strongly present in the European citizenry: a conception of a European social model and a representation of shared problems arising from

Table 7.1 Predictions for conceptions of European demos, derived from hypotheses and from the literature

	Similarity with hypothesis	Proponents	Substrate of identity formation
Worth of the Union (global competitor)	Worth of the nation	• Commission constructing tools of measurement of European economy • Iulu Winkler (EPP; see initial quote)	• Pride in success of economy (e.g., in terms of competitiveness, innovativeness or exports)
Worth of the Union (social model)	Worth of the nation	• Commission promoting European social standards • Jacques Delors, Jürgen Habermas, Maria Arena (S&D; see initial quote)	• Historically grown social model as compromise between ideologies
European political culture	National culture	• Scholars of politicization • Proponents of agonistic democracy	• Identity as result of political struggle (political culture mainly consisting of memories of past politics)

market integration. Both of these conceptions seem to have been popularized in salient past debates, such as the one concerning the ratification of CETA. In light of these results, I argue that the **construction of a European demos through the politicization of economic issues** is under way.

Arguably, these insights provide some clues about the potential **future course of public debates** in the European public sphere. The anchoring domains shared by Europeans can be drawn upon by a multitude of political actors to promote a wide range of different political projects. In the initial quotes, I presented voices from different ends of the political spectrum, from socialists over Christian democrats to right-wing populists. Certainly, some of these visions may not resonate much with the population (e.g., the EU as an economic block in a neoliberal competition of states) while others seem to fall on fertile ground (e.g., references to a social model or allusions to the suffering of the common people). Which political forces will dominate the future of Europe thus may partly depend on their capacity to mobilize the popular imagination, that is, the relevant representations of economics most widely shared by European citizens. This is where we return to the dialectics of political communities and public spheres: Politicization creates the anchoring domains of political communities, and the anchoring domains of political communities determine the success of arguments in the public sphere. I will return to this point at the end of the chapter after discussing each of the two hypotheses in a separate section.

7.2 The Worth of the Union

7.2.1 The EU as an Actor in a Neoliberal Competition of States?

A feeling of political community might be built on a perception of national economic success. In the contemporary world, national identities are frequently constructed around specific discourses of competitiveness (Kangas, 2013; O'Toole, 2003; Peet, 2002). Such discourses try to stimulate a feeling of attachment to the national community by casting the nation as an actor in a global competition of states. Economic success can generate feelings of pride or belonging while failures provide arguments for reform. "The worth of nations" (Greenfeld, 1995, p. 555) is determined in the international economic arena.

In Chapter 1, I have attempted to outline the bodies of knowledge on which such conceptions of nationalism are built. Calling the phenomenon 'the worth of nations' hypothesis, I argued that there are two main branches of knowledge production which allow for a construction of the nation as a competitor in a global competition of states. First, the national economy is constituted as a knowable object through the birth of economic statistics. The availability of data allows for the assignment of specific characteristics to the national economic space. These characteristics, second, can be compared to and measured against the features of other national economies. The international arena is thus constituted as a hierarchy of states, which, like firms, compete for sales (exports) and human capital (talented migrants). International economic rankings, moreover, assess the attractivity of national economies in terms of innovativeness, competitiveness or freedom of the economy. The availability of statistical data and the conception of the international order as an economic hierarchy can be the basis of an economic nationalism which celebrates the nation for its economic superiority vis-à-vis foreign competitors.

The construction of these bodies of knowledge is arguably taking place on EU level, too. With regard to statistics, it has been repeatedly observed that the European Commission actively pursues the construction of a European economy (e.g., Bernhard, 2011, pp. 428–429; Rosamond, 2012). National statistics are being aggregated in order to generate information about the European economic space as a whole (Rosamond, 2002, pp. 161–164). In line with this, the Commission tries to construct specifically European economic actors such as "European industry" or "European firms" (ibid.), "European workers" or "European consumers" (Jacobsson, 2004, pp. 360–362). Through the acquisition of data, "European competitiveness" or "the European labor market" become knowable objects. Thus, being able to describe the EU as a coherent economic space, the Commission frequently distinguishes the 'domestic' European economy from an outside. In other words, the EU is presented as a competitor to other economic blocks. Discourses of globalization serve to construct a vision of the international arena as a competition of states in which the EU risks falling behind (Rosamond, 2002, p. 162). Stylizing the EU as a competitor to the United States, Japan or China has been a prominent discursive strategy of European leaders ever since the 1980s (Rosamond, 2012, p. 331). With both statistical data and a discourse of global competitiveness firmly in place, the construction of the European economy mirrors the way national economies were constructed.

Why do I refer to this conception of European identity as neoliberal? Doesn't the state play a rather important role in this international competition and wouldn't this be something market radicals are not prone to like? Arguably, equating neoliberalism with the absence of state interference or laissez-faire economics would be oversimplified. I understand neoliberalism as an ideology that attempts to mobilize the state for the creation of market mechanisms in areas where these priorly did not exist (Foucault, 2006, pp. 300–324; Fougner, 2008). Thus, neoliberalism does not simply oppose state interference or regulation, but it seeks to convert the state into a market-enhancing agent. By complying with the prescriptions of international rating agencies, for example, states might attempt to boost competitiveness or innovativeness by promoting market-enhancing policies domestically (Fougner, 2008). Citizens may be encouraged to think like entrepreneurs, thus introducing mechanisms of competition into areas of life from which they were absent before. Collective action problems may be solved by turning externalities into tradeable goods, as witnessed, for example, in emission trading schemes. Such cases are not characterized by an absence of state interference, but by the active attempt of state institutions to create market mechanisms. International rating agencies and other producers of neoliberal rankings assess the success of states in fulfilling the role of a market enhancer and thus popularize neoliberal knowledge (see Chapter 1, Section 1.2.3.3). Where neoliberal criteria of assessment are applied to the state, this testifies to the success of neoliberal thought in spreading to the population.

So, are these forms on neoliberal knowledge present across the European citizenry? As most citizens know the worth of their national economy (see Chapter 3), can we expect that Europeans know the worth of the Union? Are EU citizens united in their representation of a European economy whose success in a global competition is their common aim?

In my empirical material, I only find limited evidence of such a conception of the EU's political community. While citizens clearly place their nation-states in a global competition of states, the EU is barely represented in such a way. In Chapter 3, I have shown that many focus group participants entertain a representation of an *economic world map*, which allows them to assign economic characteristics to different regions of the world. What is more, participants are able to place their own nations on this map. Knowing the characteristics of the national economy, participants frequently rank their own nation, diagnosing it to be "up front" or "behind". Such rankings are based on different criteria. Migration flows are one of them, with an inflow of migrants indicating a nation's attractiveness. Similarly, countries are rated based on the sectors in which their exports are strong. Finally, rankings can also be based on the quality of a nation's regulations, the product or labor standards. The participants in the focus group discussions thus were clearly able to place their nation-states in a global competition for talent or exports. What is more, the representations of the worth of the nation seemed to entail a feeling of belonging, conveying pride in economic strength or resonating with historical narratives. Whether the German boasting of industrial strength, the French pride in the quality of agricultural produce or the Polish quest of catching up with the West, characteristics of the national economy can be the substrate of collective self-identification. Knowledge of the worth of the nation is an important anchoring domain, and it reveals a feeling of sharing an economic destiny.

Knowledge about the state of the Union is much more limited. The EU is placed on the economic world map, yet only with regard to one of the three criteria. There is no representation of the EU as an economy which exports. Entities such as "European industry" or "European firms" are entirely absent in the material (see Table 3.2). While nation-states are compared based on the innovativeness of their exports, the EU is never placed in such a competitive setting. While it would be imaginable to depict the EU as competing for exports with China or the United States, I do not find such representations in my sample. Similarly, the EU is not placed in a competition for human capital. Migration mainly happens within the EU, and there is no representation of the European economy as an economic space in need of foreign talent. Representations such as *migration as talent* (see Appendix 1, Section A1.4.8) are exclusively applied to the nation-state. The absence of such representations indicates that **representations of a European economy are not particularly current in the European citizenry**. Economic success or failure is mainly attributed to the nation-state, and economic characteristics of the nation are more widely known than those of the EU. While knowledge of the state of the Union could be suitable substrate for the definition of a European demos, I find little empirical support for this idea.

This lack of identification with the economic success of the EU also means that neoliberal indicators are more readily applied to nation-states than to the Union. The economic world map is decisively neoliberal where the criteria for the assessment of states are based on their capacity to enhance markets (e.g., competitiveness as measured by exports, innovativeness, attractivity for human capital). Both the worth of the Union and the worth of the nation hypotheses, therefore, have neoliberal elements. But in the empirical material, these neoliberal elements are only present for nation-states (with attractivity for talent and capacity to export being causes of national pride). The popularity of such representations testifies to the capacity of neoliberal discourses to combine with nationalism (see also Kangas, 2013; O'Toole, 2003; Peet, 2002). It is all the more interesting, then, to see that this marriage of neoliberalism and nationalism does not extend to the European level. European citizens do not assess the EU by neoliberal criteria.

The absence of a vision of the EU as a neoliberal competitor is surprising given its prominence in official EU discourse. In the beginning of the chapter, I quoted a speech by Iulu Winkler, a Rumanian member of the European People's Party and an expert for trade policy. In the quote, Winkler alludes to many of the actors discussed here: to "European industry" and to "European Intellectual property rights", to "our [...] exports" and "our [...] innovation". And Winkler is certainly not alone in promoting such a neoliberal vision of a European economy, which needs to be enhanced in order to be globally competitive. Similar representations are mobilized by members of other parties in the EP (European Parliament, 2017). Moreover, as noted before, many Commission directorates to this day employ this vision of the European economy as a their main framing strategy, and, in fact, have done so since the Single European Act (e.g., Mudge & Vauchez, 2012). Yet, while such neoliberal framing strategies apparently do the trick within the European institutions, they do not seem to resonate with European citizens. In the focus groups, indicators such as exports and innovation were never applied to the European level, and the pronoun 'our' was largely reserved for characteristics of the national economy.

There is one notable exception to this lack of identification with the European economy. The EU appears on the economic world map as an economic space marked by high labor and product quality standards. In this representation of the EU, comparison with other economic blocks (e.g., the United States or China) does take place. The superior European standards, moreover, seem to be a locus of collective attachment, with participants in this context sometimes referring to the EU as 'we' or to 'our standards'. As these pronouns are usually reserved for the nation, we see that characteristics of the European economy can form the substrate of a European demos. For the citizens in my sample, then, the EU's economy is not characterized by competitiveness or innovativeness, but by the **quality of regulation**. There might not be 'European firms', but there are European standards. The EU is not understood as a global competitor for exports and talent, but rather as an economic space characterized by a specifically European social model.

7.2.2 The Worth of the Union: A European Social Model?

Just like the discourse of the EU as a global competitor, the idea of a **European social model** has gained currency since the 1980s. EU institutions have adapted this idea and they have used it to justify further integration. Arguably, one of the first European leaders to popularize the representation of a European social model was Jacques Delors (Hartlapp, 2019b, p. 545; Offe, 2005, p. 142). Yet, the concept has also been picked up by the European Council (Vaughan-Whitehead, 2015, pp. 2–3) and it has been shown to enjoy currency among Commission circles of policy experts (Duina & Smith, 2019, pp. 492–493; Jacobsson, 2004, p. 360). In the public sphere, demands on the

EU to transform into a 'social Europe' have intensified since the euro-crisis (Graziano & Hartlapp, 2015, p. 100; Hartlapp, 2019b, p. 548). Yet, despite this prominence in public discourse, definitions of the European social model remain vague (Hartlapp, 2019a, p. 60; Jepsen & Pascual, 2005). What traces of it, then, should we expect to find in the minds of European citizens? What should we look for in the empirical material when tracing a representation of a European social model?

From the academic literature, different expectations can be derived. A first conception of the European social model is based on shared historical experiences. This conception has been promoted quite prominently by Jürgen Habermas (Habermas, 1992a, pp. 10–12, 2002; see also Friese & Wagner, 2002, pp. 356–361). In Habermas conception of the political community, EU citizens should understand themselves as community of values, with these values in turn being rooted in a shared experience of European modernity. Among these specifically European experiences is the permanent need to establish compromises among different actors, ideas or systems (Habermas, 2002, p. 60; Offe, 2005, p. 142). A prominent example of such compromises is the economic system of Western Europe in the post-war years, which fused elements of socialism and capitalism. In economic terms, then, the experience of European modernity designates a compromise of economic systems, a social variant of capitalism (Nachtwey, 2016; Žižek & Horvat, 2014, p. 40). In the European citizenry, then, we should find shared memories of this time of compromise or at least a definition of Europe as a space of compromise between economic systems.

To what extent can such representations of a compromise of economic systems be discerned in the empirical material? Discussions about the relationship between the state and the market frequently entail representations of different economic ideologies. I have discerned representations of *socialism*, *capitalism* or *liberalism* in the material and – most importantly in this context – a representation of a *golden mean* (see Appendix 1, Section A1.6). In other words, when discussing complex economic issues, the focus group participants frequently characterize the pure forms of economic ideologies in a rather negative fashion (e.g., capitalism or socialism) and advocated a compromise between them. Moreover, the representation of the golden mean – the healthy compromise between economic systems – is frequently marked as a specifically European achievement. That is, it is either linked to specific historical experiences (e.g., the experience of socialism) or it is explicitly assigned to 'Europe' as an economic space.

> PSUM1: "We lived through communism, socialism, you know, they were such artificial systems which didn't work out. Right? In general. And now there is capitalism which is also not golden but that's also nothing new. But for sure it's better than those systems back in the days."
>
> – Polish soccer players discussing 'right to work'

PSTM5: "The market needs to be regulated to some extent but it should be regulated precisely regarding questions of quality, questions of standards, questions of access and of workers' rights. But it shouldn't be the case that the state with its paws is capable of controlling, of dictating every single element. Because we already went from such a form of sovereignty to a planned economy or to a centrally planned economy. And we pulled out 30 years ago."

PSTM4: "Yeah but also … For example, I am past my age of faith during which I believed in the invisible hand of the market and thought that we don't need any regulation. [PSTM1 & PSTM5 burst into laughter]"

PSTM5: "The time of faith!"

PSTM1: "The invisible hand of the free market!"

PSTM4: "Let him who was not liberal cast the fucking first stone."

– Polish soccer players discussing 'sovereignty & state vs market'

With loads of references to national history and to the representations of ideology previously described, both quotes advocate for a middle ground between state control and market liberalism. In the first quote, socialist state control is described as an "artificial system" while capitalism is not golden either. Similarly negative associations with both systems can be found in the second quote. On the one hand, the centrally planning state is described as a dangerous monstrosity, controlling the market with its paws. On the other hand, liberal ideology is ridiculed, and the memory of the unlimited faith in the free market, which ruled during the transformation, causes great laughter. Between these ridiculous extremes, PSTM5 sets out an elaborate vision of what a compromise between the systems could look like. The golden mean takes the form of a regulated market economy.

Should we view a shared experience of economic compromise as the central feature of the European social model then? Is the rejection of socialism and capitalism in their pure form a common ground for Europeans? I would be careful with sticking to such a historical conception for the simple reason that there are inter-national differences in representations of history (e.g., Gerhards et al., 2017). The quotes above, for example, are drawn from a Polish groups and similar ones can be found among German participants. Yet, as I argued in Chapter 2, memories of socialism are entirely absent from the French groups and thus the idea of a compromise of economic systems is much less frequent. While the representation of a historical compromise of economic systems seems to be current in countries with a history of socialism, this conception of the European social model might be less frequent elsewhere. Arguably, a thinner conception might be needed if we look for a representation of the European economy which might be shared among most citizens.

A second conception of the European social model defines it more thinly as a difference between the EU and other parts of the world in the desired degree of state intervention. This conception is mainly supported by empirical studies that assess the impact of nationality on public opinion in economic matters. A range of studies have found citizens of EU countries (excluding the UK) to be more favorable of state intervention and more critical of the market mechanism than citizens in the United States (and more rarely in the UK) (Duchesne, 2013, pp. 76–80; Duchesne & von Ingelgom, 2008; Lamont & Thévenot, 2000, pp. 14–15; Leiser et al., 2010, p. 135; Moody & Thévenot, 2000, pp. 285–302). Accordingly, maybe we should expect the European social model to find expression in a perception of a difference between the EU and other countries, most notably the United States. The United States might serve as a significant other, helping to define the specificities of the European economy.

Accepting this somewhat thinner definition of the European social model, I find strong evidence for it in my empirical material. I have pointed out in the last section that the EU appears on the economic world map as an economic space characterized by high labor and product quality standards. This representation is frequently complemented by a vision of *the West* as an area of unregulated capitalism, resulting in bad working conditions and low product quality regulations (see Appendix 1, Section A1.1.5). Apparently, the focus group participants define the perks of the European economy mainly in opposition to the perceived pitfalls of the United States. This construction of the European economy in opposition to the United States was most evident in the final sections of the focus group discussions when participants were asked about diverging opinions of citizens in other countries. The following discussion segments were all triggered by a question about inter-national differences in opinion.

GSUM1: "So there is a big gap between the unemployed on the one hand and the rich and the big entrepreneurs on the other. [...] I simply think those who would agree with us on all these points are members of the normal middle class. But otherwise, opinions would diverge."
GSUM3: "Well, but this middle class is almost inexistent by now. You know? [GSUM1: Well, yes.] There are only parts of it left. [...] We're inevitably approaching American conditions."
– German soccer players discussing alternative representations

FLUM1: "There are certainly some countries that are less capitalist. [FLUN1 makes an admiring sound] They are not necessarily socialist though. [...] There are always the two sides in any case."
FLUW2: "I think there are a lot of countries that rely mainly on the private sector. We are very ... How to say? Statist? So the state is very strong here."
– French teachers discussing alternative representations

PAUW1: "In the United States it's everybody for himself. Because there is no such ..."

PAUM1: "It's pure capitalism".
PAUW1: "Yes! Over there, there is no socialism, there is no insurance."
– Polish agents discussing alternative representations

In the quotes, we see that there seems to a quite pronounced representation of a difference in economic organization between the United States and Europe. The United States is depicted as "pure capitalism", lacking regulation and producing large differences between the rich and the poor. Europe, on the contrary, is described as statist or regulated capitalism (a capitalism which provides "insurance", which is "less capitalist" and which should allow for the survival of a "middle class"). The European citizens in my sample thus seemed to be convinced that there is a specifically European mode of economic organization. When asked for differences with other countries, they readily distinguish a European social model from an American counterpart.

Interestingly, even those participants which most vocally defend the free market and which are critical of state intervention are united in their opposition to the American model. Admiration for the innovativeness of the US economy often does not preclude criticism of unregulated capitalism. Most potently, this position is expressed by GAUM2, an economically trained participant who on multiple occasions voices harsh criticism of state intervention and frequently mobilizes the experience of East German socialism as a worst-case scenario. Yet, regarding the United States, he shares the skepticism of his peers:

GAUM2: "I am not against regulation in general. I think the state can and should get in involved sometimes. [...] I am happy that we do not live in the US where they have complete freedom from regulation."
– German agent discussing 'merit'

FLTM3: "But if the treaty was made how it should be, then standards would be an objective to achieve. It could go in a positive direction because it could raise standards in the entire world. Europe doesn't need to lower standards, they can also be raised."
– French teacher discussing 'standards'

Representations of a European social model thus indeed seem to be a common ground shared by a wide range of European citizens. FLTM3 is economically trained, just like GAUM2, and has been advocating efficiency-based and market friendly representations throughout the discussion. Yet, he also appreciates some core tenets of the European social model, cherishing the high European standards that may become a model for the rest of the world. A compromise of ideology, rather than the reign of unregulated (American) capitalism is thus appreciated even by those participants who do not have an affinity to socialism. Representations of the European social model seem to be accepted across a wide range of groups. In the final quotes, we see how these elements can combine to form a full-blown vision of a European political community constructed around economic issues.

> GLTM1: "I am always a bit sceptical with these free trade agreements because mentalities differ greatly between the US, Canada and us here in Europe. So eh it is important to me that this capitalist [GLTW1: Exactly], these capitalist standards – increase productivity, profits, returns and so on [GLTW1: Exactly] – that these standards don't ... I mean the economy exists to keep society functioning. And in my opinion society functions best if there is a social balance."
>
> – German teachers discussing 'standards'

> FLTM1: "For me the big blind spot are product standards. In the European Union, for example, GMOs are strictly prohibited and in Canada they are allowed. An important issue of CETA was therefore to authorize these GMO products on the European market. [...] So that is a lowering of our standards [...]. And that is the principal problem with that treaty and even worse with the one with the US which really looks scary to me."
>
> – French teachers discussing 'standards'

All elements of the European social model can be discerned in the quotes. In the first quote, a compromise of systems ("a social balance") cannot be achieved by following the American model of pure capitalism. European standards are not purely "capitalist standards". In the second quote, European standards are primarily understood as high product quality standards exemplified by a wariness of GMOs. Again, the United States (and to some extent Canada) serve as significant others. Yet, what is most striking in both quotes is the degree of identification with the European compromise or with European standards. In both cases, the pronoun 'we' is employed to refer to the European economy ("us here in Europe", "our standards"). The characteristics of the European economy and particularly the quality of European regulation thus can be the basis of collective identification. European citizens may well be united based on their concern for the preservation of a European social model.

The popularity of the conception of a European social model is good news insofar as the EU is also most commonly credited with the task of regulating the economy. In the empirical material, different representations of state functions can be discerned, and not all of these state functions are also assigned to the EU (see Appendix 1, Sections A1.5.6 and A1.5.7). The EU is not viewed as a *competitor* with other states, for example, and only rarely represented as a *re-distributor*. But as the representation of the EU as a *regulator* is quite current, there seems to be a match between the task the EU is seen fit for and the desired outcome of a strongly regulated market. The representation of the European social model thus might provide a common ground for discussion about economic policy. Arguments such Maria Arena's (cited in the beginning of the chapter) are likely to resonate with the citizens. Calls for a middle way between 'ultra-liberalism' and 'protectionism', and criticism of the placement of investors' rights above social rights are likely to be understood by the citizens of Europe.

Yet again some care is warranted. Beyond a vague commitment to a model that is more social than the American version, opinions vary greatly once this is to be translated into concrete political measures. In the beginning of the chapter, it is not only the socialist MEP Arena who mobilizes a representation of the European social model. References to superior European standards are also used by Matteo Salvini whose conclusions differ enormously from those endorsed by the left wing of the S&D fraction. The European social model thus might create a basis for the understanding of arguments, but it certainly does not provide for agreement on the political path to be pursued. Arguably, **the concrete implications of a commitment to regulated capitalism are subject to debate**. This seems to point toward yet another conception of political community.

7.3 A Demos through Politicization: Toward a European Political Culture?

The final conception of the European demos I wish to discuss here perceives the attachment to a political community as the result of politicization (Auer, 2010, pp. 1180–1181; McNamara & Musgrave, 2020; Risse, 2010, pp. 6–8; White, 2011, pp. 114–115). According to this line of theory, the European demos is to be created through political conflict, public debates and the struggle over the definition of common values. The more EU politics are politicized, the greater will be knowledge of and attachment to the European polity. Salient public debates will create the elements of a political culture.

On the level of the nation-state, the effects of politicization on the feeling of national belonging are well documented. Benedict Andersson (1991) already highlighted the importance of political debates in the public sphere for the formation of imagined communities. In the hypotheses section, I argued that nationalism can be understood as a symbolic structure that establishes shared patterns of meaning. I have referred to this understanding of the nation as a space of shared symbols as the *national culture hypothesis*. The hypothesis was tested in Chapter 2, resulting in the finding that particularly memories of past politics functioned as a crucial national anchoring domain. In other words, citizens maintain memories of the political struggles taking place in the political arena. Arguments exchanged in the public sphere and specific linguistic expressions coined in the context of debate become collectively shared references, which serve as anchoring points for future debates. Put briefly, politicization creates the elements of national political culture.

Arguably, the same process can be discerned at the European level. Politicization of European issues indeed seems to increase knowledge about the EU and thus provide common anchoring points to European citizens. The effects of this process can be discerned in three areas. First, past European politics seem to already have created some widely shared anchoring domains, most visibly in the issue area of trade. Second, there is a widely shared representation of problems arising from market integration. *Race to the bottom* representations may become an important reference point for future debates regarding the regulation of the common market. Finally, representations of the common people are shared across social groups, thus potentially creating the preconditions for a populist appeal. Whether future debates in the European public sphere, then, will be about reforming regulations, or will tip toward calls for an overthrow of the corrupt system in the name of the people, will depend on which party succeeds in mobilizing the representations shared by Europeans. Politicization is under way, but its destination is unknown.

7.3.1 Past European Politics

The salience of **memories of past European politics** as a shared anchoring domain becomes most apparent on two issues. First, the 2008 economic crisis and the consequent euro-crisis constitute shared reference points which provide knowledge about European affairs. The representation of the economic crisis is particularly salient for the construction of some parts of the economic world map. As a moment of heightened attention to European issues, the public debates surrounding the euro-crisis seem to have spread knowledge of the state of the economy in other European countries. The representation of *Southern Europe*, for example, was often connected to high levels of Youth unemployed (see Appendix 1, Section A1.1.7). Germany and Greece were mobilized as symbols for different approaches to the crisis by participants of all nations. In other words, the public debates surrounding the economic crisis seem to have provided a shared repertoire of meaning European citizens now draw upon to make sense of present debates. This seems to be in line with the findings of other studies assessing the potential of the crisis to form the elements of a European political culture (Hepp et al., 2016, pp. 187–192; Statham & Trenz, 2015, pp. 302–303).

A second source of common knowledge for European citizens seems to be the campaigns mobilizing against CETA and against the Transatlantic Trade and Investment Partnership (TTIP). Such movements criticizing the free trade deals were prominent in all three countries under study (Działo & Gawrońska-Nowak, 2017; Hübner et al., 2017, p. 844; Meunier & Roederer-Rynning, 2020). In the trade discussions, participants were prompted with a reference to CETA in the introduction. Yet, in the discussions, participants often made no difference between Canada and the United States, thus forming a representation of *the West* on the economic world map (see Appendix 1, Section A1.1.5). In fact, the construction of a European economy in opposition to the United States, which I described in the last section, might result from the public discourse surrounding the free trade agreements. In particular, in the

German and French groups, very similar symbols were mobilized to depict the difference in product standards between Europe and the West (mainly GMOs or chlorinated chicken). This might hint at the fact that the knowledge participants used to anchor questions of free trade actually came from past European debates. Politicization of EU issues seems to provide European citizens with common anchoring points for later debates.

The impact of the politicization of CETA on European citizens is exemplified by the quotes in the beginning of this chapter. The statements by S&D politician Maria Arena and by Matteo Salvini exhibit surprising similarities with some representations present in the focus group material. In particular, in the way a *social ordering of sectors* is mobilized the European Parliament debate closely resembles the discussions of focus group participants:

> GLTW2: "If I now imagine an apple farmer here in Brandenburg, but globally production costs are lower, than they have much bigger chances to succeed. So you'd have to be protective."
>
> GLTM1: "And that's exactly why you need consumer standards [GLTW2: Yes, exactly!]. I have this ecological farmer with his eco-chickens and eco-eggs on the one hand, and somewhere in the US there are these mass-produced, chlorinated chickens [GLTW3: Mass-produced eggs! Square eggs!]. I have to protect the former!"
>
> – German teachers discussing 'standards'

> GSTM1: "For us it is better if we have less toys that cause cancer. Right? Well, ok, we regulated, and we limited entrepreneurship, but we limited it for the sake of the population."
>
> DA: "Do you think so too?"
>
> GSTM2: "Hm well yeah … Rather too much than too little."
>
> – German soccer players discussing 'state vs market'

The distinction of small (ecological) European farmers from unhealthy mass production abroad was a central element of the public debate surrounding CETA and of thus also of the quotes in the beginning of this chapter. This *social ordering of sectors* (see Appendix 1, Section A1.1.4) is picked up by the focus group participants who clearly prioritize food safety (local Brandenburgian ecological eggs) over competitively priced consumer goods ("toys that cause cancer"). The second quote, moreover, appears like a defense of the precautionary principle with GSTM2 pledging for "rather too much than too little" regulation. These representations are strikingly similar to the claims advanced in the EP debate on CETA to prevent "hormone meat and GMO wheat" and not to place "investor rights above social and environmental rights". It seems that the European citizens who took part in my focus group debates did pay attention to the public debates surrounding CETA. In six out of nine trade discussions,[1] we find fears of a lowering of product standards for agriculture, which closely mirror those expressed in the parliamentary debate, often using the exact same examples and vocabulary.

The politicization of trade agreements thus seems to have made similar anchoring points available to many Europeans. Just like national cultures emerged in national public spheres, transnationally salient debates in the European public sphere are establishing a European political culture. This finding also sheds a new light on the popularity of the European social model discussed in the previous section. Just like national anchoring was rarely based on memories of grand history, representations of the European social model might also not be principally rooted in such memories. The popularity of some elements of the **European social model might be a result of recent political struggles**, rather than a collective memory of European modernity. The relationship between recent politicization, political culture and anchoring is very similar on the European and on the national level. Analogous to national anchoring, we seem to observe a form of European anchoring here.

7.3.2 The Internal Market as a Race to the Bottom: Shared Problems as the Basis for Future Politicization?

There is more to be said about the agonistic conception of the European demos. Beyond memories of past debates, the focus group material seems to reveal where there is **potential for future European debates**. Arguably, focus group participants define a number of problems they are collectively affected by. Based on such common definitions of problems, future politicization could create further visibility of European affairs and thus intensify the construction of a European political culture, which is arguably already under way.

Which are the common problems the focus group participants identify? One of the most widespread representations in the empirical material depicts the international arena as a **race to the bottom**. Race to the bottom representations can be discerned for the product, the capital, and the labor market (see Table 7.2; Appendix 1, Sections A1.2.6., A1.3.7 and

Table 7.2 Social representation of international circulation of goods, capital and labor

	Product market	Capital market	Labor market
Positive sum game	***Exchange (products)***	*Exchange (ideas & capital)*	*Migration (efficiency)*
Zero-sum game			*Migration (talent)* *race to the bottom (migration)*
Negative sum game	*Race to the bottom (products)*	*Race to the bottom (firms)*	***Migration (pointless replacement)***

Note: Representations based on personal experience are underlined.

A1.4.9). Taken together, they appear in 13 out of 18 focus groups.[2] These representations are similar insofar as they describe all states involved in the process as losers.[3] In other words, in most of the focus groups we find representations that describe the adverse of effects of the free movement of labor, capital and goods.

FSTM6: "It is more than 15 years that we are in the European community. They call that globalization, that is to say that there are no more customs between the European countries [FSTM1: That is Schengen, right?]. That means that there is meat coming in from Spain, other products come from Romania. Look for example at the workers here, you call them travailleurs détachés. What is a travailleur détaché? The people coming from Romania to work in France. But they do the same work for two times less than a French salary [FSTM1: Yeah, yeah]. […] That's why the traveilleurs détachés are called in so they can work for half the money. And it is the same for clothes, it is the same for products."

– French soccer players discussing 'workers' rights'

GLTM1: "We see that it doesn't work in the EU. Yes, ok, we can buy everything everywhere, but in the end, we don't have a social union […]. That means German meat producers can profit from the fact that Rumanians work here for the worst dumping wages and under terrible working and living conditions [GLTW2: That's how it is]. And in Rumania, they don't really profit, except those few families, if they can live from the dumping-wages."

– German teachers discussing 'investment'

PAUM1: "I chose 'boost international competitiveness [as a negative card] […]. Always this acceleration in the same direction, it really gets absurd in the end."

PAUW2: "I also took issue with 'international competitiveness' because it is a bit like … Like the race with the rabbit [loughs]. [. .]

PAUW1: "Ok, that's why I chose 'Encourage international mobility of workers'. And I dislike it because I think that everybody would leave. [PAUW2: Yes] My colleagues in the housing sector left and they were replaced by Ukrainians [PAUW2: Yes]. It is such a … This one guy left for Norway, and now he comes back to Poland every two months and he has three children. Well, that's just … [makes a suffering sound]. And he was replaced by Ukrainians and in Ukraine the situation is exactly the same as here. They have kids and family there but have to sit here and work. The problem just carries on … because soon there'll be no more poor countries from which people can come."

– Polish agents discussing 'mobility' and 'competitiveness'

The quotes above come from a coach of a French soccer team, from a teacher in Berlin-Reinickendorf and from a group of housing agents lunching in the center of Warsaw. In all quotes, I believe, we see evidence of national anchoring: the concept of *travailleur détaché*, the exploitation scandals of the German meat industry and the flows of work migration to Poland are the central anchoring points. Yet through their national lens, these European citizens describe the same problems arising from integration: The exploitation of workers from the east for the sake of lower prices and higher profits. In the race to the bottom on the product and the labor market there are few or even no winners: too low are the wages paid, too high the costs of moving abroad, too strong the pressure on working conditions. In its worst moments, the internal market thus is represented as "a race with the rabbit", a rigged competition in which all participants lose.

European citizens thus seem to perceive some processes triggered by market integration as harmful to all sides involved. As diagnosed by earlier studies (Favell, 2009, p. 12; Guérot, 2014, p. 140), the most important problems identified here are tax evasion and injustices arising from economic migration. Debating solutions to these problems in the European public sphere could boost the feeling of attachment to a political community of the EU. If a European political culture is to emerge from the struggle over common concerns, these issues might form the basis of such a politicization.

What can we infer from this about future economic debates in the European public sphere? Importantly, my argument only points at knowledge reservoirs that can be mobilized rather than predicting the success of certain political forces over others. Claiming that race to the bottom representations resonate with European citizens does not imply, for example, that the left will emerge victoriously from future political struggles. Anchoring domains and the resulting social representations can be put at the service of various political projects; race of the bottom representations may be placed in a multitude of narratives or frames (see also Chapter 1, Section 1.5). That being said, the availability of certain representations, of course, privileges some arguments to be made in the European public sphere. To say it in the words employed to describe national anchoring: if arguments resonate with the available anchoring domains, this increases their **frequency and persuasiveness**. Thus, we should expect arguments that draw on race to the bottom representations to be well-understood by Europeans and to be considered quite convincing. Arguments that do not resonate with pre-existing anchoring points should command much less popular appeal. While thus not being able to determine to the success or failure of political actors,[4] some political forces might find it easier to mobilize support for their programs as their demands mirror representations of the economy widely shared by Europeans.

What does this mean concretely? I have pointed out in Section 7.3.1 that the representation of the EU as an actor in a global competition of states does not seem to be widely shared. It seems hard to believe that political actors relying on this vision (e.g., parts of EPP and ALDE in the CETA debate) derive their strengths from popular support for such arguments. On the contrary, actors on the left of the political specter should find themselves encouraged. The restoration of (parts of) the European social model and the mitigation of adverse effects of market integration have been central demands of progressive thinkers (e.g., Habermas, 2014; Žižek & Horvat, 2014). Should the European left succeed in making such demands visible in the European public sphere, it would strike a chord with many citizens. While the left, then, might profit from the EU-wide perception of mutually harmful economic processes, other actors might capitalize on such representations, too. Most notably, representations of economic injustices are frequently accompanied by a vision of the common people, cheated by a corrupt elite. While some left-wing arguments are prone to resonate with Europeans, then, so is the people–elite discourse employed by many populist actors.

7.3.3 Cheating Common Europeans: Shared Problems as the Basis of Populist Appeal?

Apart from the race to the bottom group, there is a second type of representations which seems to provide potential for transnational mobilization and for the politicization of European economic issues. These are the representations of the **common people**, and of their opponent, the corrupt economic elite (see Chapter 4). Representations such as *the consumer*, *the working people* or *the taxpayer* are very similar among participants from all countries. Moreover, such representations of the common people are most frequently mobilized to express a feeling of being cheated. The working people are squeezed by *the manager*, consumers might be tricked by low product quality and the taxpayer shoulders the burden created by *big firms'* tax evasion (see Appendix 1, Sections A1.3.3–A1.3.5). Pitting the people against a selfish elite clearly could be a strategy of transnational politicization that might resonate with large parts of the European citizenry.

Earlier studies of transnational economic debates have identified similar forms of problem identification among European citizens of lower socio-economic status (e.g., J. White, 2011, pp. 92–104). I believe my results go beyond previous studies as they identify traces of the same discourse among participants with a variety of class backgrounds. Some teachers, some agents and some soccer players in the discussions, for example, certainly were part of rather privileged strata of society. This is why I do not speak of the "little people" like scholars previously have done (Gamson, 1992; White, 2011). I believe the terms common people or normal people are better suited to describe the phenomenon as they highlight that this discourse may surface among most strata of society. The elite in this discourse thus is very narrowly defined and the life-world experiences of the common people (paying taxes, feeding a family, working hard) seem to be relatively independent of class.[5] That is why representations of the common people are so frequent in the focus group material, and accordingly, why they might constitute such a widely shared anchoring domain in the European public sphere.

Constituting such a powerful and widely shared reference point, representations of the common people thus can be mobilized to decry the same economic problems presented in the previous section. In other words, the race to the bottom representations may be combined with those of the little people, painting a picture of the international economic arena as inherently flawed and set up simply to profit the rich.

> FSTM6: "It's the multinationals who will be happy because it's in their interest. The people interested in CETA are always the big firms, it's never the small and medium-sized companies. […] the farmers dislike it because CETA is a global thing – it will be in favor of the stock market. So for the small farmer it's dead. Same for meat producers. […] For the French producers, production is expensive, but when you go to the supermarket meat gets increasingly cheap. Why? Because there is external production. Meat will be less expensive tomorrow but in terms of quality I am not sure whether that's good."
>
> – French soccer players discussing 'SMEs'

> PSTM4: "Big corporations can dictate their condition to the state. When they take issue with workers' rights, for example, they say: 'Alright. Listen up, something!' I don't know. 'We will do it like this and like that. And you better listen because if not we'll just fuck off.' Right?
>
> PSTM5: "But it is already like that! And that's a huge problem. Mercedes comes in and says that they want to open an engine factory in Lower Silesia. So they come and say: 'Ok, make your offer! What can you give us?' Well and Poland, that is Mr. Morawiecki, is fucking shivering and starts straight away to think something up … 'Cool, thanks guys. Good idea, but wait, we'll just go to Slovakia first. [PSTM1: To Slovakia! Do you know what they offered us there?] And do you know what the Hungarians said? We will get back to you evetnually!' And then they stay silent for some fucking time. And Morawiecki is sitting there with his guys: 'Ok, we promised on TV that Mercedes will invest here. Have to offer them something good, so they come here.'"
>
> – Polish soccer players discussing 'investment'

> GSUM1: "Well, I didn't find any positive cards [laughter from group]. […] What does 'international competitiveness' mean? Non-wage labor costs – I know that from Siemens – doesn't do any good because even if they get lowered, they fire people anyway. There is always a rat-tail because they rather cater shareholders than the needs of the firm or of the people. […] Everybody should at least be able to feed his family and to pay rent. If that gets tight, then it's all for nothing.

> [...] Ehm it would also be nice, and that is not mentioned here, if the competitiveness of law ... So there would need to be the same law everywhere, the same taxes, et cetera ... Because like this they wander, it is just moving around like in a board game [Mensch-ärgere-dich-nicht]. Then off they go to the next country, because they say: 'Ah, here things are cheaper.' And off they go. Then you got some new employees over there, but you lose them in the original country. Well? That doesn't make sense. So, the law should be the same everywhere. In the end, this will take a couple of years, but in the end, it has to be the aim."
>
> – German soccer players discussing 'competitiveness' and 'mobility'

In the quotes, three groups of soccer players from different countries combine race to the bottom representations with visions of the common people. The international circulation of firms and products is depicted as a crooked undertaking, profiting only a narrow business elite while harming the common people. The first quote centers on the product market, arguing that CETA will lower "quality" (read standards), being designed to aid only the "multinationals". The race to the bottom on the product market (the lowering of standards due to competitive pressures from big business) is connected to a representation of the common people. It is the consumers who will be cheated with lower quality products and it is big business (and the political class complicit in the design of the deal) that will harvest the benefits. Similarly, in the second quote political and business elites cooperate to trick the people ("we announced on TV that Mercedes will invest here. Have to offer them something good"). Although this cooperation happens somewhat grudgingly as the Polish government is strongarmed into cooperation, the effects are the same as in the previous quote: standards (in this case "workers' rights") are being lowered and the people will bear the cost. In the final quote, the references to the common people are most explicit. GSLM1 draws on workplace experiences and explicitly cites paying rent and feeding a family as the most basic shared experiences. His description of the elite is no less clear, literally referring to the elite as "they" (without grammatical signifier). Just like in the first quotes, the elite are big firms, "the stock market" and "shareholders". Representations of the common people thus are frequently mobilized to describe the problems of market integration. Participants in all countries frequently depicted losses to the common people as gains to economic and political elites.

This cocktail of representations is quite explosive. On the one hand, there is an unfair international system, systematically favoring business interests over those of the people. On the other hand, there is a corrupt elite which – through control of both political and economic institutions – prevents changes to the system. If both representations are combined, the situation of the common people is hopeless indeed. I believe some of this hopelessness is evident in the quotes above: no solution to the problems of international markets is being proposed in the first or second quote. FSTM6 describes the rule of big business almost as a fact of life ("always the big firms, never small and medium sized companies") and participants in the Polish group trump themselves with cynicism and strong language when describing the unfairness of the international system. This tone of frustration contrasts with GSUM1's light optimism regarding the harmonization of laws within the EU. The representation of the EU as a successful regulator thus can provide a potential solution, but it is not frequent enough to be present in most groups (see Appendix 1, Section A1.5.6). Viewing successful regulation at the EU level as an option remains the exception rather than the rule.

Given the perceived absence of solution and the degree of frustration articulated at the international system, it might become understandable why radical solutions may acquire some currency.

> FSUM1: "Well, so you have the United States to begin with. Five to ten years ago in the United States, people committed suicide. They lost their homes, they didn't have anything anymore. They could no longer afford a dentist or any doctor because they couldn't pay their debts. They no longer had any money. And the false Americans, they took it all. The rich are rich, like in France, the rich are rich and the poor are poor. There no longer is a middle. Before, there were people in the middle. Today, there no longer is a middle. So let's talk about international exportation. There is a study: the Brexit. The English leave in 2019 at the latest. They told them that they would die. But today they are surviving and, even better, they are doing really well! We have to leave the euro. I think, today, we have to leave the euro. In France, we have meat, fish, cheese, agriculture. [...] We can live well with our own products in France. And with employment and everything you want. You just have to stop Europe. Europe is a charade."
>
> – French soccer player discussing 'competitiveness'

The quote above contains many of the representations thus far discussed in this chapter. FSUM1 very explicitly mobilizes a representation of the common people, stating twice that "the rich are rich" while everyone else slowly slides into poverty. This poverty is being defined by reference to the typical experiences of the common people, that is, paying rent ("they lost their homes") and bills ("they couldn't pay their debt"). Apart from that, FSUM1 also seems to reference some kind of a European social model, depicting the United States as a horror scenario and constantly alluding to a vaguely defined better past. Regarding the latter point, the quote above mainly reveals FSUM1's excessive usage of the word today, which he – in other parts of the discussion – mainly employs to distinguish the status quo from 'back in the days when everything was better'. Yet, FSUM1 clearly does not see the EU as a means to bring the good old times back. Rather, he seems to be a proponent of Frexit and of a dissolution of the EU. In FSUM1's case, frustration with the unfair economic system and with the undeserved dominance of an elite causes pronounced Euroskepticism. What is more, I believe this Euroskepticism draws on the very representations that might become the object of politicization in future European debates. While sharing many representations employed by GSUM1, FSUM1 calls on the EU to dissolve rather than to regulate. Representations of shared problems can be mobilized to advocate a wide range of solutions.

The availability of representations of the common people across European citizens thus might be a factor that contributes to the success of populist parties.[6] There seems to be far-reaching agreement in the literature that a people–elite discourse is the central element of populist discourse (e.g., Mudde, 2004; Panizza, 2005). In my focus groups, then, I find evidence that such arguments resonate with many European citizens. Representations of the international economic order as a rigged competition set up to benefit corrupt elites will be considered quite persuasive. One factor in the recent success of populist parties might be their success in mobilizing anchoring domains familiar to the European citizenry.

The course of future debates in the public sphere thus seems to be hard to predict. The representations of economics shared by large parts of the European citizenry can, in fact, be mobilized by a wide range of political actors. In the last quote, we saw how representations of the common people and of the European social model were mobilized to advocate anti-EU policies. It was the very same point I wished to convey with my choice of quotes in the beginning of the chapter. Both Matteo Salvini, anti-European populist, and Maria Arena, alter-European socialist, seemed to employ surprisingly similar representations to justify their resistance to CETA. Both diagnosed a sell-out to "multinationals" by the forces dominating the EP (the political elite, one might say). Both decried the lowering of European standards, in particular in sectors central to human flourishing. And while their speeches thus were similar, I believe it is fair to say that their visions for the EU are radically different. This should be the main conclusion drawn from the discussion of the emerging European political culture. Like national culture, the availability of widely shared anchoring domains renders certain arguments more convincing in the European public sphere. But this only gives us limited insights about the future course of debates as these resources can be mobilized by fairly different political camps.

To sum up this section, then, the conception of the European demos as the result of politicization seems to be supported by the empirical material. The construction of a European political community might take place through an intensification of public debates around economic issues. Past European debates have already created elements of a European political culture, which provide European citizens with shared anchoring points. What is more, there is considerable potential for this process to intensify in the future as many representations of economic problems seem to be transnationally shared. The

European demos might emerge in the public struggle over economic issues while the outcome of such struggles is uncertain.

7.4 Conclusion

This chapter has provided some tentative answers to the question why the European public sphere does not have a compatibility problem. If nationalism is crucial to the functioning of national public spheres, the fact that transnational communication in the EU seems to work might indicate the existence of a European demos. If social representations are cross-nationally compatible, this implies that there are anchoring domains all Europeans have access to. The chapter, therefore, discussed conceptions of the European demos which, first, define the political community via access to specific bodies of knowledge and, second, which focus on economic knowledge. The three conceptions of the European demos discussed in this chapter thus reflect different branches of EU studies and mirror the conceptions of national knowledge developed in Chapter 1 (see Table 7.1).

In the empirical material, I find evidence for two out of three of these conceptions. First, despite the prominence of such conceptions in official EU discourse, there is no evidence for a conception of the EU as an actor in a neoliberal competition of states. This is interesting as such conceptions are strongly present for the participants' respective nation-states. Whereas France, Germany or Poland are perceived as competitors for exports or human capital, the EU is not cast as such a community of economic fate struggling for success in a global race. While there is a powerful combination of neoliberalism and nationalism at the nation-state level, this conception is not present for the EU.

Second, while it is not cast as a competitor, the EU is represented as an economic space characterized by a specifically **European social model**. In the empirical material, I find three representations which are transnationally shared and which hint toward a self-definition of Europeans in economic terms: a negative representation of the 'American' model of capitalism, a representation of the EU as an economic space characterized by high labor and product quality standards, and a representation of a historically rooted compromise between economic systems. In other words, a majority of focus group participants seems to identify with a European social model, constructed mainly in opposition to the United States.

The conception for which I find most empirical support conceives the European demos as the result of politicization. Just like memories of past politics create specifically national anchoring points, I discern some transnationally shared memories of past European politics. In particular the euro-crisis and the mobilization around CETA and TTIP created anchoring points focus group participants drew upon in the discussions (with the latter partly explaining the popularity of representations of the European social model). Politicization of EU affairs, in other words, seems to create the elements of a

European political culture. Moreover, as most focus group participants share similar representations of the negative effects of market integration, there seems to be a basis for further politicization. The European demos might emerge more distinctively in future debates about adverse effects of tax competition or East–West migration.

Somewhat puzzlingly, then, the emergence of a European demos might at the same time be a precondition and an effect of the emergence of the European public sphere. Only a shared political culture allows for the functioning of communication in the public sphere, and yet this very communication creates and reshapes the symbols any political culture consists of. The EU, like a nation, might be best understood as a zone of public conflict.

Notes

1 See representation of agriculture in the social ordering of sectors: frequency: 7; standards (FAT, FLT, FST, GST, GLT, PST), prices (FST).

2 Frequency 22; competitiveness (PAU), exports (PST), interest (GSU), investment (GST, PAT, PST), mobility (FAU, GSU), privatization (PLU), right to work (FLU), sovereignty (GAT, GST, PAT), standards (FLT, FST, GAT, GLT, PLT), workers' rights (FLT, FST, GST, PAT).

3 There are some differences with regard to the definition of the winners. Whereas on the product and the capital market, winners are big firms, but on the labor market, migrant workers are assumed to profit. This causes the representation to be more nuanced for the labor market as workers from other countries are viewed as legitimate recipients of such benefits whereas big business is not.

4 Obviously, there are many additional (and potentially more important) factors which determine the success of political movements in the EU. Their capacity to mobilize discursive reservoirs present among the citizens, however, is certainly non-negligible. The fact that this chapter focuses on shared representations does not imply that I consider other factors irrelevant (see introduction to this chapter).

5 This is not to say that economic experiences are similar or independent of class. Rather, the formulations such "paying taxes" or "working hard" allow for a wide range of different experiences to be subsumed under them (and thus allow for a large variety of people to identify with them). The actual experiences (e.g., the hardship of work), however, will obviously be vary greatly with class.

6 It may, of course, given the dialectics of public communication and culture also be consequences thereof. But as studies diagnosing the presence of such representations precede the recent populist surge (e.g., Halle, 1984; J. White, 2011, fieldwork conducted in 2005), I believe makes sense to conceptualize these representations as a potential not yet fully mobilized.

Bibliography

Anderson, B. R. O. (1991). *Imagined Communities: Reflections on the Origin and Spread of Nationalism*. Verso.

Auer, S. (2010). 'New Europe': Between Cosmopolitan Dreams and Nationalist Nightmares. *JCMS: Journal of Common Market Studies*, *48*(5), 1163–1184. https://doi.org/10.1111/j.1468-5965.2010.02108.x

Bernhard, S. (2011). Beyond Constructivism: The Political Sociology of an EU Policy Field. *International Political Sociology*, *5*(4), 426–445. https://doi.org/10.1111/j.1749-5687.2011.00143.x

Calhoun, C. J. (1997). *Nationalism*. University of Minnesota Press.

Delanty, G., Hutchinson, J., Kaufmann, E., Özkirimli, U. & Wimmer, A. (2008). Debate on John Hutchinson's Nations as Zones of Conflict. *Nations and Nationalism*, *14*(1), 1–28. https://doi.org/10.1111/j.1469-8129.2008.00306.x

Duchesne, S. (2013). Social Gap: The Double Meaning of 'Overlooking.' In S. Duchesne, E. Frazer, F. Haegel, & V. Van Ingelgom (Eds.), *Citizens' Reactions to European Integration Compared: Overlooking Europe* (pp. 65–95). Palgrave Macmillan UK. https://doi.org/10.1057/9781137297266_4

Duchesne, S. & Ingelgom, V. V. (2008). Comment les discussions deviennent politiques lorsque les francais, anglais et belges parlent d'Europe. *Politique europeenne*, *n° 24*(1), 145–149.

Duina, F. & Smith, E. (2019). Affirming Europe with Trade: Deal Negotiations and the Making of a Political Identity. *Comparative European Politics*, *17*(4), 491–511. https://doi.org/10.1057/s41295-019-00180-7

Działo, J., & Gawrońska-Nowak, B. (2017). Social Expectations Concerning Free Trade Agreements. *Studia Polityczne*, *45*(3), 179–200.

Eder, K., & Kantner, C. (2000). Transnationale Resonanzstrukturen in Europa. In M. Bach (Ed.), *Die Europäisierung nationaler Gesellchaften. Sonderheft 40 der Kölner Zeitschrift für Soziologie und Sozialpsychologie* (pp. 306–331). https://doi.org/10.1007/978-3-322-80390-0_13

European Parliament. (2017). *Debates – EU–Canada Comprehensive Economic and Trade Agreement – Conclusion of the EU–Canada CETA – EU–Canada Strategic Partnership Agreement (debate)—Wednesday, 15 February 2017*. www.europarl.europa.eu/doceo/document/CRE-8-2017-02-15-ITM-004_EN.html

Favell, A. (2009). Immigration, Migration and the Free Movement of People in the Making of Europe. In J. T. Checkel & P. J. Katzenstein (Eds.), *European Identity* (pp. 167–189). Cambridge University Press.

Foucault, M. (2006). *Geschichte der Gouvernementalität. 2. Die Geburt der Biopolitik: Vorlesung am Collège de France 1978 – 1979*. Suhrkamp.

Fougner, T. (2008). Neoliberal Governance of States: The Role of Competitiveness Indexing and Country Benchmarking. *Millennium*, *37*(2), 303–326. https://doi.org/10.1177/0305829808097642

Friese, G. & Wagner, P. (2002). Survey Article: The Nascent Political Philosophy of the European Polity. *The Journal of Political Philosophy*, *10*(3), 342–364.

Gamson, G. and William, A. (1992). *Talking Politics*. Cambridge University Press.

Gerhards, J., Breuer, L. & Delius, A. (2017). *Kollektive Erinnerungen der europäischen Bürger im Kontext von Transnationalisierungsprozessen: Deutschland, Großbritannien, Polen und Spanien im Vergleich*. VS Verlag für Sozialwissenschaften. https://doi.org/10.1007/978-3-658-13402-0

Graziano, P. R. & Hartlapp, M. (2015). La fin de l'Europe sociale? Évaluation du rôle des changements politiques et organisationnels au sein du système politique de l'Union européenne. *Revue francaise des affaires sociales*, *3*, 89–114.

Greenfeld, L. (1995). The Worth of Nations: Some Economic Implications of Nationalism. *Critical Review*, *9*(4), 555–584. https://doi.org/10.1080/08913819508443403

Guérot, U. (2014). Res Publica Europaea: A Citizens-based Concept to Re-think Political Integration of Europe. In R. Fiorentini & G. Montani (Eds.), *The European Union and Supranational Political Economy* (pp. 133–154). Routledge.
Habermas, J. (1992a). Citizenship and National Identity: Some Reflections on the Future of Europe. *Praxis International*, *12*(1), 1–19.
Habermas, J. (1992b). Further Reflections on the Public Sphere. In C. J. Calhoun (Ed.), *Habermas and the Public Sphere* (pp. 421–461). MIT Press.
Habermas, J. (2002). Towards a European Political Community. *Society*, *39*(5), 58–61.
Habermas, J. (2011). *Zur Verfassung Europas: Ein Essay* (5th Edition). Suhrkamp Verlag.
Habermas, J. (2014). Jürgen Habermas im Gespräch: Europa wird direkt ins Herz getroffen. *FAZ.NET*. www.faz.net/1.2963798
Halle, D. (1984). *America's Working Man: Work, Home, and Politics among Blue Collar Property Owners*. University of Chicago Press.
Hartlapp, M. (2019a). Revisiting Patterns in EU Regulatory Social Policy: (Still) Supporting the Market or Social Goals in Their Own Right? *Zeitschrift für Sozialreform*, *65*(1), 59–82. https://doi.org/10.1515/zsr-2019-0003
Hartlapp, M. (2019b). European Union Social Policy. In S. Blum, J. Kuhlmann, & K. Schubert (Eds.), *Routledge Handbook of European Welfare Systems* (pp. 545–560). Routledge Handbooks Online. https://doi.org/10.4324/9780429290510-30
Hearn, J. (2006). *Rethinking Nationalism: A Critical Introduction*. Palgrave Macmillan.
Helleiner, E. (2002). Economic Nationalism as a Challenge to Economic Liberalism? Lessons from the 19th Century. *International Studies Quarterly*, *46*(3), 307–329. https://doi.org/10.1111/1468-2478.00235
Hepp, A. & Wessler, H. (2009). Politische Diskurskulturen – Überlegungen zur empirischen Erklärung segmentierter europäischer Öffentlichkeit. *Medien & Kommunikationswissenschaft*, *57*(2), 174–197. https://doi.org/10.5771/1615-634x-2009-2-174
Hepp, A., Elsler, M., Lingenberg, S., Mollen, A., Möller, J., Offerhaus, A., Sword, K. & Pospielovsky, D. V. (2016). *The Communicative Construction of Europe: Cultures of Political Discourse, Public Sphere, and the Euro Crisis*. Palgrave Macmillan UK. https://doi.org/10.1057/9781137453136
Hübner, K., Deman, A.-S. & Balik, T. (2017). EU and Trade Policy-making: The Contentious Case of CETA. *Journal of European Integration*, *39*(7), 843–857. https://doi.org/10.1080/07036337.2017.1371708
Jacobsson, K. (2004). Soft Regulation and the Subtle Transformation of States: The Case of EU Employment Policy. *Journal of European Social Policy*, *14*(4), 355–370. https://doi.org/10.1177/0958928704046878
Jepsen, M. & Pascual, A. (2005). The European Social Model: An Exercise in Deconstruction. *Journal of European Social Policy – J EUR SOC POLICY*, *15*, 231–245. https://doi.org/10.1177/0958928705054087
Kangas, A. (2013). Market Civilisation Meets Economic Nationalism: The Discourse of Nation in Russia's Modernisation. *Nations and Nationalism*, *19*(3), 572–591. https://doi.org/10.1111/nana.12023
Lamont, M. & Thévenot, L. (2000). Introduction: Toward a Renewed Comparative Cultural Sociology. In L. Thévenot & M. Lamont (Eds.), *Rethinking Comparative Cultural Sociology: Repertoires of Evaluation in France and the United States* (pp. 1–22). Cambridge University Press. https://doi.org/10.1017/CBO9780511628108.001

Leiser, D., Bourgeois-Gironde, S. & Benita, R. (2010). Human Foibles or Systemic Failure – Lay Perceptions of the 2008–2009 Financial Crisis. *The Journal of Socio-Economics*, *39*(2), 132–141. https://doi.org/10.1016/j.socec.2010.02.013

McNamara, K. R. & Musgrave, P. (2020). Democracy and Collective Identity in the EU and the USA. *JCMS: Journal of Common Market Studies*, *58*(1), 172–188. https://doi.org/10.1111/jcms.12978

Meunier, S. & Roederer-Rynning, C. (2020). Missing in Action? France and the Politicization of Trade and Investment Agreements. *Politics and Governance*, *8*(1), 312–324. https://doi.org/10.17645/pag.v8i1.2616

Moody, M. & Thévenot, L. (2000). Comparing Models of Strategy, Interests, and the Public Good in French and American Environmental Disputes. In L. Thévenot & M. Lamont (Eds.), *Rethinking Comparative Cultural Sociology: Repertoires of Evaluation in France and the United States* (pp. 273–306). Cambridge University Press. https://doi.org/10.1017/CBO9780511628108.010

Mudde, C. (2004). The Populist Zeitgeist. *Government and Opposition*, *39*(4), 541–563. https://doi.org/10.1111/j.1477-7053.2004.00135.x

Mudge, S. L. & Vauchez, A. (2012). Building Europe on a Weak Field: Law, Economics, and Scholarly Avatars in Transnational Politics. *American Journal of Sociology*, *118*(2), 449–492. https://doi.org/10.1086/666382

Nachtwey, O. (2016). *Die Abstiegsgesellschaft: Über das Aufbegehren in der regressiven Moderne*. Suhrkamp Verlag.

Offe, C. (2005). The European Model of 'Social' Capitalism. Can It survive European Integration? In M. Miller (Ed.), *Worlds of Capitalism: Institutions, Economic Performance and Governance in the Era of Globalization* (pp. 141–172). Routledge.

O'Toole, G. (2003). A New Nationalism for a New Era: The Political Ideology of Mexican Neoliberalism. *Bulletin of Latin American Research*, *22*(3), 269–290. https://doi.org/10.1111/1470-9856.00078

Özkirimli, U. (2005). *Contemporary Debates on Nationalism: A Critical Engagement*. Macmillan Education UK.

Panizza, F. (2005). *Populism and the Mirror of Democracy*. Verso.

Peet, R. (2002). Ideology, Discourse, and the Geography of Hegemony: From Socialist to Neoliberal Development in Postapartheid South Africa. *Antipode*, *34*(1), 54–84. https://doi.org/10.1111/1467-8330.00226

Pickel, A. (2005). Introduction: False Oppositions. Reconceptualizing Economic Nationalism in a Globalizing World. In E. Helleiner & A. Pickel (Eds.), *Economic Nationalism in a Globalizing World* (pp. 1–18). Cornell University Press.

Risse, T. (2010). *A Community of Europeans?: Transnational Identities and Public Spheres*. Cornell University Press.

Risse, T. (2014). No Demos? Identities and Public Spheres in the Euro Crisis. *JCMS: Journal of Common Market Studies*, *52*(6), 1207–1215. https://doi.org/10.1111/jcms.12189

Rosamond, B. (2002). Imagining the European Economy: 'Competitiveness' and the Social Construction of 'Europe' as an Economic Space. *New Political Economy*, *7*(2), 157–177. https://doi.org/10.1080/13563460220138826

Rosamond, B. (2012). Supranational Governance as Economic Patriotism? The European Union, Legitimacy and the Reconstruction of State Space. *Journal of European Public Policy*, *19*(3), 324–341. https://doi.org/10.1080/13501763.2011.638119

Statham, P., & Trenz, H.-J. (2015). Understanding the Mechanisms of EU Politicization: Lessons from the Eurozone Crisis. *Comparative European Politics*, *13*(3), 287–306. https://doi.org/10.1057/cep.2013.30

Vaughan-Whitehead, D. (2015). *The European Social Model in Crisis: Is Europe Losing Its Soul?* Edward Elgar Publishing.

White, J. (2011). *Political Allegiance After European Integration*. Palgrave Macmillan. www.palgrave.com/gp/book/9780230279780

Žižek, S. & Horvat, S. (2014). *What Does Europe Want?: The Union and Its Discontents* (p. 240). Columbia University Press.

Conclusion

C.1 Recap: The European Public, National Anchoring and Problems of Understanding

From climate change to economic crises: The most important political problems of the 21st century are both transnational in scope and scientifically complex. How can ordinary citizens meaningfully discuss complex issues such as monetary policy or trade regulation? How is inflation or deficit spending understood in the office kitchens and sports clubs of a transnational republic? And given large differences in national perspectives, would citizens understand each other's arguments? This book has addressed these problems of understanding in the European public sphere, attempting a realistic simulation of economic debates among European citizens.

The book's central argument is that the **European public is capable of overcoming problems of understanding**. First, this refers to the problem of issue **complexity**. I have shown that European citizens use various anchoring strategies to make sense of complex issues. While the resulting social representations of economics are diverse and differ from economic orthodoxy, there are good reasons to consider them informed. European citizens understand economics not because they think like economists, but because they are able to creatively mobilize more familiar stocks of knowledge to render complex issues intelligible.

Beyond complexity, second, the European public sphere seems to function with regard to **compatibility**, too. European citizens would be able to understand each other's arguments reasonably well when exchanging positions across borders. This does not mean that the European public sphere is free of communicative failures. Rather, it means that such failures are no more common than in national public spheres. This finding is interesting because it implies that Europeans already have a lot in common. Their perspectives are similar enough to enable public debates to function as smoothly as if they were one nation.

The central explanation I developed in this book to explain the success of the European public sphere is **national anchoring**. National anchoring describes how citizens employ memories of recent political debates to make

DOI: 10.4324/9781003335610-12

sense of complex issues. This means that politicization in the public sphere has a lasting impact on citizens' political consciousness. It popularizes specific arguments and coins linguistic expressions specific to the national language, thus forming specific cultural reservoirs citizens can draw from. This process can help overcoming complexity (by spreading knowledge of complex issues) and compatibility (by providing all participants in the public sphere with similar reference points). While national anchoring is partly responsible for citizens' capacity to make sense of complex issues, the emergence of a European political culture partly explains why Europeans understand each other.

Overall, these findings are good news for **EU legitimacy**. Almost by definition, EU politics address problems that are complex and transnational in their impact. Recent discussions surrounding issues such as COVID-19, climate change and energy security in the aftermath of the invasion of Ukraine clearly testify to the growing salience of complex issues with continent-wide implications. As the EU aspires to meet democratic criteria, it is essential that these issues be understood by the public and subjected to meaningful transnational debate. My diagnosis that the European public can overcome problems of understanding thus is a cornerstone of the EU's democratic legitimacy in the 21st century.

Apart from this optimistic assessment of EU legitimacy, the book attempts to make some more specific contributions to the academic literature. The rest of this conclusion attempts to sketch these contributions and to assess their potential consequences for ongoing debates in the respective fields. I focus on two areas of research in particular, both of them intimately connected with the study of the European public: **public opinion research and European studies**. Regarding public opinion research, I wish to highlight how a closer focus on lay representations might help us explain the success of political projects as diverse as populism or neoliberalism. Regarding European studies, I point out why the findings of this book may influence the study of European identity or European elections, making the EU look a lot closer to the ideal of a transnational democracy. In suggesting such potential applications for my findings, however, I do not wish to over-generalize them. Rather, I attempt to identify promising avenues for future research while acknowledging the limited scope of this book and encouraging tests of my results in broader contexts and using larger samples.

C.2 Outlook: Why Lay Representations Matter in Public Opinion Research

Let us take a step back and consider how the empirical material for this book was gathered. I essentially walked into a school, an estate agency or onto a soccer pitch and asked a group of people questions about issues they probably had never discussed before. The teachers, estate agents and soccer players participating in the discussions made it very clear that this was unusual.

Laughing and shaking their heads when I presented the discussion topic, they rarely failed to point out that this was the first time they were discussing trade or unemployment among themselves. For me as a social scientist I guess the equivalent situation would be a physicist storming into my office and demanding me to spell out the functioning of a nuclear power station or the true nature of gravity. In my focus group discussions, I confronted participants with highly complex topics to which most of them had never consciously paid attention in their lives.

It is all the more surprising how thoughtful, balanced, creative and even witty the discussions were. Only in a small number of moments participants found themselves at dead ends in the discussions, agreeing that 'we don't know enough'. In most cases, on the contrary, participants managed to have an informed and meaningful exchange of arguments. Positions were collectively formulated, challenged, amended; analogies were made and complex issues likened to more similar situations; metaphors were mobilized and linguistic expressions twisted. At the end of the discussions, most participants did not only state that they had enjoyed the discussion. They mostly were also of the opinion that they had learned something. In short, the capacity of my participants to overcome their perceived lack of knowledge and to explain complex economic phenomena to themselves was stunning. Lay participants were clearly able to make sense of complex economic issues.

The main reason for this capacity to make sense of complex issues is citizens' capacity to use various anchoring strategies. Lay citizens make sense of complex economic issues by employing priorly known anchoring domains. Throughout this book, we have encountered five different anchoring domains, which could be discerned in the focus group discussions. Three of these anchoring mechanisms – national political culture, the worth of nations and European political culture in Chapters 2, 3 and 7, respectively – I have subsumed under the label national anchoring. In all three cases, knowledge of the anchoring domain is spread through politicization of relatively banal policy issues in the public sphere. Apart from national anchoring, I found evidence of anchoring in a discourse of the common people (Chapter 4) and anchoring in economic theory (Chapter 5) to be prominent strategies of complexity reduction. In light of these anchoring processes, I have argued that **lay representations of economics are diverse, but informed**.

Why did I argue for these representations to be informed? This might come as a surprise given my diagnosis is that lay representations differ significantly from economic theory. Isn't this a bad sign for the quality of public deliberation? Shouldn't my results be read as a warning to educate the public better about the tenets of economic science? Along with parts of the literature on the public understanding of science, I do not believe that such a deficit model adequately captures reality (Cortassa, 2016; Irwin & Michael, 2003, pp. 27–38; Michael, 1992; Suldovsky, 2016). What I perceived in the focus group discussions was not a deficit on the part of participants. As I elaborated in the beginning of the section, I mostly found the focus group discussions to be quite informed, balanced and thoughtful. Rather than a deficit, I encountered an instance of lay epistemology, the careful weighing of different knowledge authorities and anchoring domains in a given social context (compare Irwin & Michael, 2003, p. 28). The fact that lay representations differ from economic theory should be understood as a reflection of the diverse stances on economics represented in politics and to some extent academia. Orthodox economic theory is simply to narrow a normative standard to denounce public perceptions as uninformed.

What is more, the fact that citizens are able to creatively employ various anchoring strategies should allow for optimism. This finding seems to concur with earlier studies that embrace a wider conception of citizen competence. In this understanding, a greater focus is placed on citizens' capacity to process information and form reasonable opinions on this basis (e.g., Cramer & Toff, 2017; Goren, 2012; Lupia, 2016). In the bigger picture, this means that my results align with studies arguing that democratic publics tend to be rather informed and well able to participate in debates even on complex political issues (e.g., Gamson, 1992; Page & Shapiro, 2010; White, 2011; Zaller, 1992). The public seems capable of meaningfully debating complex political issues, be it via anchoring processes as shown in this study or, for example, via other heuristics (Sniderman et al., 1993). At least for the European public sphere and at least for the issue area of economics, then, this study warrants optimism: even complex issues seem to be subject to appropriate public scrutiny by a reasonably well-informed public. While such conclusions go beyond the external validity of this study, there might be reason to believe that anchoring processes can play a similar role beyond Europe and beyond economics.

So this is why I argued lay representations to be informed. But there is another part to my claim which has equally important implications: lay representations are diverse. Arguably, the creative and diverse ways citizens make sense of complex realities need to be carefully studied in their own right. Lack of data on or attention to the idiosyncrasies of citizens' thought will result in flawed conclusions. Unfortunately, many scholars simply contend themselves with imputing their own worldview or prejudices into the minds of others. In Chapter 4, I have shown that many utilitarian approaches to public opinion formation rely on overly optimistic assumptions of citizens being near perfectly informed (e.g., Brinegar & Jolly, 2005; Ehrlich, 2010; Fraile & Ferrer, 2005; O'Rourke et al., 2001; Rehm, 2011). In Chapter 5, we have seen that other scholars exemplify the opposite extreme, this time imputing biases or reasoning fallacies into the minds of citizens without relying on appropriate data. Instead of imputing knowledge into citizens' minds, my results show clearly that lay representations are too diverse to be captured without adequate investigation. Lay representations should be the object of research, not assumption. Consequently, I believe approaches to public opinion research stressing the diversity, creativity and ambiguity of lay representations to be much more adequate. Such approaches are already widespread in some areas of public opinion research, for example, in the literature on the public understanding of science (e.g., Leiser et al., 2010; Leiser & Drori, 2005; O'Connor, 2012). For economics, this means we need to heed the call to properly study what has been called "folk economics" (Swedberg, 2018). My study further stresses the **need to carefully analyze lay representations** when studying public opinion on economic issues in the future.

The need to seriously engage with the diversity of lay representations is also evident among more discursively oriented scholars. In analyses of public discourse, a distinction is often made between official (or 'supply-side') and citizen (or 'demand-side') discourse. The bulk of studies in this area, however, focuses on supply-side discourses, sometimes for reasons of data availability and sometimes because of theoretical commitment. Based on my results, again I would urge not to lose sight of the demand or citizen side. Even though most anchoring domains which mattered in my study were ultimately spread via the public sphere, this does not mean that all public opinion boils down to supply side discourse. First, there are other relevant transmission mechanisms such as education and experience that seem partly independent of supply side discourses. Second and more importantly, the diversity of supply side discourses is one of the major reasons why demand side discourses are diverse, too. This means that some, but not all supply side discourses have an impact on public perceptions. The most prominent example of this diagnosis was neoliberal discourses at the European level. While being a staple of internal and external EU communication for decades, they seem to have little traction with citizens (see Chapter 7 or Alt, 2022). Demand side discourses (i.e., lay representation) need to be studied in their own right.

This is not to argue for a supremacy of the demand over the supply side, but rather for the need to reconcile the two. Arguably, one of the most important takeaways of this study is that we need a **theory of political resonance** that describes the relationship between supply and demand side discourses to determine when political arguments are accepted as convincing. I believe some hints for this project can be derived from the concept of national anchoring. In Chapters 2 and 3, we have seen that the success of arguments in a national context partly depends on the extent to which they resonate with national reservoirs of meaning. National anchoring increases the **frequency and persuasiveness** of arguments. This is in line with some previous studies sharing my focus on the impact of nationhood on the thought of ordinary citizens (Duchesne & Ingelgom, 2008; Moody & Thévenot, 2000). Yet, if economic arguments become more persuasive when resonating with national anchoring domains, the same might be true of party programs, political slogans, or electoral campaigns more generally. Taken together, close analyses of demand and supply side discourses may help to explain why political projects flourish in some national contexts but fail to produce significant resonance elsewhere.

In two cases, this book's empirical material already provides some clues for how such an analysis of political resonance could look like. The first, as briefly mentioned before, is neoliberalism. In many of the representations comprising the worth of nations hypothesis, for example, we find evidence of a combination of neoliberal thought with national anchoring domains (see Chapter 3). While not applied to the EU, neoliberal discourses did have traction at the nation-state level. In particular in the German groups, we have seen how the success of the national economy in a neoliberally conceived competition of states can become the source of national pride. The presence of this combination of discourses has often been noted in official sources, in party programs and in political campaigns around the globe (Fougner, 2008; Kangas, 2013; O'Toole, 2003; Peet, 2002). Most recently, the prowess of this discursive combination could be witnessed in the 2016 pre-referendum debate in Britain with many Brexiteers favoring independence not to advocate protectionism but rather to more successfully pursue liberalizing policies (Bell, 2019). Brexit was depicted as a chance to get rid of Brussels bureaucracy and to have a bonfire of regulation (Hartlapp, 2019, p. 60). The combination of neoliberal rankings with national anchoring domains, then, seems to be a prominent framing strategy in official discourse and in election campaigns. Yet, I believe my study is among the first to document that this official discourse might actually resonate with citizens' perceptions of the economic order. In doing so, this study contributes to the literature attributing the dominance of neoliberalism not only to its prominence among economic elites but also to its capacity to capture the popular imagination (e.g., Hall & O'Shea, 2013; Mitchell, 2009). Further investigations about how national pride can be constructed around neoliberally conceived economic strengths thus may illuminate one factor contributing to the success of the neoliberal project. Combining insights from supply and demand side discourse analysis may help to **explain why neoliberalism appeals to the masses**.

The second form of supply side discourse that might resonate with the social representations of the economy I found is **populism**. As we have seen in Chapters 4 and 7, a discourse of the common people is an important anchoring domain for economic issues, often resulting in a depiction of the economic order as a rigged game, which exploits the people in favor of a corrupt elite. This finding is all the more interesting as it is not limited to the working class, as was the case for earlier studies (Halle, 1984; White, 2011). In my focus group, such visions of unfair elite domination were equally common among middle class participants, which is why I speak of the "common people" rather than the "little people". While not generalizable based on my material, this finding might be a promising starting point for future research. One reason for the success of populist movements might be that their economic rhetoric mirrors the perceptions of wide segments of the population.

I believe this finding might be particularly salient in the Polish case where such views can be combined with claims to be unfairly dominated by the West. In my sample, Polish participants were most acutely aware of the adverse effects of the single market, be it through the pressures exerted by foreign capital or the brain drain caused by the free movement of labor. At the same time, memories of transformation and liberalization provided first-hand evidence of the dominance of foreign interests over those of the local population. Given this symbolic opportunity structure – which has already been well described by Polish social scientists (Gdula et al., 2017; Rawłuszko, 2019; Zarycki, 2015; Zimmermann, 2007) – claims of being economically dominated by Western elites seem to have some potential for resonance. The existence of such national anchoring points may be one factor explaining why PiS's anti-elitism commands more popular appeal than most of its (Western) European counterparts. Generally, populism might simply speak the minds of citizens, articulating criticisms of big business subscribed to by many. An analysis of political resonance combining supply and demand side data could further illuminate this.

Apart from providing hints about the success of specific political projects in a given national context, the concept of national anchoring also has important implications at the European level. The mechanism underlying national anchoring – politicization in the public sphere forming elements of national culture which later determine the degree to which political arguments resonate with the population – can be discerned in the European public sphere. Spelling out the implications of this finding is the aim of the final section.

C.3 Outlook: How Politicization Might Transform the EU

A textbook assumption in European studies is that the EU is a polity *sui generis*, that is, that it can neither be understood as simply an international organization nor as a full-fledged nation-state. Much ink has been spilled in particular to spell out the manifold ways in which the Union differs from an ideal typical version of the nation state. No public sphere, no proper elections, no demos – these are the most common accusations raised to make this latter point (Grimm, 1995, 2017; Nicolaïdis, 2013; Seoane Pérez, 2013). The upshot of such claims is clear: given its powers but lack of legitimizing institutions, the EU suffers from a democratic deficit. Yet, over the past decades, such pessimistic positions have come increasingly under scrutiny, with scholars re-assessing both the empirical state of affairs in the European polity and the idealized image of nation-states that served as a comparison. The result of such re-assessments has often been that the EU is much more similar to national societies than believed. While maintaining some unique characteristics, differences have often been overdrawn. I believe the concept of national anchoring to be a further step in this direction. On the one hand, the concept places limits on arguments stressing inter-national differences as a major hurdle to integration. These differences exist, but they are by no means insurmountable. On the other hand, the fact that processes akin to national anchoring can be observed at the European level provides reason to believe that the European polity will develop even greater similarity to its national counterparts. We might have to re-calibrate our assessments of European elections, the European demos and the European public sphere. In conclusion, the EU's alleged democratic deficit might turn out to be much less pronounced.

Let us begin with the European public sphere as this is the area in which much levelling has already been done. Since the 2000s, scholars have developed a conception of the European public sphere as transnational and established three criteria for its functioning (Eder & Kantner, 2000; Kantner, 2014; Risse, 2014a, 2014b; Statham, 2010). Two of these three criteria have been tested extensively, often with a positive outcome. This was the case with regard to the visibility of issues (criterion one; see Kantner, 2014; Koopmans, 2014; Risse, 2014a) and regarding the presence and legitimacy of foreign voices (criterion two; see Koopmans, 2014; Risse, 2014a). The third criterion (the compatibility of arguments) has received somewhat less attention, with some studies finding media framing of European issues to be largely compatible (Eder & Kantner, 2000; Kantner, 2014).

What was the contribution of this study, then? I believe this book has made a small but significant contribution to the assessment of the third criterion. The studies cited above focused on media frames and, apart from Lingenberg (2010), no other studies have thus far investigated the compatibility of citizens' representations. Yet, I believe compatibility among citizens is the decisive factor if we are to assess the capacity of a public sphere to bestow legitimacy on political institutions. Certainly, the compatibility of media frames is an important object of study as media play an important role in transmitting the debates to the citizenry. Media frames thus are a good indicator of compatibility. Ultimately, however, it is citizens' representations – and not reporting in media outlets – which needs to be compatible for a public sphere to fulfill its democratic function. It is the citizens who need to be informed and capable of understanding each other. Therefore, I believe my study makes an important contribution to the assessment of the compatibility requirement and thus to the empirical assessment of the European public sphere as a whole.

This book, then, contributed to the debate by setting out a precise definition of what it means for arguments to be compatible and by testing this conception empirically. In Chapter 1, I developed a precise definition of compatibility in the European public sphere, distinguishing disagreements from misunderstandings and establishing a national standard of comparison. In Chapter 6, I put these criteria to the test. I argued that **the European public sphere functions despite the impact of national anchoring**. On the one hand, this means that the European public sphere does indeed suffer from hermeneutic difficulties resulting from differences in national anchoring domains. Inter-national misunderstandings occur mainly due to differences in national political cultures of which citizens are not aware (i.e., the differences are not covered by alternative representations). On the other hand, such inter-national misunderstandings seem to be less pronounced than the interpretive problems to be expected in national public spheres. Comparing inter-national incompatibilities to those between economically trained and non-trained participants, I found both to be roughly equally pronounced. Considering that the research design attempted to maximize inter-national incompatibilities while intra-national misunderstandings are probably more numerous and graver beyond the sample, this is good news for the European public sphere. If we employ a realistic national standard of comparison, the European public sphere seems to function rather smoothly in terms of compatibility.

In closing one of the last gaps in the literature on the European public sphere, then, this book should further boost our confidence that such a transnational communicative space does indeed exist. By now, there is strong evidence confirming all three criteria for the existence of a European public sphere. While accusations of an absence of a public sphere – unfortunately – remain a staple of public communication and journalistic commentary, such arguments should become increasingly marginal in the academic community.

While the existence of a European public sphere thus can be confirmed with a high degree of certainty, arguments questioning the existence of a European demos or European elections continue to persist. Yet, arguably in both these areas the concept of national anchoring should boost our optimism, too. Regarding the European demos, the link to a functioning public sphere is most direct: the finding that the European public sphere functions in terms of compatibility seems to imply that there must be some anchoring domains that are shared among EU citizens. In Chapter 7, I analyzed which representations in my sample are cross-nationally shared. These are, on the one hand, representations of problems arising from market integration, in particular in the form of a race to the bottom to the detriment of states and the common people. On the other hand, there are representations of a European social model which, upon closer inspection, partly appear to be the result of the public politicization of the CETA agreement. I thus found evidence of past politicization (e.g., around CETA and the euro-crisis) and potential for future politicization (e.g., representations of common problems arising from market integration). Therefore, I concluded that the **construction of European anchoring domains through the politicization of economic issues** is under way. This can be seen as a step toward a European political culture and thus toward a European demos. National anchoring seems to have an equivalent on the European level. Just like in national contexts, the politicization on the European level can raise awareness among citizens and thus establish the elements of a transnational political culture.

The discovery of this mechanism on the European level has important implications for the study of European elections, too. This area has long been dominated by the second order election paradigm, which maintains that election campaigns, news reporting and electoral choices mainly happen within a national framework (e.g., Brug et al., 2016). Yet, in recent years studies have increasingly challenged this view, arguing that European elections might in fact have their own logic (e.g., Hix & Marsh, 2011) or be dominated by issues specific to them (Clark & Rohrschneider, 2009; Hobolt & Spoon, 2012). Thus, rather than simply being second order national contests, European elections may be transnational events, in which campaign messages and political slogans spread to the population in a similar way news do in the European public sphere. Voters may be influenced by information and events on the European level, which are then spread through national media and understood by citizens using mechanisms such as national anchoring. National anchoring thus could be a factor in explaining voters' choices in European elections. The concept of national anchoring would amend the second order paradigm as it allows for some influence of European events while still acknowledging the dominance of national knowledge in citizens' political imagination.

I believe the results I found in my French focus groups provide an excellent example of the potential usefulness of the concept of national anchoring in the study of European elections. One of the main particularities of the French focus group discussions was their frequent articulation of *race to the bottom* representations using expressions popularized in past national debates (e.g., *travailleur détaché, concurrence déloyale, délocalisation)*. These representations of an *Europe sociale* may be used not to advocate a reform of European institutions (polity politicization). But they may also be indicators of a more commonplace process which would make European elections look very similar to national contests: the voicing of specific political demands toward the future administration (policy politicization). Just like in local elections (Marien et al., 2015), citizens may use European elections to articulate demands they deem suited for the specific level of government in question. This would imply the presence of a form of voter motivation that would be both, more democratically healthy than second-order motivations and largely overlooked so far in the literature (Braun et al., 2016). A study of electoral motivations in France, Germany and Poland during the 2019 European elections (Alt et al., 2020, 2022) found that the frequency of *race to the bottom* representations in France made French citizens more likely to demand the implementation of concrete policies at the European level (e.g., a European minimum wage). The elements of the emergent European political culture thus might cause citizens to make their voting decisions increasingly based on European concerns. Greater politicization at the European level might not only cause the emergence of a demos, it would also transform the nature of European elections.

With regard to the European demos and the conception of European elections, the concept of national anchoring thus warrants limited optimism. Clearly, in both cases the empirical and theoretical literature is not as advanced as for the European public sphere. Whereas the results for the European public sphere are increasingly univocal, we have seen that in the two other cases there are powerful competing interpretations that still hold sway. The study of transnationally shared meaning structures in the EU is still in its infancy. And even if further substantiated, other conceptions of political community would have to be addressed. In particular, questions of solidarity seem to pose a challenge here as it is by no means clear that a European identity remains salient where it comes into conflict with national identifications. Similarly, we have seen that there is a host of competing explanations for behavior in European elections. And while second-order behavior might not be as dominant as long assumed, it is still an important factor to reckon with.

Given these limitations, the major reason for optimism is that the forces producing economic politicization on the European level are set to grow. The EU's economic competences and capacities have been significantly widened in the years since the inception of this study, and thus we should expect to see ever more highly salient economic debates in the European public sphere in the years to come. It is thus all the more important to be certain that the European public sphere indeed functions in the issue area of economics, and to be aware of the potential effects of such economic debates (i.e., the gradual emergence of a European political culture and the potential for greater awareness of European policy issues).

The events I am mainly referring to here are the mobilizations around climate issues and the recent COVID-19 pandemic. Following the success of the global climate strike, climate change became a dominant issue in the 2019 European election, which saw rising levels of turnout throughout the EU. Just a year later, in the aftermath of the first wave of COVID infections, the EU took an important step toward the establishment of a common fiscal policy, allowing for shared debt for the first time in its history. Yet, agreeing to borrow the money was probably the easy bit. The truly contentious discussions may await us when the money is to be distributed. With the mission to combat climate change and unprecedented funds at its disposal, EU institutions and their actions will certainly be the object of public debate more frequently in the future. Arguably, we are likely to witness an increased politicization of economic issues in the European public sphere in the upcoming years.

How significant these changes are may become clearer when looking back. When I designed the focus group discussions in early 2018, some of the trigger arguments seemed fictious. One of the arguments in the unemployment groups even read "increase state expenditure to stimulate demand". I knew back then that this barely was a realistic policy proposal at the European level. But I also knew that the competences of the EU have continuously evolved over the decades and that it may make sense to assess future scenarios. I would not have expected the scenario of a fiscal stimulus on the European level to become reality so soon. Like many other aspects of this book, their relevance became clearer to me over the course of my research in the past four and a half years. In this conclusion, I have attempted to sketch out this relevance of my findings for some of these recent events and for some adjacent academic disciplines. I hope to have provoked some intriguing questions, and I am excited to see if my predictions will hold in the years to come.

Bibliography

Alt, D. (2022). Social Model or Neoliberal Champion? Economic Visions of the European Demos among EU Citizens. *Nations and Nationalism*, *28*(4), 1494–1510. https://doi.org/10.1111/nana.12869

Alt, D., Brandes, E. & Nonhoff, D. (2020). Can the European Parliament Satisfy the People? Voter Mandates and Accountability Links in the European Elections 2019. In M. Kaeding, M. Müller, & J. Schmälter (Eds.), *Die Europawahl 2019: Ringen um die Zukunft Europas* (pp. 365–375). Springer Fachmedien. https://doi.org/10.1007/978-3-658-29277-5_30

Alt, D., Brandes, E. & Nonhoff, D. (2022). First Order for Some: How Different Forms of Politicization Motivated Voters in the 2019 European Parliamentary Election. *JCMS: Journal of Common Market Studies*, *61*(2), 362-378. https://doi.org/10.1111/jcms.13376

Bell, E. (2019). Brexit: Towards a Neoliberal Real Utopia? *Observatoire de La Société Britannique*, *24*, Article 24. https://doi.org/10.4000/osb.3196

Braun, D., Hutter, S., & Kerscher, A. (2016). What Type of Europe? The Salience of Polity and Policy Issues in European Parliament Elections. *European Union Politics*, *17*(4), 570–592. https://doi.org/10.1177/1465116516660387

Clark, N. & Rohrschneider, R. (2009). Second-Order Elections versus First-Order Thinking: How Voters Perceive the Representation Process in a Multi-Layered System of Governance. *Journal of European Integration*, *31*(5), 645–664. https://doi.org/10.1080/07036330903145906

Cortassa, C. (2016). In Science Communication, Why Does the Idea of a Public Deficit Always Return? The Eternal Recurrence of the Public Deficit. *Public Understanding of Science*, *25*(4), 447–459. https://doi.org/10.1177/0963662516629745

Cramer, K. J. & Toff, B. (2017). The Fact of Experience: Rethinking Political Knowledge and Civic Competence. *Perspectives on Politics*, *15*(3), 754–770. https://doi.org/10.1017/S1537592717000949

Duchesne, S. & Ingelgom, V. V. (2008). Comment les discussions deviennent politiques lorsque les francais, anglais et belges parlent d'Europe. *Politique europeenne*, *n° 24*(1), 145–149.

Eder, K. & Kantner, C. (2000). Transnationale Resonanzstrukturen in Europa. In M. Bach (Ed.), *Die Europäisierung nationaler Gesellchaften. Sonderheft 40 der Kölner Zeitschrift für Soziologie und Sozialpsychologie* (pp. 306–331). https://doi.org/10.1007/978-3-322-80390-0_13

Ehrlich, S. D. (2010). Who Supports Compensation? Individual Preferences for Trade-Related Unemployment Insurance. *Business and Politics*, *12*(1), 1–22. https://doi.org/10.2202/1469-3569.1289

Fougner, T. (2008). Neoliberal Governance of States: The Role of Competitiveness Indexing and Country Benchmarking. *Millennium*, *37*(2), 303–326. https://doi.org/10.1177/0305829808097642

Gdula, M., Dębskiej, K., & Trebki, K. (2017). *Dobra Zmiana w Miastku. Neoautrytaryzm w Polskiej Polityce z Perspektywy Małego Miasta*. Krytyka Polityczna. http://krytykapolityczna.pl/file/sites/4/2017/10/Dobra-zmiana-w-Miastku.pdf

Goren, P. (2012). *On Voter Competence*. Oxford University Press.

Grimm, D. (1995). Does Europe Need a Constitution? *European Law Journal*, *1*(3), 282–302. https://doi.org/10.1111/j.1468-0386.1995.tb00033.x

Grimm, D. (2017). *The Constitution of European Democracy*. Oxford University Press.

Hall, S., & O'Shea, A. (2013). Common-sense Neoliberalism. *Soundings*, *55*(55), 9–25. https://doi.org/10.3898/136266213809450194

Halle, D. (1984). *America's Working Man: Work, Home, and Politics Among Blue Collar Property Owners*. University of Chicago Press.

Hartlapp, M. (2019). Revisiting Patterns in EU Regulatory Social Policy: (Still) Supporting the Market or Social Goals in Their Own Right? *Zeitschrift für Sozialreform*, *65*(1), 59–82. https://doi.org/10.1515/zsr-2019-0003

Hix, S. & Marsh, M. (2011). Second-order Effects Plus Pan-European Political Swings: An Analysis of European Parliament Elections Across Time. *Electoral Studies*, *30*(1), 4–15. https://doi.org/10.1016/j.electstud.2010.09.017

Hobolt, S. B., & Spoon, J.-J. (2012). Motivating The European Voter: Parties, Issues and Campaigns in European Parliament Elections. *European Journal of Political Research*, *51*(6), 701–727. https://doi.org/10.1111/j.1475-6765.2012.02057.x

Irwin, A., & Michael, M. (2003). *Science, Social Theory & Public Knowledge*. McGraw-Hill Education (UK).

Kangas, A. (2013). Market Civilisation Meets Economic Nationalism: The Discourse of Nation in Russia's Modernisation. *Nations and Nationalism*, *19*(3), 572–591. https://doi.org/10.1111/nana.12023

Kantner, C. (2014). The European Public Sphere and the Debate About Humanitarian Military Interventions. *European Security*, *23*(4), 409–429. https://doi.org/10.1080/09662839.2014.890595

Koopmans, R. (2014). How Advanced is the Europeanization of Public Spheres? Comparing German and European Structures of Political Communication. In T. Risse (Ed.), *European Public Spheres: Politics Is Back* (pp. 63–96). Cambridge University Press. https://doi.org/10.1017/CBO9781139963343.005

Leiser, D. & Drori, S. (2005). Naïve Understanding of Inflation. *Journal of Socio-Economics*, *34*, 179–198. https://doi.org/10.1016/j.socec.2004.09.006

Leiser, D., Bourgeois-Gironde, S., & Benita, R. (2010). Human Foibles or Systemic Failure – Lay Perceptions of the 2008–2009 Financial Crisis. *The Journal of Socio-Economics*, *39*(2), 132–141. https://doi.org/10.1016/j.socec.2010.02.013

Lingenberg, S. (2010). Fallstudien zur europäischen Verfassungsdebatte. In S. Lingenberg (Ed.), *Europäische Publikumsöffentlichkeiten: Ein pragmatischer Ansatz* (pp. 183–226). VS Verlag für Sozialwissenschaften. https://doi.org/10.1007/978-3-531-92120-4_5

Lupia, A. (2016). *Uninformed: Why People Know So Little about Politics and What We Can Do about It*. Oxford University Press.

Marien, S., Dassonneville, R. & Hooghe, M. (2015). How Second Order Are Local Elections? Voting Motives and Party Preferences in Belgian Municipal Elections. *Local Government Studies*, *41*(6), 898–916. https://doi.org/10.1080/03003930.2015.1048230

Michael, M. (1992). Lay Discourses of Science: Science-in-General, Science-in-Particular, and Self. *Science, Technology, & Human Values*, *17*(3), 313–333. https://doi.org/10.1177/016224399201700303

Mitchell, T. (1998). Fixing the Economy. *Cultural Studies*, *12*(1), 82–101. https://doi.org/10.1080/095023898335627

Mitchell, T. (2009). How Neoliberalism Makes Its World. In C. E. K. P. of E. and P. S. and the H. and S. P. Mirowski, P. Mirowski & D. Plehwe (Eds.), *The Road from Mont Pèlerin* (pp. 386–412). Harvard University Press.

Moody, M. & Thévenot, L. (2000). Comparing Models of Strategy, Interests, and the Public Good in French and American Environmental Disputes. In L. Thévenot & M. Lamont (Eds.), *Rethinking Comparative Cultural Sociology: Repertoires of*

Evaluation in France and the United States (pp. 273–306). Cambridge University Press. https://doi.org/10.1017/CBO9780511628108.010

Nicolaïdis, K. (2013). European Democracy and Its Crisis. *JCMS: Journal of Common Market Studies*, *51*(2), 351–369. https://doi.org/10.1111/jcms.12006

O'Connor, C. (2012). Using Social Representations Theory to Examine Lay Explanation of Contemporary Social Crises: The Case of Ireland's Recession. *Journal of Community & Applied Social Psychology*, *22*(6), 453–469. https://doi.org/10.1002/casp.1125

O'Rourke, K. H., Sinnott, R., Richardson, J. D., & Rodrik, D. (2001). The Determinants of Individual Trade Policy Preferences: International Survey Evidence [with Comments and Discussion]. *Brookings Trade Forum*, 157–206. JSTOR.

O'Toole, G. (2003). A New Nationalism for a New Era: The Political Ideology of Mexican Neoliberalism. *Bulletin of Latin American Research*, *22*(3), 269–290. https://doi.org/10.1111/1470-9856.00078

Page, B. I., & Shapiro, R. Y. (2010). *The Rational Public: Fifty Years of Trends in Americans' Policy Preferences*. University of Chicago Press.

Peet, R. (2002). Ideology, Discourse, and the Geography of Hegemony: From Socialist to Neoliberal Development in Postapartheid South Africa. *Antipode*, *34*(1), 54–84. https://doi.org/10.1111/1467-8330.00226

Rawłuszko, M. (2019). And If the Opponents of Gender Ideology Are Right? Gender Politics, Europeanization, and the Democratic Deficit. *Politics & Gender*, 1–23. https://doi.org/10.1017/S1743923X19000576

Rehm, P. (2011). Social Policy by Popular Demand. *World Politics*, *63*(2), 271–299. https://doi.org/10.1017/S0043887111000037

Risse, T. (2014a). No Demos? Identities and Public Spheres in the Euro Crisis. *JCMS: Journal of Common Market Studies*, *52*(6), 1207–1215 https://doi.org/10.1111/jcms.12189

Risse, T. (2014b, November). *Introduction*. European Public Spheres: Politics Is Back. https://doi.org/10.1017/CBO9781139963343.002

Seoane Pérez, F. (2013). *Political Communication in Europe: The Cultural and Structural Limits of the European Public Sphere*. Palgrave Macmillan UK. https://doi.org/10.1057/9781137305138

Sniderman, P. M., Brody, R. A. & Tetlock, P. E. (1993). *Reasoning and Choice: Explorations in Political Psychology*. Cambridge University Press.

Statham, P. (2010). Europe's search for a public. In R. Koopmans & P. Statham (Eds.), *The Making of a European Public Sphere: Media Discourse and Political Contention* (pp. 1–11). Cambridge University Press.

Suldovsky, B. (2016). In Science Communication, Why Does the Idea of the Public Deficit Always Return? Exploring Key Influences. *Public Understanding of Science*, *25*(4), 415–426. https://doi.org/10.1177/0963662516629750

Swedberg, R. (2018). Folk Economics and Its Role in Trump's Presidential Campaign: An Exploratory Study. *Theory and Society*, *47*(1), 1–36. https://doi.org/10.1007/s11186-018-9308-8

van der Brug, W., Gattermann, K. & Vreese, C. H. de. (2016). Introduction: How Different Were the European Elections of 2014? *Politics and Governance*, *4*(1), 1–8. https://doi.org/10.17645/pag.v4i1.591

White, J. (2011). *Political Allegiance After European Integration*. Palgrave Macmillan. www.palgrave.com/gp/book/9780230279780

Zarycki, T. (2015). Modernizacja kulturowa i psychologiczna jako ideologia inteligenckiej hegemonii. *Przegląd Socjologiczny*, *64*(2), 45–68.

Zimmermann, S. (2007). The Institutionalization of Women's and Gender Studies in Higher Education in Central and Eastern Europe and the Former Soviet Union: Asymmetric Politics and the Regional-Transnational Configuration. *East Central Europe*, *34*, 131–160.

Appendix 1: Overview of Social Representations

The Economy in the Eyes of Citizens

A1.1 The Economic World Map

Definition: The *economic world map* is a normative cluster of representations depicting the global economic space as a *hierarchical ordering of regions with specific economic characteristics*. Based on two different logics of ranking, states are judged as more or less advanced. The prime indicators are different visions of *economic progress* from which assessments of the normative importance of *economic sectors* are derived (see Table 3.1). On the one hand, countries can be judged based on their export of agricultural, industrial or digital products. On the other hand, countries can also be compared based on the quality of environmental, product and social regulations.

A1.1.1 Progress as Innovation

Definition: The representation of *progress as innovation* embraces the diagnosis of an ever-changing world. The dynamism of the modern economy and the pressure it puts on individuals, countries and firms are interpreted as advancement. Innovative pressures thus should be supported and further enhanced. Creative destruction (in particular through digitalization) is viewed as ultimately beneficial. The representation is the foundation of the *innovation-based sector ordering* and the opposite of the representation *social progress*.

Linguistic Features: Metaphors of movement (advancing, stalling, falling behind, moving forward or backward), applied to countries, firms, individuals and humanity.

Frequency: 12; inflation (PSU), innovation (PAT, FAT), investment (GAT, GST, PLT, PST), merit (GSU), non-wage labor costs (GAU), privatization (GAU), variety (FST, PLT).

Quotes: see Chapter 3, Section 3.2.1.

A1.1.2 Social Progress

Definition: This vision of progress shares the diagnosis of permanent change articulated in *progress as innovation*, but judges it negatively. Permanent economic change and performance pressure are depicted as harmful; progress is viewed as currently going into the wrong direction. This representation of progress again affects multiple levels, pointing to the negative effects of performance pressure on individuals, denouncing the inutility of many products celebrated as innovative, and sketching more socially beneficial steps of development.

Linguistic Features: Metaphors of movement (like *progress as innovation*)

Frequency: 11; innovation (GLT, PLT), investment (GST), inflation (PAU), privatization (FSU, PLU), merit (GAU, GLU, GSU, PAU), variety (GLT, PLT)

Quotes: see Chapter 3, Section 3.2.1.

A1.1.3 Innovation-based Sector Ordering

Definition: The *innovation-based sector ordering* hierarchizes economic sectors based on an innovation-centered vision of economic development. The first step in this development is agricultural production, followed by industrialization and cumulating in the emergence of a digital economy. Accordingly, agricultural products are valued less than industrial products, and industrial production is viewed as less advanced than the digital economy. This sector ordering is strongly opposed to the *social ordering of sectors*.

Linguistic Features: **Metonymies** employing products as symbols of sectors and their economic worth (e.g., garlic as symbol of low-worth French exports). **Metaphors of ranking** are used to judge countries and their exports according to this sector ordering.

Frequency: 9; interest rates (GSU), non-wage labor costs (GAU), innovation (FAT, FST, GLT), investment (GAT, GST), entrepreneurship (GAU, GLU)

Quotes: see Chapter 3, Section 3.2.1.

A1.1.4 Social Ordering of Sectors

Definition: The social ordering of sectors hierarchizes sectors based on their centrality to human flourishing. It is mainly employed when the desired degree of state intervention in specific sectors is discussed. In this hierarchy, agriculture is on top followed by other sectors necessary for subsistence (housing, electricity, transport, education). All these sectors –

while not having to be state-run – should at least be tightly regulated. On the bottom of the hierarchy are "brainless" consumer products, which are viewed as inessential to human development and can be left to market forces.

Linguistic Features: Metonymies (e.g., local ecological apple being more valuable than cheap Chinese plastic gadgets); metaphors of ranking

Frequency: 8; privatization (GAU, GLU, GSU, PAU, PSU), standards (GLT), innovation (GLT); high placement of agriculture: 7; standards (FAT, FLT, FST, GST, GLT, PST), prices (FST); contested standing of housing sector: 8; interest rates (FAU, GAU), merit (GSU), state vs market (GAU), privatization (GAU, GLU), product variety (PLT), state expenditure (PSU)

Quotes: see Chapter 3, Section 3.2.1.

A1.1.5 Cardinal Directions: The West

Definition: The economy of the *The West* (mainly the United States, sometimes also the UK or Canada) is characterized by high innovativeness and a low degree of regulation. Ranked based on an understanding of *progress as innovation*, the West is at the top of the global economic hierarchy. Ranked according to the *social progress*, the West is at the bottom of the hierarchy due to its low social, environmental and product quality standards.

Linguistic Features: Metaphors of ranking and race; specific political vocabulary, drawn from past debates and symbolizing low standards (e.g., chlorinated chicken, GMOs); Silicon Valley as symbol of American innovativeness.

Frequency: The West as world leader according to innovation-based vision of progress: 6; competitiveness (FSU), innovation (FAT, GLT, PAT), investment (FAT, GAT); The West as tail light in terms of social and environmental regulation: 11; exports (FST, GST), merit (GAU, PAU), standards (FLT, GLT, GST), SMEs (FST, GLT, PAT) workers' rights (GLT)

Quotes:

FATW1: "The United States are the world's first economic power."

– French agents discussing 'innovation'

PATM1: "Frequently, innovations determine the degree of development of a country. In Poland, for example, there is sufficient economic growth, but innovations are on a very low level. And because of that we do not catch up with the countries, let's say, of the West."

– Polish agents discussing 'innovation'

GSTM2: "Yeah I think that's what's problematic about it. Those products that are sold in the US and that are full of shit, let's say [GSTM3: Yes.]. And then standards are lowered here and all of a sudden they can be sold here [GSTM1: Yes] and we then have to eat that shit."

– German soccer players discussing 'standards'

In the first two quotes, the United States is seen as the top country in the innovative hierarchy of states, mainly due to the prominence of its digital firms and because of the notoriety of Silicon Valley. Note that all the statements above contain quite explicit metaphors of ranking and race. Whether the United States is called the "first" economic power, while "we do not catch up" – the global order is imagined as a competition of states which the United States is currently leading. If – like in quote three – the social hierarchy of sectors is mobilized as a yardstick of assessment, the status of the United States is judged more negatively. The statement shows the two indicators frequently mobilized in the social hierarchy of sectors: product and social standards. The United States is depicted as a country with low product standards. This is viewed as particularly troublesome in the agricultural sector due to the fear of digesting harmful substances. The quotes thus show how the West is either depicted as a global economic leader in the innovation-based ordering of sectors or as an unregulated disaster according to the social vision of progress.

A1.1.6 Cardinal Directions: The Far East

Definition: *The Far East* (almost exclusively China) is also represented as a region with specific economic characteristics. Here again different sector orderings mobilized for judgment can be distinguished. China mainly appears as producer of mass consumer goods (e.g., toys), which, on the one hand, are industrial goods threatening European competitors (thus implying a mid-range position in the innovation-based sector ranking). In the social ranking, on the other hand, they can be depicted as consumerist nonsense or as potentially dangerous and poisonous due to low production standards.

Frequency: 8; competitiveness (FLU), exports (FAT), investment (PST), prices (GLT), sovereignty (GST), standards (FLT, GST, PST)

A1.1.7 Cardinal Directions within Europe: Northern Europe, Southern Europe, Eastern Europe

Definition: Northern, Southern and Eastern Europe are also identified as regions with specific characteristics. They are also ranked based on the two visions of progress. Yet, in Europe, migration flows function as an additional indicator, symbolizing a country's economic attractivity. *The North* (mainly Norway and Sweden) are, first, viewed as extremely advanced in terms of social and environmental regulation. They are, second, frequently cited as destinations of migration, mainly due to high wage levels and social standards. In the social ordering of sectors, then, Scandinavia is on the top. *Southern Europe* (mainly Greece, Spain and Portugal) is often depicted as a producer of agricultural goods (e.g., tomatoes or oranges), thus not being particularly advanced in the innovation-based ranking of sectors. Concerning standards, judgments are rather reserved too, frequently associating Southern European countries with low environmental standards and the use of pesticides. Finally, Southern Europe is associated with high levels of unemployment and thus as a country of origin of economic migration. *Eastern Europe* similarly seems to be located in Europe's economic periphery. In this representation, two countries are mainly cited as examples of Eastern Europe: Romania and Ukraine, the latter mainly by Polish participants. *Eastern Europe* in this representation is mainly characterized by low wages and low production costs. It is thus mainly viewed as a country of origin of economic migration.

Linguistic Features: Metaphors of ranking.

Frequency: Northern Europe: 4, alternative representations (PST), mobility (PLU, PAU), non-wage labor costs (FSU); Eastern Europe: 12, corruption (GST), exports (PST), investment (FAT, GLT, PAT), mobility (GLU, PAU, PLU, PSU), non-wage labor costs (GAU), state expenditure (FAT), workers' rights (FST); Southern Europe: 7, alternative representations (PSU), competitiveness (FLU), exports (FLU), mobility (GSU), prices (FLT, GLT), workers' rights (FST)

FSUM1: "The Nordic countries today are the first in terms of well-being."
– French soccer players discussing 'non-wage labor costs'

PSTM5: "So for example Scandinavia and these countries like Sweden, Norway, Finland and so on, they are crazy about all environmental or quality standards. Right? [PSTM4: Well yeah; PSTM1: Yes]. Every product there … I don't know, if you sell paper towels that towel must have five or seven certificates, standards and so on. […] And when the people go to the shops and they see that something doesn't have six labels, then out of principle that's a fucking crime! Like: 'we don't buy that'!"

PSTM1: "And in Greece on the other hand – fuck that!" [laughter from group]
– Polish agents discussing alternative representations

PSTM1: "If we in Poland, for example, produce good Vodka – out of potatoes, right? […] We are producing good Vodka and it sells well here. […] But now comes a Vodka from Ukraine – let's call it 'Sawskaja' – which is half as expensive and is only of slightly lower quality. But

> it's two times cheaper. So people start buying it. Why? Because production, for example, is two times cheaper in Ukraine with regard to taxes, tariffs and so on. They have to pay less to the workers, less for a production hall and so on."
>
> – Polish soccer players discussing 'exports'

A1.1.8 France, Germany and Poland on the Economic World Map

Definition: While the criteria of evaluation and representation of the international hierarchy seem to be largely shared, most participants hold quite detailed knowledge about the specific state of their national economy. Polish participants mainly described their economy as an *economy in development*. This often implied a diagnosis of a lack of public investment, resulting in low degrees of innovation, low wages and consequently a form of brain drain. Poland thus is mainly viewed as the provider of a cheap though qualified labor force. German participants, on the contrary, sometimes took considerable pride in representing their nation as *the export world champion*. In this representation, Germany is hailed for the strength of its industrial sector, which, however, is in need of qualified workers (and potentially of more investment into digital technology). French participants, finally, described their nation as a *high standard economy*. This representation was frequently mobilized to express a fear of these standards being undercut, both by low quality products and cheap labor. Accordingly, France struggles to export its goods and suffers from low wage competition abroad.

Frequency:

Poland: for progressive sector ordering and dependence on foreign firms: 4; investment (PLT, PST), non-wage labor costs (PAU), competitiveness (PLU); for Poland as origin of migration: 6; migration (PAU, PLU), variety (PLT), work (PAU, PLU, PSU); for Poland as destination of migration: 2; investment (PST), mobility (PAU); for improvements in past years & usage of term development: 6; corruption (PLT), state vs market (PAT), non-wage labor costs (PLU, PAU), right to work (PAU), variety (PLT);

Germany: For strength in export industry: 8; work (GAT, GST), exports (FAT, GAT, GST) SMEs (FLT, GLT), investment (PLT); for weakness in digitalization: 3; innovation (GAT), Privatization (GAU), standards (GAT); for destination of migration: 3; competitiveness (GLU), entrepreneurship (GSU), investment (GLT)

France: high product standards and luxury goods: 9; alternative representations (FLU), exports (FST), investment (FAT), price (FST), standards (FLT, FST), SMEs (FLT), work (FLT, FST); High work standards & destination of migration: 6; Mobility (FAU, FLU), standards (FST), state expenditure (FAT), work (FAT), workers' rights (FST)

Quotes: see Chapter 3, Section 3.2.2

Table A1.1 Social representations of actors and causal mechanisms on the product market

	Consumer benefits	Consumer faces trade-off	Consumer causes harm
Causal Mechanism	*Price (efficiency)*	*Price (quality)*	*Price (factors of production)*
International movement	*Exchange (products)*		*Race to the bottom (products)*

A1.2 Social Representations of the Product Market

Definition: The central mechanism of the product market is the price mechanism as consumers base their purchasing decisions on prices. There are different representations of how prices are formed and of how goods are traded internationally. These different representations of the market mechanism distribute benefits between producers and consumers in different countries as positive, negative or zero-sum games (see Table A1.1).

A1.2.1 The Consumer

Definition: The consumer is the central actor on the product market. Causally, her decision to buy is mainly driven by a **consideration for price**. Normatively, the consumer is **ambiguous**. The focus on low prices can be viewed as legitimate if the consumer is depicted as poor. Consumption decisions, however, can also be criticized, in particular if the *social ordering of sectors* is mobilized. Accordingly, a consumer can be described as a consumerist imbecile, harming the environment and workers in other countries by buying cheap and pointless gadgets. The representation of the consumer is strongly **anchored in personal experience**.

Frequency: 20; exports (FAT), interest rates (FSU), investment (FAT, GAT), non-wage labor costs (FSU), privatization (PLU), prices (FLT, FST, GAT, GLT, GST, PAT, PLT), standards (FLT, FST, GST, PLT), variety (FAT, PAT, PLT)

Quotes: see Chapter 4, Section 4.2.3.

A1.2.2 Price (Efficiency)

Definition: In the representation of *price as efficiency*, prices in are the result of **specialization and division of labor**. Division of labor can happen within firms, between firms, or between countries which are viewed as elements in a global production chain. The price mechanism based on specialization implies a view of the product market as a **positive sum game** where both producers and consumers benefit.

Linguistic Features: Vocabulary from and references to classical economic theory.

Frequency: 6; exports (FAT, PST), innovation (FAT), prices (FLT), privatization (GAU), variety (PAT)

Quotes: see Chapter 5, Section 5.2.2.1.

A1.2.3 Price (Quality)

Definition: In this representation, prices are perceived as an **indicator of quality**. This implies a **zero-sum game** played between consumers and producers, as low prices automatically imply low quality. The consumer will often end up being cheated by ruthless *big business* and *managers*, handing out bad quality at attractive prices. The representation is strongly **anchored in consumption experience**.

Frequency: 16; Exports (FST, PST), inflation (PAU), prices (FLT, FST, GAT, GST, PAT, PLT, PST), SMEs (FST, PAT), standards (FST, GLT, PLT), variety (PLT)

Quotes:

PLTW1: "Well 'Low prices for consumers' – yeah, it's important. But here it is somewhat less important. It's important but maybe not too much. Because if there is high quality, then the price is like information. Right? This is a high-quality product. That's why the price is high."

– Polish teachers discussing 'prices'

GSTM3: "In principle low prices are nothing bad [GSTM1: Exactly]. But like if you go to the corner and get a kebab for a euro, you really should ask yourself how it can only cost one euro."

GSTM1: "Yeah but let's take meat more generally. We're all super shocked if we see a documentary about industrial livestock farming. But how else can it be …"

– German soccer players discussing 'prices'

In both quotes, prices (and very low prices in particular) are viewed as an indicator of bad quality. Prices thus perceived are "information" telling the consumer what to expect. In terms of the distribution of benefits, the social representation of price as quality depicts the product market as a zero-sum game. Consumers either get low quality or they pay a higher price. Prices represent a simple trade-off between cost and quality. This social representation of prices seems to be based on an inference from consumption experiences. When participants mobilize the representation, they seem to have everyday life consumption situations in their mind, as the reference to the kebab shop on the corner exemplifies.

A1.2.4 Price (Factors of Production)

Definition: In the representation *Price (factors of production)*, the price of a product depends on the costs of the various **inputs needed for its production**. The factors of production can be purely economic in nature (e.g., costs of resources or transportation costs) or they can be country-dependent factors such as wage and rent levels, taxes and subsidies, or product quality and environmental standards. As it factors in country-specific costs, this representation is the basis for the depiction of the international movement of goods as a *race to the bottom*.

Frequency: 22; for subsidies and taxes: prices (GAT), SMEs (FLT), exports (FST); for wage level: exports (PST), inflation (PAU), prices (FAT, GAT, GLT, GST), workers' rights (GLT, GST, FST); standards & production conditions: prices (FLT, GST), standards (PST, GST), SMEs (GLT, GST); Economic factors (e.g., transportation costs, resources): exports (FLT), prices (GST, PLT), privatization (PSU)

Quotes:

PSTM1: "For those cheapest and lowest quality goods ... What's important is that product quality has to fulfill certain standards. Let's start with those toys from China, right? Wherever, whatever plastic, you know, there are different kinds of plastic. It shouldn't be, I don't know, the cheapest kind which costs most for the pollution our planet."

– Polish soccer players discussing 'standards'

GSTM1: "If I can buy a watch for five euro, something is wrong. In my view that can't be. Resources have their price, too. And if it is not the resources, it is the people who work there. In the end, there is a pitfall somewhere. I don't get it. But there is some kind of business model behind it, otherwise people would not do it. And the consumer is happy, but I try to avoid this kind of things ..."

– German soccer players discussing 'prices'

In the first quote, a lack of appropriate environmental standards is viewed as the cause of low prices. The somewhat awkward formulation in the final sentence ("the cheapest kind which *costs* most for the pollution of our planet") seems to reveal an understanding of environmental externalities as an element of prices. The greater the costs you impose on the environment, the lower the price of your product. In the second quote, resources and wages are cited as the relevant factors of production. The quote's final phrase contains a judgment of the consumer who might be "happy" but is potentially doing the wrong thing. Both quotes thus imply that prices can be indicators of harm being done in the process of production. In both quotes, moreover, the factors of production that cause harm (environmental and working conditions) are factors which are country specific.

A1.2.5 Exchange (Products)

Definition: If resource endowments or traditional production techniques are viewed as the central production factor, the international circulation of goods can be viewed as mutually advantageous. The circulation of products in this sense becomes a mutually beneficent *exchange* as consumers in the countries involved get access to products priorly unavailable.

Frequency 6; exports (FAT, GAT), variety (FST, FLT, PLT, PAT)

Quotes:

GATM2: "We can increase exports with those products which you cannot produce as well in other countries because they do not have the resources."

– German agents discussing 'exports'

PLTW2: "I like Whiskey for example, but – listen carefully girls – this orange-flavored whiskey which a friend of mine brought from London. But over here I didn't see that yet."

PLTW1: "Oh PLTW2, always about alcohol ... It's the main topic!" [laughter]

– Polish teachers discussing 'variety'

A1.2.6 Race to the Bottom (Products)

Definition: The representation *race to the bottom (products)* views product prices as the result of wage levels or environmental regulation (see *price (factors of production)*). Accordingly, the import of low-price products is perceived as a threat to the standards of the importing country. Continuously lowering wages, product quality standards and environmental regulation ends up harming the workers, consumers and the environment everywhere. A race to the bottom caused by the circulation of products thus implies a representation of the product market as a **negative sum game**, reducing benefits for almost all parties involved. The only actor who potentially profits from such a race to the bottom are internationally mobile firms.

Frequency: 7; exports (PST), standards (FLT, GAT, GLT, PLT), workers' rights (FST, GST)

Quotes: see Chapter 7, Section 7.3.2 and 7.3.3

Table A1.2 Social representations of the capital market

	Firms as investors	*Big firms and The manager*
Causal mechanism	*Profits (re-investment)*	*Profits (exploitation)*
International movement	*Exchange (ideas and capital)*	*Negotiation* *Race to the bottom (firms)*

A1.3 Social Representations of the Capital Market

Definition: The social representations of the capital market engender sharply contrasting normative judgments, as can be seen Table A1.2. Where firms are viewed exclusively as investors and risk-takers, a positive vision of profits as re-investment can emerge. Internationally, a positive-sum game representation can be discerned where the movement of firms is depicted as an exchange of capital and ideas. On the contrary, the capital market is represented as a negative sum game where a distinction between small and big firms is mobilized. Big firms generate profits for a small management elite by forcing states into a race to the bottom of regulation.

A1.3.1 Firms as Investors

Definition: A positive vision depicting *firms as investors.*[1] Firms invest based on cost–benefit calculations, that is calculations of expected profits based on an assessment of risk. Participants seem to conceptualize risk as the interplay of two factors: the stakes (most commonly the money invested) and uncertainty (often political or economic instability). Both factors are proportional to the overall amount of risk. Investment – which of course is based on risk-assessment – has two positive consequences: innovation and job creation. Normatively, therefore, the representation has strong links to *progress as innovation* and *the entrepreneur*.

Frequency: For investment creating jobs: frequency 6; interest (FAU, GSU, PLU), investment (FLT, PAT, PST); for investment creating innovation: 7; innovation (FAT, FLT), investment (FAT, GAT, GST, PST), variety (GLT); cost–benefit calculation: 12, entrepreneurship (GAU, GLU, GSU, PSU), interest rates (FAU, FSU, GAU, GSU, PLU), privatization (GAU), inflation (PAU, PSU)

Quote:

GSUM1: "[reads out card] 'Low interest rates' – of course. You want to invest, you have to invest … If you want to invest interest rates should be low. Right? Those are the central points. I should add 'a stable environment for firms' to 'low interest rates' of course. If they are not

> stable, then I have to ask myself: 'How will it be tomorrow?' – and I rather don't hire anyone."
>
> – German soccer players discussing 'interest rates'

In the quote, the two elements of risk-assessment become visible. The level of interest symbolizes the stakes – low rates thus facilitate investment. Uncertainty appears in the calculation as a desire for stability. Having to worry about tomorrow seems to make investment riskier. If one of the factors is not met, the investor will not create jobs. The decision to create job thus depends on a careful cost–benefit calculation. Viewing firms as bearers of risk thus can engender a rather positive social representation of their actions.

A1.3.2 Profits as Re-investment

Definition: Depiction of profits as a *positive sum game*. Profits are re-invested by firms into research and development, which generates socially beneficial innovation (strong linked to *progress as innovation*). The representation is the opposite of *profits as exploitation*. It is strongly anchored in economic theory and only used by participants with economic training.

Linguistic Features: Vocabulary from economic theory (e.g., "R&D", "research and development")

Frequency: 2; innovation (FLT), investment (PST)

Quotes: see also Chapter 5, Section 5.2.2.3.

A1.3.3 Big Firms

Definition: This negative representation of firms depicts *big firms* as profit-hungry, internationally mobile, and powerful. Big firms are powerful because they have immense administrative capacities. They can afford lawyers and lobbyists, thus allowing them to influence political decisions and to bend the existing rules in their favor. Their power is also rooted in their international mobility which allows them to strongarm the state (see *negotiation* and *race to the bottom (capital)*). Big firms, moreover, are frequently identified as those firms who are on the stock market and which are thus subjected to a pressure of generating profits whatever the costs (this immoral strive for profit being symbolized by *the manager*). Big firms are therefore prone to use their power to lower or even violate environmental and social regulations, thus violating the norms set out in the *social ordering of sectors*.

Frequency: Big firms are internationally mobile: frequency 10; investment (PST), mobility (FAU, FLU, GSU), non-wage labor costs (FLU, FSU, PAU, PSU), right to work (GAU), workers' rights (PST)

Small firms as local ecological farmers: 4; SMEs (FLT, FST, GLT, PAT); Mittelstand as positive category: 4; investment (GST), SMEs (GAT, GLT, GST)

Quote: (see also Chapter 4, Section 4.2.2 and 4.3.3, or Chapter 7, Section 7.3.3)

GLMT1: "So big firms always have a global network [GLTW2: Exactly, that's the point.]. Thus, the people controlling the firm are always quite far away from the work processes and the actual conditions of the employees. And that distance is mirrored by the wage differences. And in small and medium-sized enterprises that's different and your boss still walks through the production hall from time to time. Maybe this is an idealization, but I think in a medium-sized enterprise there is more of a corporate identity and consequently employers have more of a duty to behave responsibly towards their employees. And I don't see that with VW-managers for example [GLTW3: Yeah, they just come and go.]. If I earn 17 million ..."

GLTW3: "Yeah his mission is different. He feels responsible to himself, not to his firm [GSTM1: Exactly]."

– German teachers discussing 'SMEs'

In the quote, big firms are depicted as responsible for bad working conditions and for an unfair distribution of wages. The negative image of big firms is maintained by comparing them to smaller firms. Most frequently, small agricultural producers are mobilized in this context, but some German groups also deploy a representation of the *Mittelstand* as a significant other. Big firms are structurally different from small and medium-sized enterprises. Their management is depicted as a global elite, which privileges profits over product, environmental, and social standards.

A1.3.4 The Manager

Definition: The *manager* is a representation of a business elite characteristic of *big firms*. The manager is profit hungry and morally corrupt, the latter often symbolized by accusations of sexism.

Linguistic Features: Animal metaphors employed to demonize the manager.

Frequency: 9; entrepreneurship (GSU), interest rates (FSU, PAU), merit (FSU, GSU), non-wage labor costs (PST), privatization (FLU, FSU), SMEs (GLT)

Quotes: (see also *profits as exploitation* below)

GATM1: "I simply don't want that only a small elite ..."

GATM2: "... that in the end there is only three firms left. I understand that."

– German agents discussing 'SMEs'

FLUW2: "The big boss likes models."

– French teachers discussing 'privatization'

The quotes above mainly show that the figure of the manager is intimately linked to the representation of big firms. In the first quote big firms are called a small elite. In the second quote, the manager's abuse of power is expressed by accusing him[2] of moral corruption, in this case by linking him to sexist practices.

A1.3.5 Profits as Exploitation

Definition: In this negative-sum representation, profits result from the abuse of power engineered by *big firms* and *the manager*. Big firms squeeze employees or use their international mobility to force the state to make concessions with regard to social and environmental standards (see *negotiation* and *race to the bottom (capital)*). This representation thus seems to be based on *price (factors of production)* as big firms' ability to circumvent standards gives them an unfair competitive advantage.

Frequency: 20; competitiveness (FSU, PAU), entrepreneurship (GSU), exports (PST), innovation (GLT, PST), interest (FSU), investment (GAT), merit (FSU), non-wage labor costs (PST), prices (FLT, GLT, GST, PAT), privatization (PSU), SMEs (FST, GAT, GLT, GST, PAT), standards (GST)

Quotes: see also Chapter 5, Section 5.2.2.3.

PSUM1: "Because there can't be such a disproportion that a teacher earns 3,000 while some lady which only makes coffee for Mr. CEO gets 60,000. Like it happened in the Polish mBank."

– Polish soccer players discussing 'non-wage labor costs'

FSUM1: "Back in the days, before the euro, you bought a car for 20,000 to 30,000 Francs. And you had a new car. Today, it's 15,000 to 20,000 euros and you have the worst of cars. A real car takes at least 50,000 euros today. And the managers of the CAC40 they feed on it. They stuff themselves with it. They abuse their power."

– French soccer players discussing 'interest rates'

In the quotes representations of *big firms* (CAC40 is the index of France's 40 largest stock market firms) and the representation of *the manager* combine into a vision of profits as exploitation. Profits in this view are benefits to a self-interested and immoral elite, rather than a reward for risk-taking. Where the manager blows his money on a sexy secretary, a vision of profits as socially beneficial re-investment seems to be quite distant. The profits of big firms are viewed as an unfair allocation of money. The metaphors seem to draw from the animal kingdom (feeding or stuffing), clearly implying a demonization of the manager. While this vision cannot be described as one of mutual harm (as the manager still receives benefits), it remains a negative sum game as only a very small elite is profiting.

A1.3.6 Negotiation

Definition: Negotiations are frequently depicted by the participants as a tough process in which the stronger party presses through its will. Rather than resulting in compromise, negotiations appear as a tool for the implementation of the needs of the powerful. Negotiations most frequently pitch *big firms* against the state, with the latter using their international mobility to strongarm the state. The power of big firms in negotiations thus lies at the heart of *race to the bottom (capital)*.

Linguistic Features: Direct speech in which negotiators flatly state their demands and make threats.

Frequency: 13; corruption (GST, GLT), inflation (PAU), investment (GST, PAT, PST), SMEs (GAT, PST), sovereignty (GAT, PAT), standards (FLT, GLT, GST)

Quotes:

GATM2: "I am not certain whether this is the right place and whether the main interest is negotiating a compromise between different interests. [...] I think there where the negotiations take place, the tone is tough: 'We want to sell our cars and we want to sell them as cheaply as possible. Lower your tariffs, so people buy them. If tariffs are high nobody will buy them due to the trade deal you already have with China.'

– German agents discussing 'SMEs'

PSTM4: "Big corporations can dictate their condition to the state. When they take issue with workers' rights, for example, and they say: 'Alright. Listen up, something!' I don't know. 'We will do it like this and like that. And you better listen because if not, we'll just fuck off.'

– Polish soccer players discussing 'investment'

A1.3.7 Race to the Bottom (Capital)

Definition: The representations of *negotiation* and *big firms* can interact to depict the international circulation of capital as a *race to the bottom*. Seeking to maximize profits, big firms employ their capacity to move internationally as a bargaining chip, thus increasing their power to bend regulations. On the product market, *race to the bottom (products)* meant that the circulation of products exerts pressure on other countries to lower their standards. On the capital market, the circulation of firms has a similar effect: states need to lower their standards to accommodate firms which threaten to leave. This process is harmful for all states participating in the process. The race to the bottom on the capital market engenders a negative sum game.

Linguistic Features: Often anchored in national vocabulary (*délocalisation, concurrence déloyale*)

Frequency: 12; competitiveness (PAU), interest (GSU), investment (GST, PAT, PST), sovereignty (GAT, GST, PAT), workers' rights (FLT, GST, PAT), privatization (PLU)

Quotes: see also Chapter 7, Sections 7.3.2 and 7.3.3

PAUW2: "I also took issue with 'international competitiveness' because it is a bit like ... Like the race with the rabbit [loughs]."

– Polish agents discussing 'competitiveness'

PATM2: "Let's say it like this: sovereignty in political decisions is frequently dictated by large international corporations or it is made to their advantage. You might say that this doesn't happen, but it does."

– Polish agents discussing 'sovereignty'

In the fairy tale referred to, a rabbit dies in a race with two hedgehogs, which is set up in way so it can't win. Based on a representation of big firms as powerful and profit-hungry, the capital market thus appears as a race of states in which all participants lose out.

A1.3.8 Exchange (Capital and Ideas)

Definition: In this representation, the international movement of capital is depicted as a mutually beneficial *exchange*. Exchange in this vision includes the exchange of ideas as well as a good allocation of means satisfying the different parties involved.

Linguistic Feature: Vocabulary drawn from economic theory.

Frequency: 6; Investment (FAT, GAT, PLT, PAT), non-wage labor costs (GAU), privatization (GAU)

Quotes:

FATW1: "I think we have to attract foreign investors [FATM1: Yes]."

FATW2: "For the companies, right?"

FATW1: "Yes, for the companies. Small and medium-sized firms because ... Well, in France ... well, because it's complicated. Because if foreign ... If foreigners see that that we developed something good, this allows us to export it and that causes a virtuous circle."

FATM1: "And then you can have commercial exchanges and exchange everything that is new."

– French agents discussing 'investment'

GAUM2: "What is happening with a lot of firms which had mergers, including national jewels such as Land Rover in England, which was overtaken by Tata, they are running a lot better now. Or take Volvo, which was overtaken by the Chinese but who said nevertheless: 'We leave everything in Sweden, we leave it to you.' But for now, it has worked well for these brands. It doesn't always have to go like: 'This brand can only be overtaken by VW or Mercedes.' That is creating a sense of security in the firms, and it blocks their drive to innovate."

– German agents discussing 'privatization'

The representation of international capital flows as an exchange contrasts sharply with the representation of a *race to the bottom* because the former depicts the capital market as a positive sum game. In the first quote, the arrival of international investors is hailed for engendering a virtuous cycle. This metaphor, strongly present in some economic theories, implies that the elements of the international system can interact to create an ever-improving situation. While things get continuously worse in a race to the bottom, in a virtuous cycle they spiral upward. In the second quote, international mergers are depicted as a chance for both sides involved, thus implying an exchange of capital and expertise. In both quotes, then, the international movement of capital appears as a positive sum game.

A1.4 Social Representations of the Labor Market

Definition: Social representations of the labor market center heavily on the constellations of actors involved (see Table A1.3). *The manager* is deployed in opposition to the *working people* and practices a zero-sum strategy of exploitation. If the *entrepreneur* hires a *classical employee*, the former's passion and initiative will not bear fruit. Depending on these relationships between employer and worker, wages can either be depicted as *exploitation* or as *exchange*. Different visions of the unemployed, derived from the representations of the working people and of the classical employee, complement this tableau of relationships. Representations of international mobility are mainly based on the vision of the working people seeking higher wages abroad.

Table A1.3 Social representations of the labor market

Actor (employed)	***Working people (vs. the manager)***	***Typical employee (vs. the entrepreneur)***
Actor (unemployed)	*The precarious*	*The lazy*
Causal mechanism	*Wage (exploitation)*	*Wage (exchange)*
International Labor mobility	*Race to the bottom (migration)* *Migration as talent*	

A1.4.1 The Entrepreneur

Definition: The entrepreneur is motivated to work by inspiration. As the entrepreneur takes risk and masters it through hard work, the representation is closely related to *firms as investors*. Yet, entrepreneurship goes beyond the activity of founding or developing firms; it is viewed as a virtue, combining responsibility and hard work. Thus, all individuals could theoretically behave like entrepreneurs. Entrepreneurship thus denotes a mentality, rather than a strictly defined activity.

Linguistic Features: National vocabulary ("Ich-AG", "Startpauschale")

Frequency: Frequency: 10; Competitiveness (PSU), Entrepreneurship (FLU, GAU, GLU, GSU, PLU), exports (PLT), interest (FAU, FSU, GSU) Inspiration as motivation to work: Frequency 4; Merit (FLU, FSU, GLU), right to work (FSU)

Quotes (see also *the unemployed as lazy* below)

GSUM1: "Because in the end someone who becomes an entrepreneur has little money. You have to take that risk and lower the hurdles. [...] This has to be more or less remedied by the state. [...] If the calculation is done well, the state should say: 'Yes, we subsidize'. On the other hand, subsidies only, like the Ich-AG back in the days ..."

GSUM4: "The question is how to understand the question. Is it for people who really want to become entrepreneurs or is it for those citizens too who are working already? Should we still advance the entrepreneurial spirit? So I rather mean this style of thought of classical employees, this extreme employee mentality. Right? 'Employers are always shit'. [GSUM1: Yes] It is such a general attitude that people complain about their employer and they forget that they are being paid by him and that this can only function if you perform. [...] 'Ugh, my boss is stupid' [loughs]."

– German soccer players discussing 'entrepreneurship'

A1.4.2 The Classical Employee

Definition: The *classical employee* is *the entrepreneur*'s significant other. The classical employee is solely interested in his wage and tries to minimize the effort needed to acquire it. The classical employee undermines the efforts of the entrepreneur and thus makes a mutually beneficial work relationship impossible.

Linguistic Features: National vocabulary ("Ich-AG")

Frequency: 7; entrepreneurship (GAU, GLU, GSU, PLU), privatization (GSU), right to work (FSU, GSU)

Quotes (see the entrepreneur and the unemployed as lazy)

A1.4.3 The Unemployed as Lazy

Definition: This representation is formed when the mentality of *the classical employee* is attributed to the unemployed. In this representation, the unemployed lack initiative and are found short of inspiration to work. Normatively, it is based on the assumption that responsibility, initiative and inspiration should motivate those who seek employment, just as it motivates *the entrepreneur*.

Linguistic Features: National Vocabulary, in particular names of welfare policies ("Hartz-IV", "*500+*")

Frequency: 5; right to work (GLU, PAU, FSU), entrepreneurship (GLU, GSU)

Quotes (see also *the entrepreneur*)

GLUM1: "[reads out card] 'Advance citizens' entrepreneurial spirit' – well so they don't just subordinate themselves. [change of voice: whiny] 'Well I applied here and there. Oh no, nobody wants me'. So they think themselves: 'Ok, I want to work. There is something I am good at, something I can do. I want to work, I want to make money.' [...] What was this thing called ten, 15 years ago? One man enterprise? Ich-AG! [GLUM2: Ich-AG!] That used to be Schröder's issue back in the days." [...]

GLUM2: "Narrowly understood, this would mean to me: get self-employed! Found a company! On your own or with employees. That would be entrepreneurial spirit narrowly understood. Understood more broadly this would be being an entrepreneur, acting in an entrepreneurial manner. That is contemplating how can I acquire additional qualifications? What else could I do? Where could I go, what could I learn? Where do I have to lower my expectations? Less money, longer commuting time? So, this entire range of issues: I am responsible for myself, and I do something in order to find a job."

– German teachers discussing 'entrepreneurship'

In the quote, we see how an understanding of entrepreneurship as a mentality is mobilized to judge the behavior of the unemployed. The unemployed are supposed to take responsibility: they should make a plan, acquire the needed qualifications and make realistic concessions in order to get a job. Again, these calls for self-responsibility are advanced using the specific vocabulary of "Schröder's" period of liberal reform in the early 2000s. Contrary to this, those who behave more like a classical employee – complaining that "nobody wants me" and exhibiting a lack of effort – stay unemployed much longer.

A1.4.4 The Working People

Definition: The working people are the most frequently used representation of actors on the labor market. It is a representation of idealized normal people, of people like you and me. It is strongly anchored in personal experience, in particular the need to pay bills and taxes and feed a family. This generalization of everyday life struggles is a common denominator which allows to construct the working people as a positive normative category. The honesty of the working people sets them aside from *the classical employee* (who is not willing to work hard) and *the manager* (who cheats, exploits and evades taxes to make a living). As wages are a *factor of production*, the working people frequently become the object of exploitation. The fact that profits go to a small and undeserving elite rather than to the hard working people makes exploitation so abhorrent.

Frequency: 16; investment (GLT, PST), merit (FAU, FSU, GLU, GSU, PAU), non-wage labor costs (GLU, GSU), prices (GLT, GST), standards (GAT, GST), right to work (FLU), workers' rights (PAT, GST); working people explicitly including members of discussion group: 2; inflation (PAU), merit (FSU); Wage as motivation to work: Frequency 9; Entrepreneurship (GAU, GLU, GSU), Merit (FLU, GLU, GSU, PLU), right to work (FLU, FSU)

Quotes: see Chapter 4, Section 4.2.2.

A1.4.5 The Precarious

Definition: Where wages are low, a compassionate representation of the unemployed can be observed. In this representation, the unemployed are depicted as people like you and me, negatively affected by bad working conditions and by the outlook of low wages. Whereas the vision of the *unemployed as lazy* is based on representation of *the classical employee*, this representation depicts the unemployed as *working people* who are temporarily without job.

Linguistic Features: National vocabulary ("Hartz-IV")

Frequency: 6; alternative representations (GAU), entrepreneurship (GAU, GSU), merit (GLU, GSU), right to work (FSU)

Quote: see also Chapter 2, Section 2.3.1.

GSUM2: "So what I liked about your point is that approach of increasing incentives because – and here it gets sensitive – someone who receives *Hartz-IV* says: 'Alright I have to get up every day at six in order to have 1,300 euros.' Just inventing the numbers here. 'Otherwise, I sleep till twelve and I get 1,000 euros from the state.' [...] He will say: "Where is my incentive? Why should I hustle for an additional 100, an additional 200 euros a month?'" [...]

GSUM1: "Regulation, alright. Regulation can be there. But generally, you should have the feeling that you don't live to work but that you work to live. [...] You should not have the feeling – and a lot of *Hartz-IV* recipients have that feeling – that you live to work, that you hustle for nothing."

– German soccer players discussing 'merit'

In the quote, wages are cited as the main motivation to work. The unemployed are depicted as rational actors who consider costs and benefits of employment. Like other people, they weigh advantages and disadvantages of a new job. Like others, they might get the feeling that they just "live to work", and this, understandably, decreases their motivation to work. Their situation of joblessness thus is not viewed as the result of a flawed mentality, but as the outcome of unfair economic structures.

A1.4.6 Wages (Exchange)

Definition: Rather than as exploitation, the relationship between *the working people* and their employer is sometimes seen as a mutually beneficial exchange. An analogy between firms' and employees' well-being is employed to depict the labor market as a positive sum game.

Frequency: 5; entrepreneurship (GSU), merit (FSU, GSU, PSU), right to work (FAU)

Quotes:

PSUM1: "If you work well, you earn well. Your boss earns well, so you earn well too, right? Because if you're the boss and you have good workers, then they earn well, and you earn even better, right?"

– Polish soccer players discussing 'merit'

FAUW2: "You have to be capable as well. After all, you can't give a job to someone who doesn't fit the criteria at all. Because, I mean, it's a loss for both sides. If you propose something to someone who is not from your domain and who is not doing what he was looking for, it's a waste of time."

– French agents discussing 'right to work'

The analogy between employers' and employees' well-being works both ways: if both work efficiently together, both parties can earn more. If there is a mismatch, like in the second quote, it is a "waste of time" for both parties. Importantly, however, the labor market can be a positive sum game if wages are depicted as a mutually beneficent exchange between workers' and firms.

A1.4.7 Migration (Efficiency)

Definition: This representation stresses the *efficiency* of international labor mobility, depicting international mobility of labor as a natural market process. The mobility of labor generates a **positive sum game**, an efficient allocation of resources ultimately benefitting society. It is based on a representation of *the working people* as wage is the central motivation to migrate. The representation is exclusively employed by participants with economic training.

Linguistic Features: Vocabulary drawn from economic theory

Frequency: 2; Mobility (GAU, GLU)

Quotes: see Chapter 5, Section 5.2.2.2.

A1.4.8 Migration as Talent

Definition: In this representations, migrants are viewed as human capital which a country should attract in order to boost its economy. Normatively, the representation thus focuses on benefits to countries, rather than individuals, thus revealing proximity to the representation of the *state as competitor*. This representation has strong links to the different representations of progress and the corresponding sector orderings as these seem to determine in which economic sectors migration is beneficial. The competition of states for talent is inherently **zero-sum**, as one country's attractivity for migration causes a brain drain in another.

Linguistic Features: National vocabulary ("Fachkräftemangel")

Frequency: 8; mobility (GLU), competitiveness (GLU); brain drain: investment (PLT, PST), mobility (PAU, PLU, PSU), prices (PLT)

Quotes:

PLUW4: "Like because of … Like some years ago when we entered the Union, this labor market was opened up. That's when I noticed the best effects of my work [PLUW3: They left]. I teach English. And so those who were the best, they went away. [PLUW2: They went away; PLUW3: Yes, yes!]"

– Polish teachers discussing 'mobility'

PAUW1: "Well, we got kind of dried out in my opinion. Of course, I understand that people leave. But let's say we train a doctor, we pay for his schooling a shitload of money, and then we pay him badly, so he leaves [PAUM1: Yes]. So we don't have a doctor, but we invested in his training [PAUW2: And we already don't have money [loughs]]. And another country then employs him, gives him an income but doesn't bear the cost of education. It's a form of stealing."

– Polish teachers discussing 'mobility'

Both quotes deal with a perceived brain drain Poland has been suffering since the accession to the EU. The fact that migrants are viewed as talent is well-exemplified by the first quote where PLUW4 states that her best students left the country. The second quote also focuses on a highly trained job group: doctors. The cost of education for doctors is depicted as a form of investment by the state, an investment in human capital which will never yield profits. The benefits go to "another country", which amounts to "a form of stealing". These formulations clearly show the zero-sum logic underlying the arguments: in a competition for talent, the richer countries profit at the expense of the poorer ones.

A1.4.9 Migration (Race to the Bottom)

Definition: This representation stresses the negative effect of migration on employees in the receiving country. International mobility is seen as a mechanism which puts pressure on wage levels in high-standard countries. Normatively, the representation is a **zero-sum game** as lower wages of workers in receiving countries are balanced by higher wages which migrants receive. As migrants are viewed as honest *working people*, these benefits are considered legitimate. The race to the bottom is caused by a flawed system – it is not the fault of migrant workers.

Linguistic Features: National vocabulary ("*traveilleur détaché*", "*délocalisation*")

Frequency: 6; investment (GST), mobility (FAU, FLU, GSU), standards (FST), workers' rights (FST)

Quotes: see Chapter 2, Section 2.3.1.

A1.4.10 Migration as a Personal Prospect

Definition: The representations of *migration as a personal prospect* is anchored in the costs and benefits the participants would experience themselves if they would migrate. This representation is anchored in **personal experience** or the experiences of friends and families and thus is particularly frequent in Poland. Causally, it includes non-economic costs of migration for the individual such as distance from friends and family, language barriers and the indignity of performing less-skilled labor. In its most extreme form, migration can be depicted as a negative sum game, a pointless circle causing immense personal costs to the people who migrate.

Frequency: mobilization of personal prospects 8: exports (PLT), investment (PLT, PST), mobility (FLU, FSU, GSU, PAU, PLU); migration as pointless replacement 3; mobility (PAU, PLU), investment (PST)

Quotes: see Chapter 4, Section 4.3.2.

Table A1.4 Representations of state functions

	Fiscal policy	Law-making	EU
Representations of state enhancing market	*State as investor*	*State as competitor*	*EU as investor* (weak)
Representations of state opposing market	*State as re-distributor*	*State as regulator*	*EU as regulator*

A1.5 Social Representations of the State

Definition: Representations of the state identify two central powers: law-making and fiscal policy. Both powers can either be used to enhance or oppose the causalities of the market, resulting in the matrix depicted in Table A1.4. State revenue is mainly provided by the *taxpayer*. Interestingly, only some of these functions are also assigned to the EU.

A1.5.1 The Taxpayer

Definition: Normative figure similar to *the consumer* or to the *working people*. The *taxpayer* is an idealized normal person, working decently and paying the contributions demanded. It is based on the shared **experience** of paying taxes and bills. State revenue is viewed as mostly composed of taxpayers' contributions, thus allowing participants to legitimately judge state expenditure (as it is their money being spent).

Linguistic Features: Often referred to by pronoun 'we', stressing the origins of the representation in shared experience.

Frequency: 12; Expenditure (FAU, GSU, PAU, PLU), Investment (FAT, GST, PST), non-wage labor costs (GLU, GSU, PLU, PSU), privatization (PAU)

Quotes:

PSUM3: "At the moment it is a time in Poland where we have to pay for everything. There is nothing that is not taxed, right?"

– Polish soccer players discussing 'non-wage labor costs'

GSUM4: "Well and 'reduce non-wage costs for firms' – well not only for firms but also for citizens. For both sides, it's just too much. Taxes are too high, insurance costs are too high. There are fat surpluses being made in parts of the EU, but the citizen doesn't really get anything from it."

– German soccer players discussing 'non-wage labor costs'

In the quotes, the taxpayer is referred to using different linguistic expressions. In the first quote, the pronoun "we" is used, while in the second quote the citizen appears as a collective singular. Underlying both statements is a representation of the normal people who bear the lion's share of the tax burden. Moreover, the discussion participants seem to view themselves as taxpayers, too. Personal grievances about high contributions thus can be generalized as a concern of all people.

A1.5.2 The State as Investor

Definition: Where the state is represented as an *investor*, state expenditure is judged according to the principles of the *capital market*: it should generate mutual benefits for society and investors. Domains where such long-term benefits can be generated are mainly infrastructure and innovative industries. This reveals strong connections to the representation of *progress as innovation* and the *innovative ordering of sectors*, as well-targeted state investment is supposed to advance the economy in future-oriented sectors.

Linguistic Features: Usage of 'profits' as re-investment.

Frequency: State should invest: frequency 6; Expenditure (GSU, PLU), investment (FAT, GLT), interest rates (GSU), privatization (GAU); state institutions create innovation: 4; investment (FAT, GLT, PLT, PST); state should try its best, but firms as more effective in investing: 3; expenditure (FAU), investment (GLT), privatization (GAU)

Quotes:

FATW1: "In any case this [investment] is one of the best means for development because it suffices to look at the most indebted country in the world which are the United States which are also the world's first economic power. So investment is not a negative point, it can only be a positive point. Afterwards, ok, you also have to invest well [FATM1: There you go]. But that's something else, that's strategy. [...]

FATM1: "I think all that is ecology, that's a very interesting topic. [...] And I think we will only be able to resolve this problem if we get the investors interested in it and if we show them that they can make profits while saving the planet. Right?"

– French agents discussing 'investment'

PLUW3: "The government hands out the national money. Our money, ours! It simply is like that." [...]

PLUW4: "They want to at the same time hand out money, in the sense that they support pensions or give money for children, and on the other hand, they want to take less taxes from the people. [...] It just doesn't make sense economically [PLUW3: No, it doesn't]. Everyone who runs a household, everyone knows that there must be some form of income [PLUW3: Yes, yes, yes!]. And that's why we are afraid. [PLUW3: Exactly!] And on the other hand: If it wasn't for that, I wouldn't say the proposition is bad in itself. 'Increase state expenditure'. If it was increased in such a way that there would be for example something like public work projects. Like we make, I don't know, for example we build new streets or something else and from then on things start spinning. If it was like this and not like it is right now: 'Just take 500 złoty!' [PLUW3: Yes]"

PLUW2: "This means *rozdawnictwo* is blossoming. It just blossoms."

– Polish teachers discussing 'expenditure'

In the first quote, the state appears as an entrepreneur whose debts are a form of risk-taking, which will pay off if the money was correctly invested. As a promising domain of investment, the ecological transition is cited. The quote finishes with a statement about the mutual benefits entailed by investment as you "can make profits while saving the planet". In a similar vein, the second quote criticizes the Polish government's spending program as *rozdawnictwo*, which I would somewhat clumsily translate as outgivery. Essentially, the *500+* program is thus criticized for being target-less. In sharp contrast with the plan-less handing out of money, investment in infrastructure is depicted as the potential beginning of a virtuous circle ("from then on things start spinning"). Compliance with economic imperatives thus might entail mutual benefits. Moreover, the quote contains some very explicit references to the taxpayer as the state's main source of income. The household analogy applied to the state budget and the claim that "everybody knows" show that the taxpayer is a representation based on shared experiences; managing a budget is a question of common sense.

A1.5.3 State as Redistributor

Definition: Representation of the state employing expenditure for re-distributive purposes. This representation of the state as a *re-distributor* views welfare programs not as target-less outgivery, but as the true purpose of state spending. This is often supported by references to *social progress* and the *social ordering* of economic sectors. Expenditure should not help the market to advance innovation (as in *state as investor*) but should remedy shortcomings of the market mechanism in the most important sectors.

Linguistic Features: Usage of 'profits' as exploitation.

Frequency: state should re-distribute: frequency: 8; expenditure (FLU, GLU, PSU), merit (GLU, GSU), privatization (GLU), right to work (FLU), state vs market (PAT); subsidies to firms as waste of money: frequency 2; expenditure (FLU, GSU)

FLUB1: "[reads out card] 'Increase state expenditure in order to stimulate demand' – I just understand that the state invests in French enterprises. I say that the state should invest in social matters and that's it."

FLUW2: "Yeah but after all the state doesn't have a lot of money at the moment [a lot of confirming noise from the group]. If this increase of state expenditure was for us for example [FLUB1: Us?], or for nurses for example, for the hospitals that really need it. They are permanently in need. That's why it gets polemic here. But yeah, it is ambivalent [FLUB1: Yeah]. It shouldn't go to the market ... '

– French teachers discussing 'expenditure'

GLUM3: "So if the economy generates so much revenue, that is with all the technology we have. With the factories ... So I think this is going to be an issue in the upcoming years that through automatization a lot of value will be produced without human labor, without human hands. A factory which simply makes 10,000,000 of profit. Like that. And these profits get to the state and the state can use them to subsidize shorter work hours."

– German teachers discussing 'merit'

In the first quote, the state is depicted as an opponent of market forces. Its money "shouldn't go the market" but should be invested into "social matters" such as hospitals or schools. The latter is clearly a reference to the *social ordering of sectors.* The state thus should take care of the sectors which the market neglects – an enhancement according to the laws of the capital market ("the state invests into French enterprises") is clearly rejected. This rejection of the capital market mechanism is even more evident in the second quote. Innovation is depicted as generating huge profits, which, however, will only entail mutual benefits if they are re-distributed by the state. Without this re-distribution, the profits might be harvested by the firms – a mechanism reminiscent of the representation of *profits as exploitation*. The vision of the state as a re-distributor thus demands the state to counter-act profit-making on the capital market and to eliminate exploitation on the labor market. The state appears as an opponent of market forces.

A1.5.4 State as Competitor

Definition: The representation of the *state as competitor* depicts state regulation as a tool to increase international competitiveness. Tax and wage levels should be set to increase attractivity in an international competition for exports and human capital (see *migration as talent*). This zero-sum competition of states on the product and labor market is also at the heart of the *economic world map*.

Linguistic Features: Analogies between firms and state; reference to states as 'we' or 'they'.

Frequency: State competing for exports: work (GAT, GST), exports (FAT, FST, PST), prices (PLT), SMEs (GAT, GST), standards (GAT, GST), variety (FLT, PAT)

Quotes:

FATM1: "A state, for example France, we produce weapons. You see? We produce Boeings [sic], for example, which we export. That is a safe destination [for investment] for example. And we are among the first in the world to have this kind of technology."

– French agents discussing 'investment'

FSTM6: "But with CETA, it's dead! It's dead! It means that you have a big firm called Canada and several small firms like France or Denmark et cetera who do not have much to offer. Canada has a lot to give, a lot to sell, but in exchange they will only take garlic because they produce practically everything."

– French soccer players discussing 'exports'

Like in many quotes concerning the economic world map, the first quote contains a metaphor of ranking. France (referred to as "we") is "amongst the first in the world" regarding military technology. This technological advantage is mainly viewed as beneficial because it boosts exports. Exports are also the central concern in the second quote. Again, countries are assessed by the quality of their exports, by what they "have to offer". The analogy between states and firms, moreover, is made very explicit ("you have a big firms like Canada and several small firms like France or Denmark"). In both quotes, then, the global order is represented as a market-like competition of states. The competition of states happens according to the laws of product market (for exports) and according to the laws of the labor market (for talent).

A1.5.5 State as Regulator

Definition: In the representation of the state as a *regulator*, the state is called upon to stop this race to the bottom in different markets. This means protecting wages (labor market) and environmental and product quality standards (product market).[3] Rather than complying with market imperatives (as in *state as competitor*) the state is depicted as a counterweight to international competition.

Frequency: 18; entrepreneurship (FST), merit (GLU), SMEs (FLT, GLT, GST), sovereignty (FAT, GAT, GST, PST), standards (FLT, FST, GLT, PAT), state vs market (GAT, GST), workers' rights (GAT, GLT, PST)

Quotes:

GSTM1: "Ok but if you talk about imports more generally … I mean I don't know how, but generally it would be super interesting if you could create working conditions in low-wage countries which are not detrimental to health. Uhm rather than undermining them, this would in fact advance our worker's rights here which are pretty good. Because on average, people here get pretty decent wages in comparison with other countries. Of course, you have to talk about this: 8,90 or 8,93 – our minimum wage might not be very impressive. But it's more than you get elsewhere."

– German soccer players discussing 'workers' rights'

GLTM1: "I mean a trade agreement could protect small firms much better by setting standards or by providing stronger regulation. But regulation and free trade is somewhat of a contradiction of course [GLTW1: Yes exactly]."

GLTW3: "Yeah but you could have a standard or a seal of quality [GLTM1: Yes. Whatever] which would be a pre-condition for participation. Just like you need a vaccination if you want to go abroad [GLTW2: Yes]. So you need to comply with certain conditions, and they should rather be high. And they should not be like [change of voice]: 'I save money and buy cheap stuff'."

– German teachers discussing 'standards'

In the first quote, imports are linked to wage levels, working conditions and workers' health. Wages thus appear as a factor of production and the import of products from "low-wage countries" might be detrimental to local workers' rights. A minimum wage is cited as a form of regulation that can counter downward pressures on wages caused by the circulation of goods on the product market. Similarly, in the second quote higher standards are viewed as a means to counter negative effects of the international circulation of goods. "Standards and seals of quality" appear as an alternative to a solely price-based competition ("I save money and buy cheap stuff"). The analogy with vaccinations implies that the product market is a domain fit for state regulation like any other. In both cases, then, the state is called upon to counteract market processes. State regulation should remedy the negative effects of international competition on the product and on the labor market.

A1.5.6 EU as Regulator

Definition: Representation of *state as regulator* applied to EU. The EU is called upon to regulate the product and the labor market, in particular with an eye on environmental and social standards. The *social ordering of sectors* and the placement of the *EU on economic world map* – often as an antipode to the capitalist United States – often accompany this representation.

Frequency: For EU regulating product market: frequency 3; SMEs (GLT), standards (FLT, GST); for labor market: 2; merit (GSU), investment (GLU); for challenges of globalization: 2; sovereignty (GST, GAT)

Quotes:

GSUM3: "Well … At least … A regulated minimum wage which must be just has to create a comparability first. Since a couple of years nothing has been done in the industrial sector. There are no longer workers and employees since the ERA-system was introduced. That created comparability between blue- and white-collar workers. Something similar has to happen on the federal level in order to create a fair distribution of minimum wages. And if you want to further fine-tune it, it has to happen EU-wide. But of course, a difficulty is that laws need to be the same everywhere. Laws must be the same and taxes must be the same, so there is no way around for the firms."

– German soccer players discussing 'merit'

GATM1: "We will not solve the problems of the earth as single states. The aim has to be not only to create a Europe, but to create a world. But of course, we already see with Europe how difficult this is. In the background that should be the main aim though. Because just in terms of climate – if we want to talk about it but of course it is a very urgent topic – we will not solve these problems if there is someone somewhere who says: 'I am not joining in'. […] This might be a bit – how do you say? Idealistic? [GATM2: Visionary!] Visionary, idealistic, whatever – but visions only change the world if you ensure that standards remain affordable and realistic for all countries."

– German agents discussing 'sovereignty'

In the first quote, a strong case is made for the harmonization of regulation at the European level. The EU is depicted as a site of action best suited to implement a minimum wage and tax harmonization. Specific national vocabulary is used in making the argument. "The ERA-system" is a corporatist wage agreement negotiated for Germany's industrial sector. The mobilization of this specific regulation shows that an analogy is made between state powers and the powers of the EU. The EU should intervene as a regulator like the German state has done. The second quote also depicts the EU as a site of action, but in this case the issue to be tackled is climate change. The solutions proposed are common standards all countries can agree to – implying that the EU is an actor that should implement environmental laws. Next to the labor and the product market, then, environmental regulation is the main issue the EU is called upon to regulate.

A1.5.7 EU as Investor and Other State Functions

Definition: Apart from the state as a regulator, the other representations of the state are very infrequently applied to the EU. The EU itself is cited as an *investor* once (green technologies being the area toward which the investment is to be directed). In two German groups, an investment enhancing function is assigned to the ECB. The EU appears as a re-distributor twice, once in a call for a social Europe and once in the context of agricultural subsidies. A vision of the EU as a competitor in the international economic arena is entirely absent.

Frequency: For EU as re-distributor: frequency 2; investment (GLT), non-wage labor costs (FSU); for EU as investor: innovation (FAT); ECB as investor via low interest rates: 3; interest rates (GAT, GSU), sovereignty (FAT)

Quotes: see Chapter 2, Section 2.3.2.

A1.6 Social Representations of Ideologies

Definition: Representations of ideology are found when participants refer to specific economic doctrines such as liberalism, socialism or Keynesianism. Causally, this happens mostly when the relationship between state and market is discussed, thus linking representations of ideology to many representations of state functions (see previous section). Normatively, a pure version of ideologies tends to be viewed negatively while convergence of ideologies around a regulated market economy is appraised. Linguistically, representations of ideology heavily feature expert vocabulary and classical metaphors from economic theory.

A1.6.1 Keynesianism

Definition: The representation of *Keynesianism* is cited at multiple moments in the discussions, and some of its ideas are reproduced with a stunning similarity of wording across various groups. Causally, the central idea is that state expenditure can create a positive feedback loop, boosting production and demand. While this idea was presented on one of the trigger cards (reading 'increase state expenditure to stimulate demand'), Keynesian reasoning also appeared in groups who were not confronted with this trigger topic.

Linguistic Features: Representation of *Keynesianism* tends to be accompanied by **economic machine metaphors**. The economy can spin, inflate or be launched.

Frequency: 8; expenditure (GLU, PAU, PLU, PSU), inflation (FSU), interest (FAU), right to work (FLU), sovereignty (FAT)

> PSUM1: "[reads out trigger topic] 'Increase state expenditure to create demand'. One knows that if the state chips in more, more is going to be produced, more is going to be bought. And in this way, everything will start spinning."
>
> – Polish soccer players discussing 'expenditure'

FATM1: "But to come back to the last point about national sovereignty – it's more or less true. Generally, it's the liberal market economy. That is to say that the market is self-regulating. That's true and at the same time it is not ... The state should not intervene too much, but it has to be there to settle the problems if the market degenerates. There are plenty of economic mechanisms for that: the political re-launch, the Keynesian re-launch, for example."

– French agents discussing 'sovereignty'

The first quote contains a description of a demand-driven positive feedback loop in the economy. The second quote explicitly calls post-crisis recovery measures a "Keynesian" policy. Both quotes use machine metaphors, describing state expenditure as a "re-launch" which causes the economy to start "spinning" again. Keynesian policies thus are very explicitly cited and presented in surprising detail.

A1.6.2 Liberalism

Definition: The representation of liberalism comprises two elements. First, the market is depicted as a natural mechanism, which is self-regulating. Second, facing the natural complexity of the market, the state is depicted as incapable of properly regulating it. Normatively, state intervention is therefore decried as protectionism or as over-regulation.

Linguistic Features: The belief in the naturality of the market is expressed through personifications of the market and references to the works of Adam Smith. Metaphors of artificiality are applied to the state, underlining that the market is a natural phenomenon.

Frequency: Liberalism, protectionism, invisible hand: frequency 6; innovation (FAT), investment (GAT, PAT), sovereignty (FAT); state vs market (FAT, PAT); Market as natural and metaphors of artificiality: 6; Mobility (GAU), right to work (GAU, PAU, PSU), state vs market (FAT, GAU)

Quotes

GAUM1: "Generally, it is difficult if there is too much regulation. Or if too much is being prescribed because this distorts the entire system. [...]"

GAUW1: "Yeah, theory and praxis are just too far apart."

GAUM1: "Yeah it just moves apart because the world and the market develop differently, and no single politician or law-maker in parliament, in the Bundestag, could have foreseen that. And that finds, you find ... The market always finds a loophole and other things to go around. And then everything is turning into extremes and has other potential consequences."

– German agents discussing 'state vs market'

PATM1: "Like I think where it comes to economic issues the state shouldn't be an obstacle for entrepreneurship. One knows: the invisible hand of the market and so on [loughs]. So the state should be a kind of watchman and not someone who determines the frame. So I have a rather capitalist approach [loughs] to this question."

– Polish agents discussing 'state vs market'

These two quotes make a case for less state intervention, using the linguistic expressions cited before. In the first quote, GAUM1 describes the market as too complex to be properly understood by politicians. The market is personified in the last phrase, stating that "the market will always find a loophole". The market thus appears as a natural force which will find its way around any kind of artificial regulation. Most explicitly, however, liberal ideology is cited in the second quote in which references to both the "invisible hand of the market" and the (night)watchman state are made. Where the social representation of liberalism is mobilized, a general case against state intervention can be made.

A1.6.3 Capitalism

Definition: A negative representation of *liberalism* and the free market.

Linguistic Features: Vocabulary employed in the representation of *liberalism* acquires negative connotations (e.g., profits, consumption, supply and demand). Vocabulary with traditionally socialist connotations is being used (e.g., exploitation).

Frequency: 10; Privatization (GLU, PAU, PLU), Right to work (PSU), standards (GAT, GLT, PLT, PST), Workers' rights (GAT, GLT)

Quotes

GLTM1: "But there are certain products where these price mechanisms, the processes of free price creation, do not function and where you cannot settle everything via supply and demand. Uhm for example uhm … Education can't be regulated via supply and demand. There is food. Water cannot be regulated via supply and demand, but there have to be other mechanisms."

– German teachers discussing 'standards'

GATM1: "Here comes the socialist amongst you! So I think workers' rights should be on the same level, just to eliminate these injustices in the world. So we can truly talk about a give-and-take and lest there is only one who profits because he can produce more cheaply while others are bearing the cost."

– German agents discussing 'workers' rights'

In the first quote, GLTM1 questions the suitability of market principles (symbolized by "supply and demand") for large areas of society. GLTM1 is probably the most outspoken critic of capitalism; an even more elaborate statement of his rejection of capitalism can be found in his placement of the EU on the economic world map, where he describes the United States as a country in which "capitalist standards" rule supreme (see Chapter 7, Section 7.2.2). These standards – "increase productivity, profits, returns and so on" – show once more how liberal terminology can be bestowed with negative meaning. In the second quote, GATM1 makes a general case against global exploitation, criticizing market mechanisms for not being mutually beneficial. Here again, the term "profits" comes with negative connotations. Where market mechanisms are described as capitalism, then, a counter-vision of *liberalism* is advanced, fundamentally questioning the advantages of free markets.

A1.6.4 Socialism

Definition: The representation of socialism is often mobilized to negatively judge state intervention in the economy (see also *state as regulator* or *state as re-distributor*). In Germany and Poland, it is often linked to memories of socialist dictatorship.

Linguistic Features: Metaphors of artificiality depicting the state as an aberration of nature and thus as the opposite of the natural market; national vocabulary, in particular proverbs expressing memories of socialist times.

Frequency: 9; Privatization (GAU), right to work (GLU, GSU, PAU, PLU, PSU), sovereignty (PST), State expenditure (GSU, PLU); ridiculing liberal vocabulary: 2; state vs market (PST), privatization (GSU)

Quotes: see Chapter 2, Section 2.3.3 and Chapter 7, Section 7.2.2.

A1.6.5 The Golden Mean

Definition: Normative commitment to a regulated market economy based on the rejection of the extremes of *capitalism* and *socialism.* This representation is sometimes combined with references to the *economic world map*, locating unregulated capitalism in *the West*.

Frequency: 10; Privatization (GLU, PLU, PSU), right to work (PSU), state vs market (FAT, GAT, PAT, PST), sovereignty (FAT, PAT)

Quotes: See Chapter 7, Section 7.2.2.

Notes

1 For investment creating jobs: frequency 6; interest (FAU, GSU, PLU), investment (FLT, PAT, PST); for investment creating innovation: 7; innovation (FAT, FLT), investment (FAT, GAT, GST, PST), variety (GLT); for positive assessment of profits: 2; innovation (FLT), investment (PST).

2 I do not alter the personal pronouns in this case because the representation clearly comes with specific gender connotations.
3 Frequency: 18; entrepreneurship (FST), merit (GLU), SMEs (FLT, GLT, GST), sovereignty (FAT, GAT, GST, PST), standards (FLT, FST, GLT, PAT), state vs market (GAT, GST), workers' rights (GAT, GLT, PST).

Appendix 2: Focus Group Design

A2.1 Trade

Introductory statement: "The EU has negotiated a number of free trade deals with its partners in the past, among these CETA with Canada in 2017. In your opinion, which should be the aims of a good free trade agreement? Choose three."

- Benefits for small and medium-sized enterprises
- Create jobs
- Boost innovation in the economy
- Attract foreign firms/investment
- Low prices for consumers
- Increase exports
- Protect product standards
- Protect workers' rights
- Greater product variety

Negative round: "Which of these arguments have negative connotations for you? Choose two."

Systemic statement: "In free trade agreements, some rules of market access need to be harmonized. Some politicians think that this will reduce the state's capacity to impose regulation on the economy. Which of following arguments do you find most convincing?"

- It is bad to have treaties with countries that have lower standards [trigger standards]
- It is good to have less regulation because state institutions are susceptible to corruption [trigger corruption]
- It is bad to limit national sovereignty on economic matters [trigger sovereignty]
- Too much regulation impedes commercial activity [trigger state vs market]

Reflexive Questions:

- "Who/what people/which social group might have a different opinion than you?"
- "Do you think that there are national differences?"

A2.2 Unemployment

Introductory statement: "In the beginning of 2018, the unemployment rate within the European Union amounted to 7.3%. In your opinion, how could this unemployment rate be lowered? Choose three propositions that seem promising to you."

- Establish a right to work for all citizens
- Lower non-wage labor costs
- Ensure a stable environment for firms (e.g., no inflation)
- Ensure low interest rates to facilitate investment
- Increase state expenditure to stimulate demand
- Advance citizens' entrepreneurial spirit
- Ensure that wages reflect merit
- Boost international mobility of labor
- Increase international competitiveness

Negative round: "Which of these arguments have negative connotations for you? Choose two."

Systemic statement: "In the past, some state enterprises were privatized. Which of these arguments do you find most convincing?" [all trigger privatization]

- Government should leave most services to the market, yet ensure that they are executed by domestic firms.
- Government should nationalize some sectors of the economy.
- Government should privatize more enterprises in order for them to be run more efficiently.

Reflexive Questions:

- "Who/what people/which social group might have a different opinion than you?"
- "Do you think that there are national differences?"

Appendix 3: Characteristics of Participants

Table A3.1 Detailed information on focus group locations and participants

Country/ Group/ Topic)	*Location*	*Date*	*Age span*	*Gender ratio M/W/D*	*Left-right spread (0-10)*
FAT	Paris 16ième	June 2018	20-25	(1/2)	6-7
FLT	Meaux	March 2018	35-40	(2/2)	3-6
FST	Pontault-Combault	March 2018	25-45	(4/0)	1-5
GAT	Charlottenburg	July 2018	40-55	(2/1)	5-8
GLT	Reinickendorf	March 2018	45-55	(1/3)	3
GST	Reinickendorf	August 2018	30-35	(3/0)	2-6
PAT	Śródmieście	February 2019	30-35	(3/0)	2-5
PLT	Jabłonna	January 2019	30-35	(0/3)	5
PST	Bielany	March 2019	25-30	(5/0)	3-7
FAU	undisclosed[1]	July 2018	25-50	(1/2)	5-9
FLU	Lagny	March 2018	30-55	(1/3/1)	0-8
FSU	Meaux	May 2018	20-50	(2/1)	5
GAU	Prenzlauer Berg	July 2018	30-40	(2/1)	4-7
GLU	Steglitz	August 2018	30-60	(3/1)	3-4
GSU	Spandau	August 2018	50-55	(4/0)	3-6
PAU	Żoliborz	February 2019	35-45	(1/2)	3-10
PLU	Ursus	March 2019	30-55	(0/4)	0-5
PSU	Okęcie	February 2019	45-60	(3/0)	1-10
Total			20-60	38/25/1	Left (0-3): 20 Centre (4-6): 28 Right (7-10): 10 No answer: 6

Note

1 The small village in which this interview took place only features one housing agency. For reasons of anonymity, I do not disclose the precise location. The village, however, is a stronghold of the Front National with Marine LePen gaining around 35% in the first round of the 2017 presidential election.

Index

Note: Page numbers in **bold** refer to tables and page numbers with 'n' refers notes.

FSC
www.fsc.org
MIX
Papier | Fördert
gute Waldnutzung
FSC® C083411

Kolibri 360 GmbH
Ferdinand-Jühlke-Straße 7
99095 Erfurt, Deutschland
produktsicherheit@kolibri360.de